THE ADMINISTRATION OF
UNITED STATES FOREIGN POLICY

This book is published with the assistance of the Dan Danciger Publication Fund

The Administration of United States Foreign Policy

By RICHARD A. JOHNSON

UNIVERSITY OF TEXAS PRESS
AUSTIN & LONDON

JX
1417
.J64

International Standard Book Number 0–292–70109–8
Library of Congress Catalog Card Number 76–162689
© 1971 by Richard A. Johnson
All rights reserved

Printed by The University of Texas Printing Division, Austin
Bound by Universal Bookbindery, Inc., San Antonio

FOR IRENE

CONTENTS

Preface xi

PART I. LIMITS AND BASES OF ADMINISTRATION

1. Limits of Participation 3
2. Bases for Participation 22

PART II. INSTITUTIONAL HISTORY OF FOREIGN AFFAIRS ADMINISTRATION

3. Prologue, 1774–1939 47
4. World War II and the Years of Uncertain Commitment, 1939–1954 73
5. "Wristonization," 1954–1960 102
6. The Kennedy-Johnson Years, 1961–1969: Basic Objectives 115
7. The Kennedy-Johnson Years, 1961–1969: Personnel Programs 136

PART III. THE PARTICIPANTS AND THEIR ROLES

8. Congress and the Federal Courts 169
9. The Presidency 179
10. The Department of State and the Foreign Service . . . 195
11. USIA, AID, and Other Political Agencies 217
12. The National Defense Agencies 231
13. Other Departments and Agencies 241
14. State and Local Governments 251
15. Other Influences 256

PART IV. SOME CURRENT ADMINISTRATIVE PROBLEMS AND PROPOSALS FOR THE FUTURE

16. Problems of Policy Formulation and Review 279

17. A Proposal for Reorganizing the High Command of the Department of State 292
18. A Proposal for a Unified Foreign Affairs Service . . . 299
19. Problems of Size and Character 313
20. Problems of Selection 325
21. Problems of Personnel Training and Organization . . . 334
22. Prognosis 341

APPENDIXES

A. Investigations of Foreign Affairs Administration, 1947–1954 351
B. Investigations of Foreign Affairs Administration, 1955–1961 354
C. Long-Term Training Programs Listed for FY-'71 . . . 361
D. The Flow of Policymaking in the Department of State . . 368

List of Abbreviations 379
Bibliographical Notes 383
Bibliography 389
Index 405

TABLES AND CHARTS

TABLE

Staffing of Overseas FSO Positions Requiring S-3 R-3
    Language Skills, 1966 156

CHARTS

Department of State, 1909–1924 60
Senior Hierarchy of the Department of State, 1939 71
Department of State, December 1944 . . . . . facing page 78
Department of State, December 1969 86
American Embassy, London, January 1969 215
Consulate General, Monterrey, 1965 216
United States Information Agency, May 1969 219
Agency for International Development, November 1968 . . . 224
Peace Corps, January 1969 227

GRAPH

Junior Officer Intake 139

PREFACE

The vast field of United States foreign policy attracts many serious students, and most laymen offer judgments freely on international problems of the utmost complexity. But fewer scholars and virtually no laymen concern themselves with foreign affairs administration. Such relative neglect becomes more puzzling when one considers that the form and process of administration now serve as major determinants of the content and effectiveness of policy.

This book does not attempt to discuss, explain, or criticize substantive policy. It seeks rather to describe where and how the United States government administers policy, to discuss the major problems of administration, and to suggest the approaches to those problems that seem most likely to yield to informed study and compromise.

During the era of classical diplomacy, administration had little impact on policy formulation. Personality factors, private initiative, and political pull probably played weightier roles than did institutional pressures and systems. Since World War II, the tremendous growth in foreign affairs bureaucracies, the enormous increase in the complexity of their work, and the penetration of domestic by foreign affairs concerns have made administration an important determinant of foreign policy. As former Undersecretary of State Nicholas de B. Katzenbach put it, "The administration of . . . agencies concerned with foreign affairs does more than just *bear upon* the formulation of foreign policy. The two subjects . . . are . . . more or less inseparable."[1]

Because the scope, practice, and importance of foreign affairs ad-

[1] Nicholas de B. Katzenbach, "Administration of Foreign Policy," (Department of State) *News Letter*, no. 79 (November 1967), p. 2.

ministration have undergone a bewildering and almost complete transformation in the past quarter century, and because the studies of Tracy Lay, Graham Stuart, Katherine Crane, and other students offer excellent, detailed treatments of the pre–World War II Department of State and Foreign Service, this book includes only a brief sketch of their origins and development before 1939.

Thirty years ago the only major issue in foreign affairs administration was whether the Departments of Agriculture and Commerce should continue to maintain modest, independent, foreign services. President Roosevelt's Commission on Administrative Management vigorously endorsed executive integration in 1937. Reorganization Plan No. 2 of 1939 brought the overseas staffs of the Departments of Agriculture and Commerce into the Foreign Service. It is significant and ironic that the index of the commission's final report contains no reference to foreign relations or foreign service.

The problem of reorganizing foreign affairs administration did not assume dangerous magnitude until after Pearl Harbor, when the United States finally abandoned isolationism and assumed its full share of international responsibility. But the nation accepted world leadership reluctantly and refused to make the consequent institutional changes. It temporized, attaching incongruous additions to an outgrown structure, hoping that some day all of its foreign activities might again fit neatly into the accommodations of 1939.

The Department of State administered the information program for a time after 1945, but Congress appropriated funds for information work separately. It entrusted covert intelligence activities and economic assistance programs to new agencies. By 1949 twenty-one agencies stationed civilian employees abroad, and few domestic agencies had failed to develop some interest in the new and exciting field of international relations. In 1953 President Eisenhower removed the information program from the Department of State and relaxed field control over the operations of information and economic assistance officers. The Department of Agriculture re-established its Foreign Service in 1954.

The advent of nuclear warfare and the need for a large military establishment in being posed unprecedented national security problems that overlapped foreign policy considerations. Consequently, the military and their civilian leaders also assumed major roles in foreign affairs administration. Predominantly domestic agencies such as the Treasury Department, which had acquired vast new foreign affairs responsibilities, clung jealously to them and, with the rapid postwar expansion of international financial organizations and activities, acquired additional interests.

The Department of State and the Foreign Service lost their monopoly over foreign affairs administration; but machinery to coordinate the myriad agencies and activities involved in the foreign relations of the United States failed to evolve as rapidly as the nation's commitments and far less rapidly than the multiplicity of agencies that began to intervene in foreign affairs. Successive chief executives tried desperately to introduce more effective collaboration, but with results lamentably disproportionate to their efforts. The coordinating devices palliated but failed to eradicate the evils created by the proliferation of agencies engaged in the administration of American foreign policy and by the excessive expansion of personnel so engaged.

Many other problems emerged, including those related to the politicization of the foreign affairs bureaucracies. What happened in the past now begins to emerge. The future remains clouded. The present clearly requires far more intensive and objective study of foreign policy administration in order to provide a sound base for decisions on its form and process.

The administration of American foreign affairs requires more intensive study for at least four additional reasons; first, the nation's transcendently important international role gives the subject interest far exceeding its limitation to the system employed by a single state; second, since the administration of foreign policy now strongly conditions its substance and execution, the general public must understand how the system functions if it is to interpret the substantive policy it generates and assess accurately its chances for success; third, the machinery of American foreign policy administration differs importantly from that employed by other major states in character, complexity, and sheer size; and fourth, although the administration of American foreign policy changed radically and frequently since 1939, it remains in a not wholly satisfactory state.[2]

Twenty years ago, Professor William Yandell Elliot posed these questions: "Can the government of the United States speak with a single voice in world affairs: or will our internal irresponsibility cancel out our great power? Can we make a promise to the world and then deliver the goods? On the other hand, can foreign nations play off one part of our government against another?"[3] His questions remain unanswered. The administration of American foreign affairs patently remains a matter of primary importance to the contemporary world, but its affects the national health even more seriously because foreign and national security affairs now influence virtually all aspects of domestic life and absorb an overwhelming proportion of federal expenditures.

Neither the firmest determination to defend the United States nor the most lavish use of resources will assure peace and security unless the American people learn to conduct their external affairs in a disciplined, coordinated, and responsible manner. Crash programs, improvisations, experimentation, and frequent reorganizations may be necessary in emergencies, but bring only waste and frustration under more stable conditions. Foreign affairs will continue to preoccupy the United States indefinitely. Thus public officials must attend more diligently to the problems of coordinating, organizing, compensating, staffing, and training foreign affairs personnel.

This book obviously owes much to the pioneering efforts of such scholars as Charles Burton Marshall, James L. McCamy, Arthur MacMahon, George Kennan, William Yandell Elliott, Burton M. Sapin, John E. Harr, and many others; to the work of congressional, executive, and private committees and commissions that have examined various aspects of the administration of American foreign policy, always conscientiously and often perceptively; and to the writings,

---

[2] John E. Harr, *The Professional Diplomat*, pp. 28–44.

[3] William Yandell Elliot, *United States Foreign Policy: Its Organization and Control*, p. 5.

official and unofficial, of many officers of the Department of State and the Foreign Service.

The names of the authorities cited above and even a cursory examination of the text will reveal my approach to be pragmatic rather than theoretical. My early training and vocational experience predispose me to historical-institutional analysis. I recognize the enormous potential significance of the behaviorists' efforts to provide a sound, theoretical basis for exploring foreign affairs problems. But I am convinced that unresolved difficulties of coding and retrieving foreign affairs data, major gaps that research must still bridge in the existing theoretical fabric, and the untested status of many strands of theory preclude abandoning the pragmatic approach at this time. This does not imply that some of the findings of behaviorist scholars do not now provide useful insights and even sound bases for modifications in certain areas of foreign affairs administration. It merely asserts what I suppose most behaviorists would acknowledge, that the scientific theory of foreign affairs administration is still incomplete and in part unproven, and that at least another generation of scholarship will be needed to round out and test it.

The works of authorities, the publications of committees and commissions, and the unofficial publications of public servants used in preparing this study are listed in the bibliography. The only works cited in the text are those which have been used so extensively as to warrant special reference or those quoted directly. Bibliographical notes for each major section list uncited works most frequently consulted. No attempt has been made to list all unpublished articles, official memoranda, studies, and other documents.

Some of the information and many conclusions reflect my personal experience in the Department of State and Foreign Service between May 1940 and August 1965. During this period I served three times in management roles in the Department of State, twice as principal officer of large consular establishments, about ten months as chargé d'affaires a.i. of two embassies, once as third-ranking officer of a large embassy. I discussed many administrative problems with scores of Foreign and Civil Service officers and with the highest management officials of the Department of State, including three deputy undersecretaries of state for administration, Loy Henderson, Roger Jones, and William Crockett, several directors general of the Foreign Service, and many assistant and deputy assistant secretaries of state.

I am proud to have been part of the Foreign Service and consider that its members and those of other foreign affairs agencies generally serve their country well. I do not consider that the service or the other agencies always showed the flexibility and openmindedness needed to meet the demands imposed on them during and after World War II. The seizure of more initiative by high-ranking Foreign Service officers might have limited the dispersal of foreign policy responsibilities; had the service opened specialized career ladders to personnel required by new commitments and responsibilities, further dispersal might have been prevented. Conversely, bureaucratic rivalries and vested interests in other agencies contributed heavily both to the excessive growth of the foreign affairs establishment and to its decentralization.

I have tried to analyze objectively various problems of American foreign affairs administration, but I realize that my training and conditioning inevitably influenced some of my conclusions. In particular, the proportion of this study allocated to discussion of the evolution and problems of the Foreign Service of the United States, in contrast to the Civil Service and other participants in foreign affairs administration, may seem excessive to some readers. I confess readily that a quarter of a century in the service may have led me to overestimate its relative importance, and I hope that any distortion attributable to this experience may at least yield some compensatory insights.

The following considerations motivated my decisions on the space accorded the various participants:

1. The Foreign Service has always greatly outnumbered the Civil Service employees of the Department of State arithmetically and in terms of influence; and it remains, by a good margin, the largest career, civilian, foreign affairs organization operating at home and abroad;

2. The responsibilities of the Foreign Service include, under ambassadorial supervision, the coordination of field activities of all other civilian agencies and of some activities of Defense Department personnel;

3. The Foreign Service largely staffs the policy-making regional bureaus in the Department of State, and its officers fill a preponderance of ambassadorial and senior State Department positions;

4. The basic legislation establishing the Foreign Service also provides staffing categories used by other foreign affairs agencies, including USIA, AID, the Departments of Commerce, Labor, Treasury, and many others, to fill field positions;

5. The Foreign Service currently assigns more than four hundred officers for extended tours of duty in other agencies having foreign affairs responsibilities;

6. The Foreign Service Institute serves the foreign affairs community rather than the Foreign Service exclusively; indeed, about half of its students now come from other agencies, its lecturers and faculty represent the entire community, and it draws increasingly on academic authorities as well;

7. Since 1962 efforts to achieve compatibility between the Foreign Service, USIA, and AID have progressed notably in many areas; and

8. Although the United States now has many field services, a consensus seems to have emerged that the Foreign Service, USIA, and AID should at least be compatible, and that other civilian agencies, except CIA, should be represented abroad by the Foreign Service. Thus, the statutory title, the Foreign Service of the United States, may again become meaningful.

Many subjects treated herein have received speculative or subjective treatment because of the lack of sound monographic studies. While recognizing that many of my conclusions and suggestions may be challenged, I hope that they may at least underscore the need for much additional basic research in this important field. I also hope that this attempt at a broad synthesis may prove useful to students interested in foreign affairs as a career, to those preparing to teach international relations or public administration, and to public officials of this and other nations.

I acknowledge most gratefully useful suggestions offered by my former colleagues, Professors Robert S. Walker and Ton P. De Vos, of the Department of Political Science of Trinity University. Professor

De Vos read and criticized much of the Preface and Chapter 1; Professor Walker, much of an early version of Chapter 2. I feel deeply indebted to my old friend and colleague, Dr. J. Lloyd Mecham, professor emeritus of the University of Texas at Austin, for reading the entire manuscript and for suggesting important organizational and substantive changes. The administration of Trinity University afforded me indispensable secretarial assistance.

The views and errors in the volume must be attributed, of course, exclusively to myself, and do not reflect official opinion or the opinion of any institution or organization.

PART I

Limits and Bases of Administration

1

Limits of Participation

Foreign affairs must be administered by all powers within certain unalterable limits, under the influence of major inhibitions, and subject to essential hazards and uncertainties. Charles Burton Marshall had this premise in mind when he wrote that "there are no experts in world affairs; there are only those who, by having had to deal responsibly with affairs of state, have overcome the ignorance of their own ignorance." He emphasized that the processes of history are dynamic and cannot be altered by any static design, that foreign policy "must be lived." Human wisdom is contingent and fallible in foreign affairs. But this does not mean that the American people must resign themselves to what fate may bring. To know their limits is the beginning of freedom, and they must also fulfill their limits. To do so they must have faith in man's worth, hope "of some fulfillment transcending one's momentary incapacity to see," and charity, or "that compassionate view of other entities . . . derived from one's knowledge of not having the final answers and one's recognition of all others as being in the same boat."[1]

[1] Charles Burton Marshall, *The Limits of Foreign Policy*, pp. 125–127. Permission

General Limitations

Unfortunately the public and many officials either fail to take into account the limits of foreign affairs administration or underestimate them dangerously. Thus, when situations refuse to develop in accordance with their plans or expectations they look for scapegoats among foreign affairs administrators or seek panaceas to revive waning hopes. In both cases they further distort the conduct of foreign affairs. The same result ensues when the public or public servants react to failures with apathy or desperately urge "final solutions," such as preventive war or the escalation of an existing conflict to the point of nuclear engagement. In either case limiting factors exert profound secondary as well as primary influences.

Universal limits on foreign affairs administration can be considered conveniently under the captions of unpredictability, uncontrollability, means, public endurance, particularism, history and historicism, and communications. Most of these factors are unalterable, although some may become less important in time.

Unpredictability. The essential unpredictability of foreign affairs stems from several causes. First, man cannot be relied upon to act rationally or irrationally, egoistically or selflessly. He fluctuates wildly between passivity and terrifying volatility. Although scholars and laymen now have more knowledge of the multiple factors that influence his behavior and rely less on logic and historical analogy, as yet no models of group behavior predict infallibly how he will react at any given moment or in the future. The British, alone and virtually defenseless, faced up to the brutal power of Hitlerite Germany. The French, "ready to the last button" crumbled in 1870 and 1940. The hungry, caste-ridden masses of India and the desperately poor *campesinos* of Mexico remain relatively quiescent; Negroes of the United States, enjoying per capita incomes many times higher than the middle classes of less favored nations and far more political influence, drive cars to looting orgies and even threaten civil war. The most powerful

---

to quote from *The Limits of Foreign Policy* has been granted by Holt, Rinehart and Winston, Inc.

nation in the world renounces colonialism, spends billions on foreign assistance programs, and supports international organizations with more enthusiasm than many feeble but aggressive states. Yet the same nation also resents the burdens of world involvement, tries to impose its image on the rest of the world, and wears its heart on its sleeve. The British worker, despite the precarious economy of the United Kingdom, shows more concern with winning a thirty-hour week than with increasing his productivity. The French, who benefited enormously from the European Economic Community (EEC), at times have seemed determined to wreck it.

Nature remains almost as unreliable as man, despite his progress in limiting its destructiveness and maximizing its bounty through dams, insecticides, weather prediction and warning services, medical discoveries, and other technical advances. Man still feels most of the force of hurricanes, tornadoes, tidal waves, drouths, epidemics, infestations of plants and animals, plagues, earthquakes, volcanic eruptions, floods, freezes, snowstorms, landslides, mutations of species, shifts in the earth's axis, and like phenomena, favorable as well as tragic, but all essentially unforeseeable. An adverse climatic cycle can still change a prosperous agricultural area into a dust bowl, and a plague can reverse or stem a buoyant demographic trend. The alarming tendency of micro-organisms and insects to acquire immunities to fungicides, antibiotics, and insecticides demonstrates that man's alleged dominance over nature is not only peripheral but extremely tenuous.

Fate, chance, contingency, luck, and divine intervention all describe happenings or developments that largely defy logical explanation, prevision, and the most prudently planned courses of action. David's defeat of Goliath, the success of the revolt of the Netherlands, the failure of the Japanese to destroy the virtually unprotected American fleet covering the landings in the Philippines, the triumph of the Bolsheviks—these and innumerable other happenings must be attributed in whole or in part to chance or mischance—to the want of a nail that cost the courier's horse a shoe, to the illness, madness, or hangover of a general or statesman, to the accidental firing of a shot.

Scientific and technological discoveries, now occuring at an unprecedented and constantly accelerating rate, render even more dense the shroud that veils the future. Certain tendencies toward which current research may lead can be perceived, but no one can be certain whether or when they will be realized. Indeed, the present state of man's destructive capability raises a very real question about his survival as a species, or, if he survives, whether his institutions, learning, and innovative potential will endure. If man does not destroy himself, science and technology seem likely to bring, at unpredictable dates, more knowledge and techniques related to man's behavior, as well as to his life processes and diseases, all of which will have an incalculable effect on demographic curves. They may, sooner or later, enable man to use sea water for irrigation or to supply his cities, and, then again, they may not. They may open up vast new sources of energy or enable man to exploit existing sources more efficiently. Such developments would, of course, entail gigantic economic, social, and political consequences that no one can foresee clearly or place precisely in time.

The universal poverty of empathetic resources, together with ignorance, wishful thinking, and particularism, gravely limit the utility of efforts to assess the effects of one nation's actions on another or to interpret foreign intelligence. Such misunderstandings, distortions, and prejudices contribute substantially to the inaccuracy of diagnosis, prognosis, and remedial action. Soviet insensitivity produces major errors in projection, as in the Russians' failure to appreciate the force of Chinese nationalism. The malign influence of American wishful thinking emerged clearly in the failure of the Bay of Pigs invasion, which rested on a vastly overoptimistic assumption regarding the probable reactions of the Cuban public and armed forces.

The incredible complexity of the international situation further limits the effectiveness of attempts at prediction. The complete triumph of national self-determination since World War II doubled the number of sovereign states whose actions and reactions now must be factored into foreign affairs estimates or decisions. The fact that so many of the new nations lack political or economic viability further increases the difficulty of maintaining normal relations both with them and with other states. The interpenetration of domestic and foreign affairs problems everywhere and the transformation of the nation into man's master rather than his servant enormously complicate the administration of international affairs, as do the scientific and technological revolutions, which have made the nations increasingly interdependent and shrunk the globe to Lilliputian dimensions.

Many other major forces enter into the limitless range of factors that cloud prevision. They include, among others, the demographic explosion; the Revolution of Rising Expectations; the dynamics of the ideological struggle between communist and mixed systems; the schisms in both camps; the triumph of equalitarianism; the transition from elite to bureaucratic diplomacy; the emergence of open, conference, and summit diplomacy; the proliferation of diplomatic activity and techniques; and the revolutions in education and communications.

Finally, the fact that most foreign affairs developments are outside the control of any nation or bloc helps to make them essentially unpredictable. No nation is completely autarkical. None can mobilize the omniscience required to predict the innumerable permutations in its own national life, in the domestic polities of others, or in the clash and coincidence of national interests. None can make its will prevail abroad except within narrow vectors.

Thus, planning has limited usefulness in foreign affairs because it cannot provide for all or even most contingencies. This is not to suggest that it should be abandoned. Although its value may often be marginal, it frequently cushions shocks of the unexpected, and, when followed by resolute action, it may even exert some determinative influence. For example, careful advance planning and action to cushion the shock of the discovery of, say, synthetic coffee, could conceivably mitigate the political, economic, and social impact of such a breakthrough on the producing nations. But, if a few of the esters that contribute to the aroma of coffee should remain undiscovered for another century, such expensive preparation might be largely wasted. In any case, developmental funds needed to anticipate such a breakthrough might be needed more urgently to reach some other goal.

Uncontrollability of External Situations. Most contingencies remain not only unpredictable, but uncontrollable. The most powerful states often find it impossible to reverse untoward developments. Exporting powers deprecate but cannot ameliorate the xenophobic economic nationalism of developing states. The United States failed signally to improve land tenure systems in Latin America, prevent General De Gaulle from taking many actions damaging to its national interest, or keep Cuba out of the communist world. The seizure of the *Pueblo* by North Korea illustrated with devastating clarity the inability of the mightiest nation on earth to alter external situations along lines beneficial to it.

The influences that prevent the greatest powers from altering many foreign situations vary so widely that it would be fruitless to attempt to list them all. The factor of unpredictability contributes substantially in some cases but obviously not in all. The limits discussed subsequently, especially insufficiency of means, weigh far more importantly; but the force of modern nationalism probably imposes the most difficult obstacle to any state attempting to impose its will upon another. This force has been apparent in Vietnam, Algeria, Cuba, Albania, Rumania, Hungary, Poland, Czechoslovakia, and many other states.

Limits Imposed by Means. All nations must administer their foreign affairs in light of their capabilities. Geographic, demographic, economic, technological, scientific, and military potentials impose absolute limits on their ability to play international politics successfully. A nation's role cannot transcend either the quantitative or qualitative limits of its means. A large population may be an asset, but if it contains unusually high proportions of the very young, the very old, or the unskilled, it must be downgraded in terms of its economic and military potential. A highly developed industrial system will not remain effective with outmoded management techniques or plants or with a deficient research budget. Large military forces are only as good as the logistical systems that support them. Forces and weapons systems must be demonstrably balanced in accordance with goals and needs.[2]

No nation can hope to achieve all of its major goals. Nations that undertake commitments in excess of their means risk loss of prestige at best, and defeat at worst. Superpowers that overextend themselves also risk nuclear war. This chain of events leads from overextension to dangerous redeployment of resources, to the thinning out of mili-

---

[2] For an excellent and considerably more detailed definition of means see Karl W. Deutsch, "The Anatomy and Character of National Power," *The National War College Forum*, 6 (Fall 1968), 10–27.

tary capabilities, to the use of threats as a substitute for physical means, and to violence, if opponents elect to call the bluff. If an overextended power cuts its losses, it sacrifices prestige and national honor. In such a case, or when it loses a war, disillusionment enhances the problems of conducting a successful foreign policy.

Even when nations do not overcommit themselves, the limits imposed by means compel them to make very hard choices between alternative courses of action because profit margins in international relations are very narrow. Even a slight error in judgment or at some stage in the collection, evaluation, or interpretation of intelligence can result in an unprofitable use of means and in an inability to pursue a potentially profitable course of action. If means were not a limiting factor, all alternatives could be pursued, but since means impose hard choices, they often foreclose some options more desirable than those elected.

Public Endurance. Foreign affairs administrators must take into account not only means but also public willingness to make the sacrifices required over the period needed to reach a policy goal. The political system and the historical record play important roles here. Popular enthusiasm is evanescent and fleeting. Most major goals demand long, costly efforts for even limited gains. Unless goals can be related clearly to the vital interests of the nation, and unless this relationship can be made clear to the public, very little confidence can be placed in its staying power. The French could not continue in Vietnam because the French public doubted that a vital national interest would be served by further sacrifice. The Korean policy of the Truman administration and the Vietnam policy of the Johnson administration came under attack for much the same reason.

Dictators and autocrats do not have to take quite so much account of public steadfastness as do the leaders of democratic or representative regimes because they can enforce a larger measure of compliance, but even they must concern themselves with morale. The Soviet leaders had to promote a tremendous revival of Russian nationalism during World War II in order to resist the German invaders. Dictatorships have crumbled, moreover, with the first defeat in a foreign conflict, as did that of Napoleon III. Thus, no nation's administrators can afford to adopt goals requiring lengthy and expensive foreign programs unless they are absolutely persuaded that the general public will regard these programs as essential and will support them at great cost until they are completed. Leaders who have overlooked the importance of this limiting factor usually have had abundant reason to regret their rashness.

Particularism. The administration of foreign affairs in every nation suffers from particularism—from the peculiar distortions that the prejudices, beliefs, and distinctive character of the nation impose.

The predominant element in a nation-state's character is its nationalism. The beliefs, attitudes, and emotions that inform nationalistic sentiment vary widely from state to state and even within each state. At one extreme is the xenophobe who seeks national self-sufficiency, fears or hates the foreigner, and resolutely excludes the thought that his nation may be incorrect in any international dispute. At the other extreme is the nationalist who perceives the essential incompatibility of international anarchy with the present state of science and technology and would approve a transfer of some sovereign rights to a regional or universal international organization in the interest of world peace and well-being. Even such enlightened nationalists would retain their own national security systems unless and until effective international protection were assured. The vast majority of nationalists fall between the two extremes but probably incline more to the right. Few true internationalists exist, and they exercise no appreciable influence on the policy of any nation-state.

Nationalism probably represents the strongest group emotional force in the world today. Its importance expanded concurrently with the role of the state, which in this century has become the master rather than the servant of its constituents. Even in democratic nations, including the United States, liberal nationalism has yielded critical ground to the state. At the same time, the importance of international relations has increased tremendously, together with the difficulty of understanding them. All of these trends now combine to render national positions in foreign affairs almost unassailable by the public, even where the jingoistic sentiment, "My country! May she always be right! But my country, right or wrong," no longer prevails. They also combine to elevate the national interest above all humanistic values; and they harden and sharpen the particularist character of each state's decision making, because every policy maker assesses national interest in his own lights.

Each nation-state suffers, then, from an almost unlimited conviction of its own rightness and the primacy of its own interest, and from attachment to certain beliefs or traditions peculiar to it. The Soviet Union, for example, proclaims its Marxian orthodoxy, which it normally construes to suit the national interest, but which does limit and distort its foreign affairs decisions. The United States clings to important beliefs that will be discussed subsequently. All nation-states cherish and firmly believe in the concept of national honor. The Arab states fear Israeli imperialism; the Israelites fear and distrust Arab revanchism. Violent anti-imperialist sentiments constrain former colonial states, and underdeveloped states generally share unshakeable convictions about the exploitative character of foreign capital.

Prejudice, like nationalism and national beliefs, distorts and limits foreign policy administration. Irrational hatreds poison relationships and block rational solutions. Some derive from observable differences, such as color of skin or variant customs, others from recollections of historical wrongs, still others from religious, linguistic, or other cultural differences. Variance of any kind seems to generate prejudice, possibly because men tend to regard beings whose standards or characteristics differ from theirs as either inferior or domineering, dangerous or insignificant. Americans sometimes patronize peoples of developing countries because they do not understand their value systems. This attitude, summed up by Rudyard Kipling's phrase, "lesser breeds beneath the law," goes far to explain the antipathy with which persons of black, brown, red, and yellow skin view former colonial powers, including the United States. Religious prejudices embitter Pakistani-Indian and Israeli-Arab relationships.

Nationalism, national beliefs, and prejudice—particularism in short—lead to arrogance or hatred at worst and to imperceptiveness or resentment at best. Most frequently, particularism results in the neglect of important factors that ought to enter well-balanced foreign affairs judgments. These differences between nations seem to exert much stronger force than any international ideology, world religion, or conviction about the importance of international cooperation. It is true that ideologies, religions, and internationalist sentiments, as locally construed and applied, contribute to the unique character of individual nations, but this result is quite another matter. Thus, particularism probably imposes, after means, the strongest limit on national foreign affairs decisions.

History and Historicism. A nation's history severely restricts the options of its foreign affairs administrators. Its beliefs, prejudices, and nationalistic sentiments grow out of the past. It is the nation's group memory, based on group tradition, true or false, that gives its particularism singular force; but history also determines the nation's means, in the sense that it will have dictated its boundaries, shaped its demographic curve, its developmental potential, and its other attributes. Thus, history underlies or generates factors already discussed. It is especially influential in forming national prejudices. The sad story of relations between Mexico and the United States, as taught in Mexican schools and recounted in Mexican literature, continues to contribute more to the fear, distrust, and resentment with which most Mexicans view the United States than do racial, religious, economic, and other differences combined.

In a broader and more general sense history restricts foreign affairs decision makers to the extent that they make proper or improper use of it to find analogies they hope will aid them to resolve current or emergent problems. While it is axiomatic that history does not repeat itself, man certainly learns by experience, and history is the record of this experience. Unfortunately the record is neither complete nor dispassionate. Hence the use of history as a source of analogy offers dangers as well as advantages. What is important here is not the qualitative value of historical analogies to the foreign affairs administrator but rather that he is limited or guided by them. How many times since 1939 have statesmen invoked the analogy of Munich when calling for a strong stand against an alleged aggressor? How often have they sought to employ divisive tactics because they worked effectively in the Roman and British empires? How many other history lessons, good or bad, help to determine the conduct of international relations every day?

Problems of Communication. Communication supplies the life blood of international relations. The health of the international body requires unimpeded circulation of views and information. Yet various situations arise that produce communications blockages analogous to embolisms or distortions comparable to infections in physical organisms.

The most common and harmful communication failures probably involve the distortion of the matter to be communicated. These result from several causes. Even when a communication is made in an allegedly common language, semantic problems inevitably arise through misreadings or misapprehensions of words or phrases. In other cases wishful thinkers or persons serving special interests deliberately befog or twist meanings. Such distortions occur frequently by error or chance in the chain of command in all governments, and they also enable gigantic modern bureaucracies to frustrate decisions of political leaders.

Failure of communications between nations may result from weakness or excessive delegation in the diplomatic chain of command. A diplomat instructed by his government to enter a "vigorous" protest about a given matter normally will be able to exercise considerable judgment in determining how sharp the protest will be. If he is overly concerned with his future usefulness in the host country or considers that too stiff a protest would be counterproductive, he may temper it to a degree unacceptable to his own foreign office and thus delude his hosts. On the other hand, if he is hawkish, he may exceed the wishes of his superiors and similarly mislead the host government. Even if the formal language of the protest is prescribed, his manner of presenting it, his inflection, and his explanatory or "unofficial" comments may weaken or enhance its force. Careless drafting, the use of the imperative when the conditional is intended, poorly chosen words, and even misplaced punctuation can, of course, have much the same effect as the use of words that allow variant constructions.

Translating thoughts from one language to another compounds the problem. Most languages have words or phrases for which no exact equivalents exist. In almost all cases translation subtly alters the rhetorical effect of a word or phrase. World languages, such as Spanish, English, or French, also present innumerable variants and localisms that offer additional opportunities for conflicts and confusion. Consequently, error creeps even more frequently into translation than into communication in the same language.

Rhetoric distorts meaning perhaps more dangerously than translation. It is a mighty weapon, but those who use it often find themselves impaled on their own hyperbole. Rhetoric employs absolute terms and exaggerates the clarity of distinctions. It hardens positions and inhibits effective meetings of the mind, the goal of communications art.

Unfortunately the increasing complexity of foreign affairs administration has made it impossible for specialists to communicate to leaders clearly and effectively in all cases. Leaders, in their turn, have become increasingly handicapped in efforts to enlighten the public about the nature and significance of foreign affairs issues. Security considerations and the need for discretion while negotiating difficult and complex problems also complicate efforts to communicate with constituents. This aspect of the problem of communication has a very important impact on the validity of intelligence estimates and forward planning, because it beclouds potential reactions by leaders and the public to anticipated trends.

Other important factors that limit foreign affairs administration will not be discussed at length because they exert much of their inhibiting influence through the operation of factors such as unpredictability. For example, the revolution in diplomatic techniques and the accompanying bureaucratization of the conduct of international relations help to restrict the effectiveness of attempts at prediction, as do the demographic explosion and the Revolution of Rising Expectations. The two latter phenomena may, largely through technological progress, lose considerable inhibiting force, even though they may plague diplomats for a generation or two. The former might be classified as major limiting factors because of the rigidity, delay, and loss of empathy they have caused.

What does the preceding discussion of the general limits of foreign policy administration imply for the decision maker? It reveals a paradoxical situation, in which many options are foreclosed but in which the range of those remaining is so vast as to make prudent choice not only difficult but extremely hazardous. Arthur M. Schlesinger, Jr., seems to feel that it dictates adoption of a modern version of the British tactic of muddling through. He quotes Richard Goodwin as follows: " '. . . half of the wisdom of statecraft . . . is to leave as many options open as possible and decide as little as possible . . . since almost all important policy judgments are speculative, you must avoid risking too much on the conviction you are right.' " Schlesinger continues: "Of course keeping too many options open too long may paralyze the lobe of decision and lose the game. There *does* come a time when accommodation turns into appeasement. This is the other half of the wisdom of statecraft: to accept the chronic obscurity of events . . . in deciding when to decide the criterion must be the human consequences—the results for people, not for doctrine."[3]

Schlesinger recommends, in effect, a pragmatic approach informed by concern for people. His is good advice with which few statesmen would quarrel; but it does not relieve the decision maker of the dilemma of deciding when the appropriate time has arrived beyond which decision can no longer be deferred, nor of selecting the course that will best serve the interest of humanity. Good intentions are no proof of good results, and the best men have sometimes made catastrophic decisions in foreign affairs.

What seems clear is that only pragmatic machete work will permit penetration of the jungle of international relations until further research and testing permit greater reliance on a theoretical attack. Excessive dedication to ideology or undeviating adherence to principle cannot assure success and may well lead to catastrophe. Estimative intelligence, planning, and programming serve decision makers only within narrowly defined limits and principally to the extent that they prepare them to receive the shocks of the unexpected. Open-mindedness, flexibility, and patience are the qualities most needed by the foreign affairs administrator. A dedication to humanistic principles, if shared by all statesmen, would be admirable but would not necessarily assure that all decisions would advance the interests of humanity because the difficulties of choosing among alternatives probably always will remain far too great to guarantee that any decision will benefit

---

[3] Arthur M. Schlesinger, Jr., *The Bitter Heritage*, p. 103. Permission to cite this and other excerpts from *The Bitter Heritage* has been granted by Houghton, Mifflin Company.

rather than injure humanity in the long term. Sometimes decisions that may seem the harshest or most inhumane prove in time highly beneficial. The decision maker, believer or nonbeliever, certainly needs faith, hope, and charity to work effectively. In the last quality his humanism must find its outlet.

Unique Limits of American Foreign Affairs Administration

American foreign affairs administration must be conducted under unique difficulties that derive from its constitutional, historical, and psychological inheritances and from the position of the United States as a superpower. Its international position is impermanent, but, while the United States remains a superpower, this condition will impose special restraints.

Constitutional Limits. Constitutional restraints condition foreign affairs administration more significantly in the United States than in any other great power. The federal executive has primary constitutional responsibility for this function, but the legislative and judicial branches exercise legal prerogatives that give them enormous direct and indirect influence. State and local executive, legislative, and judicial authorities likewise enjoy specific and reserved constitutional rights that permit them to influence the course of American external relations. The bases for participation by each of the three branches at each level are examined in detail in Chapter 2.

The Historical Heritage. The legacy of the past influences American foreign affairs administration tremendously and will continue to do so, although subject to modification by present and future experience. Professor Stanley Hoffman observes that Americans, unlike Europeans, believe "that the values that arise from their experience are of universal application, and they are reluctant to recognize that they are tied to the special conditions that made the American success possible." The global entanglements that followed long, irresponsible isolationism brought disappointment and frustration because American history engendered excessive expectations. It bred an undue faith in progress that led to complacency about the power struggle and overoptimism about panaceas to assure world order. Consequently, when issues prove intractable, Americans blame the world rather than their expectations. They likewise incline to exaggerate the importance of local setbacks because they have never suffered a real defeat. They suffer from the conviction, based on wishful thinking, that history is on their side, although they righteously condemn deterministic Marxist thinking, which is at least analytical. The United States has trouble cooperating with other states as equals because it has never been friendly with equals, only dependents. Thus, the American experience in the 1917–1919 coalition became unbearable because Americans had not really accepted interdependence as the norm of international relations.[4]

Charles Burton Marshall, writing in 1954, declared that one of the persistent characteristics of the American approach to foreign relations in the past half-century has been the notion of the "existence of a philosopher's stone in world affairs—an achievable perfect formula." The mood has been usually "emotional and poetic" rather than "apposite and practical." Some had desired to banish the problem of power by declaring that it did not exist, others had wanted to rely on institutions, such as arbitration, conciliation, or international organization. Isolationism, disarmament, political accommodation, collective security, world government, and constitutional amendment to establish legislative control of foreign policy all had their adherents. Such reliance on "one shot" solutions had done no good but had often done harm by encouraging illusions. The nation seemed at times to be in danger of "letting its Walter Mitty element gain the upper hand."

Marshall emphasized that Americans seek unitary solutions partly because they have been conditioned to accept the "rationalist assumptions of a natural right ordering human affairs." This conditioning also leads to oversimplified explanations of problems, such as the Yalta sell-out and the mistakes of Versailles, which can neither be proved nor disproved. The notion that perfect foresight is attainable in the planning and perfect efficacy in the execution of foreign policy increases the pressure to seek and adopt perfect formulas. Moreover, foreign affairs especially attracts the dreamer and ideologue who is bold and imaginative because it offers such a rich field for improve-

[4] Stanley Hoffman, "The American Style: Our Past and Our Principles," *Foreign Affairs*, 46, no. 2 (January 1968), 362–366.

ment. Unfortunately, those who seek perfectibility normally take inadequate account of means or difficulties. Their failure to weigh means and difficulties is terribly important because the government is accountable and foreign policy has to be made acceptable to the American people. The main problem, therefore, is to acquaint the public with the inherent limits of foreign policy so that issues may turn on questions of how best the nation may achieve its limits "rather than on vain propositions of perfection and destructive self-reproach over failure to achieve it."[5]

Arthur M. Schlesinger, Jr., regards Americans as susceptible to the conspiratorial theory of history—to the notion that events are the result of the machinations of bad men. Both the extreme right and left refuse to recognize that history is "an untidy and unkempt process, in which decisions are taken not according to master plans, but in darkling confusion and obscurity, and where ignorance, accident, chance and stupidity play a larger role than Machiavellian calculation."[6]

Marshall attributes the tendency to exaggerate American power in the world to four major influences: first, the public's unconscious tendency to redress its own inadequacy by viewing the state as omnipotent; second, the intoxicating effect of the successful history of American foreign policy; third, the excessive faith of Americans in law and legislation—in particular "the very fact of having a lot of legislation laying down the objectives entertained by the Congress for situations internal to other countries tends to obscure the limits of our own jurisdiction"; and finally, excessive American faith in power, engineering, and social techniques to solve problems. The latter error stems in part from "a habit of mind derived from the study of history." The historian makes the past unfold sequentially and logically. He erroneously, if innocently, propagates the notion that history offers the key to the future. There is, of course, a basic contradiction between a deterministic concept of "an ascertainable pattern of the future" and the assumption that men can gain ascendency over it, but this is not always apparent. Grave danger resides in relying on any school of thought, and no weakness in acknowledging that attempts to cope with

---

[5] Marshall, *Limits of Foreign Policy*, pp. 12–18, 62, 109–127.
[6] Schlesinger, *Bitter Heritage*, p. 122.

the future must be "speculative and chancy." Fatal errors result from assuming that meticulous planning can overcome this inherent circumstance. Not perfection but utility must be sought, and utility is a modest virtue. Thus, plans must allow for any contingency and recognize human weaknesses.[7]

A recapitulation of history's inhibitive role may be helpful. In brief, the experience of the American people prior to 1939 seems to have given them excessive faith in their own values, in a panacea, which if discovered and properly administered by the bungling bureaucrats of Washington would solve all international problems, in the inevitability of progress, in the manageability of the future, and in the efficacy of domestic legislation or international agreements to control the course of international affairs. History contributed as well to widely held opinions that, when foreign affairs administration fails to bring successful results, foreign or domestic conspirators are responsible; that the processes of diplomacy are suspect or evil; that American diplomats are usually fools or incompetents; and, finally, that history is on the side of the United States, despite the rejection by the American people of the Marxist deterministic thesis and their conviction that the future is alterable.

Because certain elements in the American heritage are confused and often in conflict, the public and even many officials suffer disappointments that further hamper the successful administration of foreign affairs. In other words, restraints imposed by the historical heritage create secondary limitations by engendering frustrations that make it impossible to achieve attainable goals.

Beliefs and Values. The beliefs and values cherished by the American people do not constitute an ideology in the sense of an operational system and machine; nor are they closely tied to the concept of national interest, as are certain broad French and British objectives, for example, natural frontiers and the balance of power. Yet, like ideologies, they transcend national interest and express general views about man and society. Such beliefs and values held by Americans give the United States strength because they are widely held and thus create evangelical

---

[7] Marshall, *Limits of Foreign Policy*, pp. 18–27.

or missionary vigor, but they constitute a weakness because they do not fit all situations.[8]

Americans profess dedication to self-determination, peaceful change, the Monroe Doctrine, land reform, the Open Door Policy, the free enterprise system, democracy, God, national honor, and anticommunism. They are also strongly persuaded that the central problem of new nations is economic development, that consensus can always be achieved in international relations, and that free elections will assure the creation of viable, democratic governments.[9] A long-held conviction that developing nations benefit more from private foreign investment than from public loans has been somewhat weakened during the past decade by the force of external reactions and events.

International Position of the United States. The position of the United States as a superpower imposes other major inhibitions. As the leader of the free world coalition, it must seek consensus among its allies. It must also offer something more than lip service to the ideal of democracy in its domestic life and in treating with other nations. The public does not grasp the hard fact that the United States must achieve a measure of consensus and must be prepared to make reciprocal concessions in pursuit of a common aim. Furthermore, the man in the street mistakenly supposes that nations which have received assistance from the United States will forever be grateful and will willingly take policy guidance for indeterminable periods.

Constraints imposed by the need to take account of the character of their domestic regimes in dealing with other states frequently pose difficulties, and often dilemmas from which there exist no "good" exits. When the United States recognizes and assists democratic but weakly supported governments it risks provoking ultranationalistic reactions from extremists. When it maintains even "coolly correct" relations with dictators, such as Perez Jiménez, Rojas Pinilla, Duvalier, Batista, or Stroessner, it alienates public opinion at home, among its allies, and in uncommitted states. There may be no viable alternative to the recognition of an authoritarian regime, but the position of the

---

[8] Hoffman, "The American Style," pp. 367–376.

[9] Joseph S. Tulchin, "Inhibitions Affecting the Formulation and Execution of the Latin American Policy of the United States," *Ventures*, no. 2 (Fall 1967), p. 68.

United States as a world leader does not permit it to accept such a situation either with equanimity or good conscience.

The greatest restraint imposed on the United States by its position as a superpower derives from the fact that losses which may be inflicted on humanity by a nuclear conflict are so horrible to contemplate that all possible actions must be assessed not only with reference to their impact in areas of immediate application but also with reference to their likelihood of producing a great power confrontation. This circumstance forecloses many options open to far weaker powers. North Korea can seize the *Pueblo*, but the United States cannot retaliate in the same terms, not through fear of North Korea, but because such retaliation might result in a great power confrontation. The United States can bomb North Vietnam but not Haiphong harbor for the same reason.

To conclude, the United States, far from exercising omnipotent sway abroad, must accept, as must all other states, the hard fact that it may be able to influence some external situations and even to control a very few, but that its power must be husbanded with extreme care in order to achieve even a modest impact overseas. It is precisely for this reason that the character of the machinery and methods that it employs to administer its international relations assumes such grave importance; the narrow margin of success or achievement to be anticipated with sound, economical administration will inevitably be diminished or even dissipated by wasteful or dispersive methods.

2

Bases for Participation

LEGAL BASES

The President's Constitutional Powers. The Constitution of the United States vests responsibility for conducting foreign relations in the federal government but does not define or assign these responsibilities precisely. It grants the president, by and with the advice of the Senate, the power to appoint ambassadors, other public ministers, and consuls, to make treaties, provided two-thirds of the senators present concur, and to receive ambassadors and other public ministers. The president's role as commander in chief also looms very large today in the conduct of international relations. Because the Constitution vests the executive power in the president, it also concedes him inferentially dominant authority in the conduct of foreign relations, largely through exercise of the power of initiative.

The presidential power to appoint ambassadors, other public ministers, and consuls, subject to the Senate's confirmation, makes all chiefs of diplomatic missions his personal representatives and theoretically assures that the highest officers of the Departments of State and Defense and of other agencies share his basic views on foreign and national security policy. But the political considerations that determine most of his selections impair this unity of outlook, as do the bureaucratic loyalties of career appointees.

In the early days of the Republic, indeed until 1906, the foreign affairs bureaucracy remained so insignificant that presidential appointees completely dominated policy formulation and execution in the Departments of State, War, and Navy and in the diplomatic and consular services. Thereafter, the growing numbers and influence of Civil Service officers, accompanied by the emergence of career consular and diplomatic services, provided a modest bureaucratic base for foreign affairs and national security administration.

But it cannot be emphasized too strongly that before World War II, the continued use of presidential appointments to fill a substantial share of major positions at home and abroad and the granting of presidential commissions to all Foreign Service officers combined to maintain the importance of the appointment power in foreign affairs administration. Indeed, despite the enormous growth in the number and size of foreign affairs bureaucracies after 1939, the president's ability to prescribe and enforce foreign policy through his appointees still remains higher than in the closely related area of national security policy and other fields of public administration.

Foreign affairs agencies still rank as pygmies among the giants of the federal establishment. Some of them, such as the Arms Control and Disarmament Agency (ACDA), could fit comfortably into many of the subsections of the countless sections, innumerable divisions, scores of offices, and vast bureaus of the Department of Agriculture. All the personnel of the Department of State and the Foreign Service, the largest of the foreign affairs agencies, represent less than 3 per cent of the civilian staffs and 1 per cent of all the personnel grouped under the Department of Defense.

Since the number of presidential appointments to the foreign affairs agencies, especially to the Department of State and the Foreign Service, increased substantially after 1945 because of the emergence of many new chief of mission positions and new functions, the proportion of such appointees in the foreign affairs community also decreased less than in the national security agencies and the bureaucracy in general.

Consequently, although personnel expansion and agency proliferation reduced notably the president's ability to make and enforce policy through his appointees, attenuation of this power proceeded less rapidly and extensively in the foreign policy area than elsewhere.

The presidential power to make treaties, with the Senate's concurrence, far from suffering attrition, has become almost an exclusive prerogative through the substitution of executive agreements for treaties. Such agreements, which do not require Senate concurrence, now bind the United States in contractual relationships with other states in every conceivable range of subject matter. The federal judiciary opened the door to a liberal employment of the executive agreement procedure in decisions handed down during President Franklin D. Roosevelt's administration. In addition, Congress itself sanctioned the use of agreements to facilitate the Reciprocal Trade, Mutual Assistance, and like programs. However, many agreements contain commitments that make it necessary for the president to request legislation or appropriations from the Congress and thus compel him to take account of congressional attitudes before signing them.

Today the president invokes the treaty procedure only when, in his view or that of other parties, the undertaking should be given the prestige and presumed additional sanctity afforded by formal ratification, or when the subject matter holds such grave domestic political implications as to make it politic to submit the proposed commitment to the Senate.

The president's power to receive ambassadors and other public ministers gives him the right and responsibility to decide with which nations the United States shall maintain diplomatic relations. This authority now has to be exercised more frequently than when the infant Republic confined its formal diplomatic relations to a handful of European states. Today the United States recognizes almost six score states, and recognition problems arise all too frequently in a world in which half or more of them are unviable.

This inflation of recognition work compels the president to delegate more of his authority to his foreign affairs appointees and to place himself increasingly in their hands. The necessity of relying on intelligence and other reports and estimates from still further down the line also impairs free exercise of the recognition power. In the case of the controversial 1965 Dominican intervention, for example, President Lyndon B. Johnson and his senior advisers seem to have relied very heavily on field estimates of the situation. Indeed, the less known the country, the less likely it becomes that any substantial element of the president's judgment will be involved in a decision on recognition.

To some extent, of course, the president's power to recognize must also reflect restraints imposed by congressional and public opinion. Congress must appropriate funds for diplomatic representation, and it has always imposed very strict limitations on its appropriations to the Department of State. Thus, should the president recognize a government that a majority of the Congress or the country abhorred, he might not receive funds to support a mission to that state in the next budgetary period or lose support for higher priority programs. For example, should any president since the Korean War have elected to recognize Red China, he unquestionably would have faced serious congressional and public criticism.

Recognition sometimes affects the relations of the United States with third countries, and, in such cases, also limits this prerogative. Latin American states with constitutional governments and liberal elements in other states usually criticize the United States bitterly when it recognizes *de facto* military regimes that come to power by unconstitutional means. Thus the president has had to withhold assistance from and postpone recognition of several governments of this kind for varying periods in order to moderate criticism from other nations. He also had to break with the Trujillo regime because of third country opinion. Recognition of North Korea or North Vietnam would disrupt relations with all Asian Allies; recognition of East Germany would shatter NATO; and recognition of Rhodesia would cause enormous repercussions in Africa and in the United Kingdom. Thus, today the president's right to receive ambassadors and ministers obviously must be employed under considerable restraints and often without substantial opportunity to exercise personal judgment.

As commander in chief, the president must not only make or approve national security policy but must meld it rationally into foreign policy. Unfortunately, the scope and complexity of today's defense problems require so large a delegation of authority to appointed officials and the military bureaucracy that the presidential power often seems more nominal and ceremonial than effective. Strategic considerations and the tendency of the Defense Department's civilian and military officers to provide arms and plans for all conceivable contingencies—that is, to overinsure—seem often to prevail over broader considerations of national interest.

The formulation and execution of national security policy now appear to have devolved in a large measure to civilian and military bureaucrats. Although the president still makes the final decisions on major questions and appoints the senior military policy makers, he has become increasingly constrained by the intelligence agencies coordinated by the National Security Council (NSC), the weapons specialists of the Department of Defense, and the military strategists of the Joint Chiefs of Staff. Nevertheless, he and he alone can authorize the deployment of American forces overseas, the unleashing of nuclear weapons, and other major retaliatory action. He can, in effect, make war, although he cannot legally declare it. He can, with all legality, effect deployments of forces and take other military measures likely to bring about hostilities. For example, only the president could authorize the airlift that broke the Berlin blockade or the interposition of American naval forces between Formosa and mainland China. Only he could order the response to the North Korean invasion of 1950, the landing of troops in Lebanon, the sending of advisors and later combat troops to Vietnam, and the Dominican intervention of 1965.[1]

As chief executive, the president exercises prerogatives and initiative that reinforce the specific powers already discussed and, if he aspires to exert strong leadership and has the capacity to do so, give him enormous additional power. His position as chief of state and head of government in itself affords him exceptional prestige at home and abroad, which vastly enhances his ability to influence, advocate, and initiate. Indeed, no individual enjoys higher status or prestige today than does the president of the United States.

It must also be recalled that decisions of the Supreme Court have

---

[1] For a full exposition of this subject, see Ernest R. May, ed., *The Ultimate Decision: The President as Commander-in-Chief*; Merlo Pusey, *The Way We Go to War*.

left the federal government free of any constitutional restraints on its foreign affairs activities. Thus, the president, as chief executive, operates without legal impediments with respect to the range of his activities when functioning as the nation's first diplomat.

The vast increase in the federal bureaucracy, which has compelled the president to delegate more authority in all areas and has fused policy inextricably into public administration at all save recognizably low levels, has curtailed the president's ability to bring his own judgment to bear on a wide range of issues. But it has exalted his role as chief executive by giving him an infinitely more powerful, if less responsive, executive instrument to wield. The same consequence has ensued from the inflation in the federal budget and federal regulatory powers. The enormous federal expenditures and the awesome controls and restraints that the bureaucracy and its chief executive now manipulate give them a power over the economy and, indeed, over the entire polity far greater than even the most dedicated Hamiltonian might have envisaged.

The enormously increased complexity and burden of foreign relations, reflected in the relatively high degree of specialization that now prevails among its practitioners, as well as their inflated numbers, have given presidential legislative initiative in this area preponderant importance. The exercise of his initiative in the strict diplomatic sense has become, by the same token, his weightiest responsibility and greatest prerogative.

The Constitutional Powers of Congress. The authority of the Congress derives principally from its power to appropriate and to make all laws necessary and proper for carrying into execution the provisions of the Constitution. Congress also enjoys specific power to regulate foreign commerce and to declare war, but the Constitution does not designate the branch of government that shall make peace. The Senate has the additional right to advise and consent to treaties and to confirm nominations of the president to diplomatic and consular offices.

The Senate's right to confirm nominations unquestionably dwindled somewhat in importance with the rise of parties in the United States and the imposition of party discipline. It has also been undermined by the use of presidential agents[2] and the granting to them of personal ministerial and ambassadorial rank since World War II. It is significant to note that the Senate has never rejected a presidential nominee to a foreign affairs position, although a few nominations have been withdrawn and in one case the Senate withheld confirmation for a period of more than two years until the nominee's resignation had been received.

Obviously, it is impossible to determine to what extent the Senate's power to confirm nominations has influenced presidential judgment regarding the selection of candidates for foreign affairs positions or the extent to which it continues to do so. The fact that so many modestly qualified persons have obtained presidential commissions as ambassadors, ministers, and high officers in foreign affairs agencies argues that nominees' political rather than professional qualifications receive preferential attention in the White House and the Senate. Nevertheless, some political nominees have been appointed primarily because they had something special to bring to the performance of their duties. For example, John Winant filled a major role in London in smoothing British feathers, which his predecessor had ruffled, and in abating suspicions of American motives in the Labour Party.

A few less qualified political appointees have experienced very embarrassing moments before the Senate Foreign Relations Committee, as in the case of the nominee who could not pronounce the name of the prime minister of the country to which he had been designated. Fortunately, the standards of selection even of political nominees seem to be rising, and the totally incompetent or gauche individual who surfaces abroad because of his campaign contributions has become increasingly rare in the past decade.

The Senate's right to confirm treaties no longer gives it a major role in foreign affairs administration. The rapid rise in the number and importance of executive agreements has greatly diminished the significance of this prerogative. But it continues to exist, and, when matters of great moment, such as a nuclear proliferation or testing accord, must be negotiated with foreign powers, the treaty form solemnizes

---

[2] For a detailed and authoritative discussion of this practice see Henry M. Wriston, *Executive Agents in American Diplomacy*.

the agreement, and the Senate must then confirm it if it is to achieve validity.

Confirmation always entails elements of great hazard because it brings into play forces and prejudices of domestic politics that do not necessarily relate to the national interest. Recollections of President Woodrow Wilson's ghastly failure to achieve ratification of the Versailles Treaty, of the later failure of the Senate to approve the accession of the United States to the World Court, and of earlier rejections of carefully negotiated documents, such as William H. Seward's annexation treaty with the Dominican Republic and the McLane-Ocampo Treaty with the Juarez government, continue to haunt presidents and secretaries of state.[3] Consequently, the treaty power, although no longer exercised frequently, serves as a very real limitation on the power of the executive to commit the United States in engagements with other nations.

The power of Congress to declare war exists today as an almost complete constitutional anachronism, partly because the technology of modern warfare may compel the executive to commit the nation to total hostilities at a moment's notice, and partly because the president, as commander in chief, enjoys the right to deploy and mobilize American forces as he may consider necessary or expedient. Force deployment, without specific congressional authorization in the form of a declaration of war, led to naval warfare with France during John Adams' administration, to hostilities with the Tripolitanians only a few years later, to wars with American Indians throughout the nineteenth century, to the outbreak of fighting with Mexico in 1846, and so on, down to Vietnam. In some cases, congressional approval for deployment or shows of force came to the executive in advance of or after his action, either solicited or unsolicited, in the form of joint or concurrent resolutions or less formal expressions of congressional support.

The rapid pace and extreme complexity of international events since 1939 have, of course, compelled the president to use his powers as commander in chief in perhaps more dangerous contexts than ever before and with fewer opportunities for prior consultation with the

[3] For a full treatment of this subject see W. Stull Holt, *Treaties Defeated by the Senate*.

Congress. Yet the president, even in emergencies, must keep in mind the ultimate need for appropriations and legislation to support military action; and he normally consults the Congress when time and circumstances permit. In so doing, he probably affords more recognition to its powers to appropriate and legislate than to its residual war-making prerogative, but it could at least be said that he genuflects toward this prerogative either by describing his military actions as "peace-keeping" or employing a similar euphemism.

In sum, it cannot be emphasized too strongly that the actual commitment of American military forces to combat today, despite the constitutional prerogative of the Congress to declare war, has become almost exclusively a presidential function.[4] Naturally no president would so commit forces without a strong conviction that the Congress and the nation would ultimately perceive that the national interest demanded such action, but this does not obscure the fact that the formal declaration of war, which the Constitution contemplates as a congressional function, no longer controls such commitments of force. Since peace today not infrequently comes to nations in conflict without the signing of treaties, here, too, the Senate has lost some of its constitutional prerogative. However, when formal peace negotiations succeed, treaties still confirm their agreements.

Congress continues to regulate foreign commerce by enacting all tariff laws, and the Senate approves treaties of commerce and navigation with foreign powers, as well as consular conventions. On the other hand, the widespread use of trade and international commodity agreements and the establishment of the Tariff Commission, which interprets and administers the tariff, have compelled Congress to delegate a considerable measure of its constitutional regulatory authority. Today, in fact, the regulation of foreign commerce involves too many complications and reaches into too many cognate areas to fall exclusively within the compass of legislative control. Congress now lays down broad guidelines and distributes the requisite authority to various executive agents who administer its regulatory program.

[4] President Richard M. Nixon's deployment of troops in Cambodia and the subsequent failure of Congress to place genuine limits on his power as commander in chief, illustrate this point clearly.

The preceding discussion leads inevitably to the conclusion that the specific powers of Congress no longer give it substantial control over the administration of the nation's foreign affairs. Indeed, congressional authority in this area derives principally from the power to appropriate and to legislate. For this reason, Congress defends vigorously its custom of appropriating on an annual basis, even for programs that obviously require long-term funding. By keeping the executive establishment on a short financial leash, Congress can control programs and policies in both foreign and domestic affairs far more effectively.

By the same token, the power to appropriate gives Congress great influence over the size and character of the foreign affairs and national security bureaucracies, over the ability of the administration to fulfill any commitments in international agreements or treaties, over the nature and character of economic assistance, over the character and size of foreign intelligence and subversive operations, and over the nature and dimensions of foreign information and cultural programs.

Legislation enacted by the Congress establishes the basic structure of the Foreign Service, the United States Information Agency (USIA), the Civil Service, the Department of Defense, the military services, the National Security Council (including the national intelligence structure), the nature of our atomic energy controls, the space program, tariffs, immigration, nationality, and a multitude of other statutory members forming the framework of the legislative edifice within which foreign affairs must be administered.

In exercising its legislative prerogative, Congress normally must content itself with laying down rather broad policy directives and delegating to the executive establishment considerable authority to interpret its intent through administrative law. In effect, therefore, Congress delegates a considerable measure of its authority in most areas to the executive. The extent of delegation ascended rapidly in foreign affairs administration after World War II.

In some cases administrators now seek and find loopholes in statutes broad enough to enable them virtually to rewrite statutory law and to distort or destroy its original intent. For example, State Department administrators between 1962 and 1966, completely reorganized the officer structure of the Foreign Service. In so doing, they abandoned the original concepts of the roles of Foreign Service reserve and staff officers, and they undermined the career concept that had served as one of the strongest unifying and motivating forces of the Foreign Service officer corps.[5]

Limitations in congressional appropriations sometimes prove more difficult to evade than do statutory limitations, especially because of the postaudit operations of the General Accounting Office (GAO). But 1969 hearings on Defense Department contracting procedures raise very serious doubts about the efficacy of limitations in appropriations and GAO postaudits as well, at least as far as Defense Department operations are concerned.

The Constitution and the Federal Courts. Federal judicial power in the administration of foreign affairs derives from the constitutional right and duty of the courts to interpret the law of the land, including treaties. This power has grown enormously and become quasi-legislative. Obviously, the constitutional function of the judiciary bears less directly and powerfully on foreign affairs administration than does that of the Congress or the president, but it is not negligible.

The federal courts vastly extended the powers of the federal government to conduct the international relations of the United States. The express powers of the federal government are relatively limited, and the early tendency of the Congress was to hold the executive to its stated powers, reserving other functions to the states. The court, in contrast and relying on the doctrines of implied and inherent powers, vastly extended the federal government's authority. Implied powers derive by juridical construction from the express powers; inherent powers, from the legal theory that a sovereign state has general rights, powers, and obligations not derived from any compact between its constituent elements but resulting from the union of the whole. The executive at times has invoked the doctrine of emergency powers, but the federal courts generally have been loath to accept it. Thus, they usually employed the doctrines of implied and inherent powers until this century to define and enlarge powers of the federal government,

---

[5] A more detailed exposition of this development appears in Chapter 7.

and especially the executive, in the administration of both foreign and domestic affairs.

Late in the nineteenth century, a new legal theory of national power began to emerge in decisions of the federal courts, namely, that the law of nations confers certain powers on every sovereign nation as inherent in sovereignty and as essential to self-preservation. This doctrine found its full exposition in the Curtiss-Wright case of 1936, which offered international law as the basis of the powers of external sovereignty of the federal government. The case proclaimed a distinction between the sources of internal and external sovereign powers, finding the latter in international law, and not exclusively in the Constitution, and it vastly enlarged these powers.

This trend received substantial support and confirmation from several earlier, concurrent tendencies. The federal courts very early extended the doctrine of political questions (that a particular matter should be decided by the executive rather than by the courts) to most matters of international relations; generally upheld the ability of the government to fulfill its international obligations; showed greater respect for views of executive departments as to their obligations under international law than for their opinions in domestic questions; and elected to regard executive agreements as the equivalent of treaties for domestic law purposes. The influence of many authoritative writers who believed that powers of inherent sovereignty derived from national sovereignty and international law reinforced these influences.

In any event, the present judicially defined limits of the powers of external sovereignty, if they exist at all, are much broader than the constitutional limits. National foreign policy now overrides some of the rights of the states, some property rights, certain individual rights, the limits imposed on authority delegated by the Congress to the executive, and certain statutory requirements for the judicial review of administrative acts of external sovereignty. Thus the declaration as unconstitutional of any act affecting matters of external sovereignty has become extremely unlikely.[6]

---

[6] The preceding comments summarize and inevitably oversimplify the analysis presented by Professor Foster K. Sherwood in his perceptive article, "Foreign Relations and the Constitution," *Western Political Quarterly*, 1 (1948), 386–399.

It should not be assumed that the federal judiciary, by vastly extending the powers of the executive and the Congress, has abdicated all authority over foreign affairs. Its current quasi-legislative role remains important and will be discussed in Chapter 8.

Constitutional Rights of States, Individuals, and Foreigners. State governments have no constitutional responsibility for the administration of foreign affairs. Indeed, they are specifically enjoined against entering into "any Treaty, Alliance, or Confederation," granting "Letters of Marque and Reprisal," taxing imports or exports, engaging in war, or maintaining troops and warships without the consent of Congress. Nevertheless, the Tenth Amendment reserving to the states "the powers not delegated to the United States by the Constitution nor prohibited by it to the States," together with those articles which explicitly recognize the judicial and taxing powers of the states, give state and local governments considerable influence on foreign affairs administration, principally through the exercise of their fiscal, judicial, police, and educational powers.

Public participation, individually or corporately, in foreign policy administration probably did not engage the attention of the Founding Fathers as even a remote contingency. Nevertheless, the right of the citizenry to express its approval or to punish an administration's handling of foreign or domestic affairs through periodic elections finds its basis in the Constitution and is reinforced by the Seventeenth Amendment, providing for the popular election of senators. It is also sustained by Section 2 of Article I, which requires decennial reapportionment, and by recent judicial and legislative action reinforcing the "one man, one vote" principle.

Provisions of the Bill of Rights, which guarantee freedom of speech and the press, the rights to assemble, to petition for redress of grievances, to keep and bear arms, and to full process of law, provide the other constitutional bases from which individuals, groups, and the mass media derive their influence over the administration of federal policy.

The Constitution's recognition of the high legal status of treaties and its tacit acceptance of the rules of international law, later explicitly adopted by the Supreme Court, provide the basis for the influence that foreign governments and individuals legally exert on the administration of American foreign affairs, and, conversely, for the role that Americans legally discharge in the administration of other states' foreign affairs. Reciprocal exchanges of diplomatic and consular personnel and the reciprocal concession to resident and visiting aliens of most of the rights of nationals derive immediately and directly from the Constitution's exaltation of treaties and the ground rules of international behavior. All these constitutional rights have been defined and redefined by statute, judicial interpretation, administrative law, time, experience, the characters of personalities in office, and changes in the national and international situations.

Statutes. Federal statutes define responsibilities for foreign policy administration in greater detail but sometimes no more clearly than does the Constitution, because the foreign affairs interests of many agencies now overlap and because responsibility does not always bring authority or appropriations. All of the great administrative departments and most of the federal agencies have statutory origins. Their organic laws usually define functions, organizational patterns, and, in some cases, operational authority. Statutes allot budgetary resources to each of the federal agencies annually and determine the extent and nature of their operations.

Still other statutes determine the numbers, qualifications, pay, fringe benefits, and working conditions of staffs employed in the formulation and execution of American foreign policy. The Rogers Act of 1924, the Foreign Service Act of 1946, and subsequent legislation defined and redefined the structure of the Foreign Service. Similar enactments structure the Civil Service, elements of which engage in foreign policy formulation and execution in the Department of State and other agencies or regulate the covert intelligence and military services.

Statutes prescribe much of the work content of both Washington and field agencies. The Nationality Act, immigration legislation, laws stipulating the rights of seamen, and other statutes largely define the nature of consular work. Authorizations and appropriations for foreign assistance programs, for the exchange of students and professors, for the sale of surplus agricultural commodities, and for other activities, provide much of the substantive work of diplomatic officers. These and other laws, such as those regulating the right to bear arms and broadcast or televise, also engage the efforts of vast numbers of employees in the Department of State and in other domestic agencies.

It would be profitless to attempt to list all the federal enactments that directly or indirectly affect the administration of American foreign policy. The preceding illustrations will serve to indicate their vast range and immense importance in providing a legal basis for foreign policy administration.

Administrative Law. Administrative law affords a third legal basis for participating in foreign affairs administration. Executive orders, departmental and agency regulations, interdepartmental and interagency agreements, and directives from administrators fall within this category.

Since constitutional, statute, and administrative laws provide basic authority for the makers of federal administrative law, there is no clearly established hierarchy of legal norms in this area.

The president uses executive orders to define more narrowly the responsibilities of departments and agencies administering American foreign policy, to improve coordination, and even to establish new agencies. The Peace Corps, for example, originated in an executive order and only later received statutory approval. Executive orders regulate many other areas, such as personnel administration.

Departmental and agency regulations sometimes fill gaps in statutes or executive orders, providing more detailed guidance for foreign affairs administrators. In other cases, they open new ground. Thus, the Department of State administratively prescribes procedures for the recruitment, promotion, and selection of Foreign Service career, reserve, and staff officers. These regulations derive from authority conferred on the secretary by the Foreign Service Act and various amendments thereto. Another example of a State Department regulation opening new ground in foreign affairs administration is afforded by a regulation forbidding Foreign Service personnel to sell personal effects abroad at a profit.

Agreements between departments and agencies frequently define areas of responsibility left vague by statute or executive order. In other cases they allocate responsibility for matters or subjects that scientific or technological breakthroughs or other developments have brought into the area of international relations. Agreements also establish programs of day to day cooperation, relationships between personnel of various agencies, and the financial responsibility of agencies for specific operations. Many of the Department of State's relations with AID, USIA, the Departments of Commerce, Defense, and Agriculture, and numerous other agencies are defined by agreements. The provision of office and other facilities to employees of other agencies abroad, the commissioning of employees of other agencies as Foreign Service reserve officers, and like operations, all provide subject matter for interagency agreements. Interagency committees and liaison arrangements usually come into existence in this manner as well.

Informal orders from federal authorities provide a fourth basis of administrative law. They may take the form of circular or individual letters or memoranda, or even verbal instructions. Presidents Eisenhower, Kennedy, and Johnson all used circular letters to departmental and agency heads to define the coordinative role of the Department of State. Presidents communicate by cable, wireless, telephone, letter, and memorandum with departmental and agency heads and with chiefs of diplomatic missions.

The secretary of state and officers of his and other agencies likewise instruct subordinates and field representatives in formal instructions either cabled or mailed, or in informal but equally binding letters and memoranda. Face to face or telephonic verbal instructions along the chain of command are common in emergencies or to settle minor problems. These are usually confirmed in writing. Presidents have assigned grave and urgent responsibilities to individuals and agencies in this way in moments of crisis, sometimes by designating the secretary of state, the secretary of defense, or a White House aide to establish and head a task force to monitor or work on a problem.

Administrative law, which defines or prescribes the participation by federal agencies and officials in foreign affairs administration, also conditions, in some cases, the participation of states, localities, and the general public. Some regulations implement statutes (such as those setting qualifications for the receipt of federal subsidies for education); other directives delimit the range of state, local, and public involvement in public administration, domestic and foreign.

It must also be recalled that the states, in turn, base their activities on their own constitutional, statutory, and administrative laws, under and within the federal framework. The localities derive their powers from state constitutions, municipal charters, and legislation, which they likewise supplement with ordinances and local administrative rulings.

Extralegal Bases

The preceding summary description of the legal bases for participating in foreign affairs activities should not obscure the fact that many individuals and institutions participate without legal authority, although the activity that develops through individual or institutional initiative and prescription often receives later statutory or executive authorization. Some officials and agencies gain important extralegal influence through personal relationships with the president or other highly placed officers of the federal establishment, or through influence with congressional committees or individual congressmen.

Numerous departments and agencies without formal sanctions assumed foreign affairs responsibilities or began to engage in such activities during and after World War II. Most of these responsibilities and operations have since been legitimized by legislation, including appropriations acts, or by executive action; but some activities continue to be performed and new activities to be initiated from time to time without express authority.

Some of the roles of the public and state and local authorities in foreign affairs administration have no legal basis of any kind. State and local officials have no legal obligation, for example, to receive and entertain foreign visitors, but usually do so gladly. By the same token, the press has no legal authority to participate in the administration of foreign affairs, but certain correspondents, columnists, editors, and analysts do, in fact, exert verifiable influence on the president and other high officers. Most of the influence of the public and state and local officials, moreover, results indirectly from their exercise of predominantly domestic roles as, for example, electors of congressmen and presidents and administrators of public schools. Influence exercised by lobbyists, domestic and foreign, and by agents of foreign governments ranges from the legally authorized to the illegal. Acts of espionage and subversion obviously fall in the second category.

The Relationship of Administration and Policy Formulation

The relationship of foreign affairs administration to the formulation and execution of foreign and national security policy cannot be defined precisely. Traditionally, public administration existed in a conceptual compartment sealed off and insulated from policy. Such a concept underlay the assumption that the Department of State could exercise effective policy control over organizations having their own funds and field organizations. The concept presupposes a system in which function is rigidly allocated by position or agency and just as rigidly performed. It further assumes a considerably more rigid conformance to constitutional and statutory role definitions or limitations than pertains today. It does not concede that the executant of a policy may modify or distort policy beyond recognition or that administrators may strongly influence policy formulation.

Eighteen scholars and public officials of great distinction participated in a conference convened by the American Academy of Political and Social Science in December 1967 to discuss the theory and practice of public administration. No consensus emerged as to whether public administration could be defined at this time, or about its scope or practice. Nevertheless, the chairman, James C. Charlesworth, reported that the conferees "initially agreed that the scope of public administration cannot be determined apart from the scope of the whole political system." He also found agreement that "public administration agencies (above an easily recognized level) helped make public policy, and that the old bifurcation of government and public affairs into policy and implementation is erroneous." He further observed:

Since the objectives of public administrators are determined in large part by the administrators themselves, it is distressing to recognize that normative administrative theory is in disarray. It may deal with the ultimate dignity of man, or may confine itself to publicly agreed upon objectives, like education, or it may deal with instrumental values like clientele participation. Normativism, if it is anything is synoptic, and therefore requires a bold and comprehensive philosophic statement.

Descriptive-analytic theory also is in disarray; for old concepts of legalism and monism are lacking in reality; we need more studies of administrative ecology.

With respect to administrative methods, Charlesworth felt that general agreement had emerged that

administrative authority and response are no longer hierarchical, if they ever were; many nonhierarchical agents play in the game so the manager is a broker as well as a director. Pyramidal organization is . . . no longer apropos. The executive is not so much on top as he is in the center, being affected by "subordinates" who surround him, hence the wise executive must "consult" before taking action. Because of this and other determinants, there is a great deal of difference between the behavioral outlook of an elected as distinguished from an appointed official.

Except at modest levels, the executive deals with people he cannot order around—with coordinates, not subordinates; "colleague control" is challenging "hierarchical control." Moreover, federal-state-local relations are getting more heavily intertwined every year; constitutional law and practical administration are ever more divergent and lines of command are obscured, especially by the grant-in-aid programs, of which there are now more than four hundred.

Computerization, program planning, cost analysis, and similar techniques "create an aura of objectivity about our study of management," but such data cover "only a small part of the total factors in a decision." The conferees generally agreed, therefore, that emphasis on management ability in public administrators is yielding to "preoccupation with policy and political considerations. Indeed, we cannot separate normativism from public administration."[7]

[7] James C. Charlesworth, "A Report, and also Some Projections, Relating to the Present Dimensions and Directions of the Discipline of Public Administration," in American Academy of Political and Social Science, *Theory and Practice of Public Administration: Scope, Objectives, and Methods*, pp. 322–336. Permission to quote excerpts from James C. Charlesworth's report was granted by the American Academy of Political and Social Science.

Considerable space has been allocated to the preceding summary of authoritative views on the theory and practice of public administration, of which, of course, foreign affairs administration forms only a part, in order to underscore the fact that, while experts currently differ widely on definitions of public administration, most agree that it no longer seems possible to separate politics and administration.

The distinguished administrator and scholar, Herbert Emmerich, posited that public administration now embraces all executive acts. He noted that the tendency in American government has been "to reduce greatly the number of elected officials which characterized us in the pioneer stages of democracy and greatly to increase the number and quality of officials appointed on some kind of merit basis."[8] Although Emmerich does not proceed from this statement to the conclusion that this tendency has served to increase appreciably the political content of administrative work, one cannot perceive how it could fail to do so.

Since World War II, the mushrooming of the federal civilian and military bureaucracies, including their foreign affairs and national security components, has had the same effect by increasing both inertia and specialization throughout the now impenetrable bureaucratic jungle. Inertia, of course, tends to make an organization less responsive to direction from above. Specialization has much the same effect because superior officials cannot master all of the complex disciplines to which their subordinates tend to give their first loyalties. They must depend on them for guidance, for example, on the merits of new weapons systems and evaluations of intelligence reports. By the same token, the specialists tend to become more successful in advocating new policy or resisting changes unpalatable to them.

The tendency of the bureaucracy to expand and become more specialized owed much to Parkinsonianism but occurred mainly because government had to enter many new fields of interest and activity created by scientific and technological advances and great social upheavals. World food and health problems, the Revolution of Rising Expectations, the collapse of the colonial systems and the rise of the new nationalisms, nuclear affairs, outer space, and the need for inter-

[8] Herbert Emmerich, "The Scope and Practice of Public Administration," in *ibid.*, p. 97.

national information and intelligence services afford a few examples of problems or areas in foreign affairs with which government now concerns itself.

The Constitution did not specifically confer powers to cope with these matters, and Congress, when providing authority or funds to the executive, had to delegate broadly in crisis situations or because of the novel or even unforeseeable character of the work to be done. In some cases administrators simply had to improvise from day to day or even hour to hour. In most cases, such delegations substantially increased the policy content of administration.

Today almost 2,500,000 civilian and 3,500,000 military personnel staff the federal bureaucracy. They manage the federal budget, which absorbs about 22 per cent of the Gross National Product and exercises an even greater influence on the level of national economic activity. All postwar chief executives have complained about the insuperable difficulties they have encountered in trying to make their policy decisions effective throughout the enormous mass of the federal bureaucracy.

Policy formulation and execution now intermingle inextricably with the other duties of senior foreign affairs administrators; and even middle rank and junior foreign affairs officers, working both at home and abroad, can and do influence policy to varying degrees. The foreign affairs bureaucracy exerts its influence on policy through advocacy, decision making, the conduct of negotiations, or inertia.

Advocates express their views in estimates, speeches prepared for superiors, verbal briefings, representational work with officials and leaders of the United States and other nations, public relations activities directed toward the United States or other publics or sectors thereof, and in drafting proposed legislation or administrative law, to mention only the most important channels.

Decision making in administering statute or administrative law affords ample opportunities to modify, stultify, or initiate policy. Decisions on budget allocations, personnel assignments, staffing, programming, recruitment, promotions, assignments of oil and sugar import quotas, research funds, contracts for research or procurement, sales of agricultural surpluses, and thousands of other matters must be made on the basis of statutorily or administratively delegated or redelegated authority everyday.

Even the humblest vice consul must make decisions affecting the lives of hundreds of persons and the image of the United States abroad because of the wide discretion that the immigration and nationality laws vest in him. By the same token, the neophyte public affairs officer can affect appreciably the local atmosphere in which his and other United States programs must be executed by the manner in which he interprets USIA policy. The AID administrator in the field exercises much the same potential because much truth still remains in the old saw, "It's not what you do, it's the way that you do it!"

The conduct of negotiations with representatives of foreign states, with representatives of other agencies, or even with representatives of other offices or bureaus within his own agency sometimes affords a bureaucrat broad opportunities to effect modifications or changes in policy by accepting shadow for substance, alleging the impossibility of obtaining agreement except on terms departing from the initial instructions, or preventing agreement on substance by insisting too rigidly on nonessentials. The negotiation of Nicholas Trist with the Mexicans represents a classical case of an agent alleging the impossibility of obtaining agreement on the basis of his original instructions. During the nineteen-fifties and sixties the successful opposition of American military representatives to the acceptance of any disarmament agreements with the USSR not involving on-the-spot inspection probably serves to illustrate how basic policy objectives can be frustrated by insisting on what many would regard as nonessential, if important, conditions.

The inertia of the bureaucracy or its passive resistance to change may well serve as its most potent determinant of policy, although essentially negative. It might be helpful, perhaps, to view this phenomenon as a kind of selective, line veto power, operating more or less capriciously throughout all levels of the machine, to delay, subvert, obfuscate, or stop compliance completely through a wide range of devices. Such devices include allegations, often true, that excessive work burdens or insufficient budgetary resources inhibit compliance. Given the complexity and almost infinite layering of the average federal department or agency today, a very considerable time lapse can reasonably be anticipated between the issuance of any directive and its execution; and the two factors of size and complexity also help both honest and deceitful bureaucrats to justify their failures to move rapidly or along lines laid down for them.

The earlier discussion of the legal bases for participation in foreign affairs administration distinguished the broad categories of constitutional, statute, and administrative law as the basic sources of authority for such participation but noted that extralegal participation also occurs, although authority tends normally to legitimate or end it after a time. Generally speaking, the foreign affairs administrator's influence on policy derives only indirectly from constitutional or statute law. Indeed he makes, bends, or thwarts policy most frequently and most successfully when issuing, interpreting, or executing administrative law, or when operating extralegally. As Harlan Cleveland put it, policy for the public executive in a modern complex "turns out to be largely the decisions which he himself negotiates with other public executives. The broader guidelines that he needs are not available . . . even from the 'higher' levels of an increasingly nonhierarchical hierarchy. If he asks where he, or his organization, or America, or the world, is and ought to be heading, he finds that his best authority . . . is himself."[9]

In light of the preceding considerations, it seems clear that foreign affairs administration today undeniably embodies a very substantial if varying and undefinable political content—a content that tends to grow rapidly in the rich, permissive culture of administrative law and directives.

[9] Harlan Cleveland, "The American Public Executive: New Functions, New Style, New Purpose," in *ibid.*, p. 174.

PART II
Institutional History of Foreign Affairs Administration

3

Prologue, 1774–1939

Part II attempts a synthesis of the institutional history of American foreign affairs administration. It contributes no new evidence or major interpretive findings, except for the period since 1961, but seeks to introduce the institutional characters, fundamental concepts, terminology, and ancient dilemmas as briefly as possible. Because many of the foreign affairs agencies came into existence and many domestic agencies acquired foreign affairs interests after 1939 only a brief summary of pre-World War II developments is offered, but the bibliographical notes contain references to definitive treatments of this era.

THE HEROIC AGE OF AMERICAN DIPLOMACY, 1774–1789

When the American colonists rebelled against Great Britain, they immediately sought to exploit European rivalries to their benefit. They regarded foreign aid, economic and military, as essential to the success of their cause, and they paid for it by signing a defensive alliance with France. This involvement of the new state in European balance of power politics hampered its efforts to end the conflict with

Great Britain but did not frustrate them, principally because of the skill of its diplomats.

During its early years the infant United States achieved a quality of diplomatic representation that it has never surpassed and probably did not again attain until it developed a professional foreign service under the Rogers Act of 1924. By ironic coincidence, the highly professional execution of foreign policy during the Revolution and after 1939 also witnessed dispersion and inefficiency in domestic administration. The factors that produced these situations differed radically in both cases and the coincidence cannot be considered a parallel. It is interesting but not instructive.

The administration of American foreign policy under the Continental Congresses and the Articles of Confederation displayed two salient characteristics. First, it was exclusively congressional. Congress administered foreign policy and, indeed, discharged all other executive responsibilities through committees or *ad hoc* subordinate agencies. The other salient characteristic, the confusion that attended the domestic administration of international business, derived from the unclear definition of responsibility and its distribution between three committees of the Second Continental Congress. Overlap, duplication, and, at times, counterproductive efforts naturally resulted. In 1781 Congress established a Department of Foreign Affairs to coordinate the administration of foreign policy. This action afforded a continuity hitherto lacking, but the department still functioned under the close scrutiny of the committee-dominated Congress, itself a weak, ineffective body incapable of governing the new country.

In contrast to the lack of executive decision and authority at home, the execution of foreign policy by the tiny diplomatic and consular services displayed vigor, effectiveness, and a high degree of professional competence. This happy result stemmed from the fact that the Congress chose men of salient intellectual capacity, broad political experience (including diplomatic training as colonial agents in some cases), and great initiative. Within the constellation of diplomatic notables, the name of Benjamin Franklin scintillates, but John Jay, John Adams, Thomas Jefferson, and Henry Laurens also served with great distinction.

Diplomatic officers performed consular services, and consular officers served in quasi-diplomatic roles, especially on the Barbary Coast. Numerous so-called commercial agents performed limited consular duties, principally related to shipping and seamen. Many were aliens, but Congress consistently opposed foreigners serving as consuls, except in lower ranks.

In 1778 Franklin negotiated a consular convention with France, which the Senate eventually ratified on July 17, 1789, as the first treaty to be approved with a civilized nation under the Constitution. Based on international law, it served as a model for a statute of 1792 "concerning consuls and vice consuls," which governed the Consular Service until 1856.

CONTINENTAL EXPANSION AND EARLY GROWTH, 1790-1860

The French alliance ceased to serve the national interest of the United States even before the French Revolution embroiled France with most of Europe. The Americans had little to gain and much to lose by honoring their commitment. President Washington refused to do so, and he recommended in his farewell address that the United States follow an isolationist policy. It pursued this course until 1939, with brief lapses, although the circumstances that dictated Washington's recommendation had long since lost their validity.

Isolationism, of course, did not preclude continental expansion, inspired by the mystique of Manifest Destiny. This expansion pushed the boundaries of the nation from the Mississippi to the Pacific, eliminating, by 1854, all Spanish, French, Mexican, and British claims to territory in what is now the continental United States. By 1860 the nation had also built an enormous merchant marine and a vast foreign commerce.

The adoption of the Constitution inaugurated a new period in the administration of foreign policy, as in all other areas of political life. The domestic administration of foreign relations between 1790 and 1860 reflected the substantial respect of the executive for the privileges and powers of the Congress, congressional fear of executive ambition, and congressional determination to keep a watchful eye on all administrative concerns. Thus, the period saw executive-congressional control of foreign relations rather nicely balanced. Indeed, this balance prevailed until the twentieth century.

The president took a few major initiatives, but only after full and careful consultation with the Congress. The Congress showed excessive zeal in imposing administrative restrictions on the Department of State and its field services. No diplomatic secretary could be sent to any mission, for example, without specific congressional authorization; and Congress exercised niggardly budgetary restraints over the department and the field.

The Department of State. Congress created machinery for the administration of foreign affairs by establishing a Department of Foreign Affairs in June 1789. A few months later it changed the name of the agency to the Department of State, when it allocated certain domestic functions to it in order to save money by obviating the need for a home ministry.

When Jefferson became secretary of state in March 1790, the staff of the department consisted of two principal and three subordinate clerks, a part-time translator, and two custodians. The staff remained so small for forty years thereafter that no differentiation of functions had to be imposed. In 1833 diplomatic and consular bureaus were established, the diplomatic with 3 clerks, each having regional responsibilities, the consular with 2, to supervise 152 field officers! Congress authorized the position of assistant secretary in 1853, but the department's staff rose to only 31 by 1860, despite the vast increase in American foreign trade and shipping interests. The department's small size reflected the parsimony of Congress, the philosophy of allowing considerable initiative to officers in the field, and the preoccupation of the American nation with domestic concerns.

The Diplomatic Service. The preceding generalizations apply equally to the Diplomatic Service. Under Washington the United States maintained only five diplomatic missions. By 1860 it supported thirty-one, but all chiefs of mission and diplomatic secretaries numbered only fifty. Congressional appropriations for foreign representatives totalled $40,000 in 1790 and only $370,000 by 1861.

President Washington introduced the custom of using presidential agents for special diplomatic missions. Such agents, who had no diplomatic rank, were sometimes given the title of commissioner in later administrations. No agent enjoyed ambassadorial rank and title until after World War II. John Jay negotiated the treaty of 1794 with Great Britain, and Thomas Pinckney, the Spanish treaty, as presidential agents. When Latin America revolted, commissioners were sent to investigate the situation and promise help. Nicholas Trist negotiated the treaty that terminated the Mexican War as an agent. Naval officers served frequently as agents to negotiate with Barbary Coast or Asian states. Commodore Matthew C. Perry, for example, negotiated the treaty opening Japan to American commerce in 1854.

Diplomatic representatives continued to be chosen from among men of high capacity and attainments even during the early decades of the spoils system, because the executive did not apply it fully to the Diplomatic Service. Outstanding public men who served as diplomats included Thomas Pinckney, Rufus King, James Monroe, William Pinkney, John Quincy Adams, Richard Rush, Albert Gallatin, Gouverneur Morris, Robert Livingston, Elbridge Gerry, John Jay, and John Marshall. Most of them had no diplomatic experience, but they were usually men of affairs who had traveled widely, held important governmental offices, and accumulated much business, negotiating, and representational experience.

No one made diplomacy a career, but a few young men got some training as private secretaries. Congress authorized positions as diplomatic secretaries at major posts, but it carefully scrutinized appointments, prohibiting salary payments to any secretaries who had not been confirmed. Diplomats reported salient developments, kept "appropriate" records, issued passports to American citizens, and, in theory, supervised the consuls in their respective countries. Diplomatic secretaries served their chiefs "as directed."

The Consular Service. The Consular Service, because of the sensational growth of the American merchant marine and foreign commerce, expanded rapidly prior to the Civil War. More consular posts existed in 1860 than exist today. President Washington appointed twelve consuls and five vice consuls. By 1800 there were 52 posts, by 1820, 83, by 1830, 141, and by 1860, 282 posts and 198 consular agencies. At this time, it will be recalled, the United States employed only fifty persons in its Diplomatic Service and thirty-one in the Department of State.

Jefferson described consular duties in 1790 under four captions: officers were to report each six months the arrival and departure of American vessels; send reports on political and commercial developments as warranted, and on all military preparations; warn American shipping and merchants if war or invasion were imminent; and appoint consular agents as needed.

A statute of 1792 recognized the existence of the Consular Service, defined its duties, prescribed fees to be collected for certain services, and authorized consuls to perform duties inherent in their office or resulting from future treaties. It did not forbid officers to engage in private trade. Indeed, it authorized salaries only for two consuls on the Barbary Coast. The statute enjoined consuls to administer estates of deceased American citizens, authenticate documents, repatriate seamen, receive marine protests and declarations, and care for stranded citizens. It failed to prescribe a uniform rule for performing duties or the fees to be charged in all cases. Statutes of 1818 and 1823 added the duty of issuing consular invoices for merchandise in shipment to the United States. The expansion of American representation in North Africa, the Near East, and the Far East added judicial duties.

By 1831 the expansion of the service, the accumulation of miscellaneous instructions and statutory regulations, and the rapidly increasing importance of the service to American shipping and overseas commerce combined to inspire the issuance of a unified set of general instructions. They required the execution of a bond by all officers entering on duty and the keeping of certain records. They also specified the duties of consuls, which included, in addition to those already set forth, transmitting the consul's commission and request for exequatur to the local authorities, conserving wrecked vessels, issuing passports, protecting citizens, avoiding local controversies, reporting at least every three months to the Department of State on salient developments in "commerce or navigation," transmitting samples of new products and plant seeds to Washington, and forwarding new commercial laws and regulations. The regulations thus emphasized citizenship and commercial functions more than had previous instructions, which largely concerned shipping and seamen.

Well-founded dissatisfaction with the service may also have helped to inspire the new regulations. Only two or three State Department clerks supervised the entire service, and diplomatic missions neglected the supervisory function because they received no funds for supervisory travel. The spoils system dictated virtually all appointments, assuring that the initial qualifications of entrants would be minimal. Because most consular officers had to engage in private commerce in order to live, their personal interests frequently clashed with their official responsibilities. Consular fees were not uniform and often exorbitant. The inadequate compensation of consular representatives resulted in correspondingly poor service. As early as 1831, advocates of reform recommended a salaried service, the abolition of private trading, and the prescription of uniform fees to be paid into the Treasury; but it took twenty-five years to move Congress to enact a partial reform law!

The Act of 1856. The Act of 1856 may be described as the first legislative gesture toward creating a career consular service and as the first modest attack on amateurism in the administration of American foreign affairs. It opened a weak assault on conflicts of interest and inadequate compensation by authorizing consuls at the most important posts to receive fixed annual salaries of from $1,000 to $7,500, forbidding them to engage in trade, and requiring them to remit all fees. It authorized salaries ranging from $500 to $1,000 for officers at middle-ranking posts, and required them to remit fees, but permitted them to continue to trade. It allowed consuls and commercial agents at small posts to trade and to keep all fees collected.

The act forbade the payment of salaries to aliens as officers or commercial agents, authorized the president to issue a tariff of uniform consular fees, and permitted him to prescribe regulations for both the diplomatic and consular services. It established new schedules of salaries for chiefs of mission that remained in force until 1946!

The act set an important precedent for the recruitment of a career corps by authorizing the appointment by annual examination of twenty-five consular pupils; but Congress failed for years to provide funds for this activity and subsequently to open higher appointments to the handful of students recruited.

The act put more than half the consuls on salary and introduced uniform controls on fee collection and accountability. It failed to eliminate inefficiency because appointments and tenure continued to depend on political influence, and its defective controls did not root out corruption. Some consular salaries proved inadequate when trading was not permitted, and conflicts of interest still arose where officers were allowed to trade.

Triumph of the Spoils System, 1860–1895

During the Civil War and the three decades thereafter, the nation's rapidly expanding industrial base gave the United States an economic capability more than adequate to support great-power pretensions. The westward movement eliminated the frontier, while population growth and urbanization made giant strides. Food and fiber exports rose to new highs, and manufactured products began to move overseas. These developments occurred while the nation pursued its traditional isolationism. Indeed, they so preoccupied the national elite as to preclude serious consideration of foreign affairs. With interest focused on money making, domestic politics, and economic expansion, foreign policy administration received little attention either from the public or from Congress.

The spoils system triumphed completely over considerations of merit, and the executive normally subordinated national to partisan interests in making appointments. At every change of administration an almost complete turnover occurred in the consular and diplomatic services. Corruption and inefficiency flourished. Early Civil Service reform measures merely increased pressure on the White House for consular and diplomatic appointments. During this period President Grant sent as minister to Belgium the "most elegant gentleman that ever presided over a livery stable," and General Dan Sickles, a hero of Gettysburg, served as minister in Madrid, where his amorous intrigues with Queen Isabel II became notorious.

Congress in no way moderated the niggardliness with which it had always treated both services. It resisted all attempts to support and compensate diplomatic and consular officers at levels adequate to assure honest, efficient performance. In 1869, it reduced the staff of the Department of State from its wartime peak of forty-eight to the prewar level of thirty-one employees; it refused consistently to authorize the appointment of additional diplomatic secretaries; it suspended chargé pay for two years; it refused to allow adjustments of consular salaries or adequate office rent allowances; it made no appropriations for consular clerk hire between 1860 and 1874; it provided clerks for only thirty consulates in 1784 and for only eighty-four as late as 1896; it refused for years to appropriate funds for the appointment of consular pupils; and it failed utterly to take remedial measures to correct abuses in the Consular Service.

These abuses soon became notorious. The Act of 1856 did not ensure a strict accounting for consular fees. It also failed to prevent the entering of false claims for relief of seamen, the fraudulent administration of estates, the collection of illegal fees, the improper exercise of judicial powers, the illegal sale of passports, collusion with masters in discharging seamen, and the imposition of unauthorized taxes on Chinese immigrants. Treasury officers, who inspected consular posts to monitor fee collections, uncovered these and other deficiencies, including widespread drunkenness, low efficiency, and conflicts of interest.

Despite congressional and executive indifference and neglect, the growth of American foreign economic interests and a sharp rise in the number of Americans traveling abroad for business or pleasure compelled a substantial expansion of both services. But the exercise of initiative by field officers ceased to be encouraged or even permitted, because the advent of the steamship, the telegraph, and the cable enabled Washington to exercise closer control over the field.

American diplomatic missions increased from thirty-one to forty-one, and, in 1893, the rising power of the United States displayed itself in the conversion of its legations in Great Britain, France, Italy, and Germany into embassies. Only about half of the missions at this time had diplomatic secretaries, and only a handful of officers succeeded in dedicating their lives to professional diplomacy.

Consulates increased in number from 282 in 1860 to 323 in 1890, of which 38 were consulates general, 238, consulates, and 47, commercial agencies. Consular agencies increased from 198 to 437, principally because consular officers found fee-splitting arrangements with consular agents an easy way to supplement their inadequate official incomes.

The growth of both services and the assumption of more authority by Washington required a reorganization of the Department of State and some modest expansion of its bureaucracy. Secretary Hamilton Fish established the First and Second Diplomatic Bureaus in 1870. Each of the six officers assigned to these bureaus had separate regional responsibilities. He also split the Consular Bureau into six identical geographic areas. This division brought some improvement in the supervision of the field services by increasing the number of persons conducting diplomatic and consular correspondence from eight to thirteen.

Congress authorized the positions of second and third assistant secretary in 1866 and 1875 respectively, and it applied Civil Service acts to the lower echelons of the department. It also provided funds to permit the staff to rise by 1898 to the impressive total of eighty-eight! Some new units appeared, including tiny Bureaus of Trade Relations, Citizenship, Rolls and Library, Accounts, Archives, and Foreign Commerce.

Genesis of the Career Services, 1895–1914

The Civil War, subsequent economic growth, and its rapid increase in population gave the United States a mighty power base. Continental expansion ended with acquisition of Alaska in 1867, but the mystique of Manifest Destiny still stirred many spirits among the elite, who sought overseas outlets for the vibrant republic's energy. Their enthusiasm generated a brief experiment with traditional imperialism, the beginning of American involvement in East Asian affairs, the creation of a major naval force, and a temporary concern with the problem of maintaining the European balance of power. These activities, in turn, produced a shift in the balance of executive-congressional control over the administration of foreign affairs. Although President

Theodore Roosevelt made far greater use of the initiative in this and other areas than had any of his predecessors, the American people generally remained preoccupied with domestic concerns, and their early manifestations of interest in world politics proved ephemeral.

The movement to reform the field services received added impetus from the success of the Civil Service acts, the triumph of progressivism under Theodore Roosevelt, a continued rise in the volume and importance of American foreign commerce, a major expansion in the volume of diplomatic and consular work, and the dawning recognition that diplomatic and consular appointments made under the spoils system reflected adversely on the prestige of a great power and left important national interests unserved.

Enlightened statesmen urged reform intermittently after the Civil War. When a reform bill failed of passage in 1895, President Grover Cleveland issued an executive order putting 60 per cent of the positions in the service under a competitive examination system. This meant little because Cleveland had cleaned house upon taking office. President William McKinley followed the same practice, and all of his appointees, save one, passed the so-called examination. President Roosevelt likewise urged Congress to reform and reorganize the Consular Service, and in November 1905 he broadened the scope of the 1895 order to require the examination of all candidates for posts carrying salaries of more than $1,000 per year. In 1906, Congress finally created a career Consular Service.

The Act of 1906 classified all consular posts by salary categories ranging from $2,000 to $12,000; created a corps of five officers charged with inspecting each office every two years; required that all consular clerks receiving salaries of more than $1,000 per year be United States citizens; forbade officers receiving more than $1,000 per year in salary to engage in business or legal practice; instructed all officers, except consular agents, to pay fees into the Treasury and to account for them; and abolished the time-honored grade of commercial agent.

An executive order, complementing the statute, regulated appointments and promotions in the service in accordance with the Civil Service Act of 1883. It provided for appointments to the lowest classes by examination or by the promotion of clerks, vice consuls, and consular agents after examination, and it stipulated that all promotions to higher rank should be by merit. It also established a Board of Examiners.

Between 1898 and 1908, Congress authorized an increase in the number of diplomatic secretaries from twenty-four to sixty, the appointment of additional second secretaries, and, for the first time, a few third secretaries. It also authorized the recruitment of ten Chinese and six Japanese student interpreters, supplementing interpreter positions previously authorized. These authorizations, important in themselves, set a precedent by requiring that the appointments be made on a merit basis.

President Roosevelt ordered that all vacancies for diplomatic secretaries be filled only by transfer, promotion, or appointment after examination. President William Howard Taft extended the merit system of promotion to the Diplomatic Service, set up a Board of Examiners similar to that already established for the Consular Service, and prescribed written and oral examinations for diplomatic secretaries.

The long Republican tenure, 1897 to 1913, also favored the growth of a career diplomatic service because it greatly reduced personnel turnover and permitted the first appointments of men who had elected diplomacy as a career as chiefs of mission and to high office in the Department of State. Eighteen of the forty-one ambassadors and ministers on duty in March 1913 had served previously as diplomatic secretaries or consular officers. President Wilson sacked most of them, but the values of continuity and experience had been amply demonstrated.

Diplomatic and consular officers both welcomed the statute of 1906 that authorized the payment of transportation expenses of officers traveling to and returning from their posts under orders. Congress also authorized a modest program of purchasing sites and buildings for diplomatic properties. Before World War II, the government acquired few properties, but the act established the principle that American representatives abroad should be provided with adequate business offices and official residences.

The staff of the Department of State rose to 210 by 1909, when it included 35 officers, 135 clerks, and 40 messengers and custodians.

This growth, imposed by the heavier supervisory workload and the wider participation of the United States in world politics, required more differentiation of functions.

A reorganization of 1909 gave the third assistant secretary of state responsibility for the Diplomatic Service and established the new positions of counselor (as second officer of the department), director of the Consular Service, and resident diplomatic officer. It created four geographic divisions, replacing the ancient diplomatic bureaus, as well as a Division of Information. It reorganized and enlarged the Bureaus of Trade Relations, Citizenship, and Indexes. After the reorganization, a few area experts from the Diplomatic Service were brought back to the department to staff the regional divisions and the new position of resident diplomatic officer. This set a pattern for field staffing of the key, decision-making regional units of the department which still prevails. The accompanying organization chart illustrates how the Department of State operated from 1909 to 1924 (see Chart 1).[1]

Establishment and Consolidation of the Unitary, Elite, Career Service, 1914–1939

During World War I, the United States, a reluctant and naïve giant, entered the arena of world politics. The giant withdrew after a brief, unhappy encounter. But his world had changed. He now enjoyed the status of a major creditor; science and technology had vastly increased the frequency, complexity, and importance of international contacts; trade, investments, and business interests abroad had multiplied; and Americans could no longer be kept down on the farm —tourism had grown to a mighty flood. Even during the most isolationist phase of the period, the giant required a much larger, more sophisticated, unified, career foreign service.

The executive's role in foreign affairs continued to expand because

---

[1] Supervisory functions during this period shifted between the assistant secretaries from time to time, and unit titles changed, but the structure remained fundamentally unaltered although new functional units were added for visa issuance, protocol, and treaty work after World War I. Most of the data in Chart I were extracted from the *Register* of the Department of State, December 1909.

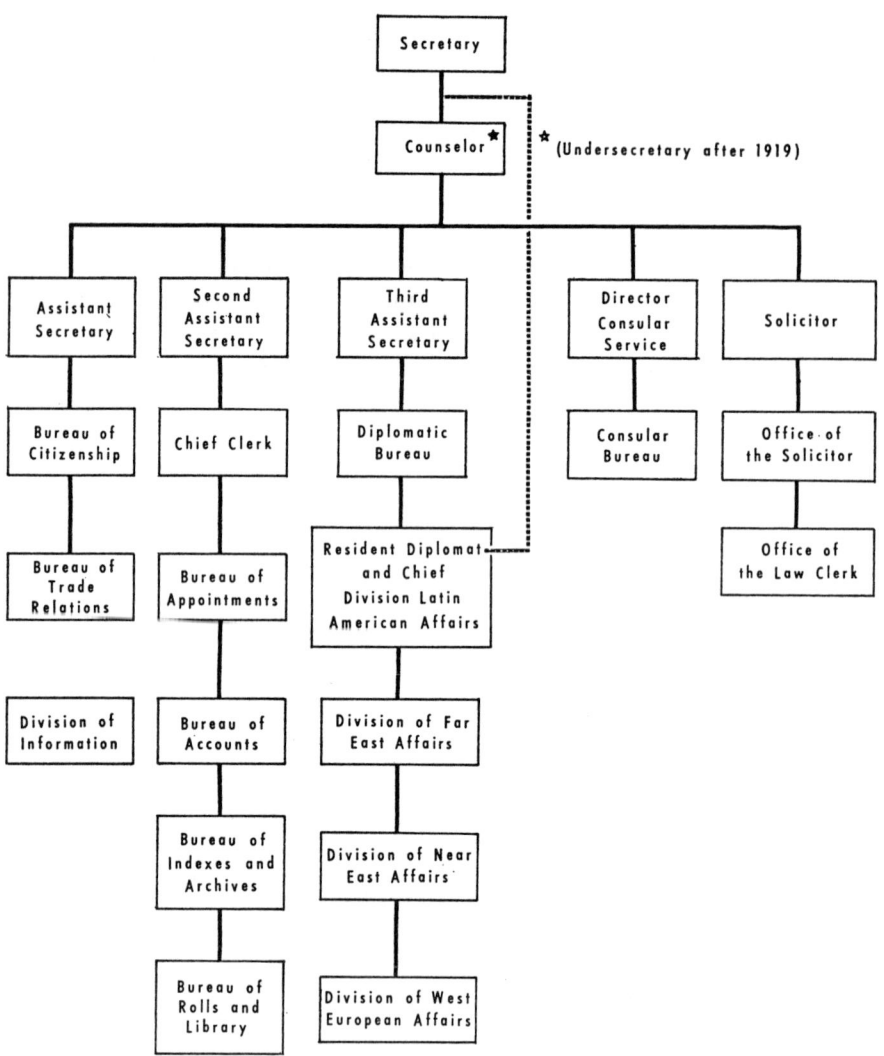

Chart 1: Department of State, 1909–1924

complex decisions had to be made more often and more urgently and because Congress could only be consulted about the most important matters. But Congress retained a major, if sometimes negative, policy-making role, which it exercised in rejecting the Covenant of the League of Nations and the World Court and by passing the Neutrality Acts of the late thirties, despite misgivings of the executive.

The period also witnessed the assumption of important foreign affairs roles by executive departments other than the Department of State. The division of roles occurred partly because of the increasing complexity of foreign affairs, which interpenetrated domestic concerns, but also because their growing importance aroused bureaucratic rivalries and spurred bureaucratic competition. Nevertheless, the Department of State's coordinating role at home and the monopoly of representation abroad enjoyed by its Foreign Service seemed well established in 1939.

World War I and the Gestation of the Career Services, 1914–1924. World War I imposed heavy burdens both on the field and on the Department of State. Diplomatic and consular officers had to relieve and repatriate American citizens, represent foreign interests, inspect prisoner of war camps, expand reporting programs, and enforce passport and visa requirements adopted as wartime security measures. The work of the Department of State increased 400 per cent in the first six weeks of the war, mostly in welfare and repatriation. Subsequently, the representation of belligerent interests, the enforcement of American neutrality programs, the assistance of relief organizations, and the protection of American citizens and interests added new burdens. After the United States entered the war, negotiations and activities involving military and economic cooperation with the allied powers absorbed much additional effort. The department's staff rose from 208 in 1914 to 440 in 1918. Field employees on duty in Washington increased from 5 to 23.

The authorization for diplomatic secretaries rose to 122 by 1918, or to twice the size of the prewar professional component of the Diplomatic Service. The Consular Service did not grow notably but became more professionalized as it filled vacancies by examination and as the work of consular agencies was transferred gradually to regular consular posts.[2]

Preoccupation with larger matters during the war precluded a complete restructuring of the consular and diplomatic services, but some pressing problems had to be solved. The Act of 1906, which fixed salaries of consular officers by posts, did not permit the necessary mobility of personnel or strict adherence to the merit system. The war accentuated the need for a flexible assignments policy and added to the serious financial burdens of many consular and diplomatic officers.

A statute passed in 1915 finally provided a statutory framework for the Diplomatic Service, recognized the merit principle, and remedied the most serious weaknesses of the Act of 1906. It put all diplomatic and consular appointments on the basis of office rather than post and authorized the free transfer of officers from post to post. It prescribed new classification systems for both services, fixing salaries for five classes of diplomatic secretaries in the $1,200–$3,000 range, and for fourteen classes of consular officers in the $2,000–$12,000 range. It authorized chargé pay of 50 per cent of the differential between the salary of the officer in charge and the absent officer. It recognized the merit principle by authorizing the secretary of state to report to the president the names of officers eligible for transfer, promotion, or appointment after examination. It eliminated an irksome provision of previous legislation by authorizing officers of the diplomatic and consular services to serve in the Department of State for periods up to four years without resigning from either service.

Congress created the rank of counselor of embassy in 1916, making diplomatic secretaries of Class One eligible for this rank, thus equating their precedence with that of their colleagues in other services. Another 1916 statute authorized the payment of special allowances at posts with excessively high living costs. This wartime grant set an important precedent because authorization to pay such allowances at specific posts later received permanent legislative approval. In 1919 Congress also authorized the travel at public expense to and from foreign posts of families of consular and diplomatic officers.

[2] In 1890, 437 agencies existed, but their number dwindled to 92 in 1921, 63 in 1930, and 28 in 1940.

The Rogers Act of 1924. The need for a reorganized, better-trained, unified, and more carefully selected foreign service became increasingly obvious during and after World War I. The larger role of the Diplomatic Service in economic as well as in political work and the need for greater technical skill in evaluating and interpreting intelligence both dictated substantial improvement. At the same time, consular functions expanded with the growth of trade, tourism, and the American merchant marine, the postwar retention of wartime passport and visa requirements, and the multiplication of services performed for other government agencies.

Deficiencies in existing legislation also required correction. Appointments to high diplomatic posts still depended on political influence and private means, and American chiefs of mission often displayed inexperience and ineptitude that exposed them to the ridicule of their colleagues and injured American national interests. Salaries of diplomatic secretaries obviously did not permit persons without private means to serve. Organic statutes precluded interchange between the diplomatic and consular services and limited promotion in the Consular Service because they authorized so few openings in the top classes. Diplomatic or consular officers appointed as chiefs of mission had to resign from their respective services and might be without employment after brief service under a political administration. Neither the Consular Service nor the Diplomatic Service could be considered adequately representative of the nation's varied regional, social, and racial interests. Finally neither service enjoyed the security of a retirement system.

The Rogers Act, effective July 1, 1924, established a decently compensated, unified, elite, career Foreign Service that could be expected, within a reasonable time, to attain a high degree of competence. It remedied most of the deficiencies of earlier legislation and permitted officers of the new service to discharge the larger roles required by the national interest.

The act merged the diplomatic and consular services in a unified Foreign Service of the United States. It gave officers below the rank of minister the title of Foreign Service officer (FSO), provided for their promotion only on the basis of merit, and for their assignment to either diplomatic or consular work.

It specified that officers were to be appointed to class and not to post. It established nine classes and an unclassified, probationary category. It authorized a salary range of $1,500–$9,000, but set percentage limits on the highest classes to prevent undue inflation of rank. It assigned as probationers all vice consuls of career, consular assistants, consular interpreters, and student interpreters. All other officers in the consular and diplomatic services were assigned to the new classes in accordance with their existing ranks.

New appointments were to be made after examination either to the probationary category or by lateral entry after five years of service in the Department of State. The act required the secretary of state to recommend to the president all new appointees and promotions and permitted the reinstatement of career officers by executive order after their appointment to other positions in government service.

It provided for the economic security of Foreign Service officers by establishing a system of retirement for age or disability. It authorized rent allowances, home leave with families at government expense after three years of service abroad, and representation allowances.

The new Foreign Service absorbed about 520 consular and 120 diplomatic officers. The new salary budget exceeded the preceding budget by only about 20 per cent, but the fringe benefits offered a substantial additional financial advantage to officers, especially the retirement and home leave provisions. In sum, the Rogers Act laid an ample and secure foundation for building an efficient service but left much to be done through administrative action and legislative adjustment.

In-Service Training. Lack of statutory authority and funds for in-service training made it impossible to train officers after they entered the old services. The Rogers Act permitted the retention of probationary officers in the Department of State for orientation, and the department established a Foreign Service School, which experimented with a one-year course, but soon settled on a three-month program. The first probationers took the course immediately after induction, but the department later began sending neophytes to the field for six months or a year for practical training before scheduling them into the school.

The school, directed by a senior Foreign Service officer, relied on officers from appropriate bureaus of the department for lectures covering various fields of consular and diplomatic operations, the organization of the Department of State and the Foreign Service, and the fundamentals of protocol. The lectures, of uneven quality and value but almost invariably dull, were not as useful as the opportunity that attendance at the school afforded to become acquainted with departmental operations and officers. Classes usually enrolled from fifteen to twenty-five students. All students left cards at the White House, were entertained at a White House function, and received hospitality from departmental officers. This helped to give them the sense of being part of a vital operation and to develop a high *esprit de corps*.

Because the Rogers Act abolished the classifications of student interpreter and interpreter, the department began offering regular one- to three-year assignments to study Chinese, Japanese, Russian, Turkish, and a few other "hard" languages. It required a trainee to spend seven years of service in a country using the language after completing his studies.[3]

The interwar period also saw the inauguration of the first in-service training programs for functional specialists. Congress voted $10,000 for specialized training in economics and finance in 1937, and $5,000 annually thereafter until 1942. Eleven officers took advanced training at major universities in these fields, laying a precedent for extensive postwar programs.

Promotion. The establishment of an effective system of promotion by merit required administrative implementation and ultimately some statutory revision. An executive order established the Foreign Service Personnel Board, staffed by the undersecretary, the three assistant secretaries, and an executive committee of three Foreign Service officers, who were to review personnel records, recommend promotions, examine candidates for probationary appointments, and pass on the lateral entry of departmental officers with five years service.

The board periodically reviewed efficiency reports prepared by principal officers and prepared a waiting list, which became the basis for promotion for a two-year period. It skimmed top names off the list

---

[3] Prior to 1926, about eighty officers had received training in Chinese, Japanese, and Turkish, about forty of whom were still in the service. Between 1932 and 1941, fifty-eight trainees accepted the hard language assignments.

whenever funds for promotions became available. Unsatisfactory ratings led to hearings, and officers who failed to meet standards reverted to probationary status.

During its first two and one-half years, the board recommended officers for promotion on the basis of their former attachment to the diplomatic or consular services, alleging that the personnel records of the Diplomatic Service were too scanty to permit adequate comparisons. This system favored former diplomatic officers, including members of the board, by about two to one. Congress, disturbed by such discrimination, recommended the immediate adoption of a single-list promotion policy and more interchange between consular and diplomatic assignments. This was done, but promotions came slowly because of the inadequacy of appropriations and because of restrictive percentage limits on the top classes.

The malfunction of the board and the failure of the Rogers Act to improve the situation of the Foreign Service clerical staff moved Congress to amend the act in 1931. The Moses-Linthicum Act attacked favoritism by removing Foreign Service officers from the board and stipulating that no Foreign Service officers below Class I should be assigned to the Division of Foreign Service Personnel, which controlled assignments, or become eligible for promotion to minister or ambassador while serving in the division or for three years thereafter. It somewhat reduced promotion blocks by reclassifying officers in eight classes and one unclassified, three-step probationary category, although it imposed new percentage limitations on classes one through six. It raised salaries to a range of $2,500 to $10,000, and it introduced annual salary step increases within class for satisfactory performance.

The act improved the position of Foreign Service clerks by stipulating that advancement in the clerical service should be by merit only, and by authorizing post allowances for clerks where needed. It set salary ranges for senior clerks at $3,000–$4,000, and for junior clerks at $2,750 or less. It further stipulated that only American citizens might serve as senior clerks in diplomatic missions.

Appointment Policy. Precedents for the appointment of career men to high office in the Department of State and as chiefs of mission existed before 1924. The Rogers Act did not end political appointments, but it encouraged a progressive increase in career appointments. Under President Calvin Coolidge, career officers held 50 per cent of the chief of mission posts for the first time; Presidents Herbert Hoover and Franklin D. Roosevelt continued to select about half of their ambassadors and ministers from the service; and the proportion of career appointees has since ascended as high as 70 per cent. President Coolidge also appointed to the highest offices in the Department of State distinguished members of the former Diplomatic Service, including William Phillips, who served as undersecretary. This precedent has also held, with the result that many high departmental officers now come from the Foreign Service.

Appointments as probationers after 1924 went only to candidates who passed a four-day written examination, an oral examination administered by the Foreign Service Personnel Board, a physical examination, an oral foreign language examination, and a background investigation of general conduct and loyalty. A few officers with at least five years of departmental service entered the middle and higher classes after oral examination, but prior to World War II new officers normally entered as probationers.

Departmental or field officers (with departmental approval) appointed American clerical personnel without examination, but after investigations of their backgrounds and qualifications. In December 1937 the service enrolled 733 American clerical employees and 703 Foreign Service officers. A few senior clerical employees held commissions from the secretary of state as noncareer vice consuls, a status roughly equivalent to that of a warrant officer in the army or navy. Principal consular officers appointed local employees. The service, in December 1937, employed 919 alien clerks and about 1,600 local service and custodial workers. Its total pre–World War II strength thus approached 4,000 employees.

Fringe Benefits. The Rogers Act authorized important additional fringe benefits but did not appropriate funds for them. Nor did it provide for all service needs. In 1930 Congress voted money for the first time for the payment of allowances for the rent, heat, and light of living quarters; and, in 1931, it appropriated $92,000 for representation expenses. The Moses-Linthicum Act liberalized the retirement system. It also authorized the granting of representation and post allowances to all Foreign Service officers and chiefs of mission, more generous home leave, and fifteen days of sick leave per year.

Unfortunately, the depression resulted in a suspension of the grants of 1931, a 15 per cent cut in salaries, and a suspension of promotions, home leave, and examinations for junior officers during 1932–1935. Foreign Service salaries fell another 30 per cent with the devaluation of the dollar. After 1935 Congress gradually restored salary cuts and fringe benefits, but officer strength dropped from 762 in 1932 to 688 in 1934, and recovered to only 723 by March 1939.

Violation and Reaffirmation of the Unified Service Principle

The growing importance of foreign affairs, their increasing complexity, and the emergence of bureaucratic rivalries and competition generated the first serious threat to the monopoly of the Department of State and its Foreign Service during the period under review.

The Treasury Department first sent agents abroad in the nineteenth century to audit the collection of consular fees. It later sent customs agents abroad to monitor the performance by the Consular Service in issuing consular invoices. Its Public Health Service medical officers went overseas initially to help enforce quarantine laws and regulations and, afterwards, to help screen visa applicants. The Treasury Department did not, however, challenge State Department control over foreign policy in any major area until World War II.

The War and Navy Departments began sending attachés abroad in the late nineteenth century to observe matters relating to the national defense, but the interest in and influence of these agencies on foreign affairs administration also remained minimal and peripheral until World War II, although naval officers often served as presidential agents.

The Departments of Commerce and Agriculture became the first to threaten the State Department's monopoly because of their keen interest in collecting information from abroad and in promoting American exports. They insisted that the diplomatic and consular services could not meet all of their reporting and promotional requirements, and they prevailed upon Congress to vote funds for foreign affairs activities directed by them. The Department of Commerce took over the Department of State's Bureau of Foreign Commerce in 1903 and received a modest sum as early as 1905 for roving "special agents" to investigate trade conditions abroad. These agents became known as "trade commissioners" in 1914, by which time they had also become resident in certain posts. Congress authorized the appointment of commercial attachés in 1914.

The Department of Commerce succeeded as well in blocking State Department efforts to coordinate interdepartmental international commercial activities, with the result that considerable duplication of effort developed throughout the federal government well before the passage of the Rogers Act.

As early as 1914, Congress appropriated funds to the Department of Agriculture for Washington and field staffs engaged in foreign agricultural economic work, but the Department of Agriculture sent resident field agents to relatively few posts.

The Rogers Act affirmed the principle that the United States should be represented abroad by a unified Foreign Service but did not eliminate existing anomalies that became increasingly dangerous and divisive as American foreign economic interests continued to expand. Moreover, the Department of Commerce persuaded Congress to appropriate funds for the establishment of a small Foreign Commerce Service in 1927, and the Department of Agriculture won a similar authorization in 1930. In 1936 the Bureau of Mines of the Department of the Interior set up a minuscule foreign service. Other departments and agencies, including the Departments of Labor and Justice, the Bureau of the Budget, the Maritime Commission, the Battle Monuments Commission, the Canal Zone Government, the Federal Trade Commission, the Tariff Commission, and others, also acquired or claimed foreign affairs roles at home and abroad before World War II but did not seriously impair coordination.

President Roosevelt halted the tendency toward the proliferation of field services in July 1939 by issuing Reorganization Plan No. 2, which brought 105 Commerce and 9 Department of Agriculture field officers into the Foreign Service. The plan eliminated duplication in both substantive and administrative work. The handful of mineral specialists of the Bureau of Mines merged with the Foreign Service in 1943, restoring temporarily a unified career service; but wartime operating agencies were already in the field by this time.

ORGANIZATION, STAFFING, AND ADMINISTRATION OF THE DEPARTMENT OF STATE AND FOREIGN SERVICE, 1918–1939

The Department of State continued to expand between the wars. Between 1918 and 1938, its staff rose from 440 to 963, partly because of the retention of wartime controls, especially passport and visa legislation, but also because of the increased importance of foreign trade, foreign travel, and foreign affairs generally. No major reorganization occurred, but visa, treaty, and protocol divisions emerged shortly after World War I, and new cultural relations, Foreign Service personnel, departmental personnel, Foreign Service administration, and passport units came into existence just before World War II.

Congress authorized the position of undersecretary as the second in the State Department hierarchy in 1919, in place of the counselor, but restored the latter position in 1937. The Rogers Act, of course, required a major shake-up in the department's administrative structure, and, to facilitate this, Congress abolished the position of director of the Consular Service, authorizing instead the appointment of a fourth assistant secretary.

The new assistant secretary of state for administration became the principal administrative decision maker because he served as chairman of the policy-making Board of Foreign Service Personnel, budget officer of the department, and supervisor of the Divisions of Foreign Service Personnel, Foreign Service Administration, and Departmental Personnel.

In January 1939 Secretary of State Cordell Hull, in compliance with a 1938 executive order, abolished the ancient position of chief clerk and created a new Division of Personnel Supervision and Management under a director of personnel for departmental personnel,[4]

---

[4] United States, Department of State, Departmental Order 782, January 26, 1939.

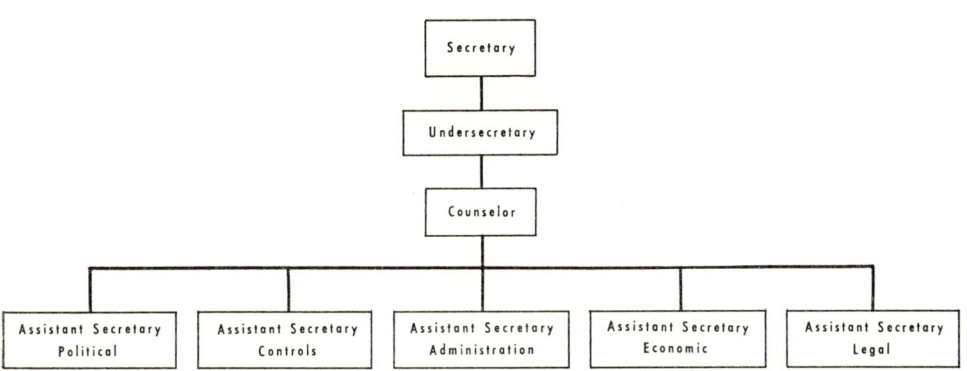

Chart 2: Senior Hierarchy of the Department of State, 1939

thus foreshadowing a long series of organizational changes that the Department of State would voluntarily or perforce adopt in order to rationalize and modernize its personnel administration. The senior hierarchy of the department in September 1939 embraced the positions included in Chart 2.

Field organization reflected the unifying concept that permeated the Rogers Act. During the thirties, diplomatic missions absorbed consulates in capital cities as consular sections, and the department began issuing dual commissions as diplomatic secretaries and consuls of career to all Foreign Service officers assigned to missions regardless of their functions.

By 1939 the present pattern of mission organization had been established. It includes a chief of mission, a deputy chief, who acts as his alter ego, political, economic, consular, and administrative sections, and sections staffed by other agencies, such as the offices of military and civilian attachés. Thus, the administration of a mission more or less resembles that of a military organization, with the chief of mission having full power to use Foreign Service personnel as the situation may require. Officers in charge continue to administer consulates general and consulates outside of capital cities. Chiefs of consular sections of missions supervise subordinate posts in each country for the chiefs of mission.

A regulation that affected the personal lives of many Foreign Service officers apparently resulted from Ambassador William Bullitt's reaction to the fact that many of the officers of the Moscow embassy had alien wives. This allegedly so disturbed the ambassador that he complained to President Roosevelt, who, in November 1936 issued an executive order forbidding Foreign Service officers to marry aliens. Since World War II, some alien marriages have been permitted, but any officer wishing to contract such a marriage must submit his resignation. Only after careful investigation of the fiancée and favorable recommendation of the officer's superior is a resignation declined and such a marriage permitted.

4

World War II and the Years of Uncertain Commitment, 1939–1954

At the outbreak of World War II the United States clung ostrich-like to isolationism, but vital national interests inexorably moved President Roosevelt to intervene "short of war." After the bombing of Pearl Harbor, the nation accepted vast international responsibilities. It did not understand that this implied a major expansion and reorganization of foreign affairs machinery. Bureaucratic rivalries, the erroneous assumption that some new activities would be temporary, presidential lack of confidence in the Department of State and the Foreign Service, and a lack of prescience and initiative in those agencies led to the adoption of expedients that vitiated the department's coordinative powers and ended unified foreign affairs administration overseas.

Isolationist sentiment revived after the war under the stresses of communist aggression, containment policy, and the collapse of naïve expectations of foreign gratitude for American efforts. Thus, the nation's commitment seemed less firm at times than later events proved it to be.

As many additional agencies of the federal government began to assume larger roles in foreign affairs administration, the coordinative role of the Department of State grew enormously in importance and difficulty, the more so because it did not control the foreign operations of other agencies. The authority of the department and the Foreign Service fluctuated with the administrative philosophy of each president and secretary of state and as a function of the relations of the president, secretary, department, and service with each other and with the Congress. Other officers of the administration, especially the secretary of defense and the director of central intelligence, began to exert major influence on the administration of foreign affairs. In the mid-fifties, dispersion of responsibility reached a maximum. Morale in foreign affairs agencies, especially among Foreign Service officers, dropped precipitately, and interest in foreign affairs careers among qualified youths plummeted.

The continued growth in the scope and complexity of foreign relations after 1939 compelled even broader use of presidential initiative. The political role of the foreign affairs bureaucracy expanded concurrently, perhaps even more significantly. The congressional role increasingly assumed the character of legitimating and amending programs of the executive.

Confusion, waste, and delay in postwar foreign affairs administration and general lack of recognition of the limits of foreign policy generated great frustration and insistent demands for reform, especially of the Department of State and the Foreign Service. A series of public and private investigations inspired some sound reforms and some that institutionalized disunity because they failed to recognize the new political role of the bureaucracy.

Despite a wide diversity of views and some dissent, general agreement emerged by 1954 that key State Department officers should be integrated with qualified reserve and staff officers of the Foreign Service in an expanded career service; a great need for specialists existed in the Foreign Service that should be met through lateral entry and integration; the Department of State should be responsible for policy; foreign operations should be conducted by other agencies; and the Foreign Service should remain outside the Civil Service.

The War Years, 1939-1945

During 1939-1940 the Foreign Service and the Department of State carried a heavy load of emergency duties—evacuating American citizens, representing belligerent interests, arranging exchanges of prisoners, conducting liaison with the Red Cross, solving complicated visa and refugee problems, and meeting increased requirements for intelligence. Better organized and staffed than in 1914, they met the emergency with modest redeployment and no significant increases in personnel.

The Foreign Service officer corps of 1939 was unified, elite, and well trained for duties that could be performed by generalists. It did not represent all geographical sections, social classes, or national and racial strains. Women, who first entered the service in 1925, also remained underrepresented. Yet, Foreign Service officers, screened through rigid examinations and subjected to a quasi-military discipline, displayed a high *esprit de corps*. They believed that they served all agencies and people of the United States, and they strove conscientiously to act in the national intrest, as they conceived it.

Virtually all Foreign Service officers had baccalaureate degrees and a few had received graduate training. Under proper leadership, and with additional in-service training, most of them probably could have adjusted to an expanded and specialized service. The nature of diplomatic life and duties requires an exceptionally high degree of adaptability and flexibility. Any Foreign Service officer, regardless of his function, must turn his hand daily to a multiplicity of chores and must often move from one function to another and from post to post. This remains true even in the larger, more specialized service of today. Probably it always will, because even a diversified service would not permit the degree of specialization found in domestic employment.

Undeniably there was little interest in or taste for management or administrative assignments in the old service. Its most successful officers had been those skilled in political and economic reporting. Ambitious officers sought assignments to these areas and tended to shun consular chores as offering relatively few opportunities for rapid advancement. The modest size of field establishments made elaborate administrative machinery unnecessary. Even the prewar embassy in London employed only about 200 representatives of all agencies, while the administration of the Foreign Service in the Department of State probably occupied less than a score of Foreign and Civil Service officers. Thus, little need for management skills existed.

The passage of the Lend-Lease Act and the proclamation of a state of national emergency early in 1941 created a rapidly growing need for personnel at home and abroad for economic assistance, economic warfare,[1] overseas information, and specialized intelligence work. President Roosevelt had little confidence in either the Foreign Service or the Department of State, which he considered to be too small, inflexible, and lacking in specialists to conduct emergency operations successfully. High departmental and Foreign Service officers lacked interest in management and operational tasks and failed to seize the initiative. A general conviction also prevailed that such work would end with the war, and that it would be imprudent to expand the career service to perform temporary duties.

In the event, the president entrusted the new operations to emergency agencies—the Lend-Lease Administration (OLL), the Economic Defense Board (EDB), the Office of Facts and Figures (OFF), and the Coordinator for Inter-American Affairs (CIAA). After Pearl Harbor, he created the office of Strategic Services (OSS), replaced EDB with the Board of Economic Warfare (BEW), and supplanted OFF with the Office of War Information (OWI) to plan and conduct, respectively, clandestine intelligence operations, economic warfare, and the dissemination of information. The president also entrusted many wartime foreign affairs tasks to other agencies, especially to the War, Navy, and Treasury Departments, and to individuals who enjoyed his full confidence, such as Harry Hopkins, Henry Morgenthau, and Admiral William D. Leahy.

The department promptly lost control over policy formulation and execution in areas entered by other departments, the new agencies, or presidential confidants. President Roosevelt made major foreign policy

---

[1] The duties included the monitoring of export controls, supervision of the flow of funds from the United States, procurement of critical commodities, and proclaimed list work.

decisions without consulting or even informing Secretary Hull, and he allowed military considerations to take precedence over foreign policy goals. He also permitted certain chiefs of mission to communicate with him directly, employed special agents with roving commissions who reported directly to the White House, and conferred high diplomatic rank on heads of subordinate missions. The control of economic assistance by Lend-Lease officials made them more influential than the chiefs of mission in several posts, and officials of emergency agencies generally found it far easier to get money and staff than did the Department of State.

These improvisations produced grave and unanticipated long-term consequences. The rational principle of coordinating foreign policy through a single department and executing it through a unified Foreign Service lost much ground. Concurrently the theory that effective policy control could be exercised by the Department of State over autonomous or independent agencies conducting foreign affairs operations won general acceptance, because the confusion, duplication, and extravagance of wartime operations did not preclude a military triumph, although they contributed greatly to the postwar international imbalance. The Roosevelt administration not only failed to invent coordinating machinery, but also impeded a postwar solution by creating many new bureaucratic and public vested interests. The loss of prestige by chiefs of mission continued to impair their ability to coordinate field operations after the war, and it taught foreign governments that the anarchy prevailing in American foreign affairs administration could be exploited to their advantage.

The Department of State and the Foreign Service shared modestly in wartime economic, intelligence, and cultural activities. This work, negotiations with the allies, postwar planning, incipient international organization activities, and the provision of administrative services to the wartime agencies soon created a pressing need for additional personnel. The department's staff rose to 2,755 by 1943, or by almost 300 per cent. This enormous expansion, together with a growing recognition that the new role of the United States in world affairs would require a more sophisticated and permanently larger Department of State, inspired two basic reorganizations in 1944. The first, hastily conceived, created offices where divisions had existed before. It placed the new regional offices directly under the secretary and undersecretary; and it gave each of the four assistant secretaries severally responsibility for units concerned with controls, transportation, and communications, with economic problems, with administration and public information, and with congressional relations.[2]

The second reorganization plan defined the roles of the new offices and their component divisions. It added two assistant secretaries to the hierarchy, assigning the Office of American Republics to one and the three other regional offices to another. It realigned some functions of the four other assistant secretaries; and it added a special assistant for international organization and security affairs with assistant secretary status.[3] Chart 3 illustrates graphically the changes summarized above.

The Foreign Service met its emergency staffing needs by employing Foreign Service auxiliary officers, principally for economic warfare, cultural relations, information, and consular work. It did so on the theory that its permanent work force should not be increased to perform emergency duties. The administration suspended the recruitment of career officers after Pearl Harbor and thereby increased the need for auxiliary staff.[4] By January 1946 the service numbered 976 auxiliary and only 820 Foreign Service officers.[5]

Well before the war ended, it became apparent that some wartime activities would become permanent, and that, in any case, a larger, more

---

[2] United States, Department of State, Departmental Order 1218, January 15, 1944.

[3] *Ibid.*, Departmental Order 1301, December 20, 1944.

[4] In 1945 auxiliary officers did approximately 90 per cent of the service's cultural and informational, 67 per cent of its economic and commercial, 25 per cent of its consular and administrative, and 10 per cent of its political work. At this time, a survey showed the following statistical breakdown of the Foreign Service workload: economic and commercial, 37 per cent; consular, 21.7 per cent; administrative, 20.8 per cent; political, 17.3 per cent; and cultural and informational, 2.9 per cent. After the department assumed OWI functions, the volume of cultural and informational work probably rose to at least 10 per cent of the total workload.

[5] Senior auxiliary officers, economists for the most part, worked mainly at economic warfare and high-level analysis. Junior auxiliary officers normally performed general consular and administrative duties, although a few served as information and cultural relations specialists. Auxiliary officers did not enjoy tenure, but they entered at higher salary levels than Foreign Service officers of comparable age and training on the assumption that their service would be temporary.

flexible service would be needed to cope with the expanded postwar volume of normal business. With a view to preparing for the future, the secretary of state established an Office of the Foreign Service in 1944, which embraced the existing Divisions of Foreign Service Personnel and Foreign Service Administration and incorporated new Divisions of Planning, Training Services, and Foreign Reporting Services. The Division of Planning began preparing draft legislation for the postwar service, and the Division of Training addressed itself to structuring an improved in-service training program. Foreign Reporting Services organized a reporting program, which it hoped might meet the information needs of all government agencies, and a system of end use evaluations of field reports.

As an interim measure, the department requested legislation to provide higher salaries for Foreign Service administrative, fiscal, and clerical personnel,[6] remove the percentage limits on Foreign Service officer classes in order to eliminate promotion blocks, and authorize exchanges of personnel between the Foreign Service and other government agencies. A statute of May 3, 1945, authorized these changes.

Postwar Administrative Changes, 1945–1946

For a time after World War II it seemed that foreign affairs administration might again be unified or at least adequately coordinated by an enlarged and more effective Department of State and Foreign Service. President Harry S. Truman abolished the emergency agencies and transferred some of their residual functions to the Department of State and the Foreign Service. Considerable expansion occurred, and new legislation made the service more attractive as a career and more effective as an administrative instrument.

When the war ended, normal foreign affairs activities reached an unprecedentedly high level; work with international organizations had emerged as an important new activity; and postwar reconstruction loomed as a task involving heavy additional duties in relief, rehabilita-

[6] Administrative support requirements of other agencies increased enormously during the war, with a consequent rise in the need for administrative employees at all levels of the Foreign Service. Civilian personnel in London under Ambassador Winant's supervision rose from two hundred to about four thousand during the war.

tion, and the repatriation of refugees. In addition the Department of State and the Foreign Service inherited important residual duties from OWI, OSS, OLL, and BEW.

The president abolished the Office of War Information (OWI) in August 1945, transferring its functions and personnel to the department and the Foreign Service. The department merged OWI domestic employees with those of the Coordinator of Inter-American Affairs (CIAA) in a new Office of International Information and Cultural Affairs. Field employees of the OWI received appointments to the auxiliary or the clerical staff of the Foreign Service. President Truman also dismantled the Office of Strategic Services (OSS), transferring its intelligence research units to the Department of State and its overseas units to the Army. When the Office of Lend-Lease Administration and the Board of Economic Warfare disappeared, the Department of State inherited a few residual responsibilities. The department and the Foreign Service between 1945 and 1948 exercised limited operational responsibility for reconstruction and interim foreign aid through the negotiation of loans and grants and through the United States delegation to the United Nations Relief and Rehabilitation Administration (UNRRA).

The Division of Foreign Service Planning, after careful study and much discussion with other agencies, members of Congress, and the Bureau of the Budget, drafted two bills, which it hoped would permit the Foreign Service to attain the size and flexibility required to meet its new responsibilities. Congress enacted both in 1946.

The Manpower and Foreign Service Acts of 1946. The Manpower Act of July 1946 sought to expand the service in its middle and higher grades by authorizing the lateral admission within two years by oral examination of 250 new officers, principally specialists in economics and management. Although more than 2,000 candidates applied, the department filled only 166 of the positions because of an alleged lack of funds. Critics of the Foreign Service, especially those who insisted that it operated as a closed corporation, charged that responsible officers dragged their feet or failed to procure adequate appropriations because they feared that the program would block opportunities for officers who had entered the lower ranks by examination. Apologists asserted that the Congress failed to appropriate enough money to support the total authorization. Neither contention has been established by objective research.[7]

The Foreign Service Act of 1946 replaced the statutes of 1924, 1931, and 1945. It sought to achieve three basic objectives.

1. It vested statutory administrative control of the service in the service itself by establishing the position of director general to be filled by a career Foreign Service officer who was to administer the service under the general supervision of the secretary and the assistant secretary for administration. It established a statutory Board of Examiners, and it replaced the policy-making Board of Foreign Service Personnel with the Board of the Foreign Service.

2. The act sought to make Foreign Service careers more attractive by increasing financial rewards, reinforcing the career principle, eliminating difficulties or disabilities that had not been remedied by previous legislation, and broadening fringe benefits.[8]

---

[7] It is possible that a simple clerical error or poor administrative planning without malicious intent by Civil or Foreign Service employees of the Office of the Foreign Service may have played a part. In the late summer of 1947, when an FSO-4 assigned to the Division of Foreign Service Personnel (FP), I prepared an inventory of Foreign Service officers on duty, pending out and pending in. It revealed more officers pending in than could be compensated with funds available for the 1947–1948 fiscal year. This apparently astonished the chief and assistant chief of FP. I have no reason to doubt that their reaction was honest and conjecture that responsibility for the failure to make all authorized appointments may rest with some anonymous employee who either failed to keep an accurate balance sheet of officers pending in and pending out or made erroneous calculations that caused the department to request inadequate budgetary support. It would be necessary to compare detailed breakdowns of the division's initial budgetary request for salaries and allowances for the Foreign Service, the department's request as submitted to the Bureau of the Budget, the bureau's approved figure, and the final appropriation to determine where responsibility should be placed, to establish that funds were, in fact, inadequate to permit recruitment of the additional manpower candidates, and to discover where responsibility should be assigned.

[8] The act provided new and more generous salary scales for chiefs of mission and authorized Foreign Service officers to serve as ambassadors and ministers without resigning from the service. It reduced the number of Foreign Service officer classes from eleven to seven, including the new class of career minister, and set a salary range of $3,300 to $13,500. It reclassified American clerical personnel into Foreign

3. Finally the act sought to increase the flexibility and efficiency of the service. It prescribed a promotion system resembling the "promotion up or selection out" technique used by the United States Navy, which required Foreign Service officers to win promotion or leave the service. Recognizing the need for more specialists, it created the Foreign Service reserve officer category with six classes, authorizing recruitment for these positions for terms of up to four years. Reserve officers were to enjoy all the privileges of career officers other than tenure and retirement benefits. The broadened opportunities in Foreign Service staff categories, it was hoped, would attract most of the permanent administrative and technical specialists the service might need. The act also established a Foreign Service Institute to plan, supervise, and administer a comprehensive in-service training program. In order to prevent Foreign Service officers from becoming cultural expatriates, it stipulated that all must spend three years of their first fifteen in service on duty in the United States.

When the act became effective, on November 13, 1946, the auxiliary service disappeared. The department incorporated into the Foreign Service as reserve or staff officers, all auxiliary officers who chose to remain and who qualified for appointment. Some junior auxiliary officers took the examinations under an accelerated program and entered directly into the career service. A few auxiliary officers entered under the Manpower Act.

Service staff officer and Foreign Service staff categories, embracing twenty-two classes with salaries ranging up to $10,000 per annum.

The act emphasized that Foreign Service officers normally would enter after the full examination process in the lowest class but permitted lateral entry in the middle and higher classes for government employees with four years of service after oral examination.

It liberalized the retirement system, continued existing allowances, and authorized new allowances for installation, transfer, and the separation of families; home leave after two years instead of three; the reimbursement of hospital and medical expenses, including transportation when employees fell ill in line of duty; reimbursement of certain official residence expenses for principal officers; salary differentials of up to 25 per cent to Foreign Service staff employees to help meet high costs of living at certain posts; and salary differentials for Foreign Service officers assigned to the department equal to the difference between their Foreign Service salaries and the Civil Service salaries for the jobs they might be filling. The department by administrative action in 1960 suspended the payment of these differentials.

The act failed to provide for enough home service by Foreign Service officers to assure the retention of their American skills and attitudes. Above all, it did not provide separate specialist routes of advancement or career ladders for Foreign Service officers. When all officers in any class compete against each other for promotion, generalists tend to progress at a more rapid rate than specialists because any officer who can do two or more jobs well seems more useful than one who is less versatile. A long and fruitless series of hortatives to selection boards to give specialists equal treatment with generalists failed to alter this tendency. The lack of separate career ladders also impeded the use of the Foreign Service officer corps to incorporate groups of experts in agricultural, information, management, foreign aid, and other fields required by the nation's commitments.

The fear of many Foreign Service officers that an influx of specialists into the service might impair career opportunities, subvert the career principle, and undermine its elite character, probably inhibited the prescription of a promotion system embodying separate career ladders by the 1946 act or by early administrative action. But the strong desire for independence or autonomy of other agencies would have limited the usefulness of a more flexible system in any case.

The 1946 act failed to accord benefits to department foreign affairs officers equivalent to the benefits received by Foreign Service career officers or to open needed opportunities for field service to them. Most Civil Service officers did not want to serve abroad or to accept the risk of being retired involuntarily (selected out) for performance that might be adequate but not good enough either to warrant promotion after a term of years or to win a competitive rating above the lowest percentiles. But they did aspire to the higher salaries, improved retirement system, and other fringe benefits enjoyed by the career officers. Many Foreign Service officers, on the other hand, viewed the frequent promotions received by some Civil Service officers in the rapidly expanding Department of State during the war and early postwar years as unmerited.

The act also failed to satisfy the aspirations of Foreign Service staff officers, although they enjoyed far more pay, privileges, and status than had noncareer vice consuls before the war. Nevertheless, some officers or their wives (which comes to the same thing) remained unhappy and dissatisfied because staff jobs offered no diplomatic and few functional openings and little social prestige. Reserve officers who aspired to careers resented the difficult lateral entry requirements.

Foreign Building Program. Immense foreign currency assets piled up during and after the war and could not be repatriated to the United States because of balance of payments difficulties. Congress, at the department's request, appropriated a portion of these to finance a major expansion in the Foreign Service buildings program. For the fiscal year 1946 alone, it appropriated $125,000,000, compared with $16,625,000 for the entire period between 1926 and 1943. By 1961 almost $250,000,000 had been appropriated for Foreign Service buildings.

Expansion of Foreign Service and Departmental Personnel. Only 792 Foreign Service career officers (FSO) remained on duty in January 1945 because of the cessation of recruitment after 1941. The Manpower Act and an accelerated junior officer examination program brought career officer strength up to 1,252 by January 1948. Reserve and staff personnel, including former OWI and auxiliary employees, considerably exceeded career officer strength. Total American and alien personnel rose to above 15,000.

State Department employees, excluding Foreign Service personnel, rose from 2,755 in 1943 to 7,623 in 1946. Since the department had about 1,000 employees and the Foreign Service roughly 4,000 before the war, it is apparent that the proportion of departmental to field employees increased from a ratio of about 1:4 to about 1:2. This change reflected the addition of some new functions, especially intelligence research, work with international organizations, and direction of the information program, including the Voice of America, but it also reflected a sensationally large rise in administrative and managerial staff.

Reorganization of the Department of State. The department, like the service, had to reorganize after the war in order to discharge its vastly increased burden of old and new responsibilities and to accomodate its enormously swollen staff. Successive secretaries and the Congress substantially completed the task by 1950. The reorganization entailed the creation of many staff and functional units and the radical expansion of others, including the Policy Planning Staff, the Executive Secretariat, the Bureau of International Organization Affairs, the Bureau of Public Affairs, which absorbed the modest Division of Current Information and began serving all media, the Bureau of Congressional relations, the Office and later Bureau of International Information and Cultural Affairs, which initially absorbed OWI and CIAA,[9] and the Bureau of Economic Affairs, in which were grouped all old and new economic and commercial coordinating and operational activities.

The elevation of existing line and operating units to higher organizational status accompanied the creation of new functional and staff units. Staffs became divisions or offices, divisions became offices or bureaus. Thus, the Visa and Passport Divisions became offices under a new Bureau of Security and Consular Affairs. The regional offices now achieved bureau status, each with its own panoply of offices, divisions, officers in charge, and desk officers for individual countries.

The rise of administrative and management functions in prestige and importance generated an impressive hierarchical ascent and proliferation of units and staff, headed by a deputy undersecretary for administration (O), who personally supervised the director general of the Foreign Service, the Foreign Service Inspection Corps, the Foreign Service Institute, and an assistant secretary (A). The assistant secretary, in turn, presided over the Bureau of Administration, a vast bureaucracy containing Offices of Personnel, Operations, Budget and Finance, Foreign Buildings, and Management. The modest prewar administrative establishment with its few scores of employees supervised by an assistant secretary, now became the department's largest area, exerting far more influence on foreign affairs administration both directly and indirectly.

The 1969 organizational pattern thus bears little resemblance to the prewar department either in structure or proportions of employees engaged in various activities. The secretary and the undersecretary

---

[9] After the separation of USIA from the department in 1953, it became the Bureau of Educational and Cultural Affairs with responsibility for administering the exchange of persons program.

Organization Chart

Secretary / Undersecretary / Undersecretary for Political Affairs

Top-level offices:
- Arms Control and Disarmament Agency
- Agency for International Development
  - Peace Corps
- Inspector General Foreign Assistance
- Protocol
- Executive Secretariat
- Deputy Undersecretary for Administration / Director General Foreign Service
  - Foreign Service Institute
  - Foreign Service Inspection Corps
  - Security and Consular Affairs
  - Administrative Offices and Staffs
- Deputy Undersecretary for Political Affairs

Under the Secretary line:
- Legal Adviser
- Counselor
- Policy Planning Center
- Congressional Relations
- International Scientific and Technological Affairs
- Intelligence and Research
- Economic Affairs
- Public Affairs
- Educational and Cultural Affairs
- African Affairs
- European Affairs
- East Asian and Pacific Affairs
- Inter-American Affairs
- Near Eastern and South Asian Affairs
- International Organization Affairs

Diplomatic Missions and Delegations to International Organizations remain at the apex, but a second undersecretary sometimes designated for economic, sometimes for political affairs, also emerged, together with deputy undersecretaries for political and economic affairs and administration. These lofty figures sit at the top of the hierarchy. At the next level, as of February 1969, a counselor, a legal advisor, a director of international science affairs, a director of the Policy Planning Council, and a dozen assistant secretaries headed line or staff bureaus controlling all offices, divisions, staffs, and other units of the department, save for those supervised personally by the secretary or by some other high officer of the department, such as the Executive Secretariat, various special assistants, or the Office of Protocol. Assignments of responsibilities within this bureaucracy have varied since 1950, but not substantially. (See Chart 4.)

Dispersal of Responsibility and Emergence of Bureaucratic Gigantism, 1947–1953

Immediate postwar developments indicating that the administration might restore the coordinative powers of the Department of State, reunify field administration, and support an elite, career Foreign Service proved illusory. Within a few months the wartime trend toward dispersal of responsibility revived and triumphed. At the same time the foreign affairs bureaucracy inflated itself to enormous proportions.

The requirement that the United States maintain large armed forces in being and the advent of nuclear warfare destroyed any hope for restoring State Department monopoly because defense policy and foreign policy now had to be considered in almost every important situation from the viewpoint of their mutual effect on national security policy.

During World War II, the War and Navy Departments and high-ranking military officers collaborated closely with President Roosevelt in making major foreign policy decisions. The war ceased to be an instrument of politics once it became total, especially after the president proclaimed the doctrine of unconditional surrender. The wartime State-War-Navy Coordinating Committee, which sought to assure that defense and foreign policy decisions remained compatible, failed to uphold the primacy of political goals.

In 1945 the War Department inherited the OSS field service temporarily, and the War and Navy Departments assumed responsibility for administering territories of the former enemy states. The postwar military services also enlarged their attaché, research, and intelligence components and began to show far greater interest in all aspects of foreign affairs administration than they had before 1939.

Congress passed the National Security Act in 1947, creating the Department of Defense, with its subordinate Departments of the Army, the Navy, and the Air Force, the Joint Chiefs of Staff, the National Security Council (NSC), the Office of Emergency Planning, the Central Intelligence Agency (CIA), and the National War College. It thus recognized the intimate civilian-military relationship in the formulation of national security policy and gave the Department of Defense a stronger statutory and institutional base for participating in foreign affairs administration. The Department of State and the Foreign Service were impelled to take increasing account of national security considerations at all times and were forced to employ additional personnel and effort both in coordination and in training personnel to work effectively with Defense Department officials.

The problem of melding postwar foreign policy and national defense policy into national security policy engaged much of the attention of Presidents Truman and Eisenhower. The former made relatively little use of the National Security Council and preferred to rely on other interdepartmental committees and less formal procedures. President Eisenhower, with his long military experience of staff work and the chain of command, wanted well-studied alternatives presented for his decision. He created the post of special assistant for national security affairs in the White House staff and the Planning Board and the Operations Coordinating Board of NSC to provide adequate staff support for NSC deliberations and follow-up procedures.

Old-line civilian departments and agencies that had encroached during the war on the monopoly of the State Department continued to engage in foreign affairs activities thereafter. Moreover, new overseas economic, sociological, and cultural programs soon emerged, which involved a far wider range of existing agencies and some new ones, such as the Atomic Energy Commission, which received statutory responsibilities or asserted claims to foreign affairs responsibilities from the outset. Such claims proved impossible for the Department of State to resist, especially when backed by appropriations.

By 1949 twenty-one agencies stationed employees abroad, and only half of the American civilian employees overseas, excluding Defense Department civilian employees but including former OWI personnel, worked for the Foreign Service. At home nineteen departments and agencies concerned themselves with all aspects of American foreign relations. In addition, forty-three administrative or administrative control, forty-six economic, fifteen social, and five military agencies engaged in specialized areas of foreign policy administration.[10]

During the years between 1945 and 1954, military departments and agencies provided the preponderance of American civilian personnel serving abroad, principally in occupation duties but increasingly in military assistance and attaché work. The largest civilian components outside of the career Foreign Service served the information, economic assistance, and covert intelligence programs.

The Department of State lost control of the information program in 1953, when President Eisenhower issued Reorganization Plan No. 8, establishing the autonomous United States Information Agency (USIA), which he piously enjoined to take policy guidance from the department. USIA's field arm, the United States Information Service (USIS), continued to operate from Foreign Service establishments but reported directly to USIA.

When Congress first authorized a foreign economic assistance program it insisted that the program be administered by a "temporary" agency taking policy guidance from the Department of State. Congress initially permitted the department to administer Point Four technical assistance because it was closely related to informational and cultural work, but President Eisenhower transferred this responsibility to the International Cooperation Administration (ICA) in 1953 under Reorganization Plan No. 7.

President Eisenhower undercut the authority of chiefs and deputy chiefs of mission over information and foreign assistance personnel by

[10] James L. McCamy, *The Administration of American Foreign Affairs*, pp. 104–133, 273.

requiring that the chiefs of mission themselves transmit orders directly to chiefs of USIS sections and ICA missions. Inferentially he gave these officers rank equal to, if not above, that of the deputy chiefs of mission. A 1954 statute re-establishing the Foreign Agricultural Service struck still another blow at the principle of unified overseas foreign affairs administration.

An unhealthy growth in the size of the foreign affairs establishment accompanied its proliferation. Several influences combined to convert normal staff expansion into rampant inflation in both military and civilian foreign affairs agencies. They included the operation of Parkinson's Law, the unfortunate connection between promotion in the Civil Service and the range of supervisory responsibility, bureaucratic rivalries, the delegation to American employees in the field of administrative tasks that might have been performed more economically at home, the extension to field employees of a wide range of new "morale-building" services,[11] the counterproductive thoroughness of government accounting and other administrative regulations, the introduction of certain management and administrative practices in field offices appropriate only for organizations with stable workloads and easily defined functions,[12] and, finally, a considerable measure of work duplication by competing or overlapping agencies.

Consequences of Proliferation and Growth. The rapid postwar growth and the proliferation of agencies in the foreign affairs community at home and abroad accentuated the problems created by wartime improvisation and short cuts and brought a host of additional problems.

Both the Department of State and the Foreign Service lost control

---

[11] These included at the largest posts (and some of the smaller) commissaries, health rooms, restaurants or snack bars, car pools, staff aid in locating housing or making travel and transportation arrangements, the lending of surplus government furniture and furnishings, and the organizing of staff social events. None of these amenities was enjoyed by the pre–World War II service. Where housing was extremely scarce, some missions also leased or bought dwelling units for personnel, and the servicing of these properties required additional staffing.

[12] The introduction of field job descriptions, for example, tended to inhibit the relocation of personnel to meet constantly shifting workloads and to encourage overstaffing.

over the administration of additional important areas of substantive policy to other agencies, some old, some new. The principle of unitary field administration of foreign policy received little service, even from the lips of authorities, between 1947 and 1954, and the coordinative responsibility of the Department of State grew enormously while its authority dwindled.

Both the necessary and the needless growth caused an unhealthy inflation of the American presence in many foreign posts, distorted the local image of the United States greatly, and complicated the tasks of diplomats and program administrators.

Although only a few diplomats enjoyed free entry before World War II, interagency rivalry and an equalitarian push for the democratization of conditions of service abroad soon resulted in virtually all American employees abroad obtaining easy access to drink, tobacco, food, clothing, and household appliances through free entry, commissaries, messes, or combinations of the three. This caused much local bitterness that was enhanced by widespread black-market currency and commodity sales by some employees.

The provision of government-owned or leased housing in many posts and generous housing allowances elsewhere segregated most Americans from the local communities, making enclave living the mode, except among career officers. Such exclusiveness and ostentation displayed by even the lowest ranking civilian and military personnel of American missions and consulates caused envy and adverse comment. Ostentation, enclave living, and local resentment all exercised an unfortunate influence both on intelligence-gathering capabilities and on the progress of other activities.

Bureaucratic gigantism at home slowed down decision making and the execution of foreign policy, induced a ponderous inertia, and discouraged individual initiative, creating new clearance layers in the several agencies, more requirements for intra-agency clearances, and even more intra-departmental units and committees.

Division of responsibility at home and abroad accentuated the difficulty and cost of coordination, produced more and more decisions representing the lowest common denominator of interagency agreement, and tended to thrust the final burden of decision increasingly either on the president, when impasses were reached, or down to the operators, when agency negotiators used imprecision to veil basic disagreement.

The rapidity with which the new foreign affairs bureaucracy expanded and the leveling influences exerted by Congress and the Civil Service inevitably produced dangerous pressure for reduction in selection standards, especially for lateral entry into the Foreign Service. At the same time, abandonment of the principle of unified foreign affairs administration produced differing sets of standards in the several agencies and a competition for personnel that tended to lower quality. Recruitment of candidates with superior attainments for the Foreign Service became increasingly difficult.

The preceding developments greatly preoccupied high officers of successive administrations, the Congress, and the general public, and they naturally had a most direct and unhappy effect on the morale of foreign affairs employees. They also motivated in large measure a long series of official and unofficial studies and attempted reforms that, in turn, created an atmosphere of uncertainty very damaging to morale.

Attrition of Elite and Career Principles in the Foreign Service, 1947–1954. The unhappy consequences of dispersion and excessive growth, disenchantment with the early results of American commitment to a world role, general ignorance of the limits of foreign policy, and the public's desire for a scapegoat produced widespread loss of confidence in the ability and patriotism of foreign affairs agencies. Demagogues exploited this situation for personal political advantage, relying on the fact that their victims had no constituencies. An inordinate and clamorous volume of criticism appeared, touching all agencies but concentrating on the Department of State and the Foreign Service because they still had the responsibility, although no longer the authority, to coordinate American foreign affairs administration. This reprobation compounded the disastrous influence on morale of bureaucratic gigantism and dispersion of responsibility.

Foreign Service officer morale suffered most severely from attrition of the elite and career principles. This attrition occurred as a reaction to general distrust of an elite corps, because the service lost control of its own fate to administrative specialists of the Civil Service, and because deficiencies in the Foreign Service Act of 1946 made it impossible to resist pressure for a mass lateral entry program. Finally, the Foreign Service probably suffered more than any other foreign affairs agency from President Eisenhower's 1953 budget slash, the McCarthy witch hunt, and the policies and personality of Secretary John Foster Dulles.

The elitism of the Foreign Service officer corps, which grew out of its exceptionally difficult selection process and high *esprit de corps*, irritated staff, reserve, and Civil Service officers, some congressmen, and many persons outside the government, who viewed it as snobbish and undemocratic. Elitism ran counter as well to the increasingly equalitarian character of the national life and helped to make the service an easy victim of political demagogues. At the same time, the service's lack of a constituency made it a tempting prey for the headline hunter.

The Foreign Service Act of 1946 sought to assure the triumph of the career principle by vesting administrative control of the service in the service, but its generous salary, retirement, and fringe benefits excited envy and ambitions of outsiders. In addition, the powerful Bureau of the Budget, antagonized by tactics employed in pushing the act through the Congress and obtaining White House approval, resented the nonconformity of service salaries and other personnel arrangements to standards that prevailed elsewhere in the government.[13] At the same time, the preoccupation of Foreign Service officers with political and economic work and their relative lack of interest in management and administration generated legitimate criticism and

---

[13] In August 1945 the bureau sent to Secretary of State Byrnes a report recommending organizational and personnel improvements in the department and Foreign Service that varied in important respects from the proposals embodied in the Foreign Service Act of 1946. In particular, the bureau recommended substantial use of lateral entry, generally uniform classification and pay provisions between the Civil and Foreign Services, more frequent assignments of Foreign Service personnel to the department and other agencies, greater emphasis on management and administrative skills in staffing supervisory posts, and establishment of a comprehensive in-service training program (Committee on Foreign Affairs Personnel [Herter Committee], *Personnel for the New Diplomacy*, pp. 142–143).

opened opportunities for ambitious Civil Service officers to enter these areas.[14]

Civil Service administrative and management experts moved into the Office of the Foreign Service in constantly increasing numbers between 1945 and 1949. The postwar need for personnel officers could not be met from the emaciated ranks of the service, and Foreign Service leadership apparently failed to realize that loss of Foreign Service control of personnel administration would bring the end of elitism, a great thrust to enhance the position and prestige of the administrator within the department and the service, and, ultimately, attrition of the career principle.

Congress legalized *de facto* Civil Service control in May 1949 by amending the Foreign Service Act of 1946 to put the service directly under the control of the secretary of state and convert the director general into an advisor, rather than the top administrator of the service. The secretary then grouped the Divisions of Foreign Service and Departmental Personnel into a single Division of Personnel, abolished the Office of the Foreign Service, and installed an administrative officer with the title of executive director in each of the critically important geographic bureaus to handle personnel and other administrative matters.

Since 1949, then, the Foreign Service has been primarily under the control of administrative and management specialists drawn from business or the Civil Service. Some of these officers subsequently became Foreign Service officers by lateral entry or accepted reserve or staff appointments, but the management and administration of the service have become thoroughly interpenetrated by their doctrine and philosophy.

---

[14] A few Foreign Service officers perceived the necessity for reconciling the interests of departmental foreign affairs officers with those of Foreign Service officers and of providing broader opportunities for Washington assignments for Foreign Service officers. A report prepared by Foreign Service officers Seldon Chapin and Andrew Foster in October 1945 proposed a gradual consolidation of the Foreign Service and certain areas of the department, but it was decided to ask for legislation limited to the Foreign Service itself. This request later emerged as the Foreign Service Act of 1946. The Chapin-Foster plan would have called for members of the proposed consolidated service to serve both at home and abroad, but it envisaged a flexible assign-

Deficiencies in the 1946 act caused growing pressure to open career officer ranks to staff and reserve officers, who were allegedly performing Foreign Service officer functions, and to Civil Service officers occupying positions in the Department of State where field experience was deemed essential. Such integration, it was argued, would bring additional badly needed administrative, economic, consular, and other specialists into the career corps, permit all Foreign Service officers to serve more frequently and for longer periods in the department in the positions vacated by the integrated Civil Service employees, and improve morale by eliminating alleged discrimination against the integrated officers. These changes implied a temporary dropping of the written examination and the foreign language requirement for admission to the career corps and amendment of the 1946 act to preclude any sacrifice of salary levels by the integrated officers. Integration hung over the service as a threat to the elite and career principles and as a depressant on career officer morale almost from the date of the passage of the 1946 act. In 1954 the blow fell.

Foreign Service and State Department morale probably sunk to its lowest postwar level during the first two years of the Eisenhower administration. Four factors combined to produce this result: a 1953 economy drive, McCarthyism, the feeling that Secretary Dulles did not have great regard for the Department of State or for the Foreign Service as institutions, and the imminence of integration.

President Eisenhower's 1953 economy drive produced a reduction in force (RIF) of all government personnel, including a suspension of junior officer recruitment for almost two years. Foreign Service officer strength declined from 1,428 in 1952 to 1,285 by March 1954. Reserve strength fell even more precipitately, from 426 in 1952 to 207 by March 1954. Departmental personnel declined in 1954 to 5,376, exclusive of Foreign Service officers, primarily as the result of Reorganization Plans Nos. 7 and 8, which removed Point Four and USIA personnel from the department, but also in consequence of the RIF. Thus, the ratio between Washington and field staffs increased from about 1:2 to about 1:2.6 between 1948 and 1954.

---

ments policy that would permit some officers to serve mostly in Washington and others primarily overseas (*ibid.*, p. 143).

The RIF probably benefited all foreign affairs agencies ultimately because it cleaned out some marginally useful personnel and checked excessive growth briefly, but its effects on the recruitment of junior officers proved most unfortunate because it left an important gap in the staffing pattern of the Foreign Service and discouraged many young people from preparing for foreign affairs careers. Moreover, the RIF unquestionably helped to undermine the morale of public servants by threatening job security, eliminating some new but useful employees, and leaving in their positions workers with seniority or veterans preference but without other claims to consideration.

The story of Senator Joseph McCarthy's investigation requires no recounting, but its effect on foreign affairs administration must be assessed. His unsubstantiated charges against departmental and Foreign Service officers proved most damaging to morale mainly because neither Secretary of State Dulles nor President Eisenhower rose to the defense of loyal officers who could not speak in self-defense and who had to share the shame of Alger Hiss and a few sexual deviates. None of the deviates was proved to be disloyal, but their peculiar weakness obviously could have made them targets for blackmailers. Several distinguished officers whose only crime was that their reporting had offended the China lobby were drummed out of the service. All Foreign Service officers were reinvestigated, and promotions were suspended for over fifteen months during the security checks.

Young people who had given some thought to Foreign Service careers decided against it in many cases, either because they feared association with characters as despicable as those maligned by Senator McCarthy or because they did not wish to subject themselves to the humiliations that officers engaged in conducting the foreign relations of the United States were forced to endure.

Perhaps the most important long-term result of the hysteria aroused by the senator came in the form of substantially enlarged security components and a rigid tightening of security regulations. The enlargement of the formidable security machinery made the foreign affairs bureaucracy even more unwieldly, and its processes, especially in selecting new personnel, considerably slower. The more rigid regulations and the atmosphere of fear and excessive conformity they created probably inhibited objective reporting by all save the most conscientious officers, required heavy expenditures of time in the observance of security rituals, prevented young people of real talent but unconventional habits from entering the service, and induced an essentially negative concentration of attention and effort on defense tactics rather than on constructive strategy.

Unfortunately Secretary of State Dulles, although active and dedicated, did little to lift and much to impair the morale of departmental and Foreign Service officers. He apparently regarded the department and the Foreign Service as his personal fiefs. Upon assuming office, he informed a gathering of officers assigned to the department that he expected their personal loyalty. This declaration sat very badly with most of his auditors whose loyalty to the government and people of the United States had always been deemed adequate proof of their patriotism by his predecessors.

The secretary's conception of the role of the Department of State and the Foreign Service, moreover, paralleled that of proponents of the theory that foreign policy can be separated from foreign affairs operations. He acceded to the removal of USIA and Point Four from the department, and apparently did not oppose the re-creation of the Foreign Agricultural Service. He cherished his role as principal presidential foreign policy advisor above all others that a secretary of state normally discharges.[15]

The secretary also engaged in an inordinate amount of personal diplomacy, thus depreciating the importance of chiefs of mission and heads of American delegations. His personality, cold and austere, did not endear him to most of his subordinates, who respected his industry and integrity but who failed to find him *simpático*.

INVESTIGATIONS AND REFORM EFFORTS, 1947–1954

The unhappy results of dispersion and bureaucratic gigantism in foreign affairs agencies, morale problems, and general dissatisfaction with American inability to shape the world in a more satisfactory image, all helped to generate a series of public and private studies of

---

[15] John E. Harr in *The Professional Diplomat* (pp. 95–99) comments perceptively on the policy-operations dichotomy.

foreign affairs administration and to intensify pressures for reform.

The Hoover Commission, 1947–1949. A commission, chaired by Herbert Hoover, Jr., and appointed in 1947, carefully examined the entire machinery of the United States government for the administration of foreign affairs. It studied both the relationship of the Department of State to the information and foreign aid programs and the administration of the department and the Foreign Service. It reported in February 1949.

The Hoover Commission found at least forty-five agencies currently interested in foreign affairs. It noted that the Department of State spent only 5 per cent of a total foreign affairs budget of seven billions in 1948, and that only 11 per cent of the 128,500 United States civilian employees abroad worked for the department. It recommended (1) that the department concentrate on policy guidance and refrain from undertaking operations at home or abroad; (2) that the Foreign Service consolidate with the higher echelons of the department in order to improve central direction of the service, promote rotation of officers in the combined service between the field and the department, and end the serious unrest that prevailed in relations between the Foreign Service and Civil Service; and (3) that the secretary of state should "legally and practically command the Department and the Foreign Service." The last recommendation, aimed at the director general, the Congress promptly implemented in May 1949.

The Rowe-Ramspeck-DeCourcy Committee. The secretary of state appointed a committee early in 1950 to study integration into the career service of departmental officers above certain levels and other Hoover Commission recommendations. The Rowe-Ramspeck-DeCourcy Committee recommended the establishment of a single, flexible personnel system for the Department of State and the Foreign Service containing both generalists and specialists. It criticized the department's failure to bring in more junior officers and to use lateral entry to provide needed specialists.

In March 1951 the secretary of state announced a plan to integrate middle- and high-level officers from the department and qualified reserve and staff officers. It provided for the identification of so-called dual service positions in the department to be filled henceforth by

Foreign Service officers and for expanding an existing program to exchange field and departmental personnel on two-year assignments.

The program's results fell far short of expectations. When the application period closed in December 1951, 2,150 candidates had applied, 693 from the department, 236 from the Foreign Service Reserve, and 1,221 from the Foreign Service Staff. By mid-1954, 449 had been examined, of whom 179 had passed and 133 had accepted appointments, but only 25 had actually been taken into the service. Forty civil servants asked for deferrals of their appointments, apparently in the hope that legislation permitting them to enter the Foreign Service at higher salary levels would pass. Many others seem to have applied to protect their careers and their opportunities for promotion. They delayed taking the examinations or accepting appointments pending the issuance of more "liberal" lateral entry provisions or the outcome of the program to designate dual service positions, which the department was supposed to have completed by November 1, 1951, but failed to execute.

The Wriston Committee, 1954. The insignificant results of the department's 1951 program, the desires and expectations aroused by additional public and private investigations,[16] the mounting official and public dissatisfaction, and the low state of morale at home and abroad all combined, by 1954, to raise pressure for reform to a new peak. Consequently, Acting Secretary of State W. Bedell Smith asked Dr. Henry Wriston to chair still another investigating committee. The committee's report of May 18 criticized Foreign Service administrators because lack of strong leadership since 1941 had injured Foreign Service morale, had failed to recruit enough Foreign Service officers at the bottom or laterally,[17] and had not attracted needed specialists in economics, labor, agriculture, commercial promotion, exotic languages, management, and administration.

It charged (1) that separate personnel systems for departmental and field personnel and for career, reserve, and staff officers hampered efficiency and damaged morale; (2) that deficiencies existed in the staff-

---

[16] Appendix A contains a résumé of these investigations and studies.

[17] Only 355 officers were recruited between 1946 and 1952 and none between 1952 and 1954.

ing and program of the Foreign Service Institute; and (3) that too few Foreign Service officers had benefited from home service assignments.[18] It also argued that the generalist theory of developing talent for top management posts had become obsolete because banks, universities, and business in general now emphasized the development of an individual around a specialty "with generalism coming later as he approaches full maturity."

The committee prefaced its own recommendations with "three fundamental points." These, it asserted, represented the consensus of "diverse groups of high competence and true public spirit" that had studied the question of unification since the Rogers Act.

1. The diplomatic service should not be absorbed by the general Civil Service.
2. The Foreign Service should not be absorbed into a generalized foreign officers corps staffing the 24 governmental departments and agencies that have American personnel abroad.
3. Above a certain level a single personnel system should cover all Departmental and Foreign Service personnel insofar as that is at all practicable.

It recommended integration within two years of approximately 1,440 departmental positions and 2,250 overseas jobs by merging certain departmental and Foreign Service reserve and staff personnel into the Foreign Service officer corps. In order to facilitate this program it called for (1) relaxation of lateral entrance standards for officers entering the Foreign Service under integration; (2) the removal in due course (later defined as three years) of departmental officers not wishing to integrate from dual service positions; and (3) the transfer of personnel at appropriate salary rates within class and not at the minimum class rate as specified in the 1946 act.

In order to assure an adequate future supply of well-trained specialists, the report recommended (1) use of the Foreign Service Reserve exclusively for the temporary services of specialists "to deal with

[18] In 1924, 52 officers or approximately 8 per cent of the Foreign Service were on duty in the department; in 1946, 130 or 15 per cent of the officers in the service were on departmental assignments; but in February 1954 only 119 officers, or less than 10 per cent, were serving in Washington.

unique problems"; (2) use of the Foreign Service Staff for positions of "lower than officer rank"; (3) broader opportunities for and "recognition" of specialists; (4) retention of the provisions for lateral entry; and (5) revitalization of the Foreign Service Institute.

The report urged the building of a more representative service through (1) more active recruitment based on closer relations with colleges and universities; (2) a shorter and more rapid examination system; and (3) the establishment of a nation-wide system of federal scholarships for Foreign Service officer candidates.

The committee considered as indispensable the recruitment of a deputy undersecretary of state for administration suitably qualified and willing to remain in the position for a considerable period.[19]

The committee failed to address itself to the salient problem of how the service was to be converted from a generalist- to a specialist-oriented organization or to the even more difficult but closely related problem of how the department and the Foreign Service could be expected to coordinate foreign policy effectively while operations remained under the control of other agencies.

[19] United States, Department of State, *Toward a Stronger Foreign Service: Report of the Secretary of State's Public Committee on Personnel, June, 1954.*

5

"Wristonization," 1954–1960

The morale of many Foreign Service and Civil Service employees of the Department of State sank to new depths during the first phase of the integration program recommended by the Wriston Committee. Nevertheless, the end result of integration probably should be assessed as favorable. Adoption of other recommendations of the committee certainly raised morale and efficiency because they helped to make the Foreign Service attractive again and to rebuild its professionalism. Unfortunately, the committee failed to provide career ladders for specialists or to tackle the still greater problems arising out of the proliferation of agencies involved in foreign affairs administration at home and abroad.

SELECTION OF NEW DEPUTY UNDERSECRETARY OF STATE FOR ADMINISTRATION

Primary responsibility for acting upon the committee's recommendations rested on the deputy undersecretary of state for administration. Recognizing this, the committee had urged that the department assign an officer suitably qualified and willing to remain in the position for a considerable period. The choice fell to a distinguished Foreign Service officer, Ambassador Loy W. Henderson, who replaced Charles Saltzman as deputy undersecretary in January 1955. Well qualified by experience, intelligence, temperament, and the respect of his colleagues, Ambassador Henderson worked with his customary zeal and efficiency. He relied preponderantly upon Civil Service management and administrative specialists of the department's Bureau of Administration for assistance, and on a few Foreign Service officers. During his tenure (1955–1961) the department adopted or made substantial progress toward effectuating most of the committee's major recommendations.

Integration and Lateral Entry, 1954–1960

In contrast to the delay that followed announcement of the 1951 lateral entry program, administrators designated dual service positions in the Department of State and the Foreign Service with commendable, indeed excessive, haste. Well before the end of 1954, they set apart 1,362 departmental and 2,609 field positions. They worked so hastily that several hundred jobs in intelligence, security, and public affairs later had to be declassified because they required either continuity in service, specialists in depth, or both. However, they located enough additional jobs suitable for dual service by 1959 to raise the home total to 1,523.

The department set August 31, 1956, as the deadline for submitting applications for integration, and the Board of Examiners completed final action on all applications before the end of 1957. About 2,400 persons applied and 1,525 entered the career service, 631 from the State Department's Civil Service, 802 from the staff, 69 from the reserve, and 23 from other federal agencies. Approximately 450 Civil Service and 165 reserve and staff officers refused to integrate.

Integration and an intensified program of junior officer recruitment raised Foreign Service officer strength to 3,436 by the end of 1957. Integrated officers then represented about 44 per cent of the total. By 1960, 326 civil servants still remained in dual service positions. The department decided not to transfer these officers to other positions against their wishes or to compel their resignation, but to allow attrition to open the positions eventually to Foreign Service replacements.

Amendments to the Foreign Service Act of 1946, adopted in 1954 and 1955, facilitated integration by permitting newly appointed officers to enter the service at intermediate salary steps. The amendment of 1955 also opened the integration program to 40 employees of federal agencies other than the Department of State and the Foreign Service. A statute of 1956 increased the authorization to 175.

The Wriston Committee recommended retention of lateral entry because it felt that situations were certain to arise that would require the "importation of mature and competent men" as specialists. The department announced the establishment of a continuing program of priority appointments to the career service for Foreign Service staff officers early in 1958; and it made 145 appointments under this program by the end of 1960, principally of administrative specialists. It also made 80 appointments under the regular lateral program, mainly management, administrative, and economic specialists.

The Junior Officer Recruitment and Examination Programs, 1955–1960

The tremendous expansion at middle and upper levels of the service obviously called for heroic measures both to assure that the service would not become an army of generals and to restore the career principle. The Wriston Committee had urged as well that the Foreign Service officer corps be given a more representative character geographically and that examinations be speeded and simplified.

The number of candidates had dwindled so alarmingly because of the McCarthy hearings and the suspension of examinations that only 750 took the September 1954 examination. The department attacked this problem by bringing information about the service directly to college and university students. A College Relations Program, staffed by about twenty-five volunteers from the Foreign Service and the Department of State, initiated a series of campus visits in the spring of 1955 to familiarize students and faculties with career opportunities in the service. Visitors usually spent from one to three days on each campus, talking with students and discussing preparation for the service with faculty members. This program, repeated in the fall of 1955 and annually thereafter, still yields useful results for a modest expenditure of manpower and travel funds.

The Board of Examiners for the Foreign Service in June 1955 accelerated and simplified the examination process in order to stimulate recruitment and broaden geographical representativeness. It replaced the three-and-one-half-day written examination with a one-day written, objective set of tests, and it dropped the compulsory foreign language paper. It saved candidates time and money by increasing the number of cities in which it offered the written examination from sixteen to sixty-five and by offering oral examinations in the field, rather than in Washington only, initially in twenty-three cities in the United States and five abroad. By March 1957, 679 new junior officers had been appointed. Since then enough qualified candidates have come forward each year to staff all junior officer vacancies.

A backlog of 300 successful candidates developed in 1957 because the department, planning to induct 460 new junior officers in fiscal year 1958, scheduled an additional written examination for June 1957. Unhappily the Congress voted only enough money for 160 new appointments. Despite efforts to eliminate the backlog by raising the pass cut-off in subsequent written examinations, delays of over a year in offering appointments persisted until the early sixties, partly because prolonged security investigations and the extended nature of the examining process also tended to delay induction. Many good candidates dropped out because they were financially unable or otherwise unwilling to wait for appointments.[1]

Dropping the foreign language requirement, reducing the cost and inconvenience of taking the examinations, and the College Relations Program all helped to increase the number of successful candidates from underrepresented regions and less elevated economic levels, but

---

[1] Deputy Undersecretary Henderson, who was deeply disturbed by this situation, charged me to devote preferential attention to the problem of narrowing the examination-induction gap when I became executive director of the Board of Examiners in December 1960.

it did not completely eliminate regional imbalance, and it did not increase appreciably the representation of minority groups.[2]

In general, the written examination barrier became less formidable with the elimination of the foreign language requirement and the essay type of paper. Moreover, the increase in vacancies compelled the Board of Examiners to approve about twice the percentage of the candidates as before the war.

Deputy Undersecretary Henderson told the Senate Foreign Relations Committee in March 1957 that, in November 1956, the staffing pattern of 4,636 designated Foreign Service officer positions was 2,951 Foreign Service, 560 reserve, 478 staff, and 426 Civil Service officers, plus 221 net vacancies. For June 30, 1962, he projected 4,087 Foreign Service, 428 reserve, 333 staff, and 124 Civil Service officers in 4,972 positions. He anticipated appointing 1,334 junior officers, 163 reserve officers, 29 officers through lateral entry, and 72 through integration in order to reach the 1962 goals. However, Congress refused to appropriate sufficient funds to permit the planned 1958 increase in officer strength.[3]

STRENGTHENING IN-SERVICE TRAINING, 1955–1960

The Foreign Service Institute (FSI) initiated a major expansion of in-service training during 1947–1954, but did not receive sufficient funds to develop its program. In fact, its fiscal year 1954 budget, $768,451, represented only 1 per cent of the department's budget for salaries and expenditures. FSI suspended the orientation course for junior officers when recruitment stopped. Its language training program got off to an excellent start but attained only modest dimensions,

---

[2] The geographical representativeness of the new officers broadened considerably. By 1960 all of the major regions had attained substantial representation, but the South lagged somewhat behind the Northeast and the West. The 926 new officers inducted between January 1957 and August 1962, who represented 25 per cent of all Foreign Service officers on duty in 1962, came from 205 widely distributed colleges and universities, although 325 came from the top ten and 215 from the next twenty-six institutions.

[3] United States, Congress, Senate, Committee on Foreign Relations, *Recruitment and Training for the Foreign Service of the United States* (staff study), 85th Cong., 2d sess., pp. 129–133.

and a program for specialized and advanced training never went much beyond the planning stage.

The Wriston Committee recommended a vigorous expansion and improvement in the institute and especially in its language program. The department sought and obtained additional funds for this purpose. By fiscal year 1958, FSI's budget rose to $4,679,545, representing about 5 per cent of salaries and expenditures. It reinitiated the basic course in 1954; greatly expanded language training; began a field training program; inaugurated a Mid-Career Course; began offering extension courses; organized functional courses in several fields; and, in 1958, initiated a Senior Officers Course, paralleling the curriculum offered at the National War College but stressing foreign policy rather than national security policy.

FSI also assigned more officers for advanced functional and area study at major universities and at service colleges.[4] Such assignments increased from the equivalent of thirty man years in fiscal year 1955 to eighty-three in fiscal year 1957. All these developments called for an expansion both in staffing and enrollment of the institute. The greatest impact of the revitalized activities came in language training where the need was greatest, especially among integrated officers and junior officers recruited after the Board of Examiners dropped the language requirement.

Expansion of the institute's activities and its elevation in the hierarchy did not, of course, assure a corresponding improvement in the quality of its offerings. It continued to rely to a large extent on officers of the department and the Foreign Service to lecture to junior officer trainees, although it began to recruit some scholars and experts to lecture in the intermediate and senior officers courses and in the functional and area courses. The assignment of Foreign and Civil Service officers to most of the administrative and some of the teaching roles

---

[4] Between July 1, 1956, and July 1, 1962, 112 officers were assigned to area studies at universities, 8 to Western European studies, 31 to Eastern European, 15 to South Asian, 14 to Southeast Asian, 14 to Northeast Asian and North Asian, 4 to Far Eastern studies, 24 to African studies, and 2 to Latin American studies. The annual program usually involved 12 or more Foreign Service officers from the FSO-4–6 classes in a year of graduate study at a major university.

in the institute probably prevented it from acquiring as dynamic and innovative a character as its role demanded.

Nevertheless, the institute effectively met its first priority, a rapid expansion in the language capability of the Foreign Service. This program began, incidentally, before either Sputnik or the publication of *The Ugly American*. By 1961 the director of the institute's language program could report that about 80 per cent of the officers had at least a useful knowledge of French, Spanish, or German, that 1,400 officers had been trained under the program, that over 60 per cent of the officers at posts using French, Spanish, and German had a working knowledge or better of the local language, and that another 14–20 per cent were nearing such proficiency.

He admitted that hard language posts were not as well staffed at the working knowledge level but pointed out that 378 Foreign Service officers or about 10 per cent of the corps had been trained in the past seven years in twenty-four of the so-called hard languages, and that 60 officers were scheduled to start language and area training in fiscal year 1962.[5]

In July 1958 the department instituted mandatory language testing when officers returned on leave. Three quarters of the Foreign Service officers had been tested by 1961. The service was then investing 800,000 man hours per year in language classes.

In the Eighty-fourth and Eighty-fifth Congresses very strong sentiment developed for establishing a Foreign Service Academy modelled on the service academies. Congressmen found the patronage possibilities of this proposal intriguing, but the department and many public-spirited citizens resisted it and the bills died.

---

[5] Deficiencies were then greatest in Arabic, Southeast Asian, and African languages. All officers, the director noted, did not need a working knowledge of hard languages at posts where they were spoken, but they did need elementary knowledge impartible in one to two hundred hours of teaching. During the third quarter of fiscal year 1961, 4,096 employees spent a minimum of an hour daily studying one of fifty-three languages. Of these employees, 1,948 were from the Department of State, 401 from USIA, and 1,013 from ICA. The remaining 734 were employees of other agencies, principally the Department of Defense. Being trained on a "space available" basis were 678 wives.

IMPROVED UTILIZATION OF FOREIGN SERVICE PERSONNEL

Integration, by opening about 1,200[6] Departmental positions to Foreign Service officers, permitted about 35 per cent of the career service to be given Washington assignments at all times. Administrative authorities established an assignments policy that called for a normal tour of duty of four years at home for middle- and senior-grade personnel and two years for juniors. They also began a modest officers' exchange program between the Departments of State and Defense.

In 1955 the Department of State organized a staff to prepare an inventory of skills in the Foreign Service, to counsel personnel, and to undertake career planning. This staff had no authority to make assignments, but it provided a locus where the needs of the individual could be considered, and it influenced the assignment process to a modest degree.

NEW FOREIGN AFFAIRS FUNCTIONS

In March 1952 President Truman established the United States escapee program in the department. Refugee work assumed enormous and pressing dimensions with the Hungarian Revolt of 1956 and the advent of Castro to power in Cuba. By March 1962 the department had assisted over 900,000 escapees. It had helped to resettle 150,000 in forty-eight countries and to facilitate the integration of 330,000 in countries that had granted them initial asylum.

The department also reinitiated and expanded science reporting, partly in consequence of the excitement caused by Sputnik but mainly because of the basic need for the program. It sent a few science attachés abroad in 1951, but the program lapsed during the economy wave and did not revive until 1959, when science attachés went to nine posts. The attachés were professional specialists recruited as Foreign Service reserve officers for minimum periods of two years. They worked as integral parts of the missions to which they were attached. In October 1960 Secretary of State Christian Herter appointed a science advisor to coordinate their efforts.

---

[6] Although 1,550 positions ultimately were designated as dual service, it will be recalled that career Civil Service officers continued to occupy several hundred.

Foreign affairs officers likewise had to assume much heavier responsibilities in Africa. The continent erupted in the late fifties in a rash of new sovereignties. The department recognized this by establishing a new bureau under an assistant secretary for African affairs in July 1958. Between January, 1959 and August 1961, the number of independent African states increased from nine to twenty-seven. This increase required the establishment of eighteen new embassies, three new consulates general, two new consulates, and two resident consuls.

Coordination

As noted earlier, President Eisenhower condoned rather than stemmed the trend toward dispersal of responsibility in the administration of American foreign policy and the separation of policy making from operational roles. He apparently considered that, by giving a free hand to Secretary Dulles, by appointing a special assistant for national security affairs, and by making much greater use of the National Security Council, he could obtain the coordination needed to reconcile divergent viewpoints and prevent conflicting activities.

According to Robert Cutler and Dillon Anderson, who served consecutively as special assistant for national security affairs between 1953 and September 1956, President Eisenhower used the council as a forum for vigorous discussion and its Planning Board as an agency to identify clearly elements of disagreement between the several executive agencies, so that such disagreements might be presented fully to the council, together with alternative policy courses.[7]

President Eisenhower also created the Operations Coordinating Board (OCB) to follow up council decisions and assure that they were executed. This interdepartmental committee was chaired, like the NSC Planning Board, by the special assistant for national security affairs. Its representation was on the undersecretarial level, but most of its work was done by an elaborate system of interagency working groups. When translating general NSC statements into tangible objectives, the

---

[7] Dillon Anderson, "The President and National Security," *Atlantic Monthly*, 197 (January 1956), 2–3; Robert Cutler, "The Seamless Web," *Harvard Alumni Bulletin*, 57 (June 4, 1955), 449–451.

OCB inevitably made as well as interpreted policy. But the board lacked command authority and could only advise operating agencies. Since its activities involved the same kind of interagency negotiating that characterized the work of the NSC Planning Board, it seems doubtful that it had much impact on the coordination of policy execution. At the same time, it probably created a false sense of security by inviting the conclusion that the problem of teamwork in the execution of policy was well in hand.[8]

Toward the end of his administration, President Eisenhower apparently decided that the devisiveness encouraged by Reorganization Plans Nos. 7 and 8 and the creation of a separate Foreign Agricultural Service had impaired coordination unduly and that the NSC and its subordinate interdepartmental committees were not working as had been anticipated. At any rate, by executive order and memorandum of November 1960, he redefined the authority and responsibility of chiefs of mission for the supervision and coordination of all official American activity in foreign countries. The order did not cover the CIA or operational military forces, but it somewhat strengthened the hands of chiefs of mission in performing their supervisory responsibilities over representatives of other agencies.

Morale

The reestablishment and expansion of junior officer recruitment, the appointment of Ambassador Henderson as deputy undersecretary for administration, the broadening of in-service training, and the more effective utilization of foreign affairs personnel all helped to revive morale. Officers of the administration also took some direct action to that end. In 1954 President Eisenhower publicly praised the Foreign Service and State Department personnel, declaring that they should have the "highest morale" in light of the important services they were performing. Secretary of State Dulles issued a laudatory statement in 1955.

[8] United States, Congress, Senate, Committee on Government Operations, *Selected Materials* prepared for the Subcommittee on National Policy Machinery, 86th Cong., 2d sess., 1960, pp. 73–178.

The Wriston Committee expressed deep concern about the effects of the security program on morale and efficiency. Its first audit report of October 12, 1954, recommended that "the security program be completed as promptly as possible." Security had already finished its crash investigations of officers on the December 1952 promotion list early in 1954, and the lists appeared shortly thereafter. This in itself did much to restore morale because most of the officers promoted had already learned through the grapevine that they had been recommended. On December 31, 1956, the department reported that it had "completed the minimum investigative requirements prescribed by Executive Order, or as otherwise determined by the Secretary of State to assure the maximum obtainable security of the Department."

The greatest boosts to Foreign Service morale came, of course, from congressional actions recommended by the administration, which raised salaries about 35 per cent, increased retirement benefits, and authorized other fringe benefits.[9]

To further restore morale and to improve efficiency, Congress

[9] Congress granted pay raises to Foreign Service officers in 1951, 1955, 1958, and 1960, and a modest adjustment in connection with a class structure revision in 1956. The sum total of these increases aggregated 35 per cent of base pay. Salaries of career ministers increased 46 per cent during this period and salaries of chiefs of mission of Classes I, II, III, and IV were raised by 10, 25, 28.6, and 33.3 per cent respectively.

Congress granted increases to Foreign Service annuitants in 1952, 1956, 1958, and 1960; and, in 1956, it authorized the computation of annuities on the basis of thirty-five rather than thirty years of service. In 1960 it provided for a reduction of the cost of the survivor's benefit and provided annuities for minor children.

In 1956 Congress authorized the operation of mess and commissary services where needed and assistance to employee-operated commissaries. It provided authority to establish recreational facilities where lacking and where such a lack damaged morale, and it permitted the use of United States transportation facilities to nearby recreation spots if local transportation was not considered safe or available.

A statute of 1955 amending the Foreign Service Act of 1946 extended hardship post differentials to career and reserve officers, although only Foreign Service staff and other agency employees had hitherto enjoyed these benefits. Congress also authorized a home service transfer allowance, educational allowances, reimbursement for the travel expenses of dependents where incurred for necessary educational purposes, free medical examinations for dependents, the crediting of military service toward Foreign Service retirement, and five- rather than four-year maximum service under reserve appointments. Another amendment in 1956 increased principal officers' residence allotments and liberalized medical benefits, which it also extended to dependents.

created the new grade of career ambassador in 1955 as the capstone of the service; and in 1956 it restored eight classes below the rank of career minister in order to permit greater flexibility in assignments and training and more frequent promotions. A statute of September 8, 1960, aimed at attracting young specialists to the career service permitted direct appointments to Class 7 of junior officer candidates meeting additional qualifications. It also prescribed stronger language and area training qualifications for appointments to ambassadorships and Foreign Service officer positions.

The department attacked duplication of administrative activities abroad by issuing an instruction in March 1955 designed to eliminate duplicatory staffing of motor pools, general services, budget and fiscal, and other overseas operations. Some modest improvement followed, but the regulations under which the several agencies operated varied too widely to permit substantial savings.

The department hoped to encourage early retirement of officers of relatively low service expectations through legislation of 1958 and 1960, which allowed a 12 per cent increase in pensions on a decreasing scale to officers who retired by May 31, 1962. The program encouraged 124 retirements in fiscal 1961, 205 in 1962, and a notable rise in Foreign Service staff retirements as well.

STUDIES AND INVESTIGATIONS OF FOREIGN AFFAIRS ADMINISTRATION, 1954–1960

Prompt adoption of the Wriston Committee's recommendations by no means stopped or even staunched the flow of studies and investigations of foreign affairs administration both private and public. Like earlier studies and investigations, they varied widely in details and emphasis; but several basic recommendations that emerged informed much of the thinking of foreign affairs administrators after 1960. The recommendations included substantial agreement on six points.

1. The same career service should staff the Department of State, the information agency (USIA), and the foreign aid agency (ICA), and more officers should be exchanged between all foreign affairs agencies.

2. Improvements should be effected in the recruitment of foreign

affairs officers, the planning of their careers, and their training while in service.

3. A great need for specialists still existed in the career service, attributable partly to failure to provide career ladders for specialists and partly to failure to make adequate use of lateral entry.

4. Excessive pluralism in the administration of American foreign policy called for measures to improve coordination at home by strengthening the Department of State's capability and powers, by substituting departmental direction for interdepartmental committees wherever possible, and by making more use of the budgetary process.

5. Coordination abroad should be improved by reinforcing ambassadorial powers and by appointing more career officers as ambassadors.

6. An expanded and more fully developed Foreign Service Institute using more effectively the resources of private scholarship should be developed.

The studies did not answer the questions of whether one agency or several should administer field operations and of how a career service could be maintained while encouraging the lateral entry of specialists.[10]

[10] Appendix B contains a résumé of the major reports and studies.

6

The Kennedy-Johnson Years, 1961–1969: Basic Objectives[1]

To the administration of American foreign policy, as to many other areas of American government, President John F. Kennedy brought a vigorous approach. He sought, above all, to improve the planning, coordination, and execution of policy, normally using the Department of State as his chosen instrument but delegating elsewhere as the spirit moved him.

He apparently looked to the creation of a "compatible family" of foreign affairs services. This meant integrating the home and field staffs of the Department of State, AID, and USIA, and making these separate services equal in quality, privileges, structure, and procedures. But he also hoped to improve the morale, quality, social representativeness, specialization, and training of all foreign affairs personnel and

---

[1] Factual information in this and the following chapter has been gleaned principally from the United States, Department of State, *News Letter*, hereafter cited as *News Letter*. A variant approach to the management innovations of the Kennedy-Johnson administrations will be found in John E. Harr, *The Professional Diplomat*, pp. 100–136.

to educate public opinion about policy issues and the problems of foreign affairs agencies.

President Lyndon B. Johnson asked the Kennedy team of foreign affairs administrators to remain at their posts when he assumed office, although he later made some changes. He did not immediately alter either the substance or the administration of American foreign policy; but he moved forward most vigorously along lines laid down during the preceding three years, delegating far more coordinative authority to the Department of State, and proposing legislation to establish a system of integrated, compatible foreign affairs agencies.

Congress did not approve the entire reorganization plan, but it created a compatible career information service. Administrative action moved the several agencies still further toward integration and compatibility. It also transformed the officer structure of the Foreign Service, seriously impairing the career principle in the process. Developments in Vietnam overshadowed and limited action in most fields of domestic policy after 1965, including the reshaping of foreign affairs administration. In the last months of 1967 and during 1968, balance of payments and budgetary crises led President Johnson to initiate a reduction in force in overseas foreign affairs establishments. This reduction, combined with an accumulation of other concerns, lowered morale in foreign affairs agencies but also generated an unprecedented activist and reformist spirit in the career Foreign Service.

Salient developments during both administrations will be summarized under the same captions to underscore the essential continuity of most of the programs, to facilitate a comparison of activities under the two presidents, and to reveal their distinctive styles.

The Kennedy and Johnson Teams

President Kennedy entrusted the Department of State to Dean Rusk, although he did not know him well and had political obligations to other candidates. He acted in some matters as his own secretary of state, making frequent use of White House assistants, but both he and President Johnson seem to have been strongly impressed by Mr. Rusk's ability and experience.

President Kennedy nominated Chester Bowles as undersecretary hoping he could initiate changes that would enable the department to discharge its coordinative role effectively. Impatient and apparently hoping for more rapid progress, he replaced Mr. Bowles in November 1961 with George Ball, who had previously served as undersecretary for economic affairs.[2] When Mr. Ball resigned in 1966, President Johnson nominated Nicholas de B. Katzenbach as his replacement.

Roger W. Jones, an outstanding career government official and former chairman of the Civil Service Commission, served in the key role of deputy undersecretary for administration until June 1962, when William H. Orrick, Jr., took over. In June 1963 a Foreign Service officer, William Crockett, replaced Mr. Orrick. Mr. Crockett, an administrative-management specialist, supervised State Department budgetary and fiscal affairs between 1958 and 1961, establishing a warm personal relationship with Congressman John Rooney, the powerful chairman of the State, Justice and Commerce Subcommittee of the House Appropriations Committee. Crockett became assistant secretary of state for administration in January 1961. His role in the administration of American foreign affairs under Presidents Kennedy and Johnson would be difficult to overestimate because he provided the only continuity between the Eisenhower and Johnson administrations. He served until January 31, 1967, when Idar Rimestad, another Foreign Service administrative-management specialist, replaced him. President Nixon did not replace Rimestad until September 1969, when he nominated William B. Macomber to the position.

President Kennedy, President Johnson, and Secretary Rusk considered that the Department of State needed all the outside help it could mobilize to meet its new responsibilities. While relying primarily on the experts of the department and Foreign Service, they brought in such outstanding men from private life and other government agencies as Adolph Berle, Roger Hilsman, Eugene Rostow, Nicholas Katzenbach, Walt Rostow, and Harlan Cleveland. They also sought expert guidance through outside task forces and investigations. Former Secre-

---

[2] Arthur M. Schlesinger, Jr., *A Thousand Days: John F. Kennedy in the White House*, p. 406; Theodore C. Sorenson, *Kennedy*, p. 288.

tary of State Christian Herter directed the most important investigation. His committee, sponsored by the Carnegie Endowment for International Peace but with full official support, focused on the Department of State, AID, and USIA and inquired into the overseas activities and personnel arrangements used by other government agencies only to the extent that it considered them relevant to its central task. It did not attempt to deal with problems of the Department of Defense, the CIA, the Arms Control and Disarmament Agency (ACDA), or the Peace Corps. It reported in December 1962.

The committee urged the creation outside the Civil Service of a family of "compatible," integrated, career, foreign affairs services, incorporating the Department of State, AID, and USIA. It recommended that senior personnel of the three services be considered for all major foreign affairs appointments but that the services continue to be administered separately. The committee envisaged the Foreign Service as the overseas vehicle for activities of primarily domestic agencies of the government, including the Departments of the Treasury, Commerce, and Agriculture. It also recommended that the coordinative role and authority of the Department of State be strengthened, especially its planning and programming capability.[3] Its specific recommendations on training, selection, and personnel management will be discussed elsewhere.

While the Herter Committee was at work, a presidential advisory board, headed by James A. Perkins, vice president of the Carnegie Corporation, studied intensively one aspect of its agenda—the preparation and in-service training of foreign affairs personnel. It reported a few days after the Herter Committee, recommending, as did the committee, the establishment of a graduate National Academy of Foreign Affairs to supersede the Foreign Service Institute and to serve the entire foreign affairs community.

Presidential Efforts to Improve Coordination

President Kennedy viewed the Department of State and its Foreign Service as his principal agency for the planning, co-ordination, and

---

[3] Committee on Foreign Affairs Personnel, *Personnel for the New Diplomacy*.

execution of American foreign policy. Achievement of this goal required raising the status of the department and Foreign Service in the executive hierarchy, although the president did not envisage restoring a single, unified field service. According to Arthur M. Schlesinger, Jr., "Kennedy had come to the Presidency determined to make the Department of State the central point below the Presidency itself in the conduct of foreign affairs."[4] He wanted the authority of the secretary to be clearly recognized in his own department and in the related areas of foreign aid and information policy, and he expected the secretary to serve as the agent of coordination in all major policies toward other nations.

To this end, the president, although he made extensive use of White House aides, confirmed and strengthened the coordinative roles of the secretary, the department, and the Foreign Service. He abolished the Planning Board and the Operations Coordinating Board of the National Security Council in the expectation that any essential work formerly done by them would be performed by the special assistant for national security affairs or by the Department of State. He also wrote to chiefs of mission, emphasizing that they were responsible for coordinating all official activities of the United States in their respective countries, except those of operational military forces, and that they might report unfavorably on or even request travel orders for undesirable employees. He specifically placed intelligence operatives under their supervision. He authorized representatives of other agencies to communicate directly with them and, in the event of decisions in which they did not concur, to ask for review by higher authorities in Washington; but he warned them to keep their ambassadors fully informed of their views and activities and to abide by ambassadorial decisions.

President Kennedy's establishment of the Agency for International Development (AID), merging the International Cooperation Administration (ICA) and the Development Loan Fund (DLF), also strengthened the department's coordinative powers. This latest in the long series of reorganizations of foreign assistance administrations

---

[4] Schlesinger, *A Thousand Days*, p. 407. Permission to quote this and subsequent excerpts from *A Thousand Days: John F. Kennedy in the White House* has been granted by Houghton, Mifflin Company.

was the first that clearly subordinated its Washington policy machinery to reasonably effective State Department control.

The president made it clear that he looked to improved coordination rather than unification of foreign affairs agencies by creating two new agencies—the Peace Corps and the Arms Control and Disarmament Agency (ACDA). Both take policy direction from the secretary of state, but their directors also have direct access to the president. While contributing to proliferation in these cases, President Kennedy resisted other pressures to establish new agencies and separate foreign services. He appeared to operate on the principle that existing divisive organizational arrangements would not be disturbed, but that the further proliferation of foreign services by established agencies would not be allowed.

President Johnson likewise viewed the Department of State as his principal agency for the planning, coordination, and execution of American foreign policy; but he relied less on White House aides, established clearer lines of responsibility, and delegated authority more liberally to the Department of State.

His special interest in Latin America prompted his first important innovation. In December 1963 he nominated Thomas C. Mann both as assistant secretary of state for inter-American affairs and coordinator of American participation in the Alliance for Progress. Mann's successors at the Bureau of Inter-American Affairs (ARA) continued to supervise the Latin American program of AID.[5]

In March 1965 President Johnson asked Secretary Rusk and Director of the Bureau of the Budget Kermit Gordon to review American programs in ten or fifteen countries before the next budget entered preparation. Each agency, he said, would "be expected to respect the levels established for each of our programs by Secretary Rusk and Mr. Gordon . . . for the ensuing year . . . and in the projection of our plans." This action underscored the importance of the department's coordinating role and attacked the problem at its source, the provision of funds. Since 1967 the bureau has consulted with the regional as-

---

[5] In October 1969 President Nixon announced his intention to ask Congress to authorize an additional undersecretary of state to coordinate all Latin American policies and programs.

sistant secretaries during its fall budget review for the purpose of trying to develop jointly an integrated program for each country.

In 1965 President Johnson expressed the desire that no government research be done that in the judgment of the secretary of state would "adversely affect United States foreign relations";[6] and he transferred the administration of the Food-for-Peace Program from the White House to the Department of State.

In March 1966 President Johnson delegated unprecedentedly broad powers to the secretary of state to direct interdepartmental activities overseas, other than military operations. He also instructed the secretary "to direct and coordinate the activities of all United States departments and agencies in international organizations." The new directive made the secretary, within certain limits, the manager rather than coordinator of American foreign affairs, because it gave him not only coordinative responsibility but the right and duty to initiate and pursue action in all areas not specifically entrusted to other agencies. It established a Senior Interdepartmental Group (SID) to direct coordination and supervise interdepartmental affairs overseas.[7] Interdepartmental Regional Groups (IRG's), headed by the assistant secretaries of state for each regional bureau, assisted the Senior Interdepartmental Group. Without unifying foreign affairs agencies and their overseas services, the president could scarcely have delegated broader coordinative and managerial powers.

In May 1967 the president instructed the secretary of state to es-

---

[6] To assure compliance, the Department of State established the Foreign Affairs Research Council, chaired by the director of the Bureau of Intelligence and Research and staffed by fourteen senior departmental officers representing the major geographic and staff bureaus. The department promptly informed other agencies of the procedures it would follow in reviewing their contract research, emphasizing that its "main function [was] not to stifle research but to encourage it" (*News Letter*, no. 57 [January 1966], p. 24).

[7] Chaired by the Department of State, SID contained representatives from AID, USIA, the Department of Defense, CIA, the Joint Chiefs of Staff, the White House, and the National Security Council. An early action of President Nixon abolished the SID but replaced it by the Undersecretaries Commitee of the NSC, also chaired by the Department of State but subordinate to the new NSC Review Group, chaired by his special assistant on national security affairs. The order retained the IRG's but provided that the Review Group would review their papers.

tablish a Water for Peace Office as an integral part of his department to "coordinate this country's efforts in the world's water programs." The new office was to "draw heavily" on the expertness of operating agencies, especially on the Department of the Interior.

In a further amplification of State Department powers, the president appointed a special assistant to the secretary for liaison with the governors, who was to serve as the link between the president and the secretary with the governors on all foreign affairs matters and to raise an "enlightened voice" in the federal government in presenting the governors' views in connection with foreign policy questions.

Although President Johnson delegated unprecedented coordinative authority to the Department of State, he, like President Kennedy, did not move toward the restoration of a unified field service or the consolidation of home foreign affairs agencies; he did, however, urge Congress to establish a family of integrated, compatible foreign affairs agencies.

STATE DEPARTMENT EFFORTS TO STRENGTHEN ITS ORGANIZATION

Between 1961 and 1969, the Department of State took many initiatives, not all successful, to improve coordination, policy planning, and the programming of overseas activities, including efforts to introduce the experience and ideas of private enterprise and the behavioral sciences into foreign affairs administration.

Planning, Programming, and Budgeting. Secretary Rusk promptly enlarged and strengthened the Policy Planning Council,[8] assigned

[8] In July 1969 Secretary Rogers merged the Council into a new Planning and Coordination Staff (S/PC), which also incorporated staff assigned to the Undersecretaries Committee of NSC. The new staff has separate sections for planning and coordination, but total staff is not to exceed twenty members chosen from inside and outside the department. The change allegedly will effect a more relevant and useful role for policy planners in the department's policy-formulating process; make directly available to the secretary and his top-level staff analysis and advice focusing on long-range and world-wide implications of important policy issues; and assist in assuring coordination and the most effective interagency participation of the department on foreign policy matters, especially in NSC. A later definition of the functions and duties of S/PC conveys the impression that its orientation will be predominantly toward the provision of day-to-day policy interpretation and crisis management.

policy planning officers to operating bureaus to take over regional and country work formerly done by the Operations Coordinating Board, and required assistant secretaries to participate more fully in policy planning. He also activated an Operations Center to support major interdepartmental task forces and to conduct informal reviews for following up government-wide action in foreign affairs.

In 1961, when President Kennedy asked the secretary to coordinate American diplomatic and military planning to meet the new Soviet threat to Berlin, Mr. Rusk established an interdepartmental task force in the department. The task force served as the focal point within the government for political, economic, and military contingency planning. It received all intelligence, coordinated information activities, and worked with British and French representatives. It broke much new ground in the tradition-bound field of diplomacy and proved to be an effective instrument for coordinating national policy. The department followed these procedures when creating task forces to deal with later crisis situations. In general, task forces with their more dynamic potential supplanted interdepartmental committees both in new action areas and in many long-established roles.

The rise in foreign affairs expenditures after World War II to a level far above the total prewar budget and the allocation of most of this money for overseas operations, as contrasted with traditional foreign affairs work, seemed to call as well for better budgeting, planning, and programming of such activities. The success of the McNamara Planning-Programming-Budgeting System (PPBS) in the Department of Defense amplified this call.

Early in 1963 a departmental task force put together the Comprehensive Country Programming System (CCPS). Field testing proved it to be cumbersome and imperfect in conception and design, but it provided a somewhat clearer view of the direction of American efforts. The department ultimately extended it to thirty countries before replacing it with the more sophisticated Foreign Affairs Programming System (FAPS). FAPS, in turn, gave place to Country Analysis and Strategy Paper (CASP), a system used (in 1970) in all Latin American posts and considered superior to its predecessors in flexibility and utility. However, grave difficulties outlined in the following paragraph and in Part IV continue to limit optimism about the ultimate applicability of such systems.

The department also established units in the Foreign Service Institute to help foreign affairs agencies find ways to improve programming and to strengthen the execution of overseas programs by applying the latest social science techniques, including systems analysis, operations research, and staff training. Deputy Undersecretary Rimestad abolished these units in mid-1967, apparently because of special limitations on PPBS work in the foreign affairs area as described in Part IV. Generally speaking, experienced officers have found the results of such work less valuable than the coordination achieved more or less incidentally in preparing the reports.

Introduction of New Information Processing and Retrieval Techniques. The information explosion after World War II, accompanied by the development of electronic data processing devices, led to recognition of the need for mechanical and electronic assistance to cope with the flood of data that threatened to swamp operations and seriously delayed decisions. In 1966 the Department of State processed 2,000 telegrams daily, making about 70 copies of each. Its Central Foreign Policy file added about 400 files drawers per annum, and the Bureau of Intelligence and Research employed 200 professionals to read and analyze 100,000 documents each month. Between 1946 and 1966 this avalanche of paper called forth 363 projects and studies on information management in the foreign affairs community, 172 in the department alone.

Under President Eisenhower, a modest Automated Data Processing Staff, using conventional card machines, began to perform experimental statistical tasks for the department's passport, communications, and transportation units. In 1962 the department acquired its first electronic computer, which it also employed on operational accounting tasks, and it installed an automated electronic message and data communications service in Paris to facilitate message exchanges between Washington and all of Europe. The department replaced its first electronic computer, already overloaded with accounting and visa work, with a more advanced system in 1965 and opened improved facilities in Bonn in 1969 to supersede the Paris center.[9]

A 1962 experiment allegedly demonstrated the possibility of using a computer for substantive data retrieval; but it illustrated as well the forbidding difficulties and expense of the process. Late in 1963, after three years of study, the Department of State installed a new uniform file system, authorizing 134 posts to follow suit as rapidly as possible. The system constituted an essential step toward the ultimate installation and efficient functioning of any automated data retrieval system. The National Archives described it as the "most comprehensive of its type ever attempted."

The Department of State also established a Substantive Information Systems Program (O/SNS) early in 1966 to plan and develop a modern system of information handling, distribution, filing, and retrieval, and to coordinate this activity throughout the foreign affairs community. It completed a preliminary design in January 1968, but an announcement of the unit's 1968–1972 program underscored the immensity of the task. Still needed were (1) further analysis of departmental and field information needs; (2) a survey of information handling methods in the field; (3) a determination of processing needs; (4) the design of a field information structure, including types of files, numbers of each, and determinations about their relationship; (5) the design of standard formats for formulating and manipulating machine language records on which files are based; and (6) the establishment of automated information files in high-priority subject areas.

In 1967 the Department of State inaugurated its new Washington

---

[9] A *News Letter* article of June 1969 (no. 98, pp. 16–17) announced that since April the Washington Financial Center had been providing computer payrolls and accounting and disbursing services to the field and that the department had been using Telstar since April to provide visa clearance computer data to European posts. The Data Processing Division was then working on the following projects: a computer model of the department's personnel system to project the career movement of FSO's over ten years; a simulation of factors affecting international trade; a tariff surveillance system; a substantive information system to store and retrieve foreign policy information regarding Vietnam; and an accounting system for the Combined Economic Reporting Program.

Communications Center, which permits much faster reception, transmittal, and servicing of communications, using television and tapes instead of teletypes. Traffic flow increased from about 60,000,000 words in fiscal year 1954 to 149,966,000 in fiscal year 1967, and to 152,845,000 words in fiscal year 1968. Traffic dropped to 136,757,000 words in fiscal year 1969 because of cuts in field personnel and reporting requirements.

A departmental officer estimated early in 1968 that the potential impact of the computer on foreign affairs work would be largely in three areas: (1) *data retrieval*—through a central bank of data for all agencies serving all agencies; (2) *data processing*—most effectively with quantitative data; and (3) *simulation and gaming*. In the long term, he predicted, its greatest impact would come from the "new intellectual climate" because machines brook no ambiguity and their logic exposes fallacies.[10]

Organizational Changes. State Department organizational changes considerably strengthened its coordinative capability and its capacity to perform new roles. Reference has already been made to the creation of the Operations Center, the Foreign Affairs Research Council, the Water for Peace Office, the development of the task force concept, the Senior Interdepartmental Group, and the Interdepartmental Regional Groups.

The department filled a conspicuous organizational gap in May 1961 by establishing, under the deputy undersecretary for political affairs, the new position of deputy assistant secretary of state for political-military affairs to coordinate its relations with the Department of Defense and take a world view of the foreign affairs implications of national security policies and activities.[11]

[10] *News Letter*, no. 81 (January 1968), pp. 20–21.

[11] This staff (1) acts as liaison with the Department of Defense in developing emergency planning, internal defense, and military assistance programs; (2) coordinates departmental policy and develops guidance in emergency planning and civilian defense; (3) supports State Department representation at military commands and war colleges; (4) studies and coordinates departmental policy on balance of payment problems arising out of national security policies or operations; (5) reviews policies and activities of the military establishment of a long-range nature, including alternate strategies and their foreign policy implications, contingency plan-

Another important change involved the Intelligence and Research Bureau, which for years had received approximately half its budget for conducting basic research for other agencies. The department relinquished these activities in 1961. Its residual intelligence research organization then concentrated on the major fields of policy-relevant research, current intelligence evaluation, increased estimative research, external research, planning to offset and counteract communist strategy, and guidance to field reporting.

Early in 1962 AID's headquarters staff moved into the Department of State's Foggy Bottom building from scattered Washington locations, and the department began to work out "back-to-back" arrangements for its Bureau of Inter-American Affairs and AID's Bureau for Latin America. Under this arrangement officers responsible for administering the Washington affairs of both agencies share the same office suites where physical proximity compels them, in theory at least, to work closely together in the joint administration of foreign affairs. In March 1963 the department also established a Latin American Policy Committee, a precursor of the Interdepartmental Regional Groups of 1966.

In July 1963 the department established a new Office of International Aviation in the Economic Bureau to replace the Aviation Division. The president later approved the establishment of an Interagency Committee on International Aviation Policy to be chaired by the Department of State.

The growing importance of international and interdepartmental scientific liaison, reporting, and coordination required the creation of the Office of International Science Affairs, with bureau status, to re-

---

ning, political-military contributions to long-range planning in the Departments of State and Defense, the foreign policy implications of United States troop dispositions, and the evolving roles of the alliance structures; (6) keeps the department informed regarding military interests in atomic energy and aerospace; (7) conducts liaison with the Atomic Energy Commission, the Department of Defense, Congress, and the White House in the preceding areas; and (8) controls exports of arms and munitions. In October 1969 Secretary Rogers raised the Office of the Deputy Assistant Secretary to a bureau and accorded its director the rank of assistant secretary.

place the science advisor.[12] It also compelled a substantial expansion of the field scientific personnel.[13]

Assistant Secretary Mann speeded decision making in the Bureau of Inter-American Affairs by abolishing office directors intermediate between the assistant secretary and the country desks, and by raising the status of desk officers, whom he redesignated as country directors. The other regional bureaus adopted this pattern after the president issued his March 1966 directive on coordination.

Several additional interdepartmental, functional policy committees, chaired by the Department of State, emerged, including the Council on International Educational and Cultural Affairs, the Foreign Affairs Information Management Effort (FAIME), the Joint Automated Data Processing Requirements Coordinating Committee, the Working Group and Committee on Population Matters, and the Foreign Area Research Coordination Group. The last-named group, representing twenty agencies, plans and administers social science research contracts.[14]

---

[12] The director of the office advises the secretary on the role of science in foreign policy, represents the department on the presidential Science Advisory Commission, chairs the Advisory Committee of the International Committee of the Federal Council on Science and Technology, coordinates the work of the science attachés, and maintains liaison with the scientific community.

[13] As of December 1966 science attachés were stationed at seventeen missions. The department also designated embassy medical officers at certain posts as deputy scientific attachés late in 1966. At other missions it designated FSO's as science liaison officers with part-time responsibility for reporting scientific developments.

[14] The Division, now Office, of External Research of the Bureau of Intelligence and Research had long served as a clearing house for public and private social science research in international relations, but without any authority to prevent duplication. When the Foreign Area Research Coordination Group was organized, the government was spending about $50,000,000 annually on some 750 social science research contracts. In December 1967 the Department of State announced a government-wide policy on contract foreign affairs research produced by the group. Under this policy all agencies were enjoined to (1) acknowledge all government support for research; (2) keep classification of research at a minimum; (3) encourage the open publication of findings; (4) make advancement of knowledge a factor in designing even action-oriented research projects; (5) consult with academic associations on problems of foreign area research; (6) avoid actions that might diminish the status of universities as centers for independent research and teaching or that might affect adversely the overseas relationships of private United States scholars; and (7) work to eliminate duplication and overconcentration of researchers and projects in any overseas area.

The asssistant secretary for administration received authority to evaluate all new programs of other agencies with regard to their probable impact on the official American presence abroad and the availability of administrative facilities to support them at any given post.[15] The Office of the Deputy Undersecretary for Administration became the focal point between the Department of State and the White House for all administrative planning and arrangements for presidential and vice presidential travel at home and abroad. Secretary Rusk also appointed a special assistant to coordinate population matters.

Integration and Compatibility

Deputy Undersecretary Roger W. Jones, when outlining the Kennedy administration's administrative goals, urged the integration of the Foreign Service into the Department of State and improvement in the career prospects of the Civil Service. He stressed the importance of continuity of service in many home positions, indicating that this meant longer tours of duty, including more Foreign Service officer time in Washington.

The department replaced separate series of circulars and news letters for the field and home offices with foreign affairs series and introduced a new performance rating form replacing separate Foreign and Civil Service forms. In March 1962 it also announced a new policy for departmental jobs. The best qualified officer was to be selected henceforth regardless of whether he was career Civil or Foreign Service, and positions were to be identified thereafter on the basis of the individual selected. This policy obviously clashed with the Wriston Committee's recommendation that dual service positions be designated permanently on the basis of the nature of their duties and that they be filled by officers obligated to perform field service. It also conflicted with views of the Herter Committee, but it solved, for the time being, the dilemma of civil servants who had refused Wristonization by giving them security in their positions, and it opened new opportunities to other civil servants.

---

[15] The fact that Foreign Service personnel were now in the majority at only 9 of 108 embassies underscored the importance of such a review. In London, for example, only 9 per cent of the staff were engaged in substantive Foreign Service activities.

President Kennedy did not attempt to obtain legislation to establish an integrated, compatible, foreign affairs system, including key home service as well as overseas employees, and covering the Department of State, AID, and USIA. It was not until March 1965 that President Johnson sent up the Hays Bill providing for such a system. The bill also authorized the direct appointment of superior junior officers to Class 6 and a packet of fringe benefits. The president concurrently nominated 760 USIA Foreign Service career reserve officers as Foreign Service officers. Neither the bill nor the nominations received congressional approval, although the bill passed the House and the president twice resubmitted the nominations.

Apparently some congressmen disliked granting permanent status to AID, and Civil Service unions opposed the legislation because they feared application of the selection out principle to all foreign affairs personnel. Some Foreign Service officers and possibly a few congressmen saw the bill and nominations as further diluting the career principle;[16] but Congressman Henry B. Gonzalez expressed the opinion that, in his view, the bill failed mainly because the foreign affairs agencies have no constituency and because few congressmen take a deep interest in the administration of foreign policy.[17]

In 1967 a Senate bill proposed the establishment of a Foreign Service information officers (FSIO) corps, paralleling the Foreign Service officers corps. Its sponsors apparently calculated that, by leaving out AID and by dropping the home and field integration feature, enough opposition could be overcome to assure passage. On August 20, 1968, the president signed into law a statute providing for "the development of separate but fully compatible personnel systems within the Department . . . and USIA."[18] Shortly thereafter, he nominated and the Senate confirmed 592 Foreign Service information officers.

Early in 1968 the Department of State announced that only Foreign Service personnel available for world-wide duty might fill designated

---

[16] See the article by Representative Thomas E. Morgan, "Congress and the Foreign Service," *News Letter*, no. 39 (July 1964), pp. 10, 47. See also John E. Harr, *The Professional Diplomat*, pp. 85–93, for a fuller discussion of the Hays Bill.

[17] Conversation with the author, April 16, 1967.

[18] *News Letter*, no. 89 (September 1968), p. 20, Public Law 90-498.

or dual service domestic positions. This change, it alleged, would improve the department's staffing, provide "reasonable career ladders" for Civil Service or other non–Foreign Service personnel in those organizations or programs where such staffing is indicated, and increase "substantially" the number of slots available for world-wide assignment.

The announcement rang with a familiar, indeed a nostalgic, tone reminiscent of 1954 personnel policy declarations. It seemed to promise a substantially integrated department staffed with Civil Service officers only in a very few positions where high performance clearly demanded specialization in depth and continuity of service. It further implied a reduction in the number of such officers and a corresponding rise in Foreign Service staffing. However, the guidelines made it clear that no employee would be moved out of a redesignated position unless another could be found for him; and further "clarification" of April 1969 authorized the promotion of Civil Service employees to or in positions designated for Foreign Service officers! Thus the wheel turned full circle again.

Although no statutory and little administrative progress occurred in integrating home with field services, the Kennedy and Johnson administrations took many actions to conform personnel systems and field administration. Efforts to conform USIA and Foreign Service selection and promotion systems actually began when former Ambassador George Allen assumed charge of USIA under President Eisenhower. He sought to equate USIS officers in quality to Foreign Service officers and to give them career status. USIA officers were classified as "career" and "limited" reserve officers, paralleling the FSO-FSR structure; and USIA began selecting its junior officers as did the Foreign Service, although its candidates completed an optional written paper in public affairs. In 1959 Mr. Allen invited the executive director of the Board of Examiners of the Foreign Service to sit ex-officio on the Joint Examining Board of USIA and began to use Foreign Service officers on USIA examining and promotion panels.

Subsequently the Department of State and USIA merged their junior officer examining and recruitment programs. The Department of State also invited AID to send representatives to the oral examining panels of the Board of Examiners, and in 1963 it broadened foreign affairs community representation on the Board of the Foreign Service.

In 1964, the Department of State and USIA agreed to the nomination, after a prior screening, of USIA's career reserve officers as Foreign Service officers and to the rating for promotion of career officers of both agencies by joint selection (promotion) boards. Later in the year, the Department of State, AID, and USIA also agreed upon a uniform set of performance standards and rating factors and substantially identical reporting forms and procedures. Such standards, recommended by the Herter Committee, obviously were prerequisite to the full development of a vigorous program of personnel exchanges and compatible personnel systems.

The Department of State and USIA also stressed the growing intimacy of their relationship by staging joint induction ceremonies for their new junior officers and giving them the same basic training at the Foreign Service Institute.

A presidential reorganization plan abolished the statutory Board of the Foreign Service and the Board of Examiners for the Foreign Service in May 1965. These boards had hitherto served not only as barriers to compatibility and integration but also as bulwarks against political dilution of the career Foreign Service. The secretary of state reconstituted the boards administratively in 1966 with representatives of AID, USIA, the Departments of Commerce and Labor, and the Civil Service Commission as full members. Their independence is, of course, substantially limited by the loss of statutory character.

In 1965 and 1966 Foreign Service career and reserve officer selection boards rated Foreign Service career reserve officers of USIA competitively with Foreign Service career and reserve officers of the Department of State. In 1967 USIA withdrew its officers from the jointly administered promotion system and began rating them again with its own boards but using "joint precepts." This change may have indicated apprehension on the part of USIA bureaucrats that such extreme compatibility might ultimately lead to unification, but possibly it only reflected dissatisfaction with the results of the joint effort. During 1966 a team of State Department, AID, and USIA officials began studying the problem of introducing more uniformity in their treatment of local (alien) employees.

Although the Department of State supplied administrative services to other agencies on an enormous scale after World War II, other major foreign affairs agencies retained large administrative staffs abroad because of differences in administrative regulations.[19] A joint USIA, State Department, and AID task force on administrative regulations, established in 1962, virtually completed its work on personal entitlements (allowances and other fringe benefits) by September, 1964. It then concentrated on regulations covering administrative operations.

The Department of State directed another initiative in this area toward developing experimental Consolidated Management Organizations (CAMO's), responsible to the ambassadors, which merged administrative services of the participating agencies. By October 1966 thirty-two had been installed. The Department of State, AID, and USIA also opened a Consolidated Administrative Service Center in Africa in 1963. It initially served twenty-four posts in eighteen West African countries as a forward supply depot and assisted them on request in solving post administrative problems.

Exchanges of Personnel

Exchanges of personnel between foreign affairs agencies increased enormously between 1961 and 1969. Exchanges began under the Foreign Service Act of 1946 but embraced only a few officers and agencies until the sixties.

The Department of State, AID, and USIA established a talent pool of the upper 25 per cent of the officers in each agency late in 1963, an-

---

[19] The Foreign Service began supplying some administrative support to other agencies before World War II. This support became big business in 1948, when the Congress created ECA. The support function grew even larger when USIA received autonomy and the Department of Agriculture set up a separate field service. Shared administrative costs in fiscal year 1965 totalled $70,000,000. The Department of State then was providing services to about 119 other agencies and units thereof. The Department of State, AID, and USIA contributed approximately 84 per cent and the remaining 117 agencies the balance of the $70,000,000.

nouncing that the best qualified officer available would be chosen thereafter to fill top vacancies in the three agencies. Several interagency assignments resulted from this program, including the designation of a USIA officer as deputy director general of the Foreign Service.

An executive order of May 1965 urged a massive increase in personnel exchanges between all executive agencies. It authorized USIA, AID, and other agencies using the Foreign Service Act of 1946 to staff field positions to negotiate agreements for mutual exchanges and appointments. The Department of State and the Civil Service Commission promptly agreed that "present and former State [Department] employees who have held career appointments in the Foreign Service may now be appointed to Civil Service positions in any federal agency under noncompetitive appointment procedures," and that civil servants might be appointed to the Foreign Service "under similar procedures."[20]

An executive order of November 1966 put 4,400 Civil Service supergrade positions in an "Executive Assignments Sytem," thus creating a pool of executives to facilitate more and easier exchanges of high-level personnel between all federal agencies. Foreign Service officers of Classes 1 and 2 came into the pool in 1968.

Foreign Service officers in other agencies jumped from 61 in 1962 to 146 in 1963, serving in 12 agencies; to 300 by March 1968, serving at home and abroad in 18 agencies, including the Office of Economic Opportunity; and to 400 by September 1969, serving in 30 agencies and 10 international organizations.[21]

Efforts to Broaden the State Department Constituency

Presidents Kennedy and Johnson both realized that foreign affairs administrators labor under serious handicaps because the public does not appreciate the limits of foreign policy, because demagogues had blackened their collective image, and because they lack the support of a broad, well-informed constituency.

[20] *News Letter*, no. 54 (October 1965), p. 11.
[21] By April 1970 over 350 Foreign Service officers had served AID in Vietnam, and the department had committed 150 of all grades to AID on a continuing basis.

Under President Kennedy the Department of State initiated Washington briefings for leaders in the mass media, nongovernmental organizations, and the general public. President Johnson's Department of State extended this program to American Legion officials, teachers of international relations, senior business executives, high school social science students, congressional assistants, representatives of Community Services to International Visitors, and editors and publishers of American foreign language newspapers.

During both administrations the department sent many more Civil and Foreign Service officers to meet with influential persons in carefully planned conferences in major cities. Over 340,000 persons attended community meetings on foreign policy between 1963 and June 30, 1967. Thirty-one teams of diplomats visited 190 communities, spoke at hundreds of institutions, and participated on more than 300 radio and television programs. The department also made far greater use of returning Foreign Service officers to address hinterland groups. In only eighteen months between January 1965 and June 1966, returning officers made 1,481 speeches and gave 1,105 interviews to media representatives.

Both administrations successfully employed public advisory councils and committees to rally support for their programs and to provide a more democratic aspect for foreign policy formulation. The public relations effort of the 1961 to 1969 period also involved a substantial rise in State Department publications, films, and tape-recording programs. Finally, the department made real efforts to improve service to the public at home and abroad in the hope of refurbishing its image.[22]

[22] The Nixon administration has continued these public relations efforts. It has also introduced a useful new series of publications, *Issues in Foreign Policy*.

7

The Kennedy-Johnson Years, 1961–1969: Personnel Programs

President Kennedy considered that foreign affairs agencies required more youth, vigor, initiative, planning, specialists, and minority representatives. He took an active, personal interest in morale and training programs. President Johnson placed less emphasis on youth but pressed vigorously toward the other objectives.

CAREER PLANNING AND PERSONNEL UTILIZATION

The Herter Committee recommended substantial improvement in career and manpower planning, which it considered prerequisite to better personnel utilization. The Department of State installed a modest performance evaluation section in 1947 and mounted a more ambitious program of career planning and counseling in 1956, but the efforts of these staffs had little impact on recruitment, selection, assignment, or promotion programs. Because of the frequent changes in the Department of State's upper administrative levels under President Kennedy, work on career planning and related Herter Committee recommendations began slowly. Progress thereafter seemed to be more publicized than effective.

In October 1963, the Department of State introduced a new functional and area machine-coded appraisal form; and it later coded all positions in the department and the Foreign Service in accordance with the form. This process allegedly permitted a computer to locate all candidates having the skills needed for any vacant position.

In December 1963, Deputy Undersecretary Crockett announced a new program of career management to convert junior and midlevel generalists into specialists through carefully planned assignments of formal and on-the-job training.

A Manpower Utilization System and Techniques (MUST), inaugurated in August 1965, purportedly established current and projected needs for foreign affairs manpower with a view to developing enough specialists to meet all needs through recruitment and in-service training. Personnel officers were to plan formal and on-the-job training assignments for all Foreign and Civil Service officers through midcareer to aid them to become experts in at least one function, comparing the projections with the inventory of personnel requirements and adjusting and balancing both in order to make them more realistic. The programming was to emphasize on-the-job training in the area of specialization but to permit assignments to other areas, thus assuring adequate breadth of experience. Programs were to be changed to reflect changing interests, failures, or "late blooming."

Inventories of positions and their requirements and of personnel and their qualifications and interests obviously must provide the basic statistical data needed to design sound recruitment, integration, in-service training, promotion, or career planning programs. An inventory of Foreign Service officers on punch cards existed in the former Division of Foreign Service Personnel at least as early as 1947 when the writer served there; and he helped colleagues in the primitive Performance Evaluation Section compile considerable information about officer capabilities and preferences. Much more data accumulated in these files between 1947 and 1956 and in the files of the Career Development and Counseling Staff between 1956 and 1963.

Statements made by senior management officers of the Department of State between 1951 and 1968 implied that personnel programs, especially those designed to meet alleged needs for specialist and technicians, rested on a factual basis supported by data derived from comparisons of job requirements with the qualifications of staff then on duty.

Consequently, an announcement of December 1968 that the department had just completed "for the first time" a "coordinated staff and position inventory covering all of its overseas and domestic jobs,"[1] raised many questions.

Unless the report exaggerated the achievement, it clearly implied that postwar major personnel programs did not rest upon sound analyses of manpower needs and employees' skills. Since the inventory reportedly took only six months to prepare, one wonders why a task of such predominant importance and urgency could not have been completed earlier. Indeed, statements of successive top administrators gave ample reason to believe that usable, if imperfect, inventories already existed.

In truth, a perfect inventory of foreign affairs positions and employees probably never will exist because of highly technical difficulties. But the writer fears that departmental administrators, for undisclosed reasons, never have made full use of the data available to them. As early as 1947, an assignments process could have emerged reflecting Foreign Service officer capabilities and preferences more accurately, but the weight of geographical rather than functional considerations prevailed.

Through the ensuing years, promotion, recruitment, integration, and many other aspects of personnel policy reflected a bland disregard for arithmetic. Thus, appointments of junior officers fluctuated wildly from year to year; promotion policy needlessly produced a badly skewed class distribution of the Foreign Service Officer corps; specialists and technicians, despite huge lateral entry and integration programs and the recent reorganization of the officer structure, still allegedly remain in short supply; and in-service training grinds out officers with the equivalent of undergraduate majors in economics,

[1] United States, Department of State, *News Letter*, no. 92 (December 1968), pp. 12–13. Hereafter cited as *News Letter*.

although recruitment still has failed to set its sights on the graduate schools.

Junior Officer Recruitment and Selection

Under Presidents Kennedy and Johnson, the Department of State made important efforts to improve the examining process, attract more able candidates to the service, and bring more specialists into the junior classes.

Unfortunately, after 1962 the apparent preoccupation of senior management officials with the task of equating the reserve and staff officers to the Foreign Service officer category, together with budgetary problems late in the Johnson administration, led to a sharp decline in the induction of officers after examination, as illustrated in the graph.

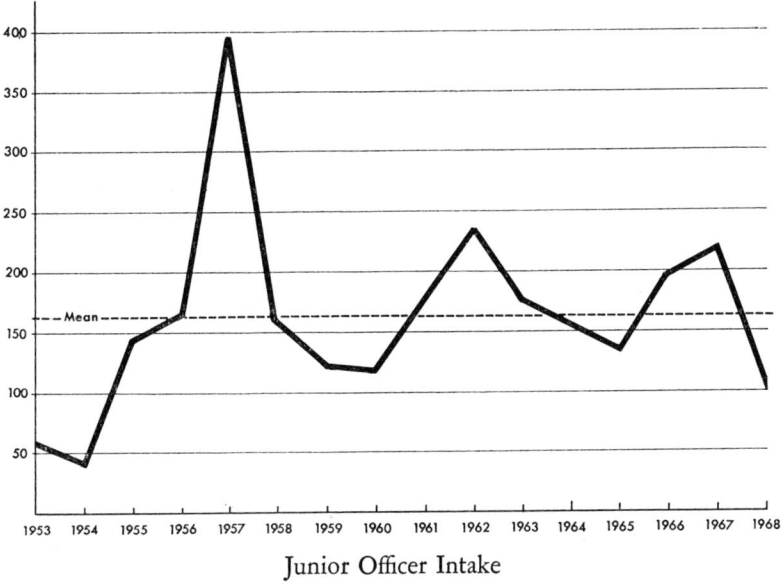

Junior Officer Intake

In fiscal year 1968, inductions fell well below the attrition rate in the Foreign Service officer corps, and, indeed, attained it only in 1962, 1966, and 1967. One must logically conclude from this that senior administrators, despite declarations to the contrary, did not attach salient importance to the career method of staffing the Foreign Service officer corps, especially since they continued to appoint junior Foreign Service staff and reserve officers while slashing the junior Foreign Service career officer induction rate.

Efforts to improve the examining system involved, first of all, an attempt to compress the time gap between the written examination and induction, which had lengthened to more than a year because of budgetary problems and a security clearance backlog. The Board of Examiners (BEX) closed the gap to about seven months by 1967, but the time lag lengthened again with the drop in inductions.

Well-founded criticisms that the one-day, objective, written examination failed to test candidates' ability to draft effectively became general by the late nineteen-fifties. BEX included an essay paper in the 1961 examination, which was not graded but which gave oral examiners a sample of each candidate's writing skill. It subsequently required candidates to edit a badly written report.

BEX resisted pressures to reimpose a compulsory foreign language examination in order to prevent the loss of otherwise well-qualified candidates. It even dropped the optional examination from the written examination in 1963. Since then, successful candidates have taken qualifying foreign language tests upon admission to the Foreign Service Institute. Currently, about 90 per cent of all successful candidates have some language competence.

In further efforts to improve the examination process, BEX substituted detailed questionnaires for unstructured letters of inquiry previously sent to candidates' references; contracted with a research institute to evaluate recruitment, rating, and promotion procedures; appointed a panel headed by Dr. Kenneth Clark to study the examining process; and increased the length of the written examination from six hours and thirty minutes to eight hours.

The Department of State obtained legislation in 1960 authorizing the direct appointment to Class 7 of highly qualified candidates in the hope of attracting more junior specialists. This program remained almost inoperative until 1962, when BEX equated the qualifications for direct appointment with those for appointment to an equivalent grade in the Civil Service and lowered the minimum age requirement to twenty-five. In order to prevent inequities, it screened the dossiers of all officers already in Class 8 and recommended promotions to Class 7 for those meeting the new standards. It sought but did not obtain authority to appoint directly to Class 6.

The department did not reorient the College Relations Program, although the Herter Committee had recommended that it direct its efforts toward graduate students or those with professional working experience in order to recruit more specialists as junior officers. Nevertheless, between January 1, 1965, and January 31, 1966, 137 of the 190 appointees had graduate training, and about 50 per cent of recent inductees have had some graduate work.

BEX sought to attract more junior officer specialists by offering optional papers for candidates having special training in management, business administration, or economics in place of the traditional examination on public administration, history, and government.

In 1964 it also set up occupational registers of successful candidates, ranking economists, administrative specialists, commercial specialists, and nonspecialists on each register on the basis of their grades in the examinations. Appointments of new officers from the top levels of the registers were made for the first time in mid-1964 in accordance with estimated needs of the service in each category. Unfortunately, the options offered under the written examination failed to attract many candidates,[2] probably because of the department's inability to offer appointments at higher salary levels.

A college intern program, inaugurated in 1961, aimed initially at attracting able undergraduates to Foreign Service careers. Twenty interns served in the Department of State in the first group. After completing the internship, it was expected that participants would return to college for a full year. The program expanded rapidly, involving

---

[2] In 1964, only 15 per cent of the examinees took the special options, 5.5 per cent in economics, 6.5 per cent in administration, and 3.0 per cent in commerce. Of the candidates who passed the 1965 written examination, 22.6 per cent had majored in political science, 17.5 per cent in history, 12.6 per cent in international studies, 4.3 per cent in law, 3.8 per cent in English, 6.3 per cent in interdisciplinary studies, and only 6.4 and 2.9 per cent respectively in economics and business administration.

about 425 youths in 1966, including 120 interns from 90 colleges and 250 young people paid with funds provided by the Youth Opportunity Campaign.

In February 1967 the department announced that it would again appoint more than one hundred interns, but almost exclusively from among persons who had passed the written Foreign Service officer examination. The change in emphasis in the program from a recruitment device to a pre-induction training experience occurred without public announcement or explanation of the motive underlying it. Presumably administrators now use it as another pre-induction screening device or to help bridge the reopened time gap between the written examination and induction.

Specialist Recruitment and Administrative Reorganization of the Officer Corps

The problem of recruiting management, labor, economics, and other specialists, and administrative, commercial and consular technicians after World War I greatly preoccupied investigators of foreign affairs administration and departmental administrators. A remarkable consensus emerged on the need for such specialists and technicians, unsupported by any definitive published statistical analysis, so far as the writer is aware. Thus, one investigating group after another and successive departmental management experts continued, and still continue, to emphasize this need, resting their case in broad terms on the increased volume and complexity of foreign affairs work and on earlier statistically unsubstantiated declarations of urgent need.

Such pronouncements never included even rough numerical estimates of the numbers of specialists and technicians needed by functional categories. More important, they failed generally to distinguish between the needs of home and field services. The former obviously require more experts in greater depth and much more continuity in service than can be accommodated or offered in the latter. Moreover, the Civil Service normally has not found it excessively hard to recruit for the home positions.

Advocates of integration and massive lateral entry also begged and still beg the question of whether the bulk of the specialists needed in the field cannot be mobilized by an officer recruitment program directed primarily toward graduate students and supported by appointment offers competive with Civil Service and academic entering salaries. Management never sought authority to appoint directly to Foreign Service officer Class 6 until 1965 and apparently has not pushed for it since the Hays Bill failed. It has still to redirect the College Relations Program toward the graduate schools.

The Department of State announced a new lateral entry program late in 1962. It promised, as usual, that the junior officer examination system would continue to provide the bulk of new talent through an annual intake of about two hundred junior officers; that direct appointments to Foreign Service officer Class 7 would be made more frequently; and that legislation authorizing direct appointment to Foreign Service officer Class 6 would be sought in order to attract more specialists at junior levels. It asserted that lateral entry would be at the rate of fifty to seventy-five appointments in the next year or two; that some lateral entrants would be recruited from within the government; and that legislation would also be sought to permit direct appointments of specialists from private life.

The following statements raise the question of whether administrators ever expected the 1962 program to succeed: "Until this authority [to make appointments of nongovernmental workers] is obtained, initial appointments will be made to the Foreign Service Reserve. Thereafter, both the direct appointment and Reserve Officer channel will be used." Reserve officers who wish to enter the career service, upon so declaring, will "henceforth be ranked for promotion by Selection Boards along with Foreign Service officers of the same class. Subsequently, those whose records so warrant will be offered appointment as a Foreign Service officer. Future appointments to the Reserve Officer Corps will be similarly handled."[3]

The 1963 selection boards reviewed the dossiers of both Foreign Service career and reserve officers in their respective classes under instructions to consider both "as officers of equal status in recognition of the fact that . . . we must include men and women who know . . .

[3] *News Letter*, no. 17 (September 1962), pp. 8–9.

the nontraditional tools of diplomatic action. These Reserve officers bring to the Foreign Service skills and specialties in short supply . . . in the career corps."[4] The boards were also enjoined to regard "a potential in a specialty as more important than general potential." Thus, State Department administrators made it abundantly clear that the statutory and the Wriston and Herter committees' conception of the reserve as a body of temporarily employed specialists would no longer guide personnel policy.

But the expansion and elevation of the reserve embraced only one phase of administrative reorganization of the structure of the Foreign Service. Earlier in 1962, the department rescinded a circular embodying the Wriston Committee's recommendations on Foreign Service staff employees. It removed promotion ceilings; eliminated restrictions on the assignments of Foreign Service staff to career officer positions; and forbade "the designation of positions as between FSO and FSS," although it promised that assignments of the Foreign Service staff corps would be made to positions of "predominantly technical character." It argued that a broader range of skills of technicians existed than had been realized, that some Wristonized former staff officers had been handicapped in competing as Foreign Service officers, that the new circular would permit them to return to the staff corps, and that need existed for a more flexible use of personnel.[5]

President Kennedy's administrative team thus effected a basic reorganization of the Foreign Service without new statutory authorization, public discussion, or congressional approval, other than that accorded in normal budgetary hearings. The independence of this action was possible because foreign affairs agencies have minuscule constituencies and because few congressmen are fully informed about their administrative arrangements.

Lateral entry remained at a low level because departmental administrators continued to recruit to the reserve and staff in order to meet alleged needs for technicians and specialists. In September 1964, moreover, they announced a new and broader program to expand staff op-

---

[4] *Ibid.*, no. 30 (October 1963), p. 11.
[5] *Ibid.*, no. 10 (February 1962), pp. 14, 35.

portunities in consular and administrative work in Washington.[6] Subsequently, the department continued to appoint many additional junior staff officers even though junior Foreign Service career officer appointments dropped sharply. An announcement of January 1967 indicated that the future commissioning of staff officers would be principally through the Federal Service Entrance Examination and oral interview procedure.

On March 31, 1960, the service enrolled about 4,900 officers, 3,608 Foreign Service career, 1,127 reserve, and 178 staff.[7] Foreign Service career officers then outnumbered reserve and staff officers by 2,303 or by a ratio almost 2.8 to 1. By April 30, 1969, officer strength stood at about 7,500, of whom only 3,292 were career officers. The 1,430 reserve officers and 2,815 staff employees in officer salary grades outnumbered career officers by about 950 or a ratio of almost 1.3 to 1! On that date, 1,977 (58%) of the career, 698 (48%) of the reserve, and 2,062 (73%) of officer level staff employees served in foreign countries. The department then had 6,994 employees of whom 3,714, or only 53 per cent were Civil Service. Of these only 2,207 had ratings higher than GS-5, which corresponds roughly to the entering Foreign Service officer level, but possibly 300 to 400 of the GS-6–9 employees served in secretarial or technical support roles.[8]

Deputy Undersecretary Crockett announced in January 1965 that

[6] *Ibid.*, no. 41 (September 1964), p. 12. The home service feature of the expanded program represented a major policy change because only 8 per cent of staff officers were then assigned to Washington, as compared with 36 per cent of Foreign Service career officers. The innovations also included provisions for stepped-up recruitment and in-service training, the initiation of assignment and career development programs resembling the programs developed for career officers, the continued use of separate selection boards for staff officers, apparently to preclude competition between staff and career officers, and an announcement encouraging reserve and career officers in consular and administrative functions to transfer to the staff.

[7] This low figure reflects the Wristonization of most FSSO's and represents all of the FSS employees in FSS grades 1–7. Possibly 20 to 30 per cent were senior clerical or technical personnel.

[8] The staff figures include all FSS 1–6 personnel. Some FSS secretaries and technicians have reached these classes, but some FSS–7's also have officer status. It would probably be safe to assume that at least 2,700 FSS employees have officer rank. The data summarized above appear in United States, Department of State, "Summary of Employment," PER/CMA Reports and Statistics Section, May 23, 1969.

staff officers were then serving "with suitable consular and diplomatic titles"⁹ and "inter-changeable in any position in which they are qualified." He added that they now had opportunities for Washington tours as well. Reserve officers had been "recognized as an integral part of the Foreign Service system" with the same promotional opportunities as Foreign Service career officers; and "with an anticipated change in legislation the Reserve officer would be given full career status along with the Foreign Service officer and the Foreign Service Staff officers."¹⁰

The anticipated change in legislation came in August 1968 as an amendment to the bill establishing the Foreign Service information officer corps. The amendment authorized the Department of State and USIA to extend unlimited tenure to reserve officers under conditions substantially equating their status to that of career officers, to appoint them to the career, staff, or Civil Service GS categories, or to terminate them within specified periods. USIA promptly converted all "career" reserve officers, not nominated as Foreign Service information officers, to unlimited status.

Senior State Department administrators announced in November 1968 that USIA's action would not set a precedent for the Foreign Service because it reflected a "peculiar USIA need."¹¹ But in December the *News Letter* reported that an administrative task force study "envisioned that there will ultimately be only three career officer categories —Foreign Service (FSO), Foreign Service Reserve Unlimited (FSRU), and Civil Service (GS)." The report contemplated that "the Foreign Service Staff officer category would disappear through attrition, conversions, and appointments to other categories."¹²

This authoritative indication of high-level management views, taken in conjunction with statements earlier in 1968 that more departmental positions were to be set aside for the Foreign Service, obviously implied both a further drive toward integration along the unhappy lines

---

⁹ In June 1964 the Department of State removed a long-standing staff grievance by authorizing the issuance of diplomatic passports to staff personnel and their families "on the same basis as Foreign Service officers" (*News Letter*, no. 51 [July 1965], p. 21).

¹⁰ *Ibid.*, no. 45 (January 1965), inner cover.

¹¹ *Ibid.*, no. 91 (November 1968), pp. 20–21.

¹² *Ibid.*, no. 92 (December 1968), p. 13.

of the Wriston experiment and another major assault on the career principle through mass lateral entry of staff and reserve officers into the career officer corps. It also implied the conversion of remaining reserve officers to unlimited tenure, despite earlier statements indicating that relatively little use would be made of this device.

RECRUITMENT OF MINORITY REPRESENTATIVES AND WOMEN

Presidents Kennedy and Johnson sought earnestly to make the foreign affairs agencies more representative in every way. They showed keen interest in bringing more members of minority groups and women into all public positions. In pursuance of these goals they named more Negroes, citizens of Latin American extraction, and women to ambassadorial positions and to major Washington offices than had any of their predecessors.

Deputy Undersecretary Jones instructed the writer, then serving as executive director of the Board of Examiners for the Foreign Service, to encourage more minority candidates to come forward, and to review the examining process in order to eliminate any discriminatory features. In August 1961 Mr. Jones also convened a Conference on Minority Employment to discuss problems involved in increasing minority representation. Conferees criticized the Foreign Service written examination as too verbally oriented and noted that few Negroes had reached high positions in the department's Civil Service. They recommended more effective recruitment and public relations campaigns directed toward the Negro and a study of the validity of the examination system. Despite earnest and fairly extensive efforts to encourage more Negroes[13] to take the Foreign Service examination, relatively few came forward, and the problem of revising the written examinations to facilitate the entry of minority candidates proved most difficult.[14]

---

[13] Considerably less effort and publicity characterized the campaign to attract more Puerto Ricans and Mexican-Americans to foreign affairs positions.

[14] The key importance of communication skills precluded substituting a less verbally oriented examination. To have lowered written examination standards, as Dr. Kenneth Clark suggested to me, seemed likely to lower the quality of all inductees. To have accorded preference to Negro candidates, as some suggested, did not

But, appointments of Negroes to ambassadorships, to major posts in the Department of State, and as reserve officers had a modest impact; and oral examining panels were urged strongly to give special consideration to Negro candidates because of the empathetic capability that they could bring to the service. The subsequent success in the orals of a very high percentage of Negroes who passed the written examinations indicate that this hortative had the desired effect.

The best approach to a rapid build-up of Negro strength in the Foreign Service seemed to be through reserve and staff appointments and through the special preparation of likely candidates in summer training sessions designed to improve their verbal skills. In support of the latter concept, the Ford Foundation provided $600,000 for a pilot program to prepare minority candidates over a four-year period. By March 1967, after 120 Negro students had passed through the Foreign Affairs Scholars Program, 14 had passed the written examination, 5 the oral, and 5 more were scheduled for the orals in the Spring of 1967.[15] The program thus demonstrated the utility of special training in preparing Negro candidates for foreign affairs work. Unfortunately, of those who qualified relatively few ultimately opted for foreign affairs careers.

Between 1961 and 1965 Negroes received eight ambassadorships and the directorship of USIA. The first Negro woman became a Foreign Service officer and ten attained top departmental or Foreign Service jobs, including an ambassadorship. Negroes likewise began serving as deputy examiners, selection board members, and officers and advisors in several bureaus. As of November 1967, minority representatives held 4.3 per cent of the department's officer positions, including 23 career, 51 reserve, and 65 staff officer positions, and 106 GS-9–18, or 246 in all, as compared with 45 in 1961. In 1967 they held 27 per cent of all State Department jobs.[16]

The problem of getting minority representatives through the written examination for the Foreign Service continues to offer great difficulty.

---

seem to be in the best interest of either minority or majority groups or of race relations in general.

[15] *News Letter*, no. 71 (March 1967), p. 11.
[16] *Ibid.*, no. 87 (August 1968), p. 22.

For this reason, the department yielded to pressures in fiscal year 1967 and began appointing minority representatives nominated by the Office of Economic Opportunity (OEO) as junior reserve officers, thus bypassing the written examination. Such appointees, inducted and trained in the same manner as examination candidates, presumably will receive lateral Foreign Service officer appointments after five years. The department made 11 reserve as compared with 103 examination appointments in fiscal year 1968; it appointed 89 junior career officers and 20 reserve officers in fiscal year 1969; and it made 20 reserve and 101 examination appointments in fiscal year 1970. It projected 20 reserve and 150 career appointments in fiscal year 1971.[17]

Women aspiring to enter either the Foreign Service or the Department of State have not suffered demonstrable discrimination since the passage of the Rogers Act of 1924. The number of women career officers in the Foreign Service has always been small. Relatively few take the examinations and many of those who enter resign when they marry, often, happily, to other Foreign Service officers. The proportion of women candidates who pass the examinations shows no appreciable variation from the proportion of successful male candidates. Critics once alleged that women found it excessively difficult to rise to the highest positions in the service and the department, but statistics no longer support this charge.

Presidents Kennedy and Johnson both showed keen interest in opening broader careers to women by appointing more to ambassadorial and important departmental positions. A departmental survey of 1964 showed that the ratio of women in higher grades in the Department of State was then more than five times the government-wide

---

[17] Letter from William D. Calderhead, acting chief, Special Assignments Division, Department of State, to author, July 22, 1970. In the letter just cited, Mr. Calderhead states the department's policy regarding junior reserve appointments in the following words: "The intake of 20 FSR Junior Officers each year represents the Department's response to a recognized need to increase the participation of minority groups in our diplomatic and consular endeavors. For each of five years (FY 1968 through 1972) 20 minority candidates will be recruited and permitted, through on-the-job training, either to prepare themselves eventually to take the oral examination or to demonstrate their qualifications for lateral entry into the FSO corps. The program is reportedly working well."

average and that the service had a similarly high percentage of women officers, including 353 career officers, of whom 41 were Class 3 or above.[18] In October 1967 President Johnson issued an executive order banning discrimination in federal employment on the basis of sex.

OTHER PERSONNEL MANAGEMENT POLICIES

Promotion. In 1962 in response to criticism about the in-grown character of the career service, the Department of State began staffing selection boards with three instead of four career officers and with two outside members, rather than one. The most important changes in the promotion system evidenced the department's desire to improve the promotion opportunities of specialists and to bring younger officers to the top faster.

Changes in 1964 promotion procedures finally introduced the concept of functional specialization or separate career ladders into the Foreign Service. The competitive rating of reserve and career officers, initiated in 1963, made such a change the more urgent. Midcareer specialists now compete against each other in several broad categories in the first stage of the rating process, eliminating the advantage previously enjoyed by generalists. Final ratings by full panels so nearly approximate subpanel ratings that recent promotion lists show a distribution of promotions by function closely resembling the distribution of specialists in each class.

Presidents Kennedy and Johnson both aspired to move able young people forward more rapidly in the Foreign Service and viewed promotion as a valuable aid in morale building. Consequently, promotion rates rose rapidly after 1961. Unfortunately, advancements became more rapid than balanced, with the result that a large surplus of senior officers developed. A junior officer quarterly review and promotion system, introduced in July 1963, produced 166 recommendations for promotions out of 276 eligible candidates in fiscal year 1964. Comparable results followed in subsequent years. Between 1964 and 1966, the average age of those recommended for promotion to Class 6 dropped

---

[18] *News Letter*, no. 35 (March 1964), p. 13. John E. Harr in *The Professional Diplomat* (pp. 171–188) offers a useful statistical analysis of the social origins and characteristics of the career service.

from 31.1 years to 28 years. Time in class fell from two and one-half years to two years and one month, and the proportion of eligible Class 7 officers promoted to Class 6 rose from 39 per cent in 1964 to 60.9 per cent in 1966.

Promotions in higher grades ranged from 19.2 per cent to 25.1 per cent of those eligible between 1964 and 1967. After 1967, because of budgetary cuts and the emergence of an excess of officers in the highest grades, promotions in all grades dropped sharply. They totaled 445 in 1968, compared with 734 in 1967, and recovered to only 539 in 1969.[19] A class profile of Foreign Service officers on April 30, 1969, revealed 781 or 24 per cent in the senior classes (FSO-2 and above), 2,287 or 70 per cent at midcareer, FSO-3–6), and only 194 or 6 per cent in classes FSO-7 and FSO-8.[20] The senior classes enrolled 22.7 per cent in 1954, 18.3 per cent in 1958, and 18.5 per cent in 1962. The junior classes in those years enrolled respectively 15.8 per cent, 14.8 per cent, and 21.2 per cent of all officers.[21]

Possibly this trend portends the future use of the career corps almost exclusively on middle and senior grade supervisory, political, economic, and management work. But Director General John M. Steeves admitted in November 1966 that the supply of senior officers already exceeded the demand. Projections to 1975, he asserted, indicated continued excessive expansion of the FSO-1 class, although some shrinkage in the middle levels should occur, assuming annual intakes of 250 junior officers (which have not been achieved). The surplus of senior officers meant greater use of compulsory retirement and what he euphemistically described as "selection up," the encouragement of a higher rate of voluntary early retirement by offering additional incentives.[22]

Compulsory and Voluntary Retirement. Instructions to 1961 selection boards raised the selection out (compulsory retirement) zone from the lowest 3 per cent to the lowest 5 per cent of the officers rated, with the obvious intent of increasing the annual attrition rate. The depart-

---

[19] In 1970 promotions dropped to 507.
[20] U.S., Dept. of State, "Summary of Employment."
[21] John E. Harr, *The Anatomy of the Foreign Service: A Statistical Profile*, p. 9.
[22] *News Letter*, no. 67 (November 1966), pp. 61–62.

ment subsequently broadened the zone to 10 per cent, but in 1968 dropped it to 3 per cent again, announcing its intention to rely on time in class to weed out the least dynamic officers.[23] In March 1967, however, it had reduced time in class prior to compulsory retirement for Class 1 officers from fifteen to twelve years and increased it for officers in Class 2 and Class 3 from eight to ten years with the obvious intent of retarding promotions to higher grades and forcing earlier retirement of some Class 1 officers. In 1968 Deputy Undersecretary Rimestad announced: "The number of promotions . . . to any particular class will be determined by . . . functional needs . . . and . . . anticipated vacancies in any one class. . . . An assessment of our present and foreseeable needs . . . indicates that the greatest number of FSO's by class should be at the 4 level."[24]

Administrators have encouraged and even forced early retirement by placing high-ranking officers in relatively menial positions. Generally speaking, they have down-graded assignments of Foreign Service officers in Class 1 and career ministers. Some spend long periods as deputy examiners of the Board of Examiners, others as Foreign Service inspectors. The new university diplomat-in-residence positions currently occupy twelve senior officers and still others work in the Foreign Service Institute. Many able senior officers, who formerly could have expected assignments as chiefs of mission, deputy chiefs of mission, or at comparable departmental levels, serve today as country directors, officers in charge of small consulates, and in especially created advisory roles.

Reorganizations of Personnel Administration. The Herter Commit-

---

[23] *News Letter*, no. 83 (March 1968), p. 35. In September 1969 the department announced that officers ranked in the lowest 5 per cent by the 1969 selection boards would be retired if they had been ranked in the lowest 3 per cent by the 1968 boards. The approval of more generous Foreign Service retirement legislation in February 1970 provided greater incentives for voluntary retirement. Consequently, 276 Foreign Service employees retired in February, March, and April 1970. The Nixon administration also introduced a bill early in 1970 providing for the retirement of career ministers at sixty rather than sixty-five. Thus, pressure for both voluntary and involuntary early retirement seems to have increased somewhat under President Nixon.

[24] *News Letter*, no. 83 (March 1968), p. 35.

tee attached great importance to improving the department's organization for personnel administration, but neither President Kennedy nor President Johnson acted on its recommendation that an executive undersecretary of state be appointed to coordinate administration as the secretary's principal staff assistant.

The department abolished the Office of Personnel in February 1964, allegedly to provide better support for the new career management program. It allocated most of its functions to two new divisions, one responsible for all Foreign Service officers, and another for clerical employees.

In June 1965 the department adopted a Herter Committee recommendation that the positions of deputy undersecretary for administration and assistant secretary for administration be combined. It abolished the Bureau of Administration and the position of assistant secretary,[25] transferring their functions to the deputy undersecretary. It also shuffled personnel management again, restoring the director general of the Foreign Service to a line position by giving him direct responsibility for about half of the personnel divisions and staffs and by creating a special assistant to the deputy undersecretary to supervise the others. No clear criteria for grouping the units could be deduced. Regional bureaus were promised an increased role in the assignments process and "ultimately authority to make specific assignments provided that such assignments conform to the individual career programs."[26]

The new reorganization was supposed to produce faster, better support for all departmental personnel and activities because it allegedly combined decentralization, management by program, and management by objective. Despite these assurances, the department regrouped all personnel functions in November 1967 in a new Office of Personnel to "operate under the Director General of the Foreign Service" and have "direct responsibility for all phases of personnel management."

---

[25] In September 1969 President Nixon refilled the vacant position of assistant secretary of state for administration and made his nominee responsible for budget and finance, operations, communications, and foreign buildings.

[26] *News Letter*, no. 51 (July 1965), pp. 6–7.

This revolution unhappily failed to move the machine any closer to a rational system.[27]

IN-SERVICE TRAINING

In stating the administrative goals of the Kennedy Administration, Deputy Undersecretary Jones asserted, "we have just begun to scratch the surface of the kind of things that we should do with in-service training."[28] He made special reference to the training needs of non-career officers and to the importance of broadening all aspects of in-service training.

Proposed Foreign Affairs Academy. The Herter Committee and the president's Advisory Panel on a National Academy of Foreign Affairs both recommended that the Foreign Service Institute (FSI) give place to a postgraduate National Academy of Foreign Affairs, and President Kennedy proposed legislation establishing such an academy to provide the Department of State, AID, USIA, and twenty other agencies with supplementary courses of training. Proponents estimated its capital cost at about $16,000,000 and its annual budget at $6,000,000. Despite the mustering of much high official support and the mobilization of a committee of seventy-seven prominent private citizens, the bill failed to win congressional approval.

Happily, the Foreign Service Institute itself adopted, in substance, the academy concept, including more interdepartmental "sharing," more reaching out for assistance from American institutions of higher learning, and greater efforts to bring the recent findings of social scientists to specialists and policy makers.

When the Foreign Service Institute celebrated its twentieth anniversary in November 1966, its budget had risen to $7,912,000. Its enrollment rose from 7,457 in fiscal year 1956 to 19,000 in fiscal

---

[27] A reorganization of the Office of the Director General of the Foreign Service announced in November 1969 established the position of deputy director general to serve as director of personnel (in lieu of the deputy assistant secretary for administration who previously exercised this function), created a new deputy director of personnel for recruitment, and transferred personnel planning from the Office of the Deputy Undersecretary for Administration to the Office of the Director General of the Foreign Service (*News Letter*, no. 103 [November 1969], p. 31).

[28] *Ibid.*, no. 2 (June 1961), p. 7.

year 1966. Other foreign affairs agencies contributed about one third of the students in fiscal year 1956, and more than half in fiscal year 1966.[29] Thus, in terms both of funding and enrollment, the Foreign Service Institute passed the goals envisaged by the Herter and Perkins committees by 1966.

On June 1, 1966, the institute for the first time also obtained adequate quarters, occupying a new, functional, twelve-story building in Arlington, Virginia. Its library holdings of twenty-six thousand volumes and three hundred periodicals then enabled it to serve twenty-five thousand readers. Established in 1954 as a branch of the State Department library, it has now achieved the status of a highly specialized collection.

The qualitative achievements of the Foreign Service Institute obviously cannot be assessed easily, but its courses and curriculum now reflect more clearly the diverse training needs of the foreign affairs community and the breadth of resources of the academic world. Probably its greatest thrust has been toward additional functional training.[30] The institute also met emergency training needs of all foreign affairs agencies by mounting a highly successful counterinsurgency seminar for senior officers, and by establishing a Vietnam language and area training center that had served eight hundred students by April 1969.

Language Training. The Foreign Service Institute made no major changes in language training programs in the sixties. It began offering Foreign Service wives language training at home and abroad, and it gave officers volunteering for hard language training additional mone-

---

[29] *News Letter*, no. 67 (November 1966), p. 46.

[30] Since 1961 FSI has added a twenty-two–week intensive economic studies program, equivalent to a strong undergraduate major in economics; seminars in science, technology and foreign affairs, international agricultural development, international law, program management, political science analysis in foreign affairs, and the computer and foreign affairs; an administrative operations and management course; a supervisory development course; a course on strategy, game theory, and decision making, which extended and replaced another in mathematics and statistics; and a world politics simulation exercise, developed under contract by Wayne State University. FSI also extended its advanced executive studies seminar, from one week to two in May 1965; and it revised and improved other management and supervisory courses. Distinguished academic authorities lecture in many of the new courses. See Appendix C for a description of FSI's 1971 training program.

tary and career incentives. By 1964 the principal shortages of hard language specialists were in Arabic, South Asian, and Southeast Asian languages.

The Department of State announced the following training objectives late in 1966: every officer going to a world language post would receive language training if needed; language designated positions at all posts were to be filled with qualified officers; and officers going to functions new to them were to receive functional training "to the extent possible."[31]

Table 1 reveals progress toward language training goals as of October 1966.

TABLE 1

Staffing of Overseas FSO Positions Requiring S-3 R-3 Language Skills, 1966*

	Hard Languages	World Languages	Totals
Number of language-designated positions	292	1,045	1,337
Number staffed with S-3 R-3's or better	158 (54%)	727 (70%)	885 (66%)
Number staffed with S-2 R-2's	33 (11%)	145 (14%)	178 (13%)
Number staffed with less than S-2 R-2	101 (35%)	173 (16%)	274 (21%)

* The S-3 capability is defined by the institute as ability to participate effectively in all general conversation; S-4 is defined as fluidity; S-5 is bilinguality; S-2 implies ability to transact routine office business, and S-1 merely to inquire directions and prices. The R or reading ratings correspond to the S or speaking ratings.

The number of officers with tested S-3 R-3[32] proficiency in at least one foreign language rose from 55.6 per cent in 1962 to 66.4 per cent in

---

[31] *News Letter*, no. 66 (October 1966), inner cover.

[32] Forty-six officers at hard language posts were rated S-3 R-3 or better but not assigned to designated positions.

July 1967; 23.2 per cent of the officers had at least S-3 skill in two foreign languages; and another 19 per cent had S-2 skill in a second language. At that date, 3,392 of the 3,568 officers on duty had been tested.

About 30 per cent of AID's overseas positions have foreign language requirements of S-2 or higher, the majority being in French or Spanish. USIA's requirements resemble those of the Foreign Service but probably are somewhat higher because of the large proportion of Foreign Service personnel engaged in administrative duties.

Junior Officer Training. A central complement training and evaluation program for all new junior Foreign officers, initiated in 1961, represented an interesting variation of the time-honored probationary field training assignment. The department lent, rather than assigned, new officers to field posts for two years for rotational training in four or five major Foreign Service functions and required evaluation reports on all training chores.

The program seemed to offer several major advantages. It afforded the new officers on-the-job training in a wider variety of functions, revealed whether they had special talents in any particular field, and gave them an early opportunity to evaluate the service as a career and a way of life. Most important, the central complement feature reduced the possibility that hard-pressed officers in charge might use new officers exclusively on visa stamping or other routine consular or administrative duties. Unhappily, the department dropped the central complement feature in 1968 because of the budgetary pinch and some congressional feeling that neophytes disliked the training in statutory consular duties. It has since assigned new officers to designated training positions at certain posts.

Objectives of junior officer training also encompass a wider range of geographical and functional experience, and a beginning of specialized competence in at least one phase of Foreign Service work. Second and third tours include another geographical area and the Department of State. The second field assignment is to a definite function, and one of the assignments must be to a hardship post.

The Foreign Service Institute inaugurated a new four-week orientation course for junior officers returning for service in the department or other agencies late in 1966. It lengthened the basic course[33] from seven to eight weeks in 1967 but halved the consular training component. It also increased the interest and value of the course by emphasizing action and participation. The institute splits the classes into teams and gives the students exercises to perform. It arranges visits to various sections of the department, to other agencies, and to Congress, and it encourages the students to question vigorously and even to challenge speakers appearing before them. After orientation, those who need it receive intensive language training. All new officers going to non-European countries receive three weeks of area briefing.

Midcareer Officer Training. Midcareer officers are primary targets in the department's drive to make every career officer a specialist. This goal compelled the institute to expand offerings and enrollment in language and area studies and functional specialization and to replace a three-month orientation course with a one-week lecture and discussion program.

The institute added Latin America and the Atlantic community to areas studied, and it organized an intensive twenty-two–week course in economics, equivalent to an undergraduate major. In 1963 it introduced three-week area studies courses emphasizing situational factors for employees and their wives who require orientation but no profound knowledge of major underdeveloped areas and Eastern Europe. In the first sessions, 383 persons participated—23 per cent from the Department of State, 52 per cent from AID, 12 per cent from USIA, 5 per cent from the Department of Defense, and 4 per cent from officers' families.

The institute still relies primarily on universities to impart nonlinguistic elements of area training, but it offers most of the language training in Washington or in its schools in Beirut, Tangier, Taiwan, and Tokyo. In 1967 the Department of State and USIA required personnel assigned to university training for an academic year or more

---

[33] This course also enrolls USIA junior officers and new Foreign Service staff officers, chosen from the top 20 per cent of candidates taking the Federal Service Entrance Examination.

to sign an agreement to serve in their agency at least three times as long as the training period.

The Foreign Service Institute has continued to draw increasing numbers of midcareer officers into area and functional courses lasting twelve weeks or more, as well as into correspondence and after-hours courses at domestic and foreign universities. The department also participates in programs offered by the Brookings Institution and the National Institute of Public Affairs under which two or three officers are chosen annually for a year of appropriate academic training.[34]

Senior Officer Training. Two innovations characterized senior officer training between 1961 and 1969. After 1961, under a presidential directive, senior State Department, USIS, AID, and military officers attended a session of the Foreign Service Institute's National Interdepartmental Seminar on the Problems of Development and Internal Defense before departing on new field assignments. By December 1967, two thousand graduates had passed through the so-called counterinsurgency course.

An innovative training–public relations–recruiting program, inaugurated in September 1964, involves the assignment of senior Foreign Service Officers as diplomats in residence to universities for an academic year. Three officers received such assignments in fiscal year 1965, and twelve in fiscal year 1969. The program serves the triple purpose of supplementing the department's public relations program, assisting the College Relations Program, and mitigating problems of finding appropriate assignments for the excess of senior officers.

Alien Employees. In April 1965 the institute brought thirty Foreign Service local (alien) employees to the United States for an eight-week training course, and it scheduled three classes of twenty locals each for fiscal year 1966. In November 1966, the Department of State and USIA made job-related training available to local employees at public

---

[34] In the six years ending in July 1966, 116 midcareer officers engaged in university economic studies, 66 in university area programs, and 10 in Atlantic community studies. The department assigned 194 officers for nonlanguage training in fiscal year 1970, as compared with 124 in fiscal year 1968. It also assigned 53 officers to hard language training.

expense by correspondence, classroom work, or through other instructional media on a full- or part-time basis. Only AID local employees previously had enjoyed such broad training opportunities.

Morale. According to Arthur M. Schlesinger, Jr., President Kennedy's attitude toward the Foreign Service was mixed. He had a basic respect for its skills but considered that some Foreign Service officers knew too little about the nations to which they were accredited. Under these circumstances, and because of his personal friendship for certain Foreign Service officers, he made great efforts to improve departmental and Foreign Service morale and capabilities.[35]

His efforts to strengthen the department's coordinative role greatly encouraged its staff, although the free-wheeling of some members of the White House staff in sensitive foreign affairs areas caused keen resentment. He appointed considerably more chiefs of mission from the career service. Whereas career officers held 40 per cent of these posts in 1955, in mid-1962, they held 68 per cent of the missions, including a substantial number in Europe.[36]

The president also showed his interest in the department and the Foreign Service by staging press conferences and other public appearances in the department, sponsoring highly beneficial salary and fringe benefit legislation, and making frequent personal appearances before foreign affairs employees.

Prompt administrative action minimized the threat to morale of the budget cut in fiscal year 1962, in marked contrast to the situation that had developed in 1953. Secretary Rusk, when announcing a modest reduction in force (RIF), emphasized that it would obviate any need to freeze travel, promotions, or the recruitment of junior Foreign Service officers. Establishment of an Out Placement Service also cushioned the RIF's impact, which did not, in fact, threaten efficiency or impose excessive burdens on remaining staffs.

President Johnson also met frequently with foreign affairs employees and backed expression of esteem with concrete actions. He delegated far more coordinative authority to the department and allowed less

---

[35] Arthur M. Schlesinger, Jr., *A Thousand Days: John F. Kennedy in the White House*, pp. 407–408.
[36] *Ibid.*, pp. 429–430.

free-wheeling by his aides. During his first two years in office, 72 per cent of his appointees, or 79 of 109 were career officers.[37] The proportion of new ambassadorial appointees from the career service dropped to 66.1 per cent by the end of 1967, but at that time 69.1 per cent of all ambassadors serving were Foreign Service officers.[38] He also signed four new pay bills, and approved additional fringe benefits, including the provision of basic household furnishings and equipment in quarters abroad.

Unfortunately, several developments subversive of the career principle negated the presidential morale-building efforts of the 1961–1969 period. They included the basic administrative reorganization of the officer structure, which grossly inflated the reserve and staff categories and altered their character; withdrawal of statutory status from the Board of Foreign Service and the Board of Examiners; the appointment of minority candidates as junior reserve officers to enable them to bypass the written examinations; the 1968 statutory authorization to confer unlimited tenure on reserve officers, together with most of the other perquisites of career officer status; USIA's prompt announcement that all its "career" reserve officers who had not been nominated for Foreign Service information officer status would be given unlimited tenure; strong indications that a new integration program would be pressed; and political intervention in the hitherto carefully protected promotion system of the selection boards, which occurred for the first time in the summer of 1968.[39]

Field officers also resented a joint 1965 State Department–AID–USIA circular prohibiting the sale abroad of employees' property, including automobiles, at profits resulting essentially from the free entry import privilege. This meant that the time-honored method long used by civilian foreign affairs personnel to recover unreimbursed expenditures on official representation or other public service at the end of an assignment no longer remained open to them, although it continued

---

[37] *News Letter*, no. 57 (January 1966), p. 2. During President Nixon's first ten months in office he named seventy-five chiefs of mission of whom forty-eight, or 64 per cent were career men (*ibid.*, no. 103 [November 1969], p. 14).

[38] *Ibid.*, no. 81 (January 1968), p. 19.

[39] *Foreign Service Journal*, 45 (November 1968), Part I, 2, 6–10; Part, 6.

to be used and even abused by diplomats of other nations. They recognized that the enormous size of the American official family and the wide extension of free entry to employees who had few representational duties had caused complaints from host countries; but this knowledge did not soften the impact of the blow on many private exchequers. Moreover, they considered that they were being unjustly deprived of property rights by administrative fiat.

A development far more subversive of field morale occurred in consequence of balance of payments and budgetary difficulties. By August 1968 presidential directives imposed reductions in the overseas personnel of the Department of State and twenty other agencies totaling 18 per cent of the Americans employed as of December 31, 1967, or 4,083 out of 22,884, and 16 per cent of the aliens employed, or 4,274 of 26,337. The agencies eased field workloads somewhat by reducing reporting requirements and by combining or consolidating some functions, but uncertainty about the prospect of additional cuts continued to depress field morale.

In addition, the Department of State announced that, because of the reduction in force, in fiscal year 1968 it would appoint only 104 junior career officers instead of 220 as anticipated. It postponed the written examination from December 1968 to May 1969 because it was still drawing on eligible candidates from the 1966 and 1967 examinations, and it made only 89 junior career officer appointments in fiscal year 1969. Administrators stressed as well the need to restrict promotion rates and to speed compulsory retirement.

No reduction in force in home offices of the foreign affairs agencies occurred early in the program, but the Bureau of the Budget took one hundred fillable vacancies from the department in August 1968 and limited the rate at which it might appoint to 70 per cent of the positions becoming vacant on and after September 1, 1968. The department's Civil Service employees also received gloomily the 1968 statements that Civil Service recruitment would be restricted to permit the staffing of more home positions by the Foreign Service.[40]

[40] See article by Allan Evans in *News Letter*, no. 90 (October 1968), pp. 18–19.
  The Nixon administration continued the pressure to reduce foreign affairs staffs in connection with its goal of lopping four billion dollars from the fiscal year 1970

To conclude, the impact of the 1968 reduction in force on all foreign affairs agencies and employees was much heavier than had been the impact of the 1962 reduction. The 1968 reduction had much more unfortunate results on the induction and recruitment of junior career officers. It occurred when a surplus of high-ranking Foreign Service officers already existed and thus increased pressures to hasten early voluntary retirement, to speed compulsory retirement, and to downgrade positions filled by such officers. Finally, it introduced an additional element of uncertainty about the future of foreign affairs careers in all ranks of all agencies and in the minds of potential candidates.[41]

Thus, despite substantial improvements in compensation and conditions of service between 1961 and 1969, Foreign Service officer morale probably did not rise to the pre–World War II or to the 1946–1947 levels. Some young career officers complained that they were being kept too long on routine work, and career officers of all grades feared that political intervention and administrative reorganizations would finally destroy the badly eroded concept of a career service. Civil Service officers feared that they might be forced to join the Foreign Service or suffer curtailed career opportunities.

The department publicly denied, late in 1964, that low morale among junior Foreign Service officers was causing a high rate of resignations. Nevertheless, Undersecretary Katzenbach acknowledged in a speech delivered in November 1967: "Our ablest young men are restive. They are asking for a richer and more varied experience than is being given them. . . . They complain of insularity in the Service, lack of real responsibility and substitution of personal security for re-

---

budget. In November 1969 President Nixon imposed a 10 per cent (roughly 5,100 positions) reduction in fiscal year 1970 in American direct hire overseas civilians, excluding Peace Corps personnel. The Undersecretaries Committee of NSC allocated the cuts among the various foreign affairs agencies. Defense had to absorb 75 per cent of the cut. The Department of State lost 540 positions, AID, 530, and USIA, 140. The department announced that normal attrition would be used to absorb the reduction.

[41] The department tried to mitigate the effects of the RIF by expanding its exchange programs, encouraging officers to take leave without pay to improve their skills, broadening in-service training, and making additional efforts to assist personnel leaving the service.

sponsibility and underutilization of their talents. *They are not afraid of change.*"⁴²

Recognition by the career service of the need for change found explicit expression in the report of the Committee on Career Principles of the American Foreign Service Association (AFSA) of October 1967, which declared distinctions between generalists and specialists outmoded and urged the rapid integration of the Department of State, AID, and USIA. Recommendations of study groups of junior officers reflected not only a willingness to accept but also a desire to embrace major changes in foreign affairs administration.⁴³ This need for change manifested itself even more significantly in an AFSA election of 1967, which a group of youthful activists, the "Young Turks," carried against the long-entrenched establishment.

The "Young Turks" at once established a committee to make specific recommendations for improvement in the organization of the nation's foreign affairs. The committee's report, submitted August 30, 1968, deplored the abandonment of the principles of a unified career service but confessed that "more of the blame than we have heretofore been willing to admit could be centered on the Foreign Service itself." It was especially critical of service resistance to change, which had prevented full use of the "marvelously flexible provisions" of the Act of 1946.

The report recommended, *inter alia*—

1. that the "present White House organization primarily concerned with foreign affairs" continue under the new administration;

2. that USIA, like AID, be placed "as an autonomous unit" within the Foreign Service;

3. that the "professional core" of AID personnel be incorporated into the Foreign Service;

4. that the basic foreign affairs structure of the Act of 1946 be restored, including the statutory status of the Boards of Foreign Service and Examiners;

5. that the director general of the Foreign Service be empowered to

---

⁴² *News Letter*, no. 79 (November 1967), pp. 4–5.
⁴³ *Foreign Service Journal*, 44 (November 1967), 30A–D.

ensure compliance by the operating agencies with regulations promulgated by the Board of the Foreign Service;

6. that an "adequate manpower utilization and planning mechanism" be established; and

7. that promotion be awarded through the middle grades after competitive ratings in functional categories, but in senior grades on the basis of service-wide competition.

In general, the report advocated establishment of a system that would restore unity while recognizing diversity and would remain open to new entrants on all levels if need should arise.[44]

But the new AFSA leadership did not content itself with preparing still another report and set of recommendations on foreign affairs administration—strangely enough, the first emanating from the service itself. It took another unprecedented step by convening an open forum of AFSA members in September 1968 to discuss the legislation granting the Department of State and USIA authority to extend unlimited appointments to reserve officers. The chairman summed up the sense of the meeting as contrary to "new departures in ... personnel administration," and to unlimited reserve appointments as unnecessary and liable to open the door to political abuse. However, he also found strong sentiment in favor of a revolutionary proposal that AFSA should have a role in decision making when the decisions affect the morale and welfare of its members or the structure and foundation of the career services.[45]

In October 1968 the chairman of AFSA's board attended the meeting of the Board of the Foreign Service that approved the USIA plan to extend unlimited tenure to "career" reserve officers not nominated as Foreign Service information officers. He called the attention of the board to the AFSA report, reiterating the view expressed therein that changes in personnel arrangements should await the new administration.

In November 1968 the AFSA-sponsored Foreign Service Day devoted a session to the now well-publicized report. Unlike previous conferences of this kind, the 1968 meeting involved a considerable

[44] *Ibid.*, 45 (November 1968), 4–60.
[45] *News Letter*, no. 89 (September 1968), p. 22.

number of non-AFSA members who had distinguished themselves in the field of foreign affairs administration. AFSA's chairman described this innovation as the beginning of "an intensive, continuing dialogue with people such as yourselves who represent an informed and concerned part of American society."[46]

Obviously, an unprecedented spirit of activism pervades the Foreign Service, as well as a broad recognition that major changes in foreign affairs administration must and can be made. To this extent, declining morale has produced at least one heartening reaction.[47]

[46] *Foreign Service Journal*, 46, no. 2 (January 15, 1969), inner cover. See also Lannon Walker, "Our Foreign Affairs Machinery: Time for an Overhaul," *Foreign Affairs*, 47 (January 1969), 309–320.

[47] John E. Harr in *The Professional Diplomat* (pp. 235–289) offers additional comment on and analysis of the morale problem.

PART III

The Participants and Their Roles

8

Congress and the Federal Courts

Congress's Role

While Congress still nominally shares control of foreign affairs with the executive, the present complexity, urgency, and mass of problems have compelled it to delegate more and more power to ever-descending executive levels. It now exercises its constitutional authority and influence largely through appropriations and legislation but has also developed other important roles that can be subsumed under the captions of criticism, advocacy, and enlightenment of the general public.

Congressional criticism normally makes itself heard through committee hearings and through the postaudit operations of the Government Accounting Office (GAO), although resolutions of either or both houses sometimes express censure. The work of the GAO permits Congress to assure itself that funds are expended for the purpose for which they were voted and to castigate any official or agency who misuses appropriated funds.

Congressional hearings and investigations were not unknown earlier, but they came into their own only after World War II. They afford congressmen ample opportunities both to voice their own opinions on matters of foreign affairs administration and to provide sounding boards for likeminded persons within and outside of the government. The publicity received by congressmen who chair or participate actively in the work of investigating or regular committees conducting interesting hearings has advanced several careers sensationally. The relatively obscure Senator Harry S. Truman, for example, rose to prominence during World War II because of his work on the Special Committee Investigating the National Defense Program and the then Senator Richard M. Nixon received a major political boon from his work in the Alger Hiss investigation.

Congress performs its task of enlightening the public about foreign relations issues more or less as a by-product of critical and recommendatory activities. That is to say, hearings of regular and investigating committees, resolutions, and publicity arising from activities of the GAO serve multiple purposes. Similarly, techniques of advocacy, which are discussed below, not only influence executive action directly but also enlist public support behind congressional initiatives.

Congressional advocates, working corporately, sometimes employ resolutions to make their views known. The Fulbright and Vandenberg Resolutions of World War II signaled the collapse of isolationism in Congress and the nation. The Monroney Resolution resulted in the establishment of the International Development Association, despite initial opposition from the Departments of State and Treasury. The Formosa Straits and Gulf of Tonkin Resolutions, although inspired by the White House, clearly expressed congressional advocacy for a firm stand against Chinese communist aggression. As congressional disillusionment with the Vietnam war deepened between 1967 and 1970, members introduced resolutions and amendments to money bills in attempts to limit the president's power of initiative, especially as commander in chief, but without significant legislative consequences. Congress also uses appropriations and the legislative power to try to advance causes or programs it favors, although not always successfully, because executive vetoes or failure to use appropriated funds sometimes frustrate such efforts.

Congressmen as individuals use the mass media and the floor of Congress to project their personal views of foreign affairs issues to the electorate and the executive with varying degrees of effectiveness. Most congressmen now use their postal franking privilege to send periodic news bulletins to their constituents, and many broadcast regular local television or radio programs. These media, together with press releases and statements to press conferences, provide ample opportunities for the exposition of their personal views. Congressmen who take an active interest in foreign relations also avail themselves of their speaking time in the House or the Senate to elaborate their opinions, which are then incorporated in the *Congressional Record* and franked to constituents.

Individual congressional advocacy and criticism reaches directly, of course, into the Department of State and other government agencies responsible for the administration of American foreign policy. Administrators frequently receive calls or visits from congressmen who wish to advocate or condemn specific policies or programs. Certain states such as Israel, Spain, and Ireland have warm partisans in the Congress who press their claims for additional military or economic assistance or diplomatic aid. Some programs, such as the surplus agricultural commodities export program and annual allotments of quotas for sugar-producing countries under the Sugar Act, normally inspire intense congressional activity. Its effectiveness depends, of course, on bureaucratic apprehensions about possible adverse effects on desired legislation or appropriations if they resist congressional pressure. Naturally the effectiveness of advocacy or criticism also varies widely with the matter being advocated and the skill and prestige of the congressman.

Congressional advocacy in general has lost so much ground to executive initiative that Professor James A. Robinson considers "that Congress' influence in foreign policy is primarily (and increasingly) to legitimate and/or to amend recommendations initiated by the executive to deal with situations usually identified by the executive; and that among the significant explanations for this relationship is the changing character of information or intelligence in modern policy-making."[1]

[1] James A. Robinson, *Congress and Foreign Policy-Making: A Study in Legislative Influence and Initiative*, p. vii. Until World War II erupted, the late Senator Borah,

The role of information in policy making has certainly expanded enormously in importance since World War I and now looms very large indeed. Congress obtains information through the Legislative Reference Service of the Library of Congress, by contract with private research organizations, and through the staffs of its committees; but the vast preponderance of its intelligence comes from the executive. It depends on the executive not only for most of the basic data needed for decision making but also for evaluation and interpretation. Individual congressmen also obtain some information from and are influenced by the public press, other mass media, the Washington diplomatic corps, and private individuals. But the fact remains that Congress depends substantially on the executive for most of its intelligence.

Probably the bipartisan policy that Congress has followed with some lapses since World War II has also reduced congressional influence over the administration of foreign policy. Bipartisanship clearly implies a congressional concern for and a subordination of domestic politics to the national interest that a partisan approach to foreign affairs does not assure. The executive's ability, freely exercised, to declare a program or measure in the national interest and to bring it under the protective cloak of bipartisanship obviously limits congressional freedom of action and strengthens the executive. However, the primary factor that has tended to limit the role of Congress while aggrandizing that of the executive has been the enormous expansion in the range, complexity, and urgency of foreign affairs issues since World War I, which can be dealt with only by executive action. This expansion has also produced the growing need for intelligence, engenders most of the staffs supplying it, and makes it impossible for a deliberative body to cope with its massive dimensions.

Historically "parliamentary institutions have lost influence relative to executive institutions." Professor Robinson considers that this trend was not inevitable and that it is not beyond modification, but leaves open the question as to whether it should be altered. He suggests that

---

for example, stubbornly insisted that there would be no war, relying on private sources of information. Permission to cite this and other excerpts from *Congress and Foreign Policy-Making* has been granted by The Dorsey Press.

it might be partially reversed by "the emergence of centralized leadership in both House and Senate."² The influence of Congress varies tremendously, of course, with changes in the national and international environment, with the quality of its membership, and with the leadership of the executive. For example, Congress asserts itself far more vigorously when public discontent or disillusionment with foreign policy administration manifests itself, but usually reposes extraordinary trust in the executive in moments of national crisis. Under Lyndon B. Johnson as majority leader, the Senate played a more impressive role than it has under his successor. By the same token, strong presidents tend to shift the balance of influence toward the executive branch.

Within the Congress, Professor Robinson considers that the Senate possesses a constitutional advantage over the House in influencing foreign policy administration because of the requirement that ambassadorial appointments receive its confirmation and because of its treaty power. The House, of course, has the advantage that money bills must be initiated there; moreover, foreign policy administration since World War II has required increasingly substantial outlays. Congressional influence on such appropriations has been consistently either to reduce, or, at best, maintain executive requests for foreign policy allotments.

With respect to substantive legislation, Congress has dominated the executive in immigration matters, where it has traditionally preferred a more restrictive policy than has the president. But much of Congress's foreign policy activity "is in determining the organizational arrangements of the policy-making process, as distinguished from effecting substantive foreign policy legislation."³ The degree of participation of Congress in the making of major decisions now seems to be relatively peripheral and its initiatives generally succeed only in marginal issues. Although the Congress initiates far more foreign affairs proposals than does the executive, the more important proposals originate in the executive. "Thus in the prescription [adoption] stage, Congress is legitimating, amending, or vetoing executive proposals."⁴

Relatively few members of Congress participate actively in foreign

² *Ibid.*, pp. iii–iv.
³ *Ibid.*, p. 12.
⁴ *Ibid.*, p. 14.

policy administration. Members of the Senate Committee on Foreign Relations originate about half of the Senate bills and resolutions pertaining to foreign relations, and the tendency is for an even higher percentage of bills to originate in the committee. Moreover, a far higher percentage of committee-sponsored than private member bills and resolutions receives the Senate's approval. The chairman and the majority party members of the committee are, of course, the primary participants in recommending and prescribing foreign policy legislation. Influence among senators varies with the nature of the issue under discussion. Robinson does not apply the preceding generalizations to the Foreign Affairs Committee of the House, but they probably would fit, given the stronger orientation of congressmen to local and domestic issues. For example, Representative Wayne L. Hays (D. Ohio) has sponsored much foreign affairs legislation and exercises important influence in the House.

A quantitative analysis of Senate action on bills and various types of resolutions led to the conclusion that measures dealing with foreign policy administration are more likely to be influenced by Congress and more likely to pass the Senate than those directly concerned with the substance of relations with foreign governments. The Senate also seems less likely to approve executive measures requiring heavy expenditures, but cost bears no predictable relationship to success for Senate-sponsored bills and resolutions.[5]

A development that has greatly increased congressional interest in and sophistication about the administration of American foreign policy merits special comment. Foreign travel by congressmen, relatively infrequent before World War II, has become commonplace since then. Two major influences worked to bring this about. First, large balances of foreign currencies generated by loans and assistance programs existed that could not be converted to dollars and were available to defray the overseas expenses of congressional visitors. Second, military air transport became available, and the military showed great zeal in arranging such trips. Some of the visits have not been exceptionally helpful, but most of them have broadened the travelers' perceptions of

[5] The preceding discussion has been drawn principally from Robinson, *Congress and Foreign Policy-Making*, pp. 12–94.

the nature and importance of the role of the United States in world affairs and of many specific problems in international relations. They have produced not only more interest in foreign relations in Congress but also a better informed Congress. First hand contact between congressmen and field officers of the Department of State and other agencies has increased reciprocal respect for the ability and problems of both. Thus, while the system of promoting, financing, and accounting for congressional visits might be improved upon, their net result clearly seems to be in the public interest.

Coordination between the Executive and Congress. The constitutional division of responsibilities for foreign affairs between the executive and the Congress requires major efforts on the part of both to prevent misunderstandings and conflict. Here the president and his White House aides play a most important role. The president makes frequent use of the telephone, correspondence, informal meetings, and various social occasions to inform congressmen about foreign affairs problems and to give them his views on possible solutions. He also tries to convert opposition congressmen to administration policy. The president uses appointments to public office, personal marks of esteem, such as trips in presidential aircraft or visits to the congressman's state or district, to win or retain support. He adds his influence as a party leader to the enormous weight of the presidential office when necessary.

In a more formal way, the president coordinates executive-congressional activity by sending draft legislation to the Congress, usually arranging for its sponsorship by key members. He sends messages from time to time to the Hill; and in his annual message he reviews the international relations of the United States and the broad outlines of his policy. Occasionally before, and customarily since, World War II, the president has appointed members of both Houses and parties to delegations to the United Nations and important international conferences.

Recently, presidents have tried to secure broad congressional approval for major initiatives by asking for resolutions supporting administration policies, for example, the Formosan Straits and the Gulf of Tonkin Resolutions. When the president feels no need for public manifestation of congressional approval, he contents himself with consultations and advance informal expressions of congressional approbation.

Departmental and agency efforts to win congressional approval for their programs usually employ the support of congressional liaison bureaus or officers. The Bureau of Congressional Relations of the Department of State, for example, serves congressmen who require information about foreign affairs matters or help for their constituents. It works principally with staffs of congressional committees and the personal staffs of congressmen, although it also brings congressional viewpoints to the attention of departmental officers.

High officials of executive departments and agencies spend much of their time testifying before congressional committees or trying to persuade congressmen in less formal surroundings to support administration policies. In January 1965 Secretary of State Rusk spent twenty-two hours on congressional relations and made eleven visits to the Capitol, although Congress sat only half of the month. The preceding figure did not include the time the secretary spent preparing for his congressional meetings. Secretary of State Acheson estimated that he spent approximately a sixth of his time in congressional relations. Congressmen and their aides frequently request help directly from assistant secretaries and geographic desk officers of the Department of State, rather than through the formal liaison channel. The departments of State and Defense both promote and support congressional overseas travel to broaden congressional-executive understanding.

Congress seeks in several ways to narrow the information gap between the foreign affairs expert and the legislator. Congressional committee staffs and aides of individual congressmen spend much time obtaining information about foreign affairs developments from the executive. Hearings on appropriations, legislation, and special hearings, such as those convened on the Vietnam situation, serve the same purpose. Individual congressmen maintain personal contacts with officers of the executive branch from the president down, which also facilitate coordination, as does their participation in overseas visits and international conference and organization work. Some congressmen try to supplement their knowledge of the international situation by accepting invitations from foreign diplomats stationed in Washington and by cultivating mass media representatives.

Unfortunately, congressional efforts to narrow the information gap succeed only partially. Probably these efforts never can attain perfection, given the tremendous volume and uncertain meaning of the current intelligence intake and the predominantly domestic interests of most congressmen, who must concern themselves above all with matters affecting their re-election.

The effort to achieve executive-legislative understanding, although time consuming, must be considered indispensable. Coordination remains far from perfect, but it is essential to the continued functioning of a system obviously ill-designed to cope with the problems created by the dimensions and complexity of the current international role of the United States.

Proponents of the cabinet system of government argue that the introduction of ministerial responsibility would improve coordination between the executive and legislative branches. But this would imply a basic revision of the constitutional system, and it is by no means certain that the plural and diverse society of the United States would permit a cabinet government to operate effectively. In any case, there seems to be little sentiment for such a change.

The Federal Courts

Chapter 2 traces briefly the course of federal judicial decisions that extended the powers of external sovereignty of the federal government far beyond those contemplated by its designers and concurrently strengthened the role of the executive. But the judiciary did not thereby abdicate all authority over foreign affairs. On the contrary, it continues to play a major role both directly and indirectly. It has, for example, handed down decisions on cases brought under the nationality and immigration acts that have been based primarily on considerations of constitutional law and have compelled consular officers to modify their activities correspondingly. Some rulings of the Supreme Court with respect to naturalization now make it virtually impossible for an alien to expatriate himself other than through a formal process of renunciation. Similarly, a citizen can no longer be deprived of his passport or refused a passport on specified administrative grounds.

It must also be recalled that international law as interpreted by the federal courts binds as well as liberates foreign policy administrators. The Supreme Court, for example, in a case involving the seizure by United States naval vessels of Cuban fishing boats during the Spanish-American War compelled restitution on grounds derived from rules of international law.

The indirect influence of the federal judiciary on our foreign relations is perhaps greater even than its direct influence. Decisions on matters such as school segregation, other civil rights causes, and cases involving major economic policy have an important impact on foreign attitudes toward the United States and consequently on the conduct of American policy toward foreign powers. Judicial decisions also affect substantially the capability and resources of American diplomatic and national security policy makers and administrators. Furthermore, federal administrators, congressional leaders, and in certain cases, policy makers in other nations must take into account decisions and known views of members of the judiciary of the federal courts when deciding problems in the field of foreign relations. The court thus exercises a definite restraining and guiding influence even when it has no cases before it.

In summary, the major constitutional function of federal courts in the administration of American foreign policy has been to enlarge federal jurisdiction and to liberate it almost completely from restraints by the states or the Constitution. Courts have tended to strengthen executive control of foreign policy, but they have retained and still retain, principally through their quasi-legislative power, important influence on foreign affairs administration. Moreover, decisions and the presumed orientation of the federal courts exert strong inhibiting and guiding influence on administrators' and legislators' attitudes and condition those of the governments of foreign states.

9

The Presidency

THE PRESIDENT'S ROLE

The sign that President Truman displayed on his desk—"This is where the buck stops"—epitomizes the primary role of the president, who makes final decisions on all matters of grave importance. His personal dynamism and charisma set the tone and largely determine the viability of initiatives in foreign and domestic policy. Only he can coordinate foreign and national defense policies, weave them into the incredibly complicated web of domestic policies and politics, and provide the leadership required to modify, reverse, or initiate national policies.

Most of the decisions that confront the president today represent choices not between good and bad but between bad and worse alternatives. He seldom, if ever, receives clear or complete criteria upon which to base a sound conclusion, because subordinates sometimes differ radically in their analyses of the same intelligence and because important data normally do not become available until after the event. Moreover, coordination now presents horrifying obstacles because of the proliferation of agencies engaged in foreign affairs administration, the unavoidable confusion of national defense and foreign policy considerations, and the vast, continually growing impact of external matters on domestic affairs.

Until World War I, a president could perform his triple role as a decision maker, coordinator, and innovator with only a few secretarial assistants. President Theodore Roosevelt recognized the need for professional staff in the White House, but it was not until 1939 that an act establishing the Executive Office first gave the president adequate assistance. It authorized the appointment of six senior aides and up to three hundred other staff members, and it transferred the Bureau of the Budget (established in the Treasury Department in 1921) to the Executive Office.

The Executive Office grew rapidly during and after World War II, especially after adoption of the National Security Act of 1947. Its employees numbered 1,027 in 1947, but rose to 3,389 by 1966. The figures for both years do not include employees of the Central Intelligence Agency, which the press estimated to be in excess of 12,500 in the Washington headquarters alone during the nineteen-sixties. The total of civilian government employees rose from 2,262,625 in 1947 to 2,535,690 in 1966, exclusive, of course, of CIA employees.[1]

The preceding statistics reveal the magnitude of the presidential management task, the enormous mass of inertia that must be overcome in stimulating innovation, and the tremendous capability of the civilian bureaucracy for generating problems. It must also be noted that military forces in being during this period fluctuated around three million and that military bureaucrats contribute importantly to the president's workload, although perhaps not in proportion to their numbers.

The wide variance in the influence and style of chief executives makes it difficult to generalize about the role of the presidency and how it is performed. Every chief executive brings to his high position a different conception of his role, but every president is also bound by the human condition, by law, custom, and external and internal developments, and by the existence of the huge civilian and military bureaucracies, including the bureaucracy of the Executive Office. These circumstances reduce appreciably the importance of individual differences.

---

[1] United States, Congress, Senate, Committee on Government Opeartions, *Report* No. 26, 89th Cong., 2d sess., April 25, 1966.

Thus, a broad description of the role of the presidency and how it is discharged today will have considerable applicability, at least to the post-World War II administrations.

Some presidents participate so actively in foreign affairs administration that they become, in effect, their own secretaries of state; others disseminate foreign affairs responsibilities widely throughout the executive branch. Some use the military approach to the organization of work in the Executive Office; others prefer to receive a variety of opinions and recommendations on major issues. Some distrust or dislike the idea of a unified, elite, career Foreign Service; others endorse it. Some presidents show great ability to work with the Congress; others exert tremendous influence over the general public but succeed less well in conducting congressional relations; and still others enjoy excellent public and congressional relations but display little dynamism or initiative.

Presidents also display important characteristics in common. All reach their high office after having had some conditioning in the American political power struggle. Presidents Harding, Truman, Kennedy, Johnson, and Nixon served in the Senate. Presidents Johnson and Nixon also served as vice president. Presidents Hoover and Eisenhower had long service in the federal government. President Coolidge served as governor of Massachusetts before fate raised him to the White House. Chief executives upon taking office already know where power resides and how to use it effectively, and this induces some uniformity of approach to the responsibilities of the position. Tradition, domestic exigencies, and the influence of foreign pressures and rigidities likewise combine to impose more uniformity of approach and action on presidents than personal differences would lead them to adopt.

Finally, concern with the national interest and the desire to protect and embellish their personal historical images set wide but important guidelines that individuality cannot transcend.

The President's Family and Friends. Historically, presidents' wives, their children, and their siblings have played relatively minor or insignificant roles.[2] Some presidents have used their sons as aides, but the influence of these young men generally has not been regarded as

[2] Except for Mrs. Wilson while the president was incapacitated.

highly significant. Possibly the Kennedy administration may rank as the one in which family connection provided the greatest access to roles in foreign policy administration and the greatest influence on presidential thinking. Robert and Edward Kennedy, Sargent Shriver, and other members of the Kennedy family, including the president's father, former Ambassador Joseph P. Kennedy, are all considered to have exerted some influence on the president's thinking. Robert Kennedy and Sargent Shriver also discharged important roles in the executive establishment.

If family influence on chief executives has been relatively limited, it is equally true that persons bound to presidents by ties of personal friendship have often been appointed to important foreign affairs positions or have exercised influence without corresponding responsibility. Colonel House served as President Wilson's principal foreign affairs advisor and as a presidential agent. President Franklin D. Roosevelt entrusted the Treasury Department and certain limited foreign affairs responsibilities to Henry Morgenthau, a friend and neighbor. He also permitted Morgenthau to influence immediate postwar German policy for which he had no official responsibility. President Roosevelt relied heavily as well on other friends and associates, such as Harry Hopkins and Admiral Leahy to perform tasks normally entrusted to State Department or diplomatic officers. Presidents Truman, Eisenhower, Kennedy, and Johnson all used personal friends to assist them in discharging some foreign affairs responsibilities.

Agencies of the Executive Office

The White House Staff. The special assistants to the president and other officers of the White House staff fill roles related in varying degrees to the administration of American foreign policy. The style of the president dictates the influence of his immediate staff. The president's special assistant for national security affairs, the special consultant to the president, and the armed forces aide, although primarily concerned with national security problems, inevitably become involved in foreign affairs as well. Other special assistants and the press secretary also engage in foreign affairs administration as requested by the president or as their talents, interests, opportunities, and personal relationships to the president may permit.

In the Kennedy and Johnson administrations, several White House staffers moved to the Department of State in high policy positions. Their roles indicated that they had already established their competence in foreign relations in the minds of their chiefs. Because President Johnson attached great importance to the qualities of discretion and abnegation, it cannot be ascertained how much or in what areas the White House staff influenced his decisions and activities.

Publications of Kennedy White House aides, especially of Arthur M. Schlesinger, Jr., and Theodore Sorensen, indicate that their personal roles and those of other staffers were highly important. According to Schlesinger, the center of foreign affairs administration "lay not in Foggy Bottom but in the White House." He emphasizes the great importance of the role performed by McGeorge Bundy as special assistant for national security affairs, but adds: "Nor was the work of foreign policy at the White House confined to the Bundy staff. The President wanted Ted Sorenson at his right hand every time there was a major crisis or a major speech. Because of his special concern with Latin America, he directed Richard Goodwin and me and later Ralph Dungan to follow hemisphere developments for him. Dungan, in addition, watched the foreign aid program and advised on the selection of top government officials. Jerome Wiesner and his Science Advisor's staff dealt with armament and disarmament. Meyer Feldman kept a hand in on the Middle East and on tariff and trade issues. I acquired the United Nations and occasional European matters, especially Italy, as particular problems."[3]

The Office of Management and Budget. The president traditionally relied heavily on the Bureau of the Budget to impress upon executive departments and agencies his wishes regarding coordination, programming, and policy. President Nixon's creation in 1970 of the Office of Management and Budget, which includes the Bureau of the Budget, should enhance the already impressive role of the bureau. This highly

---

[3] Arthur M. Schlesinger, Jr., *A Thousand Days: John F. Kennedy in the White House*, p. 422.

influential component of the Executive Office exercises a major influence on matters of policy, program, and administrative procedures through its International and Military Divisions, which are primarily responsible for examining annual budgetary presentations and requests for new legislation. The higher officers of the bureau, of course, devote much attention to the administration of American foreign policy as well, and it is they who make the major policy decisions. The annual budgetary exercises, in which all executive departments and agencies have to justify their requests for the ensuing fiscal year, afford the bureau an opportunity to enforce presidential guidelines and, one suspects, bureau thinking as well, while departmental and agency budgets are still in the formative stage and before they go to the Congress.

Recently, preliminary screening of all requests for money for foreign affairs activities has been done conjointly with State Department officials. Normally the screening involves a reduction of estimates. The process is important because it permits the chief executive not only to establish and enforce a general budgetary ceiling but also to review all programs undertaken by the executive establishment, thus theoretically precluding duplication or counterproductive activity. That it does not always do so is one of the facts of American bureaucratic life. Yet few would deny that the bureau prevents much duplication and wasteful competition.

When exercising its function as a monitor of proposals for new legislation the bureau also follows presidential guidelines and tries to assure that the proposed legislation will not permit duplicatory activity or affect other programs or activities adversely.

The Bureau of the Budget tries to impose uniform and efficient management and administrative standards on government agencies. For example, the bureau was greatly troubled by the draft legislation that resulted in the Foreign Service Act of 1946, because it seemed likely to perpetuate a difference in treatment between Foreign Service and Civil Service employees. Consequently it tried to persuade the president to withhold his approval from the draft and the subsequent act. It did not succeed in this case, but it did manage to have certain changes incorporated in the bill. Under the Office of Management and Budget greater uniformity in management policy and stricter budgetary controls may well be enforced.

The Council of Economic Advisors. The President's Council of Economic Advisors, a body of three members established by the Full Employment Act of 1946, exercises an indeterminate but important influence on the president's decisions with respect to the global size of the budget, major budgetary allocations requiring foreign exchange or affecting the balance of payments, national productivity, tax policy, and commercial policy. It also prepares an influential annual report to Congress.

Its impact on the administration of foreign policy depends largely on the respect and confidence that the president and Congress repose in its chairman and his two colleagues. But the council's members have always been drawn from among the ranks of economists with highest academic status, and their recommendations, untinged by bureaucratic logrolling, normally combat the force of institutionalized budget making and the perpetuation of outworn programs and policies. They enjoy at least a respectful hearing and frequently stimulate action by Congress or the executive.

The National Security Council. The National Security Act of 1947 established the National Security Council (NSC) to advise the president on the integration of domestic, foreign, and military policies relating to the national security. It is composed of the president, vice president, secretary of state, secretary of defense, director of the Office of Emergency Preparedness, and such other members as may be invited from time to time by the president. The director of the Central Intelligence Agency and the chairman of the Joint Chiefs of Staff usually attend council meetings, and the council theoretically directs CIA activities. The role and power of the council varies widely with the character and style of the president. President Eisenhower made considerable use of it. He also established the NSC Planning and Operations Coordinating Boards, which President Kennedy abolished. President Kennedy made less use of the council, although its secretariat proved helpful in resolving or formulating clearly differences of opinion before they reached the president.

According to Arthur M. Schlesinger, Jr., President Kennedy not only convened the National Security Council less frequently than did President Eisenhower, but convened it only when he was on the brink of decision. Kennedy saw no sense in placing unformulated problems before the miscellaneous body of men designated in the statute and preferred to set up task forces specifically qualified to deal with particular problems. These task forces, unlike the interdepartmental committees of the Eisenhower administration, had action responsibilities and thus improved the speed and coordination with which policy was made.[4]

President Johnson's style with respect to the use of the National Security Council resembled that of President Kennedy. President Nixon has largely restored the NSC role.

The Central Intelligence Agency. The Central Intelligence Agency operates under broad directives of the National Security Council and thus forms part of the Executive Office. In practice the agency has a unique budgetary and committee relationship with Congress, and its director functions in many respects as an independent agency head. He attends meetings of the National Security Council, has easy and frequent access to the president, and, although he does not enjoy equal status with the secretaries of state and defense, works in the same rarified atmosphere.

The influence of the director, like that of all other high administrative officials, varies with his personality, his capacity, and the closeness of his personal relationship with the president. Allen Dulles, for example, because of his family connection with the secretary of state and the high confidence that President Eisenhower reposed in him, had great influence. His agency's views likewise prevailed against those of certain other members of the intelligence community when President Kennedy launched the ill-fated Bay of Pigs invasion.

The formal responsibilities of the director include coordination of the entire federal intelligence community, which incorporates not only the intelligence components of the Department of Defense, the Department of State, and the Central Intelligence Agency, but also of the

---

[4] *Ibid.*, pp. 420–421.

FBI, the Atomic Energy Commission (AEC), the National Security Agency,[5] and the Secret Service.

Each agency has clearly allocated functional responsibilities for intelligence collection, evaluation, interpretation, and dissemination. The Department of State has responsibility for overt political, economic, and sociological intelligence; the Department of Defense for military intelligence; the FBI for counterintelligence; the Atomic Energy Commission for intelligence in its special area of competence; the Secret Service for intelligence relating to the security of the president; CIA for covert intelligence and operations; and the National Security Agency for electronic intelligence and cryptographic work.

The Joint Intelligence Board, which meets weekly under the director, theoretically coordinates the community's efforts. Other coordinative techniques include interagency exchange of raw and evaluated data and finished intelligence, the circulation of daily reports, day-to-day contacts between agency personnel, and formal and informal field liaison and cooperation .

When members of the intelligence community disagree on evaluation of data or its interpretation, a "split" in the final report results. Intelligence agencies try to minimize splits so that the president and other high officers of the administration may have the benefit of a unified presentation. This sometimes results in watered down papers of marginal utility to the decision maker. Splits on important matters often come to the National Security Council. Such a split reportedly existed when the decision had to be made on the Bay of Pigs invasion. The failure of the invasion, allegedly recommended by the CIA, constituted a hard blow to its prestige. Subsequently, the subsidizing of student and other educational groups also brought an abundance of bad publicity with a resultant increase in pressure for more stringent congressional control over the agency, its budget, and its activities. The Senate Foreign Relations Committee, in particular, aspired to a voice

---

[5] This agency, a dependency of the Department of Defense, was established in 1951 and operates under maximum security regulations.

in CIA matters, but its initiative failed largely because of the strength of entrenched congressional prerogative.

The National Aeronautics and Space Council.—The National Aeronautics and Space Council, whose members are the secretary of state, the secretary of defense, the administrator of the National Aeronautics and Space Administration (NASA), and the chairman of the Atomic Energy Commission (AEC), exists to help the president coordinate aeronautics and space policy and to develop initiatives in those areas. Its activities, while far less important than those of the National Security Council, clearly affect the country's national security, international relations, and economic postures.

The Office of Emergency Preparedness. The Office of Emergency Preparedness (OEP) shares responsibility with the Department of Defense for civil defense and has primary responsibility for advice and long-range planning. It plans for the coordination of the economy in the event of war. Such planning includes preparation for price control, priorities, rationing, economic warfare, and other duties. The director of the office is a member of the National Security Council and in this capacity theoretically may influence foreign policy, depending on his personal interests and ability. Generally, the office's role in foreign and national security affairs may be described as latent, but its activities could produce major consequences in times of national emergency.

The Office of Science and Technology. After World War II it became apparent that the president required highly specialized assistance on problems related to the effective use of science and scientists in national security and domestic matters. President Truman met this need by naming a special assistant, and President Kennedy created the Office of Science and Technology in 1962 to provide greater status and assistance for his advisor. The office, in addition to offering advice to the president, studies and coordinates programs of various federal agencies concerned with science and technology, maintains liaison with leading scientists, and attempts to stimulate effective work in scientific fields within and outside the government.

Office of the Special Representative for Trade Negotiations. The Office of the Special Representative for Trade Negotiations coordinates and conducts negotiations with other signatories of the General Agreement on Trade and Tariffs (GATT). During the Kennedy Round of negotiations in Geneva, concluded in 1967, it played a highly important role. It could exercise considerable influence over any program that may emerge to remove nontariff barriers to international trade.

The Cabinet. Some presidents have consulted their cabinets from time to time about foreign affairs problems, but such consultations on major topics have become increasingly infrequent and the cabinet no longer exercises important collective influence in foreign affairs. Its individual members often play important roles outside their statutory range of duties. Robert Kennedy, while attorney general, for example, helped to organize the counterinsurgency training program at FSI and participated in other foreign affairs activities, including the task force on the Cuban missile crisis. The secretaries of defense and the treasury since World War II have generally played major roles in foreign affairs.

Executive Coordination

The most difficult problems in American foreign affairs administration arise from the need to assure that all participants of the executive branch work toward the same ends, employ compatible techniques, and refrain from duplicating each other's efforts. These are the goals of coordination. Confusion about aims and counterproductive activities may and do preclude the successful pursuit of objectives. Duplication prevents the allocation of limited resources to other important projects. It also requires unnecessary expansion of the American presence and excessive activity abroad. Either or both may produce adverse foreign reactions that thwart the hopes of project administrators.

Presidential Techniques. The president tries to keep activities of the executive in phase and complementary by personal supervision and through extensive use of the Executive Office. He reviews all matters of importance and renders decisions on all major disputes, normally using the National Security Council to clarify issues. Where the president cannot act personally, he delegates supervisory authority. Normally he relies upon the Department of State to coordinate foreign affairs activities in general, and on chiefs of mission to assure coordination abroad. But the agencies of the Executive Office and many advisors and committees in other functional areas also enforce foreign policy decisions.

The president issues executive orders to define jurisdictions not defined by statutes. He also uses informal communications for this purpose. With congressional authorization, he issues reorganization plans, many of which are aimed at improving or facilitating coordination.

Agency Techniques. Agencies normally exchange information copies of incoming and outgoing correspondence and policy documents. In some cases, dozens or even scores of copies of such documents have to be made. Many departments and agencies assign liaison officers to other agencies to keep themselves informed about the activities of these related agencies. For example, the Departments of Defense and State exchange officers for this purpose. The liaison officer then assures that his agency receives copies of all relevant documentation of the host agency.

Agencies use clearance as the single most important coordinative technique. All matters of interest to more than one agency must be cleared, and most matters today concern many agencies. Sometimes clearance can be given informally by telephone, but usually it involves the physical circulation of a document and its initialing by an officer of the clearing agency. Since World War II, clearance has come to absorb an alarming proportion of the time of many foreign affairs administrators. Unhappily, it also delays responses, impairs their effectiveness, and forecloses options. Unfortunately, the need for multiple concurrences on any foreign affairs decision also results in watering down decisions to narrow areas of common acceptance in order to preclude sending split papers to higher authority.

The most damaging effects of clearance probably become apparent when interdepartmental committees and boards are involved. By 1951 the Department of State sat on 131 such committees, 56 of which it chaired. The delays involved and the dilution of decisions finally taken usually surpassed those engendered by other clearance techniques. The Kennedy and Johnson administrations reduced the number of committees appreciably, made far greater use of task forces, and gave broader decision-making powers to chairmen, usually to the State Department representative. This tendency reached its peak in 1966 when President Johnson "directed the Secretary of State . . . to assume authority for the overall direction, coordination and supervision of interdepartmental activities of the United States Government overseas."[6] In a sense, President Johnson made the Department of State manager of the nation's foreign affairs. President Nixon restored considerable power to NSC and increased and institutionalized the role of his special assistant for national security affairs.

Departments and agencies sometimes improve coordination in areas of doubtful or disputed jurisdiction by negotiating agreements defining their mutual responsibilities. In this manner the Departments of State and Commerce delineated their joint duties for the promotion of American foreign commerce and the selection and assignment of officers engaged therein. Hundreds, if not thousands, of bilateral and multilateral agreements between the Department of State and other agencies help to reduce interdepartmental committee and other clearance work.

Interdepartmental and interagency personnel exchanges considerably facilitate coordination. Formal or informal agreements sometimes provide for exchanges of personnel in operational positions. In other cases, they provide for staff exchanges for formal or on-the-job training, or for interagency participation in personnel policy, recruitment, selection, or evaluation work. For example, the Departments of State and Defense exchange officers in operational roles and send them to each others' highest staff schools. The Department of State sends contingents annually to the National War, Army, Navy, Air, and Industrial Colleges. The Department of Defense sends officers to the Senior Officers Seminar, the counterinsurgency seminar, and many other courses offered by the Foreign Service Institute. Both agencies also exchange faculty members.

Officers in USIA, AID, and the Departments of Commerce and Labor participate in the work of the Department of State's Board of

---

[6] *News Letter*, no. 59 (March 1966), p. 1.

the Foreign Service, Board of Examiners for the Foreign Service, oral examining panels, and selection (promotion) boards. The Department of State, in turn, sends representatives to oral examining panels of USIA and to its Joint Board of Examiners. Such exchanges educate officers in the problems of other agencies and help to reduce institutional particularism.

Field Coordination. Field coordination presented no serious problem before World War II because chiefs of mission and consular officers in charge exercised supervisory responsibility over all American government employees within their jurisdictions. During World War II the supervisory and representational authority of chiefs of mission and principal consular officers declined abruptly with the rapid growth in numbers and resources of other agency representatives over which they had no effective control.[7] Field supervision continued to deteriorate after the war with the advent of CIA, and the military and economic assistance programs. It probably reached its nadir in 1953 with the creation of USIA and ICA and when chiefs of USIS and ICA field missions were accorded virtually autonomous status. Ambassadorial authority also suffered attrition in countries where large American military forces were stationed, as in West Germany, Korea, Taiwan, and Turkey.

An obvious need existed to restore more adequate supervision to field operations. The chaotic situation in Greece during the early phase of the Greek-Turkish Aid Program produced one useful expedient in the form of the country team, a committee of heads of all major agencies meeting periodically or at the call of the chief of mission, and serving as an advisory council and primary agency for coordination. Virtually all American embassies now have country teams. In the absence of a unified field service, these teams fill an important need, but they suffer from the same basic weaknesses as any interagency committee.

They are supplemented by the formal clearance procedure, normally

[7] I observed, for example, that the influence of Ambassador Winant with British authorities declined notably shortly after the arrival of Averill Harriman in London as director of the Lend-Lease Mission and dispenser of billions of dollars to the British government.

administered by the ambassador's alter ego, the deputy chief of mission, and by the interagency staff meetings conducted on lower levels. The political counselor of an embassy, for example, will usually conduct periodic staff meetings at which all agencies engaged in intelligence collection and evaluation are represented for the purpose of pooling data and arriving at joint evaluations of major developments. Mission sections also exchange information through personal contacts and through information copies of important documents. Personal efforts of the ambassador and his officers, formal or informal, planned or *ad hoc*, verbal or written, official or social, likewise contribute to interagency understanding and conjoint action.

President Kennedy's letter to chiefs of mission of March 27, 1961, emphasized their responsibility for supervising and coordinating official activities in their respective countries and helped to restore the effectiveness of these officers. The letter for the first time placed field intelligence operatives under the supervision of chiefs of mission, and it exempted only operational military forces from their purview. Subsequent statements by Presidents Kennedy, Johnson, and Nixon probably have done as much to confirm ambassadorial authority as can be expected while field services continue to report to different agencies.

Unhappily, field coordination still suffers from the fact that some 120 different agencies of the United States government send representatives abroad, although obviously not to every country. Although the ambassador may have full responsibility for supervision and coordination, the loyalties of officers of other agencies attach primarily to their own principals. Moreover, an ambassador's disciplinary power remains limited to the authority to return to the United States any employee who may comport himself so outrageously as to merit such extreme action. The ambassador has little power to reward, despite the greater utility of the carrot as compared with the stick. Ambassadors do not even receive complete information about all activities, reports, and recommendations of all agency representatives. Some still employ codes to which officers of the Foreign Services do not have access, and all conduct official-informal correspondence with their agencies that does not pass over the desks of the ambassador's reviewing officers. Thus, operators continue to play major roles in making policy and are still capable of thwarting policy, as reviewed and approved by the Department of State. This weakness exists and will continue to exist as long as representation abroad is divided along functional lines based on the fallacious assumptions that operations and policy can be administered separately and that State Department review of policy decisions of other agencies will assure that actions of their field representatives conform to the major lines of national policy.[8]

[8] John E. Harr in *The Professional Diplomat* (pp. 290–311) offers an excellent and more detailed discussion and analysis of field coordination.

10

The Department of State and the Foreign Service

The Department of State enjoyed a virtual monopoly of foreign affairs administration until World War II, when it lost control of wide functional areas. The proliferation and inflation of departments and agencies engaged in foreign policy administration made the department's coordinating role infinitely more difficult, as did the enormous expansion in the range and volume of international commitments and relations. The Department of State and its Foreign Service have also grown enormously in size and organizational complexity with the result that the coordination and management of their own efforts present serious problems.

Nevertheless, it remains essentially correct to affirm that the character and personal endowments of the secretary of state and the closeness of his relationship with the president and the Congress still largely determine the ability of the department and the Foreign Service to discharge their roles. Since World War II the nation has had four secretaries who did not enjoy optimal relationships with their presidents, Cordell Hull, Edward Stettinius, James Byrnes, and Christian Herter.

Whereas General Marshall worked well and effectively both with President Truman and the Congress, Dean Acheson's unhappy relationship with the Congress made it impossible for him to resist effectively the dispersive tendencies of his period. Furthermore, the Truman administrations abounded with crises caused by communist aggression, with the result that the military aspects of national security generally tended to prevail over other considerations. Although John Foster Dulles had the full confidence of President Eisenhower, he failed to secure for the department and the Foreign Service authority requisite to enable them to coordinate foreign policy administration because he failed to challenge the theory that operations and policy making can be separated effectively. Secretary Rusk enjoyed good relations with Presidents Kennedy and Johnson and with Congress.

The secretary's effectiveness is limited or enhanced by the leadership qualities of his principal assistants, especially the undersecretaries, the deputy undersecretaries, and the assistant secretaries of state. All of these high officers owe their appointments to the president, rather than to the secretary, and this situation, of course, limits the secretary's ability to form a completely unified team.

Fortunately, the growing importance of foreign affairs seems to have brought improvement in the competence of persons selected for high foreign affairs positions. This statement cannot be documented and represents an impression rather than a substantiated conclusion. Foreign Service officers certainly hold more ambassadorships today, and the tendency to reward political loyalty with assignments in the Department of State, the Foreign Service, USIA, or AID seems generally to be diminishing. A full comparative and analytical study of the prior preparation of foreign affairs political appointees to ambassadorial, AID mission chief, and home office positions over the past three decades would be needed to draw soundly based conclusions about the relative competence of recent appointees.

The Department of State

Functions. The Department of State discharges four major foreign affairs responsibilities: it makes and executes political policy, except in a few highly specialized areas, and it supervises policy making in those areas; it coordinates the efforts of all agencies engaged in foreign affairs administration; it makes and executes policy in functional areas not claimed by other agencies; and it supervises the Foreign Service of the United States, which executes political policy abroad, conducts such other operations as are entrusted to it by the department and other agencies, and supports representatives of other agencies administratively.

Organization, Structure, and Political Roles. The structure of the Department of State, although now quite complex, is often described in terms of line or decision-making regional units, and staff or functional units; but the distinction becomes blurred when officers serving in staff capacities to the secretary or other high officers engage in decision making and when decisions emerge from functional areas. Virtually all units discharge coordinating responsibilities.

The secretary and his close collaborators on the seventh floor of New State head both the line and staff elements. This group includes the undersecretaries, the counselor, the deputy undersecretaries, and the director of the Planning and Coordination Staff.[1] These officers make the highest policy decisions and resolve conflicts at lower levels in the department.

The great mass of day-to-day political decisions emerges from the regional bureaus, largely staffed by Foreign Service officers, which make political policy and coordinate functional and interagency policy in Africa, Latin America, Europe, East Asia and the Pacific, and the Near East and South Asia.[2] The Bureau of International Organization Affairs, which conducts United States relations with the United Nations, occupies an unenviable position, because considerations of national interest still dominate decision making in the United States, as elsewhere, even when the issues affect international organizations. As

---

[1] Formerly the Policy Planning Council.

[2] See Appendix D for an excellent description of the flow of policy making and the clearance process within the department, drafted by Charlton Ogburn, Jr., extracted from United States, Congress, Senate, Committee on Foreign Relations, *The Formulation and Administration of United States Foreign Policy*, study No. 9, prepared by the Brookings Institute, 86th Cong., 2d sess., 1960, pp. 172–177. Although some titles and minor details in this description have changed, the process remains essentially unaltered.

emphasized earlier, President Johnson greatly strengthened the coordinative authority of the regional bureaus.

Rapid advancement in the Foreign Service traditionally has come to officers assigned to the geographic bureaus. Ambitious officers seek duty progressively as country desk officers, office directors, deputy assistant secretaries, and assistant secretaries, interspersed with correspondingly important field diplomatic assignments.

The responsibilities and workloads on the geographical desks are enormous but challenging. Trade union leaders and the Civil Service Commission would resist the pressures and working hours required. Enthusiasm for their work and large measures both of patriotism and personal ambition are requisite for success in this exacting *métier*.

The functional units of the department exert varying degrees of influence on decision making in the regional bureaus and at higher levels, make decisions in functional areas, and collaborate fully in coordinative work.

The Economic Bureau guides political decisions affecting commercial, financial, and general economic policy. It also participates in a wide range of coordinative activities by representing the department on interdepartmental economic committees and task forces.

The Bureau of Intelligence and Research makes available to the regional and functional bureaus, spot, estimative, and basic intelligence that influences decision making in varying but usually unascertainable degrees. It represents the department on the Joint Intelligence Board and on other interagency committees of the intelligence community. It also monitors and coordinates government-wide social science contractual research in international relations. The Bureau of Politico-Military Affairs conducts liaison with the national security agencies. (Note 11 of Chapter 6 lists the bureau's specific functions.)

The Bureau of Congressional Relations conducts liaison with the staffs of congressional committees and with the personal staffs of congressmen, tries to provide information and service to the Congress and to its members upon request, presents the department's point of view to Congress, brings congressional views to the attention of departmental officers, and helps to coordinate the selection of congressional delegates to international meetings.

The Bureau of Public Affairs conducts the department's relations with the press and other media and tries to project a favorable image of the department to the general public. It answers public inquiries about foreign policy or departmental activities and conducts information programs directed at key sectors of public opinion.

The Bureau of Cultural Affairs administers the exchange of persons program and maintains liaison with other government agencies interested in cultural exchange activities. It exerts only peripheral influence on the work of geographical bureaus.

The Office of Science and Technology supervises the activities of science attachés abroad, keeps the regional and functional bureaus informed of scientific and technological developments having a bearing on policy considerations, and coordinates the department's efforts with those of other scientific elements in the federal government.

The Legal Advisor and his staff provide the department with advice on municipal and international law as it affects policies or programs that may be under consideration.

The Bureau of Security and Consular Affairs discharges two major functions. Its security units screen all new departmental and Foreign Service employees, establish and maintain security procedures, and maintain physical security, including the "debugging" of official offices and residences. Its units supervising consular affairs discharge statutory responsibilities relating to immigration, nationality, the protection of American citizens, shipping and seamen, notarial services, and related consular duties. The Bureau of Security and Consular Affairs also supervises field performance of consular services and the observance of security regulations. It maintains liaison with and coordinates the efforts of other departments and agencies in these areas, especially the FBI and the Immigration and Naturalization Service.

The deputy undersecretary for administration supervises the Bureau of Security and Consular Affairs and all other control and administrative components of the department, including the Office of the Director General of the Foreign Service, the Foreign Service Institute, the Foreign Service Inspection Service, and a multitude of units that engage in various specialized administrative support operations. The officers of this area, under the immediate supervision of the assistant secretary for administration and his deputy, select, assign, promote, and retire or discharge personnel for the department and Foreign Service; they supervise all housekeeping functions of the department and the Foreign Service, including budgetary and accounting work, position classification, automated data processing, the foreign buildings program, and the medical program.

Staffing Arrangements. Three types of employees staff the Department of State. A few high officers owe their positions to political preferment. This does not mean that they are necessarily less effective than their career colleagues. Indeed, some have offered the highest conceivable qualifications, for example, Averill Harriman, George Ball, Chester Bowles, and Walt W. Rostow, to name only a few. Others owe their preferment to political considerations, but the spoils system no longer seriously impairs effective operation of the Department of State because the occasional dud usually lands in a position of less than critical importance and is carefully surrounded with able subordinates.

Many officer positions and virtually all clerical positions are filled by Civil Service employees, recruited, paid, and otherwise treated in accordance with regulations prescribed by the Civil Service Commission. They do not usually serve abroad and tend to concentrate in functional or staff positions requiring continuity of service and a high degree of specialization, for example, in estimative intelligence work or in highly technical legal, economic, management, administrative, and security positions.

Foreign Service officers dominate the regional bureaus. Foreign Service officers assigned to functional and staff areas of the department tend to come from the ranks of the integrated officers brought in under the Manpower Act, Wristonization, or lateral entry, and to be specialists in management, administration, economics, or commercial work.

Important changes have occurred both in the ratio of Foreign and Civil Service employees engaged in foreign affairs administration and in their functional deployment. At the turn of the century, departmental employees, virtually all from the Civil Service or political, numbered only two hundred. Diplomatic and consular employees outnumbered them by at least six to one. At the outbreak of World War

II, the department still employed less than one thousand persons; only a handful of Foreign Service officers served in Washington, mainly in the minuscule geographical divisions, and the ratio of American field to home employees remained about four to one. It has since varied from as low as two to one to the present figure of about two point seven to one, but it has obviously shifted importantly. However, while the number of Civil Service employees increased both numerically and relatively since World War II, the Foreign Service consolidated its control over the key regional bureaus, and, since Wristonization, the service also holds many important functional positions. Consequently, its decision-making role in the Department of State now far exceeds in importance that of the Civil Service.

THE FOREIGN SERVICE

Functions. The Foreign Service serves as the field arm of the Department of State and of many other executive departments and agencies. It provides field administrative support for elements of all agencies. Originally the service was conceived to represent all the executive establishments abroad, but this concept no longer governs. The activities that successful performance of its role presently require include the performance of statutory duties, reporting, commercial work, negotiation, representation, administration, and, last in this sequence but probably first in importance, the supervision and coordination of all American official activities and personnel abroad.

The statutory responsibilities of the Foreign Service include the documentation of aliens by the issuance of visas to those who wish to come to the United States as visitors, students, or permanent residents; the issuance of passports to American citizens and their renewal or amendment; the registration of births and deaths of American citizens; the administration of estates of Americans who die abroad without leaving resident heirs; the performance of certain notarial services; extradition work; the taking of testimony under oath from witnesses in the consular district under letters rogatory issued by courts in the United States; services for shipping and seamen; the protection of American citizens; ascertaining the whereabouts and welfare of Americans in response to inquiries from friends and relatives; the performance of certain services for the Veterans Administration and the Social Security Administration in connection with the delivery of checks to and the verification of the continued existence of their clients abroad; and other duties of less demanding and time-consuming importance.

Of the preceding functions, the visa, the passport, and other citizenship services are, of course, the most onerous and most important in their impact on public relations. The image created by the Foreign Service in the minds of American citizens who come to a consulate or a consular section for protection or passport services is directly related to the speed, efficiency, and friendliness with which service is performed. By the same token, nationals of other countries who come to apply for visas are attracted or repelled by the manner of their reception.

Reporting absorbs much of the time of many Foreign Service employees. Such intelligence work includes the collection, evalution, and interpretation of data. The Foreign Service does not engage in underground or covert intelligence collection, which is the task of the Central Intelligence Agency and its overseas operatives, but Foreign Service intelligence may be classified to protect the informant, the information, or the credibility or significance accorded it.

Foreign Service reporting covers economic, political, and sociological areas, including intellectual, cultural, scientific, and educational developments. Specific requests of the department, other executive agencies, and congressional or public inquiries generate the bulk of reporting. Voluntary or semivoluntary reports respond to general directives that require the Foreign Service to report and interpret salient developments and trends that may have an impact on the United States or its foreign policy.

Field reports may take the form of spot news or intelligence designed to keep Washington abreast of current developments. Such intelligence, usually transmitted by cable or wireless, is, of course, encrypted in a code appropriate to its security classification, if classified. Periodic reports of developments normally are submitted on reproduceable master sheets so that enough copies may be run off in Washington to serve all users. Such reports may survey agricultural or industrial production, political developments, commercial movements, banking, currency, or balance of payments trends, major intellectual or cultural trends, or other fields of interest.

From time to time, officers of embassies or consular establishments prepare "think pieces" or estimative reports; in these, they assess the significance of basic trends they have observed for a time in terms of possible impact on the host country or on American interests and policy. They use such assessments to support recommendations for changes or modifications in United States policy. All reports, whether spot, periodic, or estimative, must contain evaluations of the sources from which they are derived so their value may be assessed.

Political and economic reporting offered the quickest and surest route to advancement in the pre–World War II Foreign Service. Indeed, such reporting still serves as the most effective medium for bringing a field officer's talents and preparation to the attention of his superiors. Consequently, most young officers regard reporting assignments as more desirable than consular or administrative duty, despite repeated hortatives about the importance of other activities.

Commercial work ranks as a third major function. Its volume and importance fluctuate as the balance of payments requires greater or reduced emphasis on trade promotion and tourism. Commercial officers engage in promoting tourism, resolving trade disputes between American and foreign businessmen, seeking trade opportunities for American business, assisting American businessmen to make appropriate contacts in the local community, aiding foreign businessmen who may contemplate visiting the United States to plan their trips efficiently, maintaining commercial reference libraries for the benefit of local and American businessmen, and performing a wide range of highly specialized reporting services.

Local employees of long service and high competence usually do the leg work for commercial reporting. Commercial reports include World Trade Directory Reports, which resemble Dun and Bradstreet evaluations but cover foreign firms; trade lists, which are rosters of local businessmen engaged in the same line of manufacture or commerce; trade opportunity reports; periodic revisions of basic reports on doing business in the local community; and reports on changes in price levels, or in commercial or tariff laws and regulations. Commercial officers also conduct a wide range of correspondence with local businessmen, and they correspond with businessmen in the United States through the Department of Commerce.

Negotiations formerly engaged the attention only of political officers or of principal officers of consulates, but the expansion of foreign affairs commitments and interests into other functional areas has made negotiation a commonly shared duty. In fact, officers assigned to economic and commercial work often negotiate more today than do political officers, but even cultural or consular officers not infrequently engage in negotiations.

The preceding generalization applies with greater force to representational work, which embraces *presentations*, or the introduction of colleagues and visiting Americans to local persons, *protocol*, or the practice of diplomatic good manners, and *contact* work, or the cultivation of professionally useful acquaintances.

Social contact with citizens of the host country, colleagues and visiting Americans, and members of the local diplomatic or consular corps formerly absorbed rather pleasantly an important but not excessive portion of the time of senior political, economic, and consular officers. The range of officers so engaged and the amount of time spent on the activity rose sensationally after World War II. The increased importance of nonpolitical activities required an extension of representational work to the new fields. At the same time the emergence of many new states and the expansion of the foreign services of older states, often for reasons of prestige, greatly inflated all diplomatic and consular corps and their representational activities. Some of the diplomats of the new states, and even officers of old states, have little to do except to cultivate their colleagues, of whom their American colleagues often are most important to them because of the emergence of the United States as a superpower.

Increased requirements for intelligence likewise necessitate much more contact work, but the growing tendency to substitute large affairs for intimate and congenial dinners and soirees has made such work less useful even as it has become more onerous. Extension of free entry, commissary services, and similar privileges, together with the more generous representation allowances of all agencies enabled more foreign affairs employees to entertain without incurring prohibitive personal sacrifices. The fantastic increase in foreign travel, official and unofficial, by American citizens also enlarged the representational burden, as did the rise in the number of American businessmen, scholars, retirees, and other private citizens resident abroad. Much official entertaining thus became a matter of taking in one's own social washing.

All the preceding functions require far more staffing than was the case before World War II, with the possible exception of statutory consular services; but none has equalled or begun to rival management and administration as a devourer of manpower. Prewar Foreign Service establishments were so small that they required little or no management activity, and the top administrative role usually could be discharged by the principal officer or his deputy as a minor responsibility. The work of preparing accounts and payrolls normally absorbed the attention of one or two clerks, often local employees. In a few large missions, noncareer vice consuls were designated to serve as administrative attachés, but even London had less than two hundred American and British employees before the war, and not all of the Americans, even then, were Foreign Service. Management and administration probably absorbed less than 5 per cent of the working time of all officers and noncareer officers prior to 1939. Certainly, very few Foreign Service officers in the Department of State engaged in management or administration because the Divisions of Foreign Service Personnel and Foreign Service Administration employed only a handful. A somewhat higher but still modest proportion of American and local clerical staff performed administrative support work, but their numbers remained low because the Foreign Service enjoyed few fringe benefits and supported relatively few employees of other agencies administratively before World War II.

Today management and administration absorb at least half the working hours of all employees of the Foreign Service. Most staff and a substantial minority of reserve and career officers are so employed. Moreover, a preponderance of American and local staff support personnel are engaged in administrative tasks. Several factors contributed to this revolutionary change. First, Foreign Service establishments now serve as hosts abroad to a multitude of employees of 120 agencies. About one third of all American Foreign Service employees stationed abroad are now engaged in this administrative support work,[3] and the proportion of local employees so engaged probably is higher. Moreover, the problem of coordinating the activities of these agencies increases the need for Foreign Service clearance and supervisory personnel, thus raising the administrative support requirement for such traditional functions.

Fringe benefits won by foreign affairs employees and their dependents since World War II have also inflated the administrative component. The number of foreign-owned and leased office and residential properties that must be administered and maintained now represents an investment well in excess of $250,000,000, and government-owned furnishings are provided in publicly owned, publicly leased, and many privately leased quarters. The real estate, buildings, and inventory require the full time and attention of many general services employees and the part-time efforts of others. But Foreign Service employees also receive additional personal services and substantially more generous allowances for representation, rent, heat and light, education, travel, official residence expenses, medical outlays, cost of living, and post differentials, which must be administered and accounted for.

The supervision of the sale of personal property abroad by Foreign Service personnel, the extension of benefits to Foreign Service local employees, previously enjoyed only by American employees, including retirement, health benefits, and educational opportunities, and the initiation of language training programs in most posts, have all added their share to the impressive collective burden of administrative overheads chargeable to postwar paternalism. Furthermore, the tendency of Washington to "devolve" administrative duties and impose its administrative norms on the field has also contributed to the administrative inflation.[4] Moreover, the function of supervising and coordinating

---

[3] In April 1967, 2,667 of 7,065 American Foreign Service employees overseas were employed in administrative support roles (United States, Department of State, *News Letter*, no. 78 [October 1967], p. 57).

[4] See Chaper 4.

all American activities within the jurisdiction of an embassy or a consular establishment obviously forms part of the management problem. (See Chapter 9 for a detailed discussion of this aspect of foreign affairs work.)

Thus far, comment on the roles of the Foreign Service has focused on its duties in diplomatic missions and consulates. As of April 30, 1969, about two thirds (6,573 of 9,894) of all American Foreign Service employees were engaged in these duties. But Wristonization has increased the proportion of Foreign Service officers on home duty from less than 15 per cent to about 42 per cent; today, moreover, 52 per cent of reserve and 27 per cent of staff officers serve at home.[5]

Many more officers now receive assignments to other agencies for periods of a few months to two or three years. Others serve on delegations to hundreds of international conferences or meetings of international organizations. Some of these meetings last for months and even years, for example, the Kennedy Round trade negotiations.

In-service training absorbs more than 5 per cent of all the Foreign Service officers and a somewhat lower proportion of reserve and staff officers. Training assignments last from a few days to two or three years. In addition, much training is undertaken in the field, especially in languages. Such language instruction is offered during the work day, but officers are expected to study on their own time.

The "man-in-motion" also represents an important percentage of Foreign Service employees on the rolls. This term includes those in transit to or from their posts, on local, home, or sick leave, or for any reason granted leave without pay, for example, to perform military service. With home leave currently being granted regularly every two years, and with junior officers receiving new assignments at intervals of two years or less, the man in motion becomes a staffing factor of critical significance.

Staffing. Six categories of employees staff Foreign Service posts: political appointees, Foreign Service officers (FSO), Foreign Service reserve officers unlimited (FSRU), Foreign Service reserve officers

---

[5] United States, Department of State, "Summary of Employment," PER/CMA Reports and Statistics Section, May 23, 1969.

(FSRO), Foreign Service staff officers (FSSO), Foreign Service staff employees (FSS), and local employees (FSL-alien).

Political appointees currently serve as chiefs of mission at about one third of the embassies. Criteria for the selection of political ambassadors vary somewhat with occupants of the White House, but services, financial or otherwise, to the party in power normally predominate, although conspicuous exceptions can be cited. As suggested earlier, the writer considers that standards for political appointments to foreign affairs positions generally have risen during the past decade, and that special situations will always arise in which a carefully chosen political appointee may perform better than a career officer.[6]

Foreign Service officers hold the preponderance of ambassadorships, virtually all deputy chief of mission jobs, all officer in charge positions at consular posts, and most section chief jobs in missions and consular establishments. Thus, they occupy virtually all the positions staffed by State Department employees from which political and politico-economic policy can be made or influenced abroad. Responsibility for the coordination of other agencies' activities resides as well in these roles. In July 1962, 54.2 per cent of the 3,670 FSO's on duty had entered through the examination route and 45.8 per cent through integration or other lateral programs, of which Wristonization accounted for 32.3 per cent.[7] The 3,262 FSO's on duty in 1969 probably represented a somewhat higher proportion of examination appointees because a substantial number of Wristonees opted to return to reserve or staff status.

All FSO's upon appointment receive three presidential commissions subject to Senate confirmation. A commission as a Foreign Service officer, specifying the appointee's class, determines his salary. Each FSO also receives commissions as secretary in the Diplomatic Service and vice consul of career. As he rises in the service, he receives new commissions.

Officers assigned to any position in a diplomatic mission normally receive diplomatic and consular commissions according to their FSO rank (FSO 7's and 8's as vice consul and third secretary) in order to

[6] See also Henry Villard, *Affairs at State*, pp. 177–188.
[7] John E. Harr, *The Anatomy of the Foreign Service: A Statistical Profile*, p. 12.

facilitate their employment in either capacity should the need arise. Officers assigned to consular posts are assigned only with consular titles.

The following rank order of diplomats established at the Congress of Vienna still prevails:

1. papal legates and nuncios and ambassadors
2. papal apostolic internuncios, ministers plenipotentiary, and envoys extraordinary
3. ministers resident
4. chargés d'affaires and chargés d'affaires *ad interim*

Diplomatic secretaries rank in the following order: counselor, first secretary, second secretary, and third secretary. Attachés take precedence after diplomatic secretaries in theory, but in practice they rank frequently with counselors and first secretaries.

No exact correspondence of the titles between diplomatic and consular officers exists, but, in general, FSO's whose rank entitles them to counselor or first secretary status can likewise expect commissions as consuls general, if they are in charge of a post or chief of a supervisory consular section at a mission. Second secretaries and third secretaries normally rank as consuls and vice consuls respectively.

International law and custom accord diplomats certain rights and privileges, including free entry of personal effects through customs, exemptions from local taxes, inviolability of person, immunity of residence, immunity from criminal, police, and civil jurisdictions, exemption from giving testimony, and other less significant immunities.[8]

Consuls enjoy fewer privileges and immunities under international law and custom. Consequently, the Department of State has concluded specific consular conventions with a number of states defining consular rights and has included clauses covering consular rights in many treaties of commerce and navigation. Generally speaking, only career consuls benefit from most treaty and customary privileges. These include the right to protection from local authorities, the inviolability of archives and offices, the right to display the flag and arms, and sometimes but not invariably free entry, exemption from taxation,

[8] Graham H. Stuart, *American Diplomatic and Consular Practices*, pp. 222–258.

from civil, criminal, and police process, and from serving as witness.[9]

When serving at consulates or at consular work, FSRO's and FSSO's receive commissions issued by the secretary of state as vice consuls and consuls and, when assigned to embassies, "appropriate" diplomatic titles, usually as attachés or assistant attachés. Although only FSO's may be commissioned as consuls general, FSRO's and FSSO's serve as consuls and vice consuls at the same salary levels as FSO's. Reserve and staff officers now enjoy the same privileges and immunities as FSO's.

FSO's, as of April 30, 1969, staffed 1,942 officer positions overseas; FSRO's, 698; and FSS employees, in the officer salary grades 1–6, 2,061. Other FSS employees numbered 1,808; foreign nationals, 10,950; consular agents, 13; resident American staff, 21; and unclassified employees, 13. Overseas employees then totalled 17,488 in all.[10]

In general, FSRO's staff economic and administrative positions, although some serve in roles requiring greater specialization in depth, for example, as labor, transportation, or science officers. FSSO's serve primarily in administrative and consular roles. Staff employees provide secretarial and clerical help for all sections and fill certain technical roles that do not require officer rank.

Organization of Field Establishments. The organizational pattern of the field units of the Foreign Service relates so intimately to the performance of its roles that it warrants a fairly detailed description. All diplomatic missions of the United States are now headed by ambassadors, with a few unimportant exceptions, and all consular establishments outside of capital cities are headed by principal officers who hold the title either of consul general or consul.

Thirteen consular agencies staffed by part-time agents still exist, but their roles are so minor that they need not be discussed. A recent tendency to reopen one-officer, special-purpose consular posts has not yet altered the basic pattern, except in Mexico. Such posts are supported administratively and staffed by the embassy or the nearest

---

[9] *Ibid.*, pp. 379–393. President Nixon asked the Senate in May 1969 to approve the Vienna Convention on Consular Relations.

[10] U.S., Dept. of State, "Summary of Employment."

consulate general. They exist to perform only a limited range of statutory (visitors' visa or protection) or other services (representation or reporting on an unusually important functional or geographic area), which cannot be discharged conveniently from the supporting post.

The organizational pattern both of missions and of consular establishments displays marked similarity, depending on size and the area served. The ambassador, of course, is the president's principal representative in the host country, and it is he who ultimately has the responsibility for pulling together all American activities in the country, assuring that they are complementary rather than competitive, that they advance American objectives, that no waste or duplication exists, and that the personnel of all agencies conduct themselves in a manner that will bring no discredit upon the United States. A consular officer in charge represents the ambassador before the national and local authorities in his district and reports both to the embassy and the Department of State. Some consular establishments (for example, Hong Kong) are both larger and more important to the United States than are many small missions.

At larger missions, ambassadors usually have personal staffs, which may include anywhere from one to four junior- and middle-grade officers who serve as personal assistants or "ambassadorial doormats." These dedicated young men or women work impossible hours and strive to anticipate every need of their overburdened chiefs. Their primary role is to attend the multitude of personal and telephone callers tactfully and thus save as much time as possible for the ambassador. But there are innumerable chores to be performed in connection with the maintenance of the official residence, the scheduling of ambassadorial trips, the arranging of representational affairs, and similar tasks that require much coordination with the wife of the chief and with administrative and other officers of the embassy. The drafting of less important ambassadorial correspondence occupies any free moments.

All ambassadors are assisted by deputy chiefs of mission (DCM's), who usually receive the temporary, personal rank of minister in large missions, if they do not already have career minister status. Almost all are FSO's, although USIA or AID, in a few cases, have provided DCM's. The deputy chief is the ambassador's alter ego, chief advisor, and chief of staff. He serves as chargé in his absence and performs most of the routine coordinative work for him, in the sense that he reviews incoming and outgoing correspondence, presides over numerous informal and formal staff gatherings, is in constant communication with heads of sections, and advises the ambassador contantly when problems involving coordination arise.

Foreign Service components of the typical mission include the political section, usually presided over by a counselor for political affairs, who ranks customarily as the third officer of the embassy and assumes charge in the absence of the ambassador and his deputy, or becomes acting deputy should the deputy be away. His section does the bulk of political and liaison reporting, including labor, and coordinates all mission intelligence activities, although the deputy chief and the ambassador usually take a hand in both of these functions. In addition to reporting, political officers negotiate political questions, although here, too, if matters are to be discussed on a sufficiently high level, the deputy or the ambassador may participate. Protocol functions normally center in the political section or in the ambassador's outer office, and political officers perform an unusually high proportion of representational duties, including shepherding visiting delegations of congressmen or dignitaries from the United States.

Economic sections under counselors for economic affairs always include commercial units and agricultural reporting units if the Foreign Agricultural Service does not have personnel at the post. In several embassies that supervise foreign aid programs, the work of the economic and AID missions has been consolidated under the direction of a single officer of AID or the Foreign Service who holds the title of economic counselor and mission director. The traditional functions of an economic section include, of course, preparing economic reports covering all aspects of the economy of the host country, conducting negotiations on matters of economic concern, such as commercial treaties, patent rights, and air transit rights, performing commercial functions, and rendering assistance to the ambassador in coordinating all American economic activities in the host country.

The consular section of a diplomatic mission performs statutory consular services under the direction of a counselor of embassy for consular affairs. The counselor also helps the ambassador to coordinate the activities of subordinate consular establishments located elsewhere in the host country. Consular sections of diplomatic missions do not engage in the broad range of activities that consular offices outside the capital cities are required to undertake, but confine themselves to statutory duties. However, they perform representational work, and they conduct specialized negotiations with local officials as part of their responsibilities for protecting American citizens.

The administrative section of a mission, usually headed by a counselor for administrative affairs, normally employs as many or more persons as the rest of the average Foreign Service establishment. Its subsections include budget and fiscal, accounting, personnel, general services, security, files or archives, communications, and library units.[11]

The preceding description of the organizational pattern of a diplomatic mission applies to large missions. In small missions section chiefs bear the diplomatic title of first, or second, or even third secretary. The structures of large consular establishments located outside capital cities

---

[11] A budget and fiscal unit, normally small, prepares an embassy's annual budgetary submissions to the department; records expenditures and obligations against budgetary allotments; requests any transfers, increases, or decreases in allotments that may appear necessary; and, in general, tries to maintain the fiscal health of the establishment. Accounting sections process all vouchers for expenditures, payroll changes and payrolls, and petty cash transactions. Personnel components employ and discharge local employees; administer personnel programs, including morale-building programs; and organize the submission of personnel preference and performance reports, position descriptions, and similar personnel reports. General services units maintain government-owned or -leased property and operate motor pools, custodial, janitorial, commissary, restaurant, snack bar, and like services. Security sections normally include Marine Guard detachments and are responsible for the physical security of the embassies and the residences of ambassadors and high-ranking officers. They also investigate local employees before employment or any employees whose conduct may so require. At the request of the Department of State, field security officers also conduct field investigations of American citizens applying for employment with the department or the Foreign Service. Files units maintain file copies of correspondence, usually for four years, after which old files are either shipped to the National Archives or destroyed if they have no permanent value. Files are organized and maintained on the basis of a system uniformly applied throughout the Foreign Service. Communications units receive and transmit clear and encrypted communications to the Department of State, encrypt and decode classified communications, take responsibility for the safe custody of codes and coding devices, and make up, dispatch, and receive diplomatic pouches. Library units maintain compact reference libraries for the use of all sections of the mission.

resemble this pattern and their various sections perform substantially the same functions, except that separate sections often perform the major statutory functions of visa issuance and citizenship. Consular officers, of course, confine their official relationships to regional officers of the national government and to state or provincial, local, and municipal officials within the consular district. In consulates general most sections are headed by consuls or vice consuls. In the smallest posts functional differentiation disappears, and much doubling and even trebling in brass must be undertaken by the consul and his one or two vice consuls.

The preceding description of the organizational pattern of Foreign Service field establishments covers, of course, only the Foreign Service components of such establishments. Other federal agencies that station personnel abroad normally attach them to diplomatic missions or consular establishments as additional sections or units, or as attachés.

Normally other agency representatives are housed in the mission or consular premises and supported administratively by the Foreign Service. Operational military units, military assistance advisory groups, Peace Corps personnel, tourism and trade center officers of the Department of Commerce, and certain other employees usually occupy separate quarters and often have large administrative staffs, even when they receive some support from the Foreign Service.

Many agencies, including the Departments of Agriculture, Commerce, Defense, Justice, Labor, Transportation, and Treasury, by agreement with the Department of State obtain attaché titles for their officers or nominees stationed in diplomatic missions. USIS officers use other diplomatic and consular titles as well. Personnel not accomodated in mission or consular premises and AID, Immigration and Naturalization Service, and Public Health Service officers even when so accommodated do not use diplomatic or consular titles.

It would be profitless to enumerate all of the more than one hundred federal agencies that maintain a few representatives abroad. The various methods by which they are integrated into Foreign Service overseas establishments emerge from the preceding description of the manner in which major non-Foreign Service components are accomodated.

Charts 5 and 6 illustrate typical mission and consulate organizational patterns.

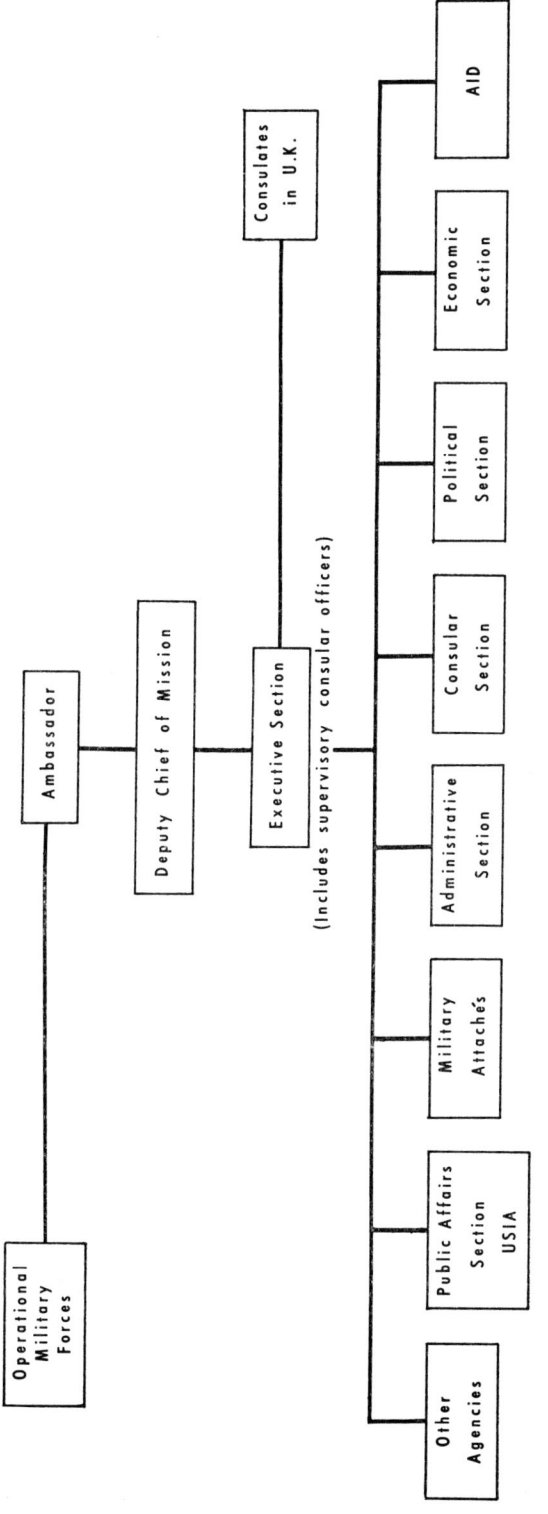

Chart 5: American Embassy, London, January 1969

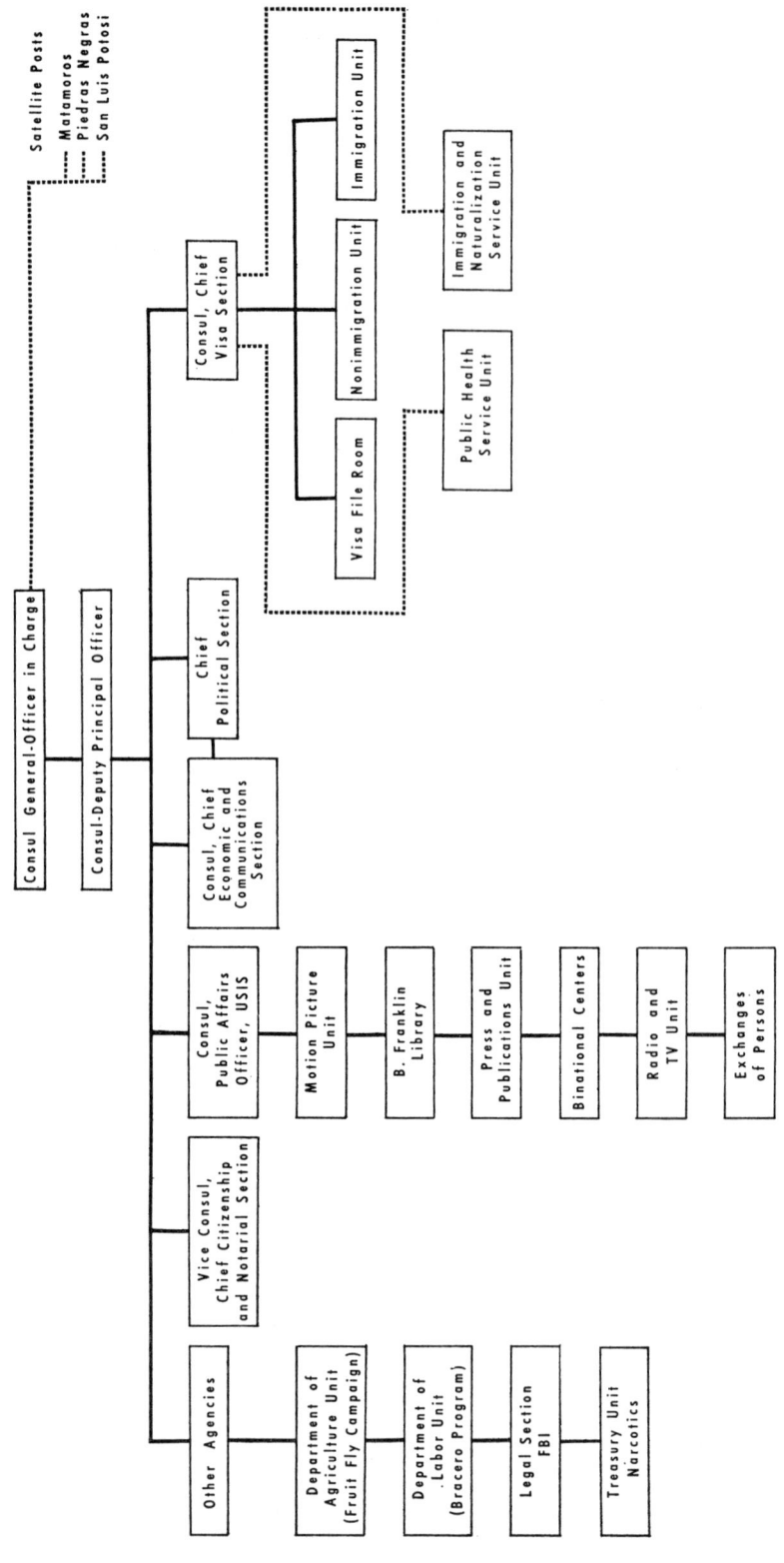

Chart 6: Consulate General, Monterrey, 1965

11

USIA, AID, and Other Political Agencies

Since World War II, the Department of State has shared its political responsibilities with the United States Information Agency (USIA), the Agency for International Development (AID), the Peace Corps, and the Arms Control and Disarmament Agency (ACDA), which take policy guidance from it but which operate autonomously. Except for ACDA, these agencies also have foreign services and their total representation abroad engaged in substantive work now outnumbers that of the Foreign Service by about four to one.[1] Nevertheless, respon-

[1] In April 1967, of 46,779 Americans attached to overseas posts only 7,065 or 15 per cent were Foreign Service employees, including 2,661 administrative support employees. Thus, only 9 per cent of the Americans abroad were working at traditional Foreign Service tasks. The Peace Corps had 12,417, or 26 per cent of the total; USIA, 1,365, or 3 per cent; and AID, 4,885, or 7 per cent. Defense Department employees totalled 19,552, or 43 per cent, and all other agencies contributed only 1,465, or 3 per cent. Even the total of "other agency" representation equalled the pre-World War II total of American Foreign Service deployment abroad (United States, Department of State, *News Letter*, no. 78 [October 1967], p. 57 [hereafter cited as *News Letter*]).

sibility for executing political policy abroad and coordinating the activities of representatives of other agencies remains in the Foreign Service.

USIA AND USIS

The United States Information Agency (USIA) formulates United States information policy under State Department guidance and conducts operations through the mass media to assure that the United States position on major international issues is clearly understood and, hopefully, accepted abroad. USIA supervises its overseas component, the United States Information Service (USIS), which uses the mass media and direct contacts abroad to explain the United States position. USIA also coordinates all American overseas information policy and activities. Its director takes policy guidance from the secretary of state but has direct access to the president.

The headquarters organization of USIA, as the accompanying chart reveals (see Chart 7), resembles the Department of State in that decision-making functions are concentrated primarily in regional directorates supported by similar staff and functional units. It also includes specialized staff units to supervise and support information centers abroad and conduct three major media operations. The Voice of America prepares and broadcasts information and policy-oriented programs throughout the world in English and a wide range of foreign languages. It also operates a chain of relay stations abroad. A motion picture unit plans, prepares scripts for, and arranges for the production of films used by USIS.[2] A press and publication unit prepares and arranges for the publication in many languages of documents and other materials for foreign distribution.

The staffing of the USIA also resembles that of the Department of State. At the top, a few political appointees share responsibility for major decisions with high-ranking Civil Service and USIS officers. The preponderance of middle- and low-level USIA employees comes from

---

[2] Most of the films are obtained under contract because USIA's producing facilities are limited. USIA films may not be exhibited at home, although an exception was made by statute for the USIA film on the assassination and funeral of President Kennedy.

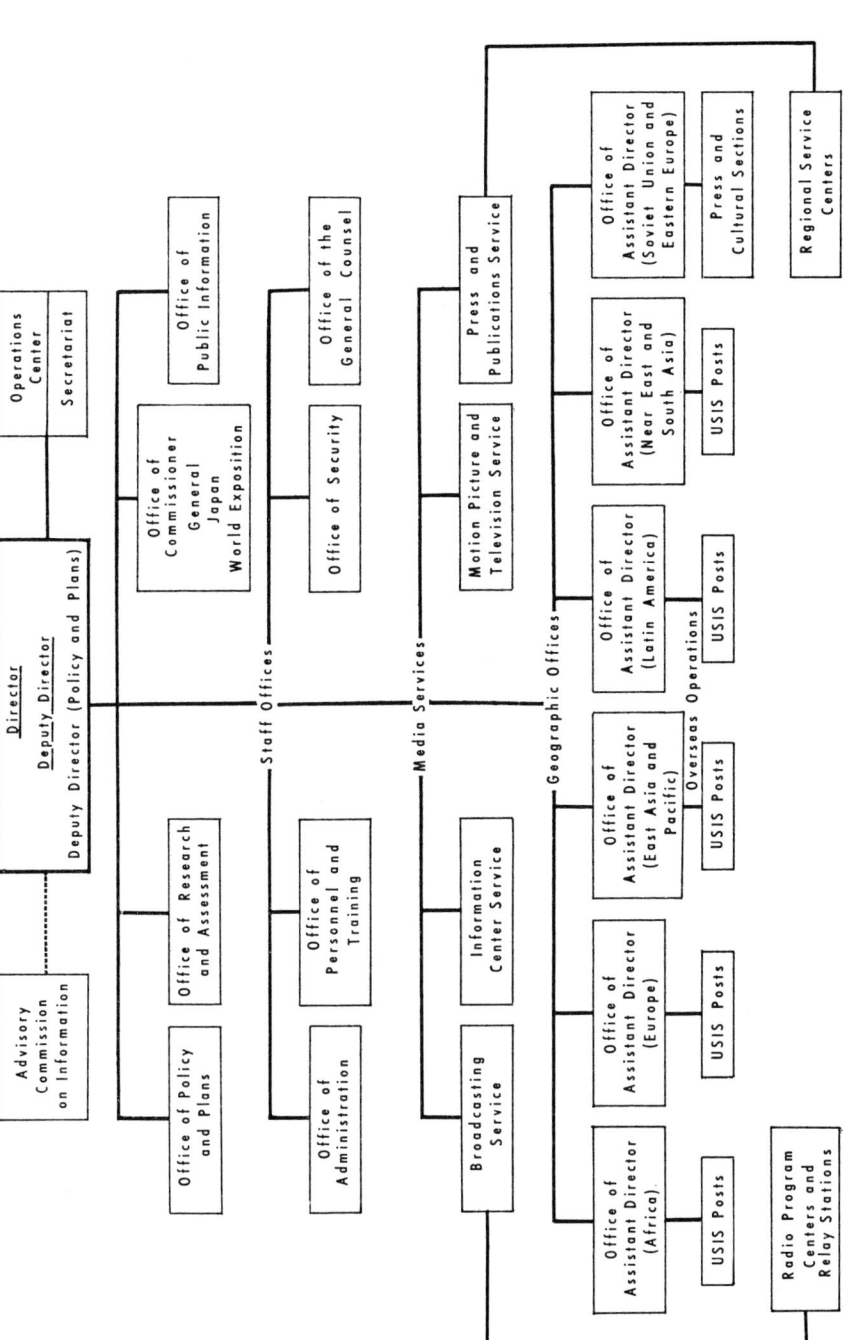

Chart 7: United States Information Agency, May 1969

the Civil Service. On April 30, 1969, 2,794 of USIA's domestic employees were Civil Service and only 459 of USIS's American employees served at home.[3] Thus the Civil Service outnumbered field employees in the home office by six to one.

USIS is staffed by personnel recruited by and responsible to USIA but serving under the provisions of the Foreign Service Act of 1946 as amended in 1968 to establish the Foreign Service information officer (FSIO) corps and to permit Foreign Service reserve officer unlimited (FRSU) appointments. USIA also employs many locals and some contract personnel. USIA on April 30, 1969, employed 835 FSIO's, 118 Foreign Service reserve officers unlimited (FSRU), 499 Foreign Service limited reserve (FSLR) (then in process of conversion to FSRU, FSSO, or termination), and 560 FSS employees, of whom 415 had reached the FSS-1–6 or officer-level salary range.[4]

A survey of the 1,858 American employees of the USIS in 1946 revealed that USIS personnel was then serving at 228 Foreign Service posts. A random sample of 220 career reserve officers, now presumably FSIO's, indicated that they compared favorably with Foreign Service officers in their qualifications and exceeded them in experience in communications, teaching, and research.[5]

Most USIS employees serve in public affairs sections of missions and consulates, which usually contain several functional units. A press unit follows the trend of local press comment on the United States and its major policies, maintains liaison with the local press and periodicals, prepares releases and feature stories for local publications, and

---

[3] Data supplied by USIA/Management Division, June 19, 1969.

[4] *Ibid.*

[5] Of the USIS sample, 80 per cent were male; 16 per cent single; average age, 43; average length of service, nine years with USIA or some other foreign affairs agency; average overseas service about nine years; 77 per cent had had experience outside the government in media, teaching, or research for an average of four years; 91 per cent had undergraduate degrees, 37 per cent had masters, and 19 per cent had Ph.D.'s; 10 per cent had made Phi Beta Kappa; 73 per cent had performed military service; 43 per cent had spent an average of four and one-half years in the field of commercial communications; 89 per cent had a rated proficiency in one or more foreign language; 66 per cent, two or more, 25 per cent, three or more (*News Letter*, no. 35 [March 1964], p. 21).

distributes clichés, mats, photographs, and printed materials received from USIA for republication.

Cultural attachés maintain liaison with university and other educational leaders, conduct presentations of cultural materials such as books and portraits, arrange cultural events, including visits of American artists or theatrical troupes financed by the president's fund for promoting international cultural exchanges, prepare articles for learned journals, and represent the mission at cultural events.

Motion picture (mopix) sections maintain film libraries, lend films to schools, trade unions, churches, and other reputable institutions, and frequently operate mobile units that carry out to the countryside programs suitable for mass audiences. Mopix sections lend projectors, amplifiers, screens, and splicers, as well as film, and frequently provide operators for local screenings. On special occasions, they arrange gala showings in commercial theatres or other major centers for which the chief of mission or principal officer will issue invitations.

Radio and television sections maintain libraries of records and video and radio tapes of music and other program materials from which they supply local radio and television stations. They receive most of their material from USIA but, with the help of local employees, prepare some programs locally to improve their timeliness and to meet local needs and tastes more successfully.

Exchange of persons units help select and screen students, teachers, and other leaders for visits to the United States under the Fulbright and other programs. They perform this service abroad for the Department of State, which administers the programs at home through the Bureau of Cultural Affairs. The activity entails administering English language tests in most cases, close cooperation with security officers to insure that no one selected for a grant may have subversive tendencies, and close consultation with other sections of the mission or consulate, especially with the political and economic sections and other units of USIS to assure that the objectives of their programs are met.

A major function of public affairs sections is, of course, the supervision of binational cultural centers, USIS information centers, and USIS libraries. USIS libraries range in size from a few hundred to many thousands of volumes and are designed primarily to afford local students access to a carefully selected range of representative works about all aspects of American life and culture. In some countries such libraries are maintained only in the capital cities; in others, branches are also operated in provincial centers where they are supervised by the public affairs sections of consulates. Such libraries frequently include record collections and tapes. The frequency with which anti-American elements attack them attests to their effectiveness.

Binational centers, of which there are now several score, especially in Latin America, originated during World War II under the coordinator of inter-American affairs. Organized by the joint action of local and American residents of a community and governed by binational boards, they strive to promote intellectual and cultural cooperation between the two countries, normally financing most of their activities by offering lessons in English and in the language of the host country.

USIS supports binational centers by granting scholarships or financing special training programs, by paying the salaries of American directors acceptable to the boards, by loans or gifts of books, furniture, and teaching materials, or by combinations of the three. Until recently directors of binational centers were engaged under contract by USIS in order to preserve their unofficial status. Recently they were converted to Foreign Service staff or reserve officers in order to give them tenure, salary, and retirement benefits. Some centers still operate without American personnel and subsist on modest allotments for special training programs and scholarships for needy English language students.

The binational centers usually engage in active cultural and intellectual programs, in addition to language instruction, which in some institutions reaches thousands of students. They offer art exhibits, lectures, dramatic performances, and a wide range of social activities. They usually have small libraries and record or tape collections as well.

Information centers of USIS normally include library components and record and film libraries. They exist where libraries or binational centers do not operate and provide alternative sources of American cultural influence.

The public affairs officer serves as the ambassador's principal adviser on public relations, and he or one of his subordinates often helps draft the ambassador's addresses, press releases, and correspondence with the media or cultural leaders.

THE AGENCY FOR INTERNATIONAL DEVELOPMENT

The Agency for International Development (AID), under policy guidance from the Department of State, develops American economic and military foreign assistance policy, organizes training programs for foreign nationals in the United States, and supports field operations of its personnel abroad. As Chart 8 indicates, AID's five regional units embrace only the developing areas. A separate office also exists for the United States coordinator for the Alliance for Progress; but, since the merger of AID's Latin American Division with the Bureau of Inter-American Affairs and the appointment of the assistant secretary for that area as coordinator, this distinction has ceased to make any real difference.

AID also requires the normal staff support units and additional units to support its special operational functions, including the Offices of the War on Hunger, Private Resources, Engineering, International Training, Labor Affairs, and Public Safety. Chart 8 reveals its domestic organization as of November 1968.

AID functioned at home on May 31, 1969, with 2,589 Civil Service employees, 589 Foreign Service reserve, and 88 Foreign Service staff employees, plus 42 other agency employees, to comprise a staff of 3,308. Its field establishment at that time totalled 12,777 direct hire employees, including 8,424 (alien) local, 3,635 Foreign Service reserve, 676 Foreign Service staff, 42 Civil Service, and 938 other agency employees. AID also makes considerable use of contract employees abroad. It contracts with universities and research centers to send out teams to conduct operations abroad and engages many locals on contract. Contract employment on May 31, 1969, increased AID's total overseas force by 2,201 United States and 4,909 aliens to a grand total of 20,825.[6] Political appointees fill most of the highest positions in

---

[6] "AID Employment—As of May 31, 1969," Enclosure to letter dated July 18, 1969,

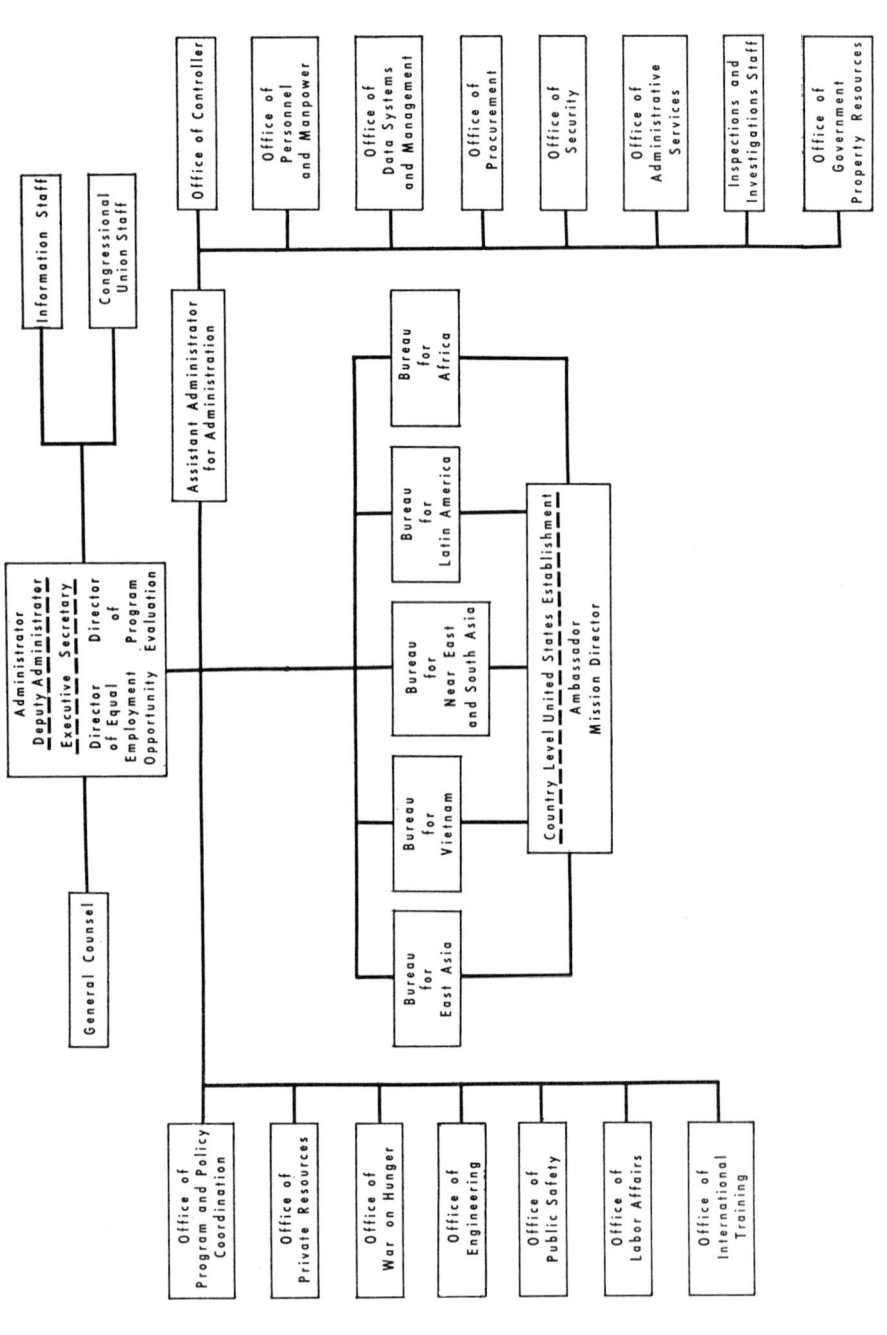

Chart 8: Agency for International Development, November 1968

AID and many of the mission director positions in the field. In fact, AID has become one of the last important patronage resources of the executive.

AID is, of course, deeply engaged at this time in the pacification program in Vietnam. Elsewhere, the gamut of its operations runs a very wide range corresponding to local internal defense and development needs. But AID is a political instrument, designed to advance political objectives of the United States, especially its containment policy. Thus, programs cannot be assessed solely in terms of their publicly stated objectives. In some cases, American policy may be served primarily by successful development or by strengthening internal defense capabilities. In others, this may be merely a secondary goal, desirable though it may be, because the primary or urgent end sought may be the recipient's support in an international organization or simply the maintenance in power of a regime regarded as more favorable to the American interest than a potential successor group.

AID development programs seek to close the growing technological and scientific gap between the developing and the advanced states.[7] Within the limits of its appropriations, AID makes loans and grants calculated to help host countries undertake nonbankable economic and social projects;[8] and it tries to encourage private American and other foreign capitalists to invest in infrastructural or industrial enterprises. It also sponsors private technological and materials resource pools.[9]

AID's military assistance programs concentrate on the provision of training, arms, and munitions essential to maintain internal stability and to counter insurgency. The Department of Defense staffs the military assistance advisory groups (MAAGS), which provide the overseas training in these areas.

---

from Joseph S. Toner, director, Office of Personnel and Manpower, AID, to me.

[7] AID employs American experts abroad in training missions and assists foreign nationals to train in the United States and third countries, for example, Mexico. It also engages in translation programs of technical and scientific works, and it provides consultatory services to foreign governments in many fields.

[8] It has lent Mexico, for example, large sums to finance the construction of low-cost housing and to establish a revolving fund for loans to small farmers.

[9] For example, city-to-city programs, programs under which retired technicians or managers lend their services to a foreign state, programs to collect tools or implements or instruments needed by underdeveloped countries, and so on.

AID field representatives collaborate in the negotiation of assistance agreements with host countries and assist chiefs of mission in coordinating economic assistance programs, in planning development programs for host countries, and in performing appropriate representational duties.

The Peace Corps

The Peace Corps, under policy guidance from the Department of State and when invited by foreign governments, engages in projects to assist them to improve or expand their educational, cultural, social, or economic opportunities. President Kennedy conceived of the Peace Corps as an agency which, while taking policy guidance from the Department of State, would operate independently of it and would not overtly promote American national interests in the host countries. He felt that AID's operations too obviously reflected our national interest, and he sought a device to channel American enthusiasm and philanthropic spirit in to the developing nations in a way that would minimize any reflection of such political inspiration. It goes without saying, however, that American political interests, conceived in the broadest sense, can only be furthered by the success of operations which, if undertaken with State Department approval, help to improve the national image of the United States. Consequently, it is appropriate to consider the Peace Corps as a political agency dedicated to achieving a major political goal of the United States.

The Peace Corps staffs its Washington headquarters and overseas posts with a few political appointees and employees detailed from other agencies, including Foreign Service officers, but mainly with Foreign Service reserve and staff officers who do not have tenure. The corps, as of May 31, 1969, had 1,218 employees serving thirty- to thirty-six–month tours, including 111 aliens. It deployed 443 of its "permanent" Americans overseas and the balance, 664, at home. It used 244 of 248 "temporary" employees at home.[10]

Like the other agencies under discussion, and as Chart 9 reveals, its decision-making functions are concentrated largely in regional units

[10] Letter from Leon M. Parker, deputy director, Office of Administration, Peace Corps, to author July 3, 1969.

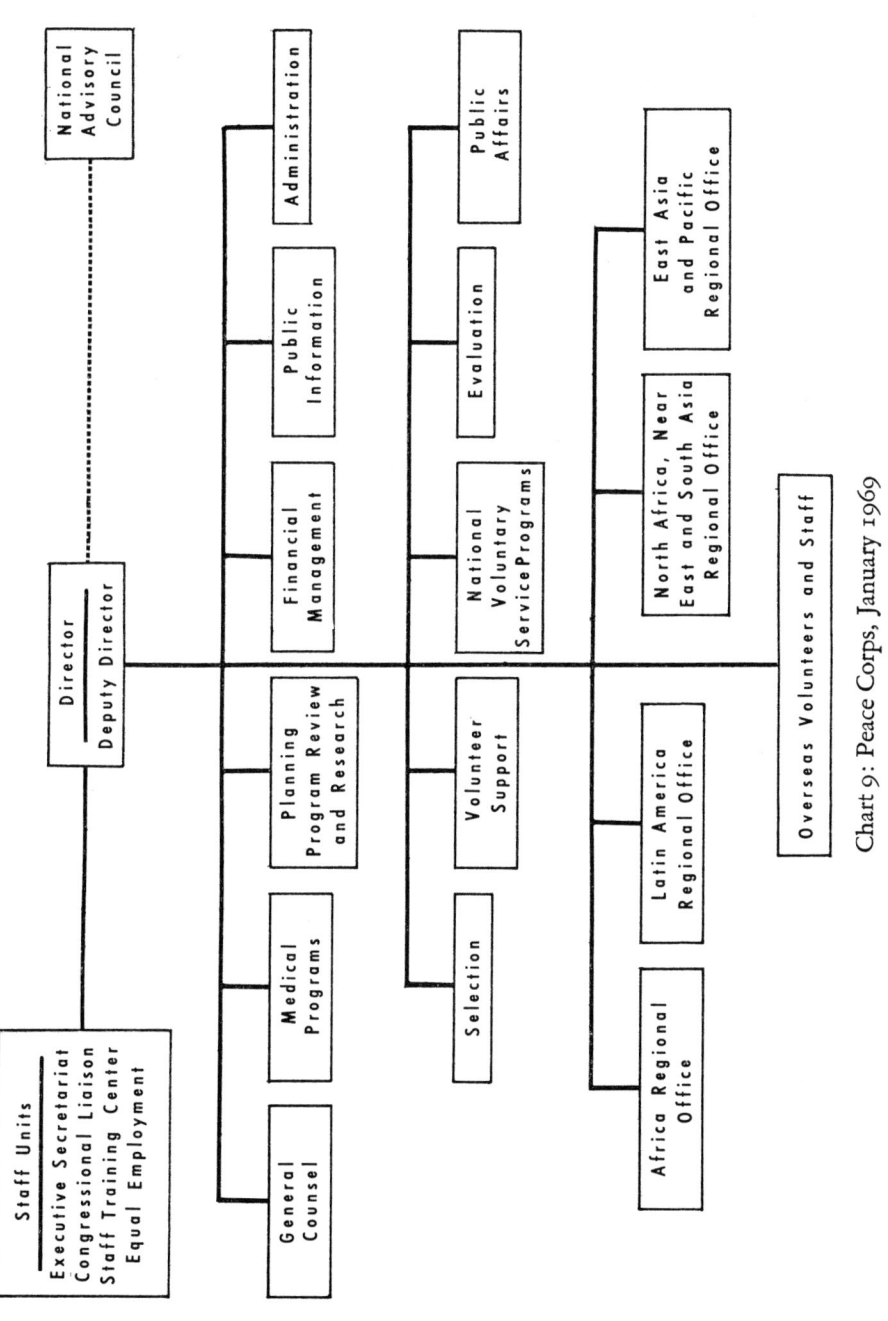

Chart 9: Peace Corps, January 1969

supported by the usual staff sections and by specialized operational sections, specifically designed to meet the unique needs of the agency. The Peace Corps has proved to be especially innovative and effective in selecting and training its employees.[11]

Field operations of the Peace Corps are administered by a very small staff of full-time employees. Although Peace Corps detachments in the host countries receive support from and operate under the supervision of diplomatic and consular missions, they remain detached administratively. This separation emphasizes the philanthropic and non-political character of Peace Corps activities. But chiefs of mission are responsible for the conduct of Peace Corps programs in the nations to which they are accredited and for supervising the personal conduct of Peace Corps personnel. The bulk of Peace Corps representatives abroad are, of course, volunteers. Volunteer strength on May 31, 1969, stood at 10,861, of whom 10,066 were in service and 795 in training. They represented almost a quarter of the American civilians serving overseas under State Department supervision.

Youthful Peace Corps volunteers become objects of special interest to Foreign Service recruitment officers, and they are encouraged to apply for designation to take the Foreign Service examination or the Federal Service Entrance examination. Successful candidates for the Foreign Service are also deferred, should they wish to enter the Peace Corps for a tour of duty. Peace Corps experience and training patently increases their empathetic capability, linguistic qualifications, and knowledge of foreign affairs processes.

The activities in which Peace Corps vounteers engage cover a tremendous range of educational, social, and economic development projects, usually those requiring little capital investment, but considerable enthusiasm and some modest degree of technical skill not possessed by citizens of the host country. The volunteers have been so well received on the whole, and their work has been so greatly appreciated that other nations have followed the example of the United States and initiated operations resembling those of the Peace Corps. Since imitation is the

---

[11] It made very effective use, for example, of psychological testing. Nevertheless, Congress has refused to appropriate money for such testing to other foreign affairs agencies, including the Department of State.

sincerest form of flattery, this approach to economic and social assistance obviously has demonstrated its worth.

THE ARMS CONTROL AND DISARMAMENT AGENCY

The very small Arms Control and Disarmament Agency (ACDA), located physically in the State Department building, is staffed principally by political appointees, the Civil Service, and the Foreign Service. Its total staff does not exceed one hundred persons, and it is primarily a policy-making and coordinating unit, which functions in close liaison with appropriate bureaus of the department, officers of the White House, and other government agencies. Officials of the agency also attend international conferences and meetings of international organizations in representation of the agency. Since most higher officers of the agency are chosen from the Foreign Service or the department, coordination presents no real problem, and for practical purposes, ACDA operates as another bureau, despite its separate agency status.

OTHER POLITICAL AGENCIES

The Foreign Claims Settlement Commission of the United States collaborates with the Department of State in this very restricted area of political interest. Three interdepartmental committees also share with the department a certain measure of control or influence over the foreign political affairs of the United States and to some extent assist in its coordinative task.

The Advisory Commission on Inter-Governmental Relations includes representatives from municipalities, counties, state legislative bodies, state executives, the Congress, the executive branch, and citizens at large. It has a small permanent staff and meets infrequently, but it provides a channel through which all areas of public opinion can make themselves felt in the administration of American foreign policy.

The Advisory Commission on Information, staffed largely by persons chosen from outside the executive branch, exists principally to give a broader basis to policy decisions of the United States Information Agency.

The Commission on International Rules of Judicial Procedure consists of the principal legal officers of the executive department and prominent attorneys specializing in international law. Like the other broadly based committees, it serves as a consultative group and presumably provides some bases of popular support for executive activities in this area.

12

The National Defense Agencies

Since World War II, national security considerations have weighed enormously, at times preponderantly, in foreign affairs deliberations. National security embraces and is embraced by foreign policy, the servant of national interests, of which national security is the most vital. National security also comprehends military, economic, and civil defense policy. The melding of decisions in these crucially important areas cannot be made in any executive agency but only by the president, who is assisted by the National Security Council, the special assistant for national security affairs, and such other persons as he may select.

Power and war until recently had almost no place in the compartment that American scholars and statesmen reserved for foreign affairs. Geographical position, domestic concerns, and an isolationist policy, made viable by British naval superiority, permitted the United States to dispense with all save token military forces until the end of the nineteenth century. The government built a modern navy at the turn of the century but did not discover a need for a large peacetime army and air force until after World War II. Thus, no major need for the coordination of national security and foreign policy existed in the nineteenth century, and recognition of the fact that military and foreign affairs policy planning would have to be integrated to make both effective dawned very slowly. The Department of State viewed initial War and Navy Department suggestions for the establishment of coordinative machinery as attempts at intrusion into its exclusive domain. In fact, exchanges of letters between the secretaries of the three departments served as the only medium of coordination until the Wilson administration.

During World War I, a Joint State and Navy Neutrality Board emerged to offer coordinated advice on diplomacy and international law, and other conferences and committee meetings began to set patterns of teamwork in areas of common concern. But no permanent machinery came into existence between World War I and 1939. Indeed, the Department of State gave great offense to the Navy Department by its resolute refusal to accord it wider consultative status on naval disarmament matters. Proposals for the establishment of coordinating bodies continued to surface from time to time, but none won adoption.

During World War II, President Roosevelt bypassed the Department of State, and strategic exigencies completely overrode foreign policy considerations. Efforts at coordination did not begin again until 1944, when the president created the State-War-Navy Coordinating Committee (SWNCC) to prepare military government directives and surrender terms. SWNCC soon moved into other areas as well and may thus be regarded as the immediate predecessor of the National Security Council.[1]

The Military-Industrial Complex

President Eisenhower in his final and probably most important statement from the White House warned his countrymen about the tremendous influence of the military bureaucracy and the great industrialists who supply goods and services to the Department of Defense.

[1] For an excellent, far more detailed summary of these developments, see Ernest May, "The Development of Political-Military Consultation in the United States," *Political Science Quarterly*, 70 (June 1955), 161–180.

He spoke in general terms of the danger to our polity inherent in this powerful combination of bureaucratic and private vested interests. His words carried tremendous force not only because of his high office but also because they could not conceivably reflect even the slightest antimilitary or, indeed, antibusiness bias. He did not specifically assert that the military-industrial complex influenced foreign affairs administration, but the importance of the role assigned to it in formulating and administering national security policy would guarantee a substantial overlap into fields shared with foreign affairs, such as disarmament, nuclear testing, control and proliferation, deterrence, estimative intelligence, and the definition and administration of containment policy.

Professor John Kenneth Galbraith argues most convincingly that, while any public or private bureaucracy is guided by "a life and purpose and truth of its own . . . the most spectacular examples of bureaucratic truth are those that serve the military power—and its weapons procurement." They include first, the belief that "the dangers of a continued weapons race with the Soviet Union . . . are less than those of any agreement that offers any . . . opening for violation." Secondly, "the belief that the conflict with Communism is man's ultimate battle. Accordingly, one would not hesitate to destroy all life if Communism seems seriously a threat." Thirdly, "the national interest is total, that of man inconsequential."

Galbraith emphasizes that the complex "is an organization or a complex of organizations and not a conspiracy." He finds that "mutual enrichment" and some graft occur but emphasizes that the conspiracy theory exaggerates the role of the defense industries. "The reality," he suggests, "is a complex of organizations pursuing their sometimes diverse but generally common goals. The participants . . . are mostly honest men."

The complex includes not only the military and specialized defense contractors but also the defense divisions of primarily civilian firms. It also embraces the intelligence agencies, Defense Department research contractors in the universities, and institutions such as Rand, the armed services committees of Congress, and, according to Galbraith, "Foreign Service Officers who provide a civilian or diplomatic gloss to the foreign policy positions which serve the military need."

The country desks, he says, citing Ralph Dungan, are "often strongly influenced by the Pentagon." Galbraith attributes to former Secretary Rusk "a high respect for military acumen and need" and asserts that Rusk "in some degree regarded diplomacy as subordinate to military purpose."[2]

In the writer's view, the Foreign Service generally has resisted rather than collaborated with efforts of the military to influence foreign policy. The extent to which the country desks yield to military influence may reflect their response to guidance from political superiors rather than their own predilections. But undeniably the Pentagon exerts strong influence on foreign policy one way or another.

Indeed, the secretary of defense and his department probably influence American foreign affairs administration more than any other official or agency of the executive establishment, other than the president and his office and the secretary of state and his department. The secretary of defense by statute advises the president and the Congress on national security problems, and he and his colleagues exert strong influence over public opinion as well.

Expenditures on national defense, which absorbed in 1970 about 8 per cent of the GNP and 35 per cent of the budget, have a tremendous impact on both domestic and foreign affairs. The civilian constituency of the Department of Defense embraces not only the managers of defense industries but, less firmly, the vast mass of their shareholders in defense industries. The unprecedented size of the military establishment since World War II has also added an enormous and growing number of active and retired career military personnel to the Defense Department's constituency. Thus, the department can mobilize in behalf of its policies and programs a force capable of exerting enormous pressure on Congress, the mass media, and other spheres of the executive branch, including the presidency.

THE DEPARTMENT OF DEFENSE

Role. Administrative decisions in the Department of Defense,

---

[2] John Kenneth Galbraith, "How to Control the Military," *Harper's Magazine*, 238 (June 1969), 32–46. Permission to quote from this article has been granted by John Kenneth Galbraith.

within limitations imposed by Congress regarding contract allocations, rates of spending, and even, to some extent, the functional and geographic disbursal of its vast resources, give the department and its components enormous leverage in Congress and the executive. Finally, the day-to-day administration of certain programs and facilities (for example, the Military Air Transport Command, which provides transportation to Congressmen, and V.I.P. billets) further enhances the department's capability to influence powerful civilian individuals and groups.

Department decisions on national defense policy affect for good or ill the entire power base upon which the conduct of foreign affairs largely depends. The importance of defense contingency planning would be equally difficult to overestimate because it tends to set irrevocable courses of action and to give excessive weight in some cases to military as opposed to political considerations.[3]

Many Defense Department operational roles bear heavily on foreign affairs administration. Military commanders in combat zones have complete responsibility not only for troop but also for civilian operations. Consequently, they make much foreign policy by interpretation and action. Where Defense Department elements are garrisoned abroad, their presence contributes to the content of political and economic relations with host countries by modifying the local image of the United States and by altering economic and financial relationships. In still other areas, the Department of Defense exercises governmental or occupational responsibilities, for example, in Okinawa, the Bonin Islands, and the Panama Canal Zone. The control of prisoners of war and overseas surveying and engineering duties similarly affect foreign affairs administration. Defense Department officers also advise on settlements of foreign claims and have rendered assistance in international trials of war criminals.

[3] This situation occurs because the military reinsure against all possible military contingencies and overprotect against eventualities. The final result may be to increase, rather than to lessen, danger to the national security by making military victory an end rather than a means. For example, in 1914, the Russian general staff allegedly found itself unable to stop the general mobilization it had ordered in response to Austria's invasion of Serbia. Consequently, Russia could not meet Germany's ultimatum and suffered the catastrophe of World War I.

The Department of Defense and its components engage on a large scale in traditional and new diplomatic activities. These include the stationing of attachés abroad to collect military intelligence, the collection of electronic and cryptographic intelligence for the entire government, the organization and staffing of military advisory groups to conduct military assistance programs, the maintenance of permanent liaison with the International Hydrographic Organization and the International Meteorological Organization, and the assignment of members, advisors, and observers to delegations to disarmament and other international conferences, and to international organizations that engage in activities having national security implications.

The Department of Defense sponsors the National War College, the Industrial College of the Armed Forces, the Armed Forces Staff College, and the Inter-American Defense College. Its three component services operate war colleges, staff schools, and an enormous system of other training facilities. Not only military personnel but also employees of other foreign affairs agencies and of many foreign governments use these facilities. The general public currently receives a limited exposure to the faculties of some defense educational institutions through National Defense Seminars conducted in various localities, through Reserve and National Guard training programs, and through correspondence courses.

Foreign affairs officials who take this training also receive full indoctrination in national defense considerations and military attitudes. Foreign military personnel, many of whom rise to the highest positions,[4] receive not only technical training but conditioning that affects their attitudes toward the United States and its institutions. Defense Department components also train attachés and military government and military assistance personnel, and they conduct extensive language training programs in collaboration with the Foreign Service Institute.

---

[4] Of 305 foreign naval officers who attended the Naval War College between the academic years 1956–1957 and 1968–1969, 104 had attained flag rank by May 1969 and 19 had headed their navies. Others had distinguished themselves in other branches of government or in business (United States, Department of State, *News Letter*, no. 97 [May 1969], pp. 18–19).

All training programs normally include briefings on foreign policy administration.

The Department of Defense not only functions as primary collector and evaluator of intelligence but also plays a role in the Joint Intelligence Board second only to CIA. Officers from the Joint Chiefs of Staff, the army, the navy, and the air force sit on this important board. The Department of Defense, therefore, has four times the numerical representation of the Department of State. Intelligence collection, evaluation, and interpretation by the department and its components support and condition its contingency planning. It contributes most weightily to some presidential decisions with respect to the existence of international crises or opportunities, and it supports department positions in national intelligence estimates. Defense Department research on weapons and weapon systems development obviously has major foreign affairs implications.

Organization. The components of the Defense Department that exercise the greatest influence in foreign affairs administration include the secretary and undersecretary, the Armed Forces Policy Council, the assistant secretary for international security affairs, the assistant secretary for research, the Joint Chiefs of Staff, the Joint Staff and its intelligence unit, the National War College, and the Industrial College of the Armed Forces.

Each of the three service departments influences foreign affairs administration in varying degrees through its secretary, undersecretary, international affairs component, legislative liaison office, training facilities, judicial facilities, intelligence organization, public information section, and research units. Each also has special organizations[5] that engage in activities having foreign affairs content or implications.

Overseas elements of the Department of Defense and its components include attachés at diplomatic missions, military assistance advis-

---

[5] Such components of the Department of the Army include the director of Civil Defense, the National Security Administration, the Corps of Engineers (which is responsible for international surveys, mapping, and canal routes), and the Provost Marshal General (who is responsible for prisoners of war). The Department of the Air Force, among other specialized units, incorporates the Office of the Assistant General Counsel for International Civil Aviation.

ory groups, joint United States military groups (which supervise the construction and operation of military bases abroad), garrisons in countries where the United States has obligations to maintain forces, surveying and engineering units in Latin America and elsewhere, personnel assigned to international organizations and conferences, troops engaged in occupation and civil government duties, and, at present, operational forces in Vietnam.

In addition to military personnel, the Department of Defense employs tens of thousands of American civilians overseas to operate its billets, dependent schools, messes, post exchanges, commissaries, the Panama Canal, civil governments, and other facilities, or to construct new facilities. Postwar expansion of the department's civilian component abroad vastly increased the American presence in many nations, with a consequent major impact on the American image.

The Department of Defense also employs masses of alien civilians in its facilities and in construction projects. Its relationships with local employees do much to set the tone for American diplomatic relations with the host countries, especially in countries such as Korea, Panama, Japan, Vietnam, and West Germany, where they are employed in such relatively large numbers and where national sensibilities are so vitally involved.

Military and civilian personnel of the department, because they so greatly outnumber other official American representatives abroad, contribute preponderantly to the formation of foreign attitudes toward the United States. The impact of all overseas military operations on foreigners' knowledge of or beliefs about American military capabilities probably exercises far more influence in determining their orientation toward the United States than the Department of State, AID, and USIA exert conjointly.

Military outnumber civilian employees of the Department of Defense by a ratio of about three to one,[6] but the influence of these

---

[6] On January 1, 1966, all Defense Department and Defense Department component civilian employees totalled 1,057,482 (United States, Congress, Senate, Committee on Government Operations, *Organization of Federal Executive Departments and Agencies*, Report No. 26, 89th Cong., 2d sess., April 25, 1966). At that time military forces in being exceeded three million men and women.

civilian employees on foreign affairs administration may well equal or exceed that of their military colleagues because they staff the highest positions in the department, dominate its international security, electronic intelligence, and research components, and head the service departments.

Military officers, who normally spend about 10 per cent of their peacetime duty at in-service training, have, in recent years and especially at staff and war colleges, received considerable training in world politics. Many have also had attaché or other foreign affairs duty or have participated in exchange programs with civilian foreign affairs agencies. Consequently, the level of political sophistication of senior military officers has risen notably since World War II, while civilian thinking on foreign policy has been influenced increasingly by defense considerations. Thus the gap between military and civilian thinking on foreign affairs has narrowed somewhat, and the military approach to a political solution no longer results inevitably in the perversion of force into an end rather than a means. Indeed, some high military leaders appear to be quite as persuaded of the need to limit warfare as are their civilian colleagues.

THE ATOMIC ENERGY COMMISSION

The Atomic Energy Commission (AEC) plays a very important role in national security policy but a far more modest one in foreign affairs administration. Within its own domain, nevertheless, it both makes and vetoes foreign policy.

AEC's interests in foreign affairs focus primarily on intelligence about foreign nuclear capabilities, international negotiations involving peaceful uses of atomic energy or the control of atomic weapons, and the activities of the International Atomic Energy Organization and Euratom. The possibility that AEC's research teams may change the course or content of defense, or foreign policy, or both, by achieving breakthroughs in the peaceful or military uses of atomic energy remains constantly before us.

Its assistant general manager for international activities, Division of Intelligence, and Office of Congressional Relations discharge most of its foreign affairs responsibilities and probably exert the most direct influence on the rest of the foreign affairs community.

The Federal Aviation Administration and the National Aeronautics and Space Administration

The respective responsibilities of the Federal Aviation Administration (FAA) and the National Aeronautics and Space Administration (NASA) for civil aviation and the use of outer space involve them deeply in national defense and foreign policy, not least through the tremendous potentialities of their gigantic research programs. Daily these roles grow more important and probably will continue to do so. FAA and NASA draw their staffs from the Civil Service, except in a few policy-making positions that are filled by political appointees. They have personnel exchange agreements with the Departments of State and Defense under which a few Foreign Service officers and a considerable number of military officers serve them. Both collaborate with the Department of State to assure that experts, usually commissioned as reserve officers, staff civil air attaché and other appropriate positions in missions abroad. FAA and NASA also provide personnel for delegations to international conferences and meetings of international organizations concerned with international civil aviation or outer space respectively.

Defense Materials Service of General Services Administration

Defense Materials Service, through foreign purchasing and stockpile management, influences not only the economic defense capability of the United States but also its relations with countries supplying critical commodities to the United States. The timing and volume of purchases, the selection of suppliers, and the manner in which the Defense Materials Service turns over or disposes of stockpiled commodities all have important foreign affairs implications. Civil servants staff the General Services Administration and its components. The foreign purchasing activities of the Defense Materials Service do not normally require the permanent residence abroad of its employees in peacetime.

13

Other Departments and Agencies

THE ECONOMIC AGENCIES

The Treasury Department. Historically the Treasury Department became the first agency of the executive branch, other than the Departments of State, War, and Navy, to send officers overseas. Before the middle of the nineteenth century, it sent inspectors abroad to audit collections of consular fees and later to check on the accuracy of consular invoices. But it was not until this century that the Treasury Department began to develop a major interest in foreign affairs administration.

Its principal roles derive from its responsibility for setting or recommending policy on the medium of exchange, taxation (including the customs tariff), the balance of trade, the balance of payments, and the public debt, which gives it a keen interest in international interest rates. Treasury Department interests likewise embrace the traffic in narcotics and counterfeiting. Its responsibility for the security of the chief of state involves it in counterespionage.

The secretary of the treasury occupies a position of enormous prestige, and the wide range of his domestic responsibilities normally assures him frequent access to the president. When strong personal ties exist between the chief of state and the secretary of the treasury, as in the case of President Roosevelt and Secretary Morgenthau or President Eisenhower and Secretary Humphrey, the secretary's influence in foreign and domestic affairs tends to expand and sometimes to overlap jurisdictions of other departments or agencies.

Treasury Department components that exercise major influence on foreign economic policy include the Office of the Undersecretary for Monetary Affairs, the Office of the General Counsel, the Internal Revenue Service (IRS), the Bureau of Customs, the Bureau of Narcotics, the Secret Service, the Bureau of the Public Debt, the Office of International Finance, and the National Advisory Council on International Monetary and Financial Problems.

Permanent overseas representatives of the Treasury Department include investigators of the Bureau of Narcotics, who cooperate with foreign police authorities in frustrating the activities of international narcotics rings, and attachés stationed at major embassies, who engage primarily in international financial and monetary reporting but who also participate in representational work and in negotiations of concern to their agency. The Treasury Department also sends abroad on temporary missions representatives of the Internal Revenue Service to help American and foreign civilians prepare income tax returns; provides personnel for American delegations to international organizations and conferences on financial, taxation, and monetary matters; and sends representatives of the Secret Service abroad to prepare for and accompany the president on foreign visits.

The Treasury Department shares several of its roles with other departments and agencies, particularly the Federal Reserve Board, the Controller of the Currency, the Tariff Commission, and the FBI. It is often difficult to determine where its mandate runs, but in the areas delimited above it is always consulted by the Department of State and normally exercises preponderant influence.

The Department of Commerce. The Department of Commerce, although it is of relatively recent creation, was the first department seriously to challenge the State Department monopoly of foreign affairs administration. It established its own foreign service before World War II and asserted preeminence in important areas of foreign economic policy at home. The Foreign Commerce Service merged with the Foreign Service in 1939, and relations between the Departments of State and Commerce today seem to be amicable and well regulated by interdepartmental agreement. The Department of Commerce maintains a few officials abroad, but with full State Department approval and clearance. It participates fully in the selection, training, and promotion of Foreign Service officers assigned to commercial duties.

The Department of Commerce's primary interest and responsibility in the administration of foreign economic affairs has always been, and continues to be, the expansion and protection of American foreign commerce. It also collects and exchanges meteorological, geodetic, census, and standards data.

Commerce Department components that engage most actively in the promotion of exports include the regional, commodity, and functional offices under the assistant secretary for international affairs, especially the Office of International Trade Affairs. The department also maintains regional offices throughout the United States to assist businessmen to enter or participate more effectively in export trade. Commerce Department components with peripheral or secondary interest in the administration of foreign economic affairs include the Patent Office, the Bureau of Standards, the Coast and Geodetic Survey, the Weather Bureau, the Bureau of the Census, and the Business and Defense Services Administration. Since World War II, a few Foreign Service officers have been assigned to export promotion units for operational duties, training, and liaison.

Since the merger of the Foreign Commerce Service with the Foreign Service in 1939, the Department of Commerce has not maintained a field service, but during the Kennedy administration it sent a few officers abroad to promote tourism to the United States. These officers receive administrative support from the Foreign Service but maintain offices apart from mission and consular establishments. From time to time the department also sends overseas representatives of its international expositions unit to help mount American exhibits at trade fairs and other expositions. Under the terms of the current State-

Commerce Department agreement, the Department of Commerce nominates Civil Service and other experts to the Department of State for appointment as reserve officers to serve as commercial attachés at key missions, but Foreign Service employees perform the preponderance of commercial functions in the field. The Department of Commerce, in turn, participates in the selection and promotion of Foreign Service officers and in the deliberations of the Board of Foreign Service.

The Department of Agriculture. The Department of Agriculture, like the Department of Commerce, challenged the Department of State's monopoly of foreign affairs administration at home and abroad early in this century. It established a Foreign Agricultural Service, which, like the Foreign Commerce Service merged with the Foreign Service in 1939, but unlike it, re-emerged in 1954. The components of the Department of Agriculture that concern themselves primarily with foreign affairs include those administering the Foreign Agricultural Service, commodity divisions, policy research and training divisions, and a management office embracing, among other units, the foreign market information division. A few Foreign Service officers fill on-the-job training assignments in the Department of Agriculture.

The department's foreign interests include promotion of the sale abroad of American agricultural commodities, arranging for the overseas sale or distribution of surplus agricultural commodities owned by the federal government, the size and allocation of foreign quotas for the importation of cane sugar, the collection of information about foreign agricultural developments, participation in the work of international organizations and conferences, collaboration in overseas technical assistance programs, the provision of assistance to neighboring countries to enable them to control or eliminate plant or animal plagues that threaten the United States, and the administration of an effective plant and animal quarantine system (sometimes with protectionist rather than sanitary motives).

The Department of Agriculture sends abroad officers of its Foreign Agricultural Service (FAS), who have Civil Service status, to staff sections in certain missions and consulates where agricultural reporting or negotiating requirements are exceptionally heavy. It also fields Civil Service employees for technical assistance or plague control programs.

The technical assistance people usually are detailed to AID, but the plague control personnel normally reside abroad under special agreements with host governments. In all cases, the Foreign Service provides administrative support.

Functions of agricultural attachés include reporting, negotiation, and representation. Representatives of The Department of Agriculture also serve on delegations to international conferences and organizations concerned with agricultural problems. At posts where the FAS is not represented, the Foreign Service continues to discharge all the functions that it performed for the Department of Agriculture between 1939 and 1953.

The Department of the Interior. The influence of the Department of Interior on foreign economic policy derives partly from its responsibilities to protect and develop water and power resources, including research on the critically important problem of desalinization of sea water. Its efforts to protect migratory fish and wildlife resources involve it with Japan, the Soviet Union, Canada, and Mexico and with other Atlantic and Pacific powers when questions of the protection of oceanic aquatic life arise. The Department of the Interior also regulates imports of foreign petroleum and has a major interest in the volume of minerals imports and exports. A minor but interesting function of the department is its sponsorship of the Board on Geographic Names.

Components of the department primarily engaged in foreign economic activities include those which function under the assistant secretaries for mineral resources, fish and wildlife, and water and power. The department once had a small overseas service of minerals attachés, but it merged with the Foreign Service in 1943. The department requests a considerable volume of reporting from the Foreign Service and influences appointments of petroleum and minerals attachés at a few posts.

The Department of Transportation. The Department of Transportation unites a number of previously independent agencies with bureaus of old-line departments, including the Federal Aviation Administration, the St. Lawrence Seaway Development Corporation, the Federal Railroad Administration, the Federal Highway Administration, and the Coast Guard. Its foreign affairs interests embrace international transportation problems of the United States, foreign transportation developments, the law of the sea, safety at sea, and the provision of technical assistance in highway and other transportation fields.

It has no overseas field organization but considerable reporting requirements, which the Foreign Service discharges. Its representatives attend international conferences and organization meetings on transportation matters; and it influences appointments by the Department of State of attachés at posts where the volume of transportation reporting, negotiation, and representation work may warrant. The Coast Guard operates frequently outside territorial waters and polices territorial waters. It also participates in the International Iceberg Patrol.

Independent Economic Agencies. Several independent agencies play restricted occasional roles in the administration of foreign economic affairs. Like the Treasury Department, the Board of Governors of the Federal Reserve System, by manipulating the rediscount rate, affects international interest rates and capital movement. The Export-Import Bank authorizes credits in support of certain economic aid programs. In its conventional role of financing American exports, it greatly assists the trade promotional efforts of the Department of Commerce. The Tariff Commission, through decisions on classifications and rates applicable to various imports, advances or hinders programs of trade liberalization. The Federal Communications, Maritime, Power, and Trade Commissions, working within the areas of their specific responsibilities, also affect the foreign relations of the United States incidentally to discharging their domestic roles. These independent agencies for the most part do not maintain permanent staffs abroad, but they occasionally send employees overseas on special missions or as representatives to meetings of international agencies or conferences. The Foreign Service meets their reporting requirements.

The Social and Service Agencies

Social and service roles tend to cut across the boundaries of political and economic affairs. Indeed, most activities in international relations impinge upon each other. The allocation of departments and agencies to this and other categories, therefore, has been made with reference to their primary fields of interest but with full recognition that much overlap exists, that nothing done in any foreign affairs area fails to have an impact directly or indirectly on all other fields, and that most agencies play roles outside their major areas of interest.

The Department of Justice. The Department of Justice, while primarily oriented toward areas of domestic social concern, also engages in counterespionage intelligence and other activities having a direct impact on political and economic foreign relations. The Department of Justice admits, deports, and controls resident aliens, incarcerating those convicted on federal charges. Its roles also include the apprehension of international criminals, administration of alien property, extradition of foreign criminals, and enforcement of antitrust legislation.

The components of the Department of Justice engaged in the preceding activities include the Immigration and Naturalization Service, the Border Patrol, the Board of Immigration Appeals, the Bureau of Prisons, the Federal Bureau of Investigation (FBI), the Office of Alien Property, the Office of the Attorney General, and the Antitrust Division.

The FBI staffs legal sections of missions and consular establishments abroad, where it cooperates with foreign police and Interpol in the apprehension and extradition of international criminals and conducts counterespionage intelligence. The Immigration and Naturalization Service also stations a few officers abroad at certain diplomatic and consular posts to assist the Foreign Service to find solutions to abstruse immigration and visitors visa problems and to monitor the return of visiting aliens.

The Department of Labor. The Department of Labor determines the need for foreign transient and immigrant labor in the United States. This role gives the department effective control over the movement of certain categories of aliens, especially from Mexico and the Caribbean. The Department of Labor also conducts research on foreign labor movements, maintains liaison with foreign labor leaders, assists American labor leaders to establish appropriate contacts abroad, and sends representatives to meetings of the International Labor Organization.

The Office of International Labor Affairs manages these activities. A few Foreign Service officers are usually assigned to it for on-the-job training. The Department of Labor is represented on the Board of Examiners for the Foreign Service, the Board of the Foreign Service, and on Foreign Service selection boards. It does not maintain a field service, but it nominates to the Department of State qualified persons for appointment as labor attachés in countries where labor activities are sufficiently important to warrant such representation. In other nations the Foreign Service meets the Department of Labor's reporting requirements.

The Department of Health, Education, and Welfare. The Department of Health, Education, and Welfare (HEW) discharges a disparate variety of foreign affairs roles. It has an enormous potential role in the International Education Act, but Congress has not yet appropriated funds for activities envisaged thereunder. Three components of HEW discharge its present responsibilities.

The Office of Education, through the assistant commissioner for international education, collects and exchanges data about educational developments and administers the exchange of persons program for educational personnel.

The Public Health Service (PHS), through the Divisions of International Health and Foreign Quarantine participates in international medical and sanitary activities and enforces quarantine and sanitary regulations. PHS provides medical officers to many embassies and consulates who assist in the medical examination of applicants for immigration visas, help enforce quarantine and sanitary regulations, serve as deputy science advisors, and function as medical advisors to the Foreign Service establishments. PHS also sends personnel to meetings of the World Health Organization (WHO) and to international health conferences.

The Social Security Administration has many foreign pensioners on its rolls. It forwards their checks through the Department of State. The Foreign Service distributes the pension checks and conducts investigations, as staff permits, to assure that the beneficiaries are still alive. The administration also sends teams to the field occasionally to assist in such investigations.

Other Social and Service Agencies. The International Service Division of the Post Office Department's Bureau of Transportation conducts negotiations with foreign carriers and foreign postal services. The department also sends representatives to meetings of the International Postal Union (IPU).

The Veteran's Administration, like the Social Security Administration, has many foreign pensioners on its rolls, and it, too, relies normally on the Foreign Service to distribute checks and conduct investigations. It also sends representatives abroad from time to time to assist in this activity.

The American Battle Monuments Commission, unlike most independent agencies, maintains a fairly large staff of foreign employees, both American and local. On January 1, 1966, 437 employees of the commission served overseas in the improvement or conservation of battle monuments and cemeteries where American veterans are buried. Employees of the commission are supported administratively by the Foreign Service.

Agencies and Boards with Peripheral International Interests

Many of the scores of independent agencies, boards, and commissions predominantly engaged in domestic activities, exercise peripheral but significant influence on the administration of foreign policy in narrow functional or geographic sectors.

Decisions of the Canal Zone Government, for example, affect political relations not only with Panama but also with other nations of Latin America. The Subversive Activities Control Board conditions relations with states that sponsor subversive activities in the United States. Operations of the Selective Service System and the Federal Civil Defense Administration also affect political policy and relations at times.

Activities of the Panama Canal Company, the Securities and Exchange Commission, and the Mexican-American Boundary Commission influence the course of both political and economic foreign relations. Many social and service institutions and agencies likewise exert peripheral influence, including the American National Red Cross, the

Gorgas Memorial Institute, the National Academy of Sciences, the National Science Foundation, the National Research Council, the Smithsonian Institution, and the Interdepartmental Committee on Scientific Research and Development.

14

State and Local Governments

The Constitution entrusts the conduct of foreign relations exclusively to the federal government, but state and local authorities influence foreign affairs administration significantly, sometimes directly, usually indirectly. The vertical separation of powers at the federal, state, and local levels and the triple system of checks and balances at each level inevitably result in jurisdictional overlap and confusion, even where definitions of responsibility are relatively clear.

The Educational Role

The most important influence of state and local governments on foreign affairs administration derives from their control over public education. No other great power delegates such enormous influence over the minds of its citizens to its states, provinces, or other subdivisions, and it is precisely from this difference that much of the uniqeness of American foreign affairs administration and foreign policy derives. Each of the states sets the curriculum in its public schools, and most of them prescribe the texts as well. State authorities also set professional standards for teachers, and for other professional practitioners, including medical doctors, lawyers, and dentists. The officials who perform these functions usually act under strong legislative directives or influence.

County and municipal authorities administer the public primary and secondary schools and many junior colleges. They also select textbooks, to the extent that they are not prescribed or provided by the states, and they engage teachers and local school administrators. Thus, state and local authorities determine what goes into the heads of all primary, secondary, college, and university students who do not attend parochial or private institutions. State standards, moreover, exert a strong influence in the private educational sector. Consequently, the vast majority of Americans receive all their formal instruction about foreign countries, international affairs, civics, civic responsibilities, and political theory[1] from systems organized, operated, or dominated by state and local officials. Most of these officials usually have no great knowledge or experience even of national affairs, and virtually all of them lack training and experience in international relations.

It would be astounding if the end products of American public education did not often reflect regional and particularist limitations and attitudes. Indeed, it is amazing that the public has supported so many costly international programs since World War II, especially since Congress does not permit foreign affairs agencies to engage in major campaigns to enlighten the public on international issues. Thus, after a quarter of a century of world commitment, the American public still has little conception of the limits of foreign policy, many illusions about the general efficacy and utility of planning and policy making, and dangerous delusions about the ability of the United States to control events outside its own borders.

Such enlightenment as exists emanates from private institutions and those few public school systems that have been able to overcome most of their regional and national parochialism. Some scholars and publicists, operating through the mass media, also exert a broadening influence on the general public. But these sources of enlightenment

[1] For example, convictions about the general applicability and value elsewhere of the ill-defined American way of life.

do not remedy all the deficiencies of the educational system. The system remains much too weak to provide a basis of public understanding broad enough to give statesmen the flexibility they need to administer the nation's foreign policy as dynamically as the times require.

Impact of Police and Judicial Powers

The police and judicial powers of state and local authorities extend to resident and visiting aliens as well as American citizens. The treatment that aliens receive from local authorities conditions their attitudes and those of their mother countries to the United States and at times affects the course of international relations. Discrimination against Mexicans by certain state and local officials long constituted one of the most serious obstacles to a *rapprochement* between Mexico and the United States, and it still causes resentment from time to time. Discrimination against Japanese and Chinese aliens in California and elsewhere helped to complicate relations with China and Japan.

The lack of a national police force greatly enhances the capability of local enforcement and judicial agencies to influence the administration of foreign affairs because most federal statutes and regulations must be enforced by state and local authorities. This permits, among other things, continued local discrimination against minorities in education, housing, employment, and law enforcement. The effects on foreigners of nonobservance and violations of federal law, including constitutional law, are profound. Most of them do not understand the complexities of a federal system and tend to view American declarations about liberty, equality, democracy, and nondiscrimination as hypocritical and fraudulent. Moreover, the vast majority of the world's peoples, who are brown, black, red, yellow, or of mixed blood, doubly resent such apparent misrepresentation. The impact of the credibility gap thus created on foreign policy administration probably requires no illustration.

The lack of a national police also makes local and state authorities responsible for maintenance of public order—for the prevention of crime, the apprehension and punishment of most criminals, the prevention of unlawful assembly, and rioting. Since local and state police forces are of uneven capability in terms of size, equipment, and training, some fall down disastrously at times in discharging these responsibilities, and some commit abuses. Uneven standards tend to create totally erroneous conceptions abroad about the national unity and purpose of the United States and its ability to organize and utilize its vast power. Police or judicial abuses committed on aliens result, of course, in protests and sometimes in the impairment of relations.[2]

Impact of Legislative Powers

States and localities often influence foreign affairs administration through their legislative activities. Municipal and county zoning regulations, especially in the Washington area, greatly complicate the task of the Department of State in finding suitable accomodations for diplomats of color. These regulations have unquestionably had an adverse effect on the attitudes of such diplomats, their governments, and their peoples. Miscegenation laws and other discriminatory state legislation affect foreign attitudes adversely.

In contrast, state laws and local ordinances promoting international trade fairs and expositions, or international trade and cooperation programs, sometimes have a beneficial influence abroad. The creation of good neighbor commissions by border states to combat discriminatory practices and promote international cooperation, and the mounting of international expositions at Chicago, San Francisco, New York, Seattle, Philadelphia, San Antonio, and elsewhere presumably have had favorable results. California has even engaged in an international development program in collaboration with Chile, and many municipalities have joined in AID's sister city program.

State agricultural, petroleum, and mining laws regulating production or prices have a direct impact on economic and political relations.

State and local tax measures sometimes conflict with the provisions of consular conventions or encroach on diplomatic immunities guaranteed by international law. In such cases, they engender consular and diplomatic protests and often require the intervention of the Department of State or recourse to the federal courts to set matters right.

[2] See John B. McConaughy, "International Law as Practiced in State Courts," *South Carolina Law Quarterly*, 10 (Winter 1958), 189–224, for a much more detailed and authoritative discussion of this subject.

Impact of Executive Action

Executive officials of states and localities influence the course of international relations through their actions and attitudes. Their warmth or coldness in receiving alien visitors in their jurisdictions can promote international harmony or cause serious diplomatic incidents.[3] Ill-considered statements by state or local officials that wound the sensibilities of foreign dignitaries or nations cause resentments that enhance the difficulties of federal foreign affairs administrators.[4] State executives initiate extradition proceedings for crimes committed in their states by aliens or American citizens residing abroad. They also cooperate with federal authorities in extraditing Americans or foreigners who have committed crimes elsewhere in the United States or abroad. As heads of the enforcement agencies of their states, they set the tone for the enforcement of both federal and state legislation and the manner in which enforcement is undertaken.

[3] The withdrawal in June 1966 by Mayor John V. Lindsay of New York of a luncheon invitation to King Feisal of Saudi Arabia because of pressure from Zionists caused serious repercussions throughout the Arab world.

[4] Attacks on the person of the British sovereign by the mayor of Chicago, the late "Big Bill" Thompson, during the twenties caused considerable ill feeling in the United Kingdom and the Dominions.

15

Other Influences

The relative importance and totality of influence on foreign affairs administration of the American public and of alien elements cannot be measured accurately. Some tentative impressions will be offered in the hope that they may stimulate more research in depth in these interesting but difficult areas.[1]

THE GENERAL PUBLIC

Political parties, the mass media, and pressure groups probably exert more influence on day-to-day administration of foreign affairs than does the public at large. This may also be true for the long term, but the role of the individual as a voter, and especially as an independent, ticket-splitting, or bolting voter should not be underestimated in try-

[1] Gabriel Almond and a few other students have undertaken pioneering research on public participation in foreign policy administration. But much monographic work will have to be done before categorical statements can be offered about either the relative importance of various public sectors, their exact relationships to governmental participants, or their influence on foreign relations.

ing to weigh the factors that determine major trends. The presidential elections of 1920, 1952, 1960, 1964, and 1968 all offered broad but definite choices on the direction of foreign policy to the electorate, and its decisions clearly had recognizable impact on foreign affairs administration under Presidents Harding, Coolidge, Einsenhower, Kennedy, Johnson, and Nixon. The elections of 1916 and 1940 also offered foreign policy issues; but external circumstances compelled both Presidents Wilson and Roosevelt to disregard their pledges to keep the nation out of war, and the public supported them enthusiastically in the event.

In addition to voting, the general public exercises the rights of free speech, petition, and assembly to influence foreign affairs administrators, although with considerably less effect, because on major issues it seldom displays broad enough consensus to move the official community. Nevertheless, letters and personal appeals to congressmen and executive officials do receive consideration and sometimes elicit favorable action, especially if they only relate to individual protection, passport, pension, or visa cases. Mass protests usually are not spontaneous, but unaligned individuals are sometimes drawn into demonstrations organized by pressure groups. Such activities rarely exert much positive influence on the administration of foreign affairs and may even consolidate support for administration policy when they seem to threaten law and order.

Since World War II, the general public has exerted an incalculable but significant influence on foreign attitudes and actions through the personal contacts of American citizens with foreigners. Millions of American servicemen have been stationed abroad for periods of several months to several years; and the number of bureaucrats, tourists, students, businessmen, employees of American corporations, and retirees visiting and residing abroad has risen sensationally. The impact of these hordes of visitors on their hosts and on foreign affairs generally has not yet been studied as thoroughly as the phenomenon warrants.

Unquestionably it caused a large dollar outflow, which has now required the adoption of restrictive foreign capital export policies by the United States. Conversely, the contribution these dollars have made to other economies has been largely beneficial, except in the special situations of wartime Korea and Vietnam where the dollar deluge also brought dangerous inflation.

It is also evident that the flood of visiting and resident Americans has helped to change foreign attitudes toward their own way of life, and toward the United States. This is especially true in the new, developing counties, but also in some ancient states with relatively low living standards. The spectacle of embassy secretaries and military noncommissioned officers driving large automobiles and living in quarters that only the most prosperous levels of society can afford to occupy unquestionably raised popular desires and expectations in Greece, Spain, Italy, and other nations. The sight of American citizens in the flesh enjoying luxuries seen before only in photographs or over television obviously has greater impact than a media acquaintanceship. The effect is compounded when the persons obviously do not belong to the American power structure. Thus, the presence overseas of so many millions of Americans has contributed importantly to generating expectations, and those, in turn, complicate the problems of all foreign affairs administrators.

The conduct of Americans abroad has been no more naïve or boorish than that of tourists from other nations, despite the many jibes and ill-humored caricatures that have appeared in foreign newspapers and journals. The number of serious incidents abroad involving American servicemen has not been disproportionate, and their adverse effects have been minimized by prompt and usually fair settlements of claims against the military. Nevertheless, the net public relations consequences of the presence abroad of such a multitude of Americans must be assessed in light of the World War II British comment on the American soldier in Great Britain: "There is nothing wrong with the Americans,—except that they are over-sexed, over-paid, and over here!"

It would be absurd to assume that any nation could send so many of its citizens abroad in so short a period without causing friction, incidents, and some damage to its image. But the preceding comments are not intended to demonstrate that the effect of the presence of multitudes of Americans overseas has on balance been bad or in any case that it could or should have been avoided. The intention, rather, has been to suggest that it affected the administration of foreign affairs.

No one can deny that the economic benefits to some foreign countries, derived from tourism and from the garrisoning of American troops, have represented the critical difference between national bankruptcy and relative solvency, or that American forces protected Western Europe, South Korea, South Vietnam, Taiwan, and Japan from actual or probable conquest or takeover. Moreover, to the extent that Americans overseas have broadened their knowledge of the problems of foreign countries, prepared themselves for work in foreign affairs, or even to vote more intelligently, such experience has also been reflected in the course of foreign affairs administration. Consequently any growth of tensions attributable to the American presence abroad must be accepted as the price of the benefits derived therefrom.

THE MASS MEDIA

Newspapers, periodicals, and books and the people who write them probably exert more direct and continuous influence on foreign affairs administrators than do the television and radio industries. Most of the key officers of the Department of State and other agencies begin the day by scanning the *New York Times* and the *Washington Post.* They read James Reston, Arthur Krock, and Art Buchwald, and they view Herblock's cartoons with keen interest and appreciation, although not necessarily with approval. They read Jack Anderson in the devout hope that they will not find their names in his column. Publications such as *Foreign Affairs, Harper's Magazine, The New Yorker*, and *Commentary* are also read widely by decision makers in foreign affairs agencies. Analysts such as Richard Rovere, Walter Lippman, and Walter Millis command respectful attention. Books by academic authorities, such as Arthur M. Schlesinger, Jr., Henry Wriston, Dexter Perkins, Bernard Brodie, James McCamy, and many other scholars unquestionably influence actions and policy. While it is quite impossible to determine the extent to which publications and their authors influence decision making, it seems abundantly clear that sensitivity to press comment or to possible academic literary reactions serves to limit, define, or preclude action in many cases and to stimulate it in perhaps fewer instances.

American foreign newspaper correspondents work closely with reporting officers of missions and consulates. They have access to social classes and categories of data that official representatives of the United States government cannot explore. Conversely, diplomatic and consular officers are privy to some intelligence sources not accessible to journalists. Consequently, within the limits of security regulations, much exchanging of impressions and data takes place between responsible foreign correspondents and diplomatic and consular officers to their mutual advantage, the good of the public service, and the enlightenment of the public.

The extent to which publications influence public, as contrasted with official, opinion on foreign affairs is harder to assess. The voters at times have shown themselves to be indifferent to a preponderance of journalistic opinion. Journals overwhelmingly opposed Presidents Franklin Roosevelt and Harry Truman but this did not prevent their success at the polls. Editorial influence normally is vitiated because journalists usually tend largely to cancel each other out. If 40 per cent of the publications favor, for example, isolationism, and 60 per cent favor involvement, the net weight of influence exerted in favor of involvement will be represented by the differential rather than by the majority. Such a differential may or may not be significant enough in the face of other influences to move public opinion.

The existence of a free press means that foreign affairs administrators must often withhold from correspondents information that they regard as potentially harmful to the national interest if released prematurely. This process impairs their relations with the press and sometimes with the public. The national interest and journalistic free enterprise conflict at times because the press thrives on sensation whereas the successful progress of diplomatic negotiations depends on the maintenance of a prolonged atmosphere of calm and privacy, followed by mutual concessions. The premature disclosure of negotiating terms or the undue excitement of nationalistic sentiments tends to harden positions and preclude successful negotiation. The publication of operational plans or policies prematurely may also deprive them of their potential efficacy. These disadvantages must be accepted by all nations as the price that must be paid for the inestimable boon of a free press.

Television and radio probably have less impact on decision makers, although a few editorial commentators, such as Walter Cronkite, Eric Sevareid, the late Edward Murrow, David Brinkley, and Howard K. Smith are listened to with respect, as are such programs as "Meet the Press." But television and radio may be more effective in influencing mass opinion. They provide the preident, the secretary of state, other major figures responsible for foreign affairs administration, and their critics media for reaching many more voters in a much more personal and persuasive way than they might hope to do through the journalistic press or on a speaking tour. The masses do not read political addresses or public policy statements, and only a small percentage can be reached by a personal speaking tour. But they may listen to a radio or a television speech by a public figure, especially if it replaces a motion picture or an athletic contest. Consequently, the impact of these media on the general public probably exceeds that of newspapers, which always offer the distractions of comics and a sports section and which in any case cannot reach the many functional illiterates. Such influence normally validates or supports the administration's foreign policy because the president has virtually unlimited access to the air and his critics do not.

Overseas, a few radio and television correspondents collaborate with diplomatic and consular officers in exchanging information, as do foreign newspaper correspondents, but their numbers are fewer and the exchanges normally are less significant.

Freedom of the air brings conflicts of interests between foreign affairs administrators and media representatives, but these conflicts are less serious than the those between foreign administrators and journalists because of the greater preoccupation of newspapers with gathering news first-hand and the substantial reliance of radio and television on press services.

Political Parties

Political parties traditionally have played a significant role in helping the general public discover its views on major issues of foreign policy. Presidential campaign slogans, such as "Fifty-Four Forty or

Fight," "He kept Us Out of War," and "I will end the war in Korea," illustrate how parties have exploited foreign affairs issues for political purposes.

But party discipline within the Congress strengthened the role of the executive in foreign affairs and also of the party leader, as contrasted with congressional and local party officials. The advent of congressional bipartisanship and the declining importance of political appointments to foreign affairs positions further diminished partisan influence. The increasing volume and complexity of foreign affairs and the corresponding need for a tremendous volume of intelligence also reduced substantially the role that political parties can and do play in foreign affairs administration.

Governor Nelson A. Rockefeller commented recently on the declining role of the political party, which he attributed to the growing technical information gap between bureaucracies and leadership and to leadership's lack of capacity both to absorb such information and to transmit it to the public. He concluded, "it is not surprising that more and more voters feel frustrated. Political parties, traditionally the strongest links between the electorate and the government, are losing their hold. The proportion of voters unaffiliated with either party is increasing, and indications are that those who are affiliated tend to cross party lines more and more often."[2]

To conclude, the major parties, during congressional and especially presidential elections tend to seize upon major foreign policy issues and to exploit them for partisan purposes, although perhaps more responsibly today than was the case when major blunders in this area were not irreparable.

Pressure Groups

American Corporations. A few score American industrial corporations play major foreign affairs roles because of the magnitude of their overseas operations and the critical importance of such operations to host countries or to the United States. Recently large and middle-ranking American banks have vastly extended their overseas operations as

---

[2] Nelson A. Rockefeller, "Policy and the People," *Foreign Affairs*, 46 (January 1968), 235.

well, although this development has attracted little public and no scholarly attention.

Gigantic Standard Oil of New Jersey controls the production of approximately five million barrels of crude petroleum per day, about half in the Western Hemisphere and half in the Middle East. In Venezuela and the Middle East its policies have tremendous impact on the economic and political well-being of local governments and on the course of their relations with the United States.[3] Other major oil companies play similar roles, and the great automobile, electrical equipment, computer, and farm machinery manufacturers also produce and sell all over the world.

However, the heaviest concentration of American investment is in Western Europe. So important has it become to Western Europe's economy that one student has suggested that in fifteen years the world's third industrial power, after the United States and the Soviet Union, will be not Western Europe but American industry in Europe.[4] The

[3] In its issue of December 29, 1967, *Time* ("The Long-Term View from the 29th Floor," pp. 56–59, 63) described ESSO as likely to be involved in "everything from a Middle East coup to whether Jersey should eventually construct a 1,000,000 ton supertanker or what the President of the U. S. has on his mind." It credited ESSO with eighty-five years of experience in foreign operations, 150,000 employees, 750,000 stockholders, $3.8 billion in assets, and annual earnings, as last reported, of $1.1 billion on sales of $13.6 billions. According to *Time*, 52 per cent of ESSO's assets are foreign, and it operates through 300 subsidiaries. It has 126 vessels under fourteen flags, supplies 65,000 service stations, and markets its products in over 100 nations.

[4] John Diebold, "Is the GAP Technological?" *Foreign Affairs*, 46 (January 1968), 276–291. Diebold alleged that the relative importance of American activity in Europe can be measured by the size of direct American private investment and sales of American subsidiaries in Europe. He pointed out that both had grown three times faster than the rate of European economic growth over the past eight years; that although sales of American subsidiaries did not represent more than 5 per cent of total economic activity in any country, the "increasingly obvious penetration of American goods," ranging from "toothpaste to computers" provided a "basis for European alarm"; that American products manufactured under license in Europe brought the United States fees of $251,000,000 annually as compared with the $45,000,000 it pays Europeans for licensing fees; and that direct private American investment in Europe increased from $1.7 billion at the beginning of 1951 to $13.9 billion at the end of 1965. *Time* noted that Americans now control 80 per cent of Europe's computer business, 90 per cent of its micro-circuit industry, 40 per cent of the automobile industry, and important shares of chemical, farm machinery, and oil production. In the United Kingdom they own 50 per cent of all modern industry, employ one out of

volume of overseas American investment rose from $8.4 billions in 1945 to $27.4 billions in 1958, and $64.8 billions in 1967. This increase placed a corresponding strain on the American balance of payments, mitigated partly by growing remittances of American corporations from abroad, which, in 1966, somewhat exceeded net investment. Perhaps the most important direct impact on the administration of foreign affairs resulting from this movement has been not economic but political; especially grave have been European reactions stemming from fear that the take over of their economies may be complete or resentment of what they consider to be American arrogance. General De Gaulle capitalized on such fear and resentment, but his was not the only voice raised in criticism and in warning.

Jean Jacques Servan-Schreiber, however, views American initiative and presence as indispensable. He exhorts his fellow Europeans to upgrade their educational systems and to pay more attention to management, urging socio-political reform and greater respect for free enterprise as essential to enable them to catch up with the momentum created by the greater initiative of United States companies. He attributes American success in Europe to managerial skill and a complex interplay of big government, business, and education.[5] His book, *The American Challenge*, published in France in 1967, aroused tremendous interest and may even have contributed ultimately to the defeat of General De Gaulle.

Another important aspect of the current phenomenon, is the increasing international or transnational attitudes of American industrial and banking firms with large overseas investments. They employ nationals of many countries in positions of high responsibility, not necessarily in their own nations. They enter into close working arrangements with alien corporations for joint production, marketing, or other purposes, and thus further internationalize their interests and attitudes.

---

seventeen workingmen, and manufacture 10 per cent of all British goods. They squeeze twice as much profit out of their investment as the British, send home $225 million annually, and reinvest the balance ("Long-Term View," *Time*, December 29, 1967).

[5] Jean Jacques Servan-Schreiber, *The American Challenge*; see also, Charles P. Kindleberger, *American Business Abroad*.

They plan their production, marketing, and financial operations on regional and even world-wide scales, with minimal regard to national boundaries and interests. Thus, their interests obviously transcend those of any nation-state, including the United States, and, if one were to indulge in wild speculation, he might even hazard that the gigantic industrial or financial corporation with international interests and connections, rather than the functional or regional international organization, or the utopian world federation of nations, may well emerge as the transitional building block in any new international construction.

Special Economic Interest Groups. Hundreds of special economic interest groups bring pressure to bear on Congress and the executive agencies and exercise substantial influence in many areas of foreign affairs administration. The range of interests of these groups is as broad as the nation's economic spectrum. Lobbyists represent all major and many minor industries, agriculture, service occupations, mining, petroleum, labor, and, far down the scale of effectiveness, the consumer. Their impact on foreign affairs administration is both direct and indirect and affects political as well as economic relations. For example, domestic beet and cane sugar growers, by lobbying successfully for higher production quotas, affect the American market for foreign-grown sugar and American political relations with nations to which sugar exports are highly important. Domestic petroleum producers achieve similar results when they agitate effectively for the curtailment of foreign crude imports, both in Congress and with officials of the executive charged with the administration of legislation governing the importation of crude oil and petroleum products.

Following the expropriation of foreign petroleum properties in the nineteen-thirties by Bolivia and Mexico, petroleum industry lobbyists also delayed rational diplomatic settlements of these problems for several years. In 1967 and 1968 a combination of industry representatives induced many members of the Congress to support tariff legislation that would have restored a large measure of protectionism, and the possibility of such a development immediately drew anguished and angry protests from Latin American and other less developed states. Innumerable additional illustrations of the manner in which special economic pressure groups influence foreign affairs could be offered, but the preceding examples should suffice to illustrate the importance of their activities.

Some lobbyists owe most of their effectiveness to the actual or potential voting strength of ther clients, for example, those representing agricultural or labor groups. Others seek to equate the interests of their principals with those of the nation, with varying degrees of assiduity and success. The lobby for the American watch industry, for example, has long maintained that its importance to the national defense warrants special tariff protection.

Most economic pressure groups also dispose of funds that they can contribute to the campaign expenses of congressmen who cooperate with them. This gives them tremendous leverage in Congress, especially in the House of Representatives, and also with political appointees of the executive, who must consider the needs of their national committees. Even career officers of the bureaucracy, who must please their political chiefs if they are to win promotion, cannot allow themselves to be insensitive to the wishes of large contributors to campaign funds or lobbyists who represent wide constituencies.

The economic pressure groups derive some of their power from their ability to influence or, in some cases, control the mass media, and the media themselves are well represented in Washington. A former special assistant to President Johnson, for example, presides over the Motion Picture Producers Association of America. Economic interest groups influence the media through their large advertising appropriations; and some giant enterprises include press, radio, or television components in their complex, highly integrated corporate structures.

To conclude, economic special interest groups unquestionably influence foreign affairs administration. Their power cannot be assessed accurately, both because sufficient monographic study has not been attempted and because much of the information from which any categorical conclusions would have to be drawn probably will never become available. In some cases no records exist about lobbying activities while in others scholars have no access to them. A conversation between a lobbyist and a congressman resulting in a vote in favor of certain legislation in exchange for a promise of a campaign contribution is not likely to result in the production of a permanent record or even to be revealed under oath. Similarly, a request by a lobbyist to a highly placed official of the executive backed by an offer of financial support or by an open or implied threat of adverse publicity is unlikely to get into the record.

Nationality and Racial Groups. Nationality and racial groups have influenced foreign affairs administration most significantly throughout our history. The role of the Irish immigrant in keeping alive and further exaggerating anti-British sentiment in the United States is too well known to require elaboration. The strategic positions occupied by Irish-American politicians in the Democratic party, especially in metropolitan centers of the eastern United States, enabled them to exert disproportionately heavy pressures in Congress and on the executive branch in opposition to British interests and in favor of the liberation of Eire.

Resident German aliens and German-Americans probably delayed the entry of the United States into World War I, and, like the Irish, contributed to anti-British sentiment.

Zionists can claim major responsibility for American recognition of Israel and for the highly favorable treatment that the new state has received since its birth. Conversely, the Zionists, to the extent to which they have served the cause of Israel, have impaired American relations with the Arab nations and facilitated the penetration of the Middle East by the Soviet Union.

Anglophile sentiments, even in the early days of the Republic, always affected foreign affairs administration. Alexander Hamilton's maneuverings, although ultimately unsuccessful, are a case in point. Anglophile sentiments stimulated opposition to the War of 1812, helped bring the United States into World War I and World War II on the side of Great Britain, and have since contributed largely to the continued "special relationship" between the two powers that so enraged General De Gaulle.

The influence of national sentiments also reveals itself very clearly in the national origins immigration act of the twenties, which sought to maintain the basically northern European complexion of the American population.

Mexican-Americans and Puerto Ricans have, until recently, played only modest political roles and thus have not greatly influenced foreign affairs except in a negative sense.[6] But their roles have become increasingly important in the past decade.

The influence of the Negro on American foreign affairs began to be felt before he became an active participant in the nation's political life. The debates and compromises in the Constitutional Convention on the prohibition of the slave trade and the representation issue reflected this passive role; so did the Mexican War and the intersectional conflict, to the extent that slavery produced it. Since the Negro has become a full citizen of the United States, he has influenced foreign affairs actively and increasingly. Moreover, as noted elsewhere, discrimination against the Negro has affected the American image abroad most unfavorably and further complicated foreign affairs administration.

Negro spokesmen generally have been strong advocates of self-determination, anticolonialism, and American support for black countries. Since World War II, the rising political power of the Negro minority has given it much greater leverage in foreign as well as in domestic affairs. This leverage helped to assure the new African nations immediate recognition and economic assistance from the United States. It also contributed to the deterioration of American relations with the Union of South Africa, Portugal, and Rhodesia. As noted earlier, a drive to increase Negro participation in the work of foreign affairs agencies, initiated under President Kennedy, thus far has achieved only modest progress, but many barriers have been lowered and the future holds better promise.

The only racial groups other than the Negroes that have influenced American foreign policy administration importantly have been the Chinese and Japanese. The Oriental Exclusion Act represented a popular reaction to competition from Chinese and Japanese coolie labor that threatened wage standards and working conditions. The racial issue probably would not have arisen had not the early Japanese and Chinese immigrants been so industrious and thrifty and had they not clung so tenaciously to their own values. It was these qualities that produced

[6] Discrimination against Mexicans and Mexican-Americans in the United States embittered United States–Mexican relations for years, and all of Latin America regarded pre-Commonwealth Puerto Rico as a victim of United States imperialism.

the discriminatory legislation and in turn damaged the relations of the United States with Japan, China, and the rest of Asia.

Religious Groups. Religious groups, possibly because of the separation of church and state or the pragmatic and materialistic bent of the American ethos, have played a less significant role in foreign affairs administration than in some other states, for example, Catholicism in Spain, Lutheranism in Sweden, or Calvinism in Scotland and Geneva. Nevertheless, religious groups have made their influences felt even in the United States. The liberalization of immigration policy, for example, owes much to the Jewish religious community, which consistently pressed Congress and the executive to open the doors to their persecuted coreligionists abroad.

Roman Catholic prelates and laymen have been in the forefront of the extreme anticommunist element. Roman Catholicism also contributes substantially to Irish nationalism and helps to explain the friendly orientation of many Irish-American politicians and congressmen toward the present regime in Spain. These political leaders influenced the administration of American policy during the Spanish Civil War and have consistently supported Francisco Franco since his triumph.

Protestant sects generally take little collective interest in foreign affairs. In the past, however, they frequently sought State Department and Foreign Service assistance or protection for their missionary efforts abroad and consistently opposed the opening of diplomatic relations with the Vatican. Protestant leaders of the National Council of Churches generally take a relatively internationalist and liberal position on international issues, while the Roman Catholic hierarchy tends toward a more conservative orientation. The Protestant churches do not speak with one voice and therefore lose much of their power as a pressure group. The Roman Catholic hierarchy is much more effective in this sense, as is the Jewish community.

The influence of church leaders and clergymen on their congregations varies widely and is impossible to assess accurately. Like political parties, the mass media, and other pressure groups, clergymen oriented toward foreign affairs must compete for small areas of attention, and their results probably will always remain largely unassessable.

In summary, the role of religious groups probably has been most direct and influential in promoting liberal immigration legislation and more flexible administration thereof, in obtaining assistance and protection for missionary efforts, in strengthening anticommunist activities, and in building support generally for peace and international cooperation.

Ideological, Professional, and Educational Groups. Groups that seek to advance ideological, professional, philanthropic,[7] or educational interests without special economic motivation are numerous, but they exert much less influence than do special economic interest and other pressure groups,[8] principally because most of them are not large or strongly financed. Many of these groups maintain Washington lobbies and some are capable of exerting limited pressure on Congress and certain executive agencies. The National Education Association, for example, could almost be classed as a special economic interest group. Other groups, such as the learned societies, including the American Historical Association, the American Political Science Association, and the American Chemical Society, operate with modest budgets and in restricted spheres. The American Historical Association, for example, worked long and, on the whole, effectively with agencies of the executive, particularly the Department of State, the National Archives, and the Department of Defense, to make available more foreign affairs documents for research at earlier dates. Like achievements can be attributed to other learned organizations. The impact of these activities on international relations is small, except to the extent that the scholarly research they facilitate eases or exaggerates international tensions. In any case their influence tends to be indirect rather than direct.

This is not true of ideological groups, such as the American Civil Liberties Union (ACLU) and a wide variety of other permanent and *ad hoc* ideological bodies, such as the League of Women Voters and Americans for Democratic Action. Some ideological groups are exploited by undercover agents and subversive groups that organize united fronts for the purpose of influencing foreign policy in areas of

---

[7] American foundations play roles that merit further study (see Francis X. Sutton, "American Foundations and U. S. Public Diplomacy," address).

[8] The American Medical Association, while professional in membership, acts as an economic pressure group.

mutual concern. For example, communist, Nazi, and Fascist groups united with right-wing America First elements before Hitler attacked the Soviet Union to try to keep the United States out of World War II. The difficulty of assessing the degree of influence exercised by most ideological pressure groups acting severally or in united fronts is overwhelming. Against evidence of any positive effects of their efforts one must weigh their counter productive aspects, especially when demonstrations, riots, or other excesses consolidate opinion behind administration policy.

Alien Elements

Foreign nations and peoples influence the administration of American foreign policy just as Americans influence the foreign relations of other states. They exercise such influence through official representatives, undercover operatives, propaganda programs mounted abroad and in the United States, lobbyists, cultural programs, and individual participation by private foreign nationals and corporations.

Public Officials and Employees. Foreign diplomatic and consular representatives affect foreign policy administration in most nations using techniques long sanctioned by international law and custom. These include diplomatic protests and declarations, negotiations, representational work, reporting, informational and cultural activities, and, in a few cases, economic and military aid programs.

The effectiveness of the sum of such efforts varies widely with their scope and dimensions, with the skill of the personnel engaged, and with the intimacy of the personal relationships of the diplomats with high officials of the host governments.

Expanding the scope of traditional diplomatic and consular activities by adding informational, cultural, covert intelligence, and, where appropriate, economic and military assistance operations, seems to yield sufficient additional increments of influence and intelligence to compensate for the substantial additional costs and the problems that inevitably arise with the escalation of an alien official presence in another nation. The latter problems emerge with greater clarity and seriousness, of course, in small, developing states where the factor of conspicuousness inflates with each degree of difference in affluence, dermal shade, and proportion of aliens to nationals occupying good housing, driving big cars, and using the finest diversion centers of the capital.

That the skill or gaucherie of diplomatic and consular personnel has direct bearing on their ability to influence foreign affairs administration in host countries seems obvious. The accomplishments of Talleyrand at the Congress of Vienna, Benjamin Franklin in Paris, Dwight W. Morrow in Mexico, and Jean Jules Jusserand in Washington all illustrate the enormous potential of the skilled diplomat to move other nations in desired directions. Extraordinary ineptitude, such as that displayed by Jules Poinsett and Henry Lane Wilson, who intervened clumsily in Mexican domestic politics, obviously had the opposite effect.

Personal relationships can still contribute substantially to a diplomat's effectiveness, although perhaps not so notably as in the era of absolute monarchies. For example, the British and French ambassadors enjoyed personal friendships with President Kennedy that greatly enhanced their influence during his administration, a situation that did not pertain after his death.

A few words will suffice to illustrate how the performance of traditional diplomatic and consular functions affects foreign affairs administration in host countries. Protests and declarations, even by the most negligible powers, must be given some consideration because of their possible impact on the general image of the host country or its policies or programs in third countries. Representational work, that is to say, entertaining, accepting hospitality, and exuding charm, can often prove highly productive because diplomats concentrate on public opinion leaders, key administrators, and those legislators most likely to influence parliamentary attitudes.

Reporting on salient developments in a host country, to the extent that it is full and perceptive, enables home governments to assess the capabilities and intentions of the host country more accurately and to respond more knowledgably. Such responses, whether intelligent or not, have a direct impact on the host country. Underestimates of capabilities or the seriousness of intentions can lead to adventurism. Overestimates stimulate arms races, pre-emptive warfare, or unwarranted pessimism. For example, the failure of German intelligence to warn Hitler against the inevitability and potential weight of American intervention in World War II not only resulted in the ultimate destruction of the Third Reich but also obviously had an equally important impact on American foreign policy.

All major powers conduct covert intelligence and subversive operations abroad. Such activities, unsanctioned by international law, have been practiced for millenia, often most effectively. Students report that the bulk of American covert political, economic, and social intelligence comes from the CIA. They credit CIA as well with mounting subversive operations that included, among others, overthrowing the Mossadeq government in Iran, and the Arbenz regime in Guatemala, and with having sponsored the Bay of Pigs fiasco.[9] Soviet undercover operatives mounted the 1948 Communist takeover in Czechoslovakia, played a major role in fomenting the Greek disturbances of 1945–1948, pilfered atomic secrets from the United Staes, allegedly penetrated the State and Treasury Departments in the persons of Alger Hiss and Harry White respectively, and engaged in many other successful and abortive clandestine intelligence operations and subversive activities. Activities of the British, French, German, Red Chinese, and other major undecover services similarly affect foreign affairs administration of the states that they penetrate.

The Soviet Union, Red China, and Cuba also control surfaced organizations; the Soviet Union uses the American Communist Party and the Red Chinese employ splinter factions. The Russians made particularly effective use of the American Communist Party before and during World War II to organize a united front that first hindered the preparedness program and aid to Great Britain and later promoted American-Soviet friendship and spurred war production. Since World War II, it has used the American Communist Party flexibly to counter American foreign policy objectives. Western undercover agencies at times either subsidize existing political groups or sponsor new ones

---

[9] Harry Howe Ransom, *Central Intelligence and National Security*, pp. 88–89; David Wise and Thomas B. Ross, *The Invisible Government*, pp. 1–90, 110–113, 165–183.

to win the support of actual or potential leaders, especially of military officers.

Lobbyists for foreign governments and interests work just as assiduously to influence American leaders, administrators, and congressmen as do lobbyists for domestic interests. They are required to register as foreign agents, but this does not seem to impair their efficiency. Like lobbyists for domestic interests, they often dispose of large sums of money that can be applied to campaign expenses or other objects. Before his assassination Generalisimo Trujillo, for example, maintained a very large, well-paid lobby in Washington to work for larger sugar quotas for the Dominican Republic, an objective that he pursued with considerable success.

Foreign leaders and governments supported by the United States sometimes rely on their real or assumed indispensability to pursue courses of action that affect the administration of American foreign affairs adversely or require unanticipated adjustments in it. Such leaders and governments act, quite naturally, in their own interests, rather than in consonance with American national interests; and not infrequently American policies and programs based on assumptions of their continued acquiescence are thrown out of phase. President Roosevelt did not always have his way with his British ally during World War II, despite Britain's desperate position; and President Johnson encountered difficulties with both Generals Ky and Thieu.[10]

Other Aliens. Foreign journalists in the United States influence American foreign affairs administration because their reports to their home papers may move public opinion and modify official policy toward the United States. The playback then influences American opinion and policy.

Foreign tourists to the United States help to alleviate balance of payment problems as do foreign investors; foreign gold speculators accentuate them.

Political exiles have sometimes complicated American foreign relations by attempting to mount expeditions to their home lands in viola-

[10] Arthur M. Schlesinger, Jr., wrote early in 1967 that "General Ky . . . has become one of those Frankenstein's monsters we delight in creating in our client countries, very much like the egregious General Phoumi Nosavan, who single-handedly blocked a settlement in Laos for two years" (*The Bitter Heritage*, p. 116).

tion of American and international law. Conversely foreign insurgents or bandits, such as Pancho Villa and Raisuli, have often introduced even greater tensions in international relationships. Foreigners taking asylum in American missions abroad often exacerbate American relations with their own governments. Cardinal Mindzenty, by taking asylum in the American legation in Budapest unquestionably made any United States–Hungarian *rapprochement* more difficult.

Activists abroad who burn USIS libraries or deface American embassy or consular premises influence public opinion there and in the United States in diverse ways; but it is usually impossible to determine the net effect of such demonstrations on the administration of American foreign policy. Their actions frequently appear to boomerang. Even when the demonstrators apparently attain the desired result, it is not always possible to ascertain whether or not they were officially inspired or, in other cases, merely reflected an opportunistic exploitation of an issue sure to be resolved in the manner advocated.

The role of the immigrant to the United States who retains his loyalties to the mother country can be highly significant in some contexts, as suggested in the discussion of the role of minority groups. Leaving loyalties aside, the immigrant still plays a significant if unconscious role in foreign affairs. The American balance of payments is affected adversely by immigrant remittances and benefits disbursed to Social Security, Railroad Wage Board, Veterans' Administration, and other federal, state, and local beneficiaries residing abroad. But these transfers must be set off against the stimulus they give to foreign demand for American merchandise and services. Immigrant labor also helps to keep prices of American export commodities competitive and to restrict imports, especially of stoop labor farm products.

Over the long term, the effects on foreign states of immigrant letters and remittances and especially of returning immigrants have certainly been noteworthy, even if not precisely measureable. It is impossible to allocate to immigration to the United States an exact share of responsibility for generating rising expectations in the country of emigration and for mutations of its policy vis-à-vis the United States. In some cases, especially Mexico, they have been highly significant.

PART IV

Some Current Administrative Problems and Proposals for the Future

16

Problems of Policy Formulation and Review

Foreign affairs administration in the United States generates so many difficulties and problems that even a complete list of them would attain impressive proportions. A detailed examination of major problems and of the more rational solutions proposed would call for enough studies to fill several library shelves. A thorough exploration of personnel administration alone would require multivolume treatment. Thus, the discussion in Part IV does not pretend to be exhaustive, but rather it suggests a few salient problems about which more study would be helpful and in which some progress may reasonably be expected.

Most Americans entertain strong views on foreign policy. They confide excessively in the ability of the United States to influence external affairs to its own advantage, and they blame policy and its authors when foreign states misbehave. They fail to appreciate the grave difficulties and uncertainties inherent in arriving at any decision, the narrow limitations of policy, or the differences and interrelations between basic policy, interpretive, operational policy decisions, contingency planning, policy review, and the planning, programming, and budgeting of overseas operational programs.

Nature and Sources of Basic Policy

Basic policies, which theoretically guide interpretive decisions on foreign affairs problems, contingency planning, and operational decisions, rarely have to be made and usually survive long beyond their years of maximum utility. Thus, the isolationist policy inherited from President Washington endured for at least half a century after the nation's power and international interests dictated that it pursue a more positive role.

When consciously made, basic policy often reflects the compulsions of external circumstances as much as or more than an act of volition. The policy of containing the Soviet Union, adopted by the Truman administration, represented not so much a conscious effort to promote the national interest as a defensive reaction to Soviet aggression. Both isolationism and containment, which generated innumerable interpretative operational decisions, illustrate clearly the importance of continuous, thorough review of existing policy.

Basic policy may also be interpreted out of all harmony with its original content. The Monroe Doctrine in its various permutations affords an excellent example of how basic policy may be distorted or even perverted by interpretation and reinterpretation over a long period. The problem of interpretation also underscores the importance of systematic, periodic policy review.

Responsibility for making or revising basic policy resides, as Chapter 2 emphasizes, in the president and the Congress. The Department of State, the Foreign Service, and the high echelons of other agencies play major roles as policy advocates, advisors, and critics, but do not consciously originate basic policy; yet their activities sometimes generate or link chains of events that move higher authorities to make or change policy.

The Department of State and the Foreign Service seldom exercise enough power today even to dictate major interpretational decisions without prior presidential approval or lateral clearance, but, despite these grave limits on their authority, the public holds them responsible for conducting the nation's foreign relations. Thus, they frequently serve as whipping boys for demagogues and the mass media when international affairs do not develop along lines favorable to the United States.

POLICY OR CONTINGENCY PLANNING

Unfortunately some highly intelligent and well-informed scholars and publicists exaggerate the importance of policy or contingency planning. They underestimate the proportion of interpretive, operational decisions that must still be made pragmatically with hard-won knowledge, experience, and judgment, taking basic policy into account, but under contingencies unforeseeable by the most assiduous and able planners.

Former Congressman David S. King, then serving as ambassador to the Malagasy Republic, observed in 1967 that many people call for clear exposition of policy without realizing that diplomacy resembles navigating a dangerous stream to a "well-known and clearly defined destination." It would be dangerous to rely on excessively detailed plans because many decisions must be made with "good sense and quick wit, with ample room to maneuver."[1] John C. Ausland, director for combined policy, Office of Politico-Military Affairs, uttered an even stronger statement on the limits of contingency planning, which he characterized as helpful only part of the time and mainly to cushion shock and acquaint participants with the other players. "For the most part," he asserted, "you will be reacting to situations precipitated by the actions of other countries."[2]

Unawareness of or refusal to accept the fact that so many decisions have to be made in light of unforeseeable developments sometimes leads critics to allege that the Department of State does not staff itself or the Foreign Service with enough officers capable of policy planning or that planners are diverted by other duties. There is some truth in

---

[1] United States, Department of State, *News Letter*, no. 76 (August 1967), p. 4 (hereafter cited as *News Letter*); see also George Morgan, "Planning in Foreign Affairs: The State of the Art," *Foreign Affairs*, 39 (January 1961), 271–278.

[2] *News Letter*, no. 79 (November 1967), p. 16.

these allegations, because Congress normally refuses to vote funds for adequate staffing of politico-economic positions. Critics have also urged the transfer of policy officers from line to staff positions in order to free them from excessive daily work pressures and bureaucratic prejudices.

Among advocates of more prevision and less reaction in the conduct of American foreign affairs, Professor James L. McCamy occupies a distinguished position. He considers that planning generally has been neglected by the department and the Foreign Service and strongly criticizes those who contend that policy must be made pragmatically as events unfold. He charges that men "who cope with daily events and fail to see that events reflect the great unfolding patterns of change in the world are unable to think ahead."[3]

Professor McCamy recommends the formation of a corps of about 400 specialists in policy within the career service of whom about 320 would be stationed in missions abroad, 20 in Washington, and 60 in training at intervals throughout their careers. These officers would be selected through the British country-house examining technique but without the participation of psychologists.[4]

Professor McCamy does not weigh the difficulties and limits of contingency planning as heavily as do some other academic students and most practicing diplomats. Does not the training, long experience, and expert knowledge of at least some career diplomats give them perceptivity that enables them to arrive at sound decisions in many unforeseeable contingencies? Certainly a good many have looked over the horizon and have "seen the great unfolding patterns." But perception alone does not assure that action can or will be taken, or that action, even if timely and intelligent, will necessarily change the emerging pattern of history. None can deny, of course, that events often require hastier and less contemplative decisions than officers like to render and

[3] James L. McCamy, *Conduct of the New Diplomacy*, p. 251.

[4] Under the country-house system, groups of a half dozen postulants are invited to a country estate for a weekend with a panel of examiners, including a psychologist. Their behavior under normal circumstances and while engaged in working individually and collectively on assigned problems is then observed. The observations of the examiners can then be used to construct profiles of the candidates on the basis of which comparisons and final selections are made.

that some officers lack either courage, perceptivity, or both, as is the case in all organizations.

The real questions, it would seem, are the following: how far ahead can the government plan; where should planning be done; can the government recruit more perceptive officers; and where should planners be placed in the chain of command.

Professor McCamy offers as an illustration a significant study that might be undertaken by a policy planner in Cairo: he would project what a new irrigation system would mean ten or twenty years from now to the Middle Eastern nations, should a feasible system of converting sea to fresh water be discovered and economic means of employing atomic fuel be invented to pump it from the coast to inland reservoirs. Clearly such a change would entail revolutionary implications not only in Egypt but also around the world and in all phases of human existence. But it seems doubtful that the man in Cairo, given the world-wide permutations of the subject and the inability of highly specialized scientists and technicians to estimate the timing or even the probabilities of breakthroughs could contribute anything very useful to the conduct of American diplomacy through such a study now or in the future. Could he not contribute more usefully by exploring the policy implications of some aspect of Egyptian political, economic, or social prospects over the next three to five years?

During the writer's service as director of the former Office of Functional and Biographic Intelligence of the Department of State, he encouraged specialists of the Division of Functional Intelligence to assess the implications of probable technological breakthroughs but with very marginal results, mainly because of the impossibility of pinpointing the likelihood or timing of any discovery. The importance of bringing imminent and actual breakthroughs to the attention of foreign affairs administrators cannot be contested. This would seem to be one of the roles of the department's Bureau of International Scientific and Technological Affairs. Analysis of the social, economic, and political implications of such developments remains within the province of intelligence research. Any policy emendations emerging therefrom would still have to be initiated by line officers in the regional bureaus or at the highest levels of the department. The Policy and Coordination Staff might be brought in for a contingency study or an opinion but not necessarily. In any case, the vast implications of most scientific and technological discoveries virtually preclude much useful field work in this area, except in gathering raw intelligence, and science attachés serve this purpose.

Professor McCamy's objective of recruiting foreign affairs officers with higher perceptivity certainly merits wholehearted endorsement. This objective could be approached by requiring more area or functional specialization before appointment and by revising testing procedures along lines he suggests. For reasons set forth later, it may not be feasible to introduce the British country-house system intact, but some of its advantages could certainly be sought, both through a remodeled oral examination and through more careful observation in the final probationary state.

With some exceptions, policy planning officers probably should not work outside the chain of command because, no matter how brilliant their recommendations, their status would reduce the possibility of effectuating them. The Department of State does not need an inflated Policy and Coordination Staff but more officers of high perceptivity in line positions. Must officers in the chain of command always be overwhelmed by daily routine and emergencies and thus be unable to focus on policy objectives? They will be so inundated unless Congress authorizes sufficient additional line positions to take pressure off the especially trained and recruited officer group Professor McCamy regards as essential. But it should be easier to obtain appropriations to expand the line sections of the department and its missions abroad than to provide personnel for ivory-tower staff sections. Moreover, if planning officers can serve in the chain of command, their work will almost surely influence daily operational decisions of their peers and superiors more effectively. In any event, this view seems to be shared by George Kennan, organizer of the Policy Planning Staff and perhaps its most distinguished alumnus.[5]

Beyond question, a great need exists for a higher degree of perceptivity in contingency planning, reporting, and analysis. Professor

---

[5] George F. Kennan, *Memoirs (1925–1950)*, p. 493.

McCamy's suggestions contain many useful leads to constructive action.[6] Although the writer does not fully share his optimism about the potential of planning, he considers that much more can be achieved than has been accomplished with some judicious changes in examining procedures, staffing patterns, and reporting requirements. Above all, there must be recognition that perceptivity is a quality highly to be prized and cultivated.

PLANNING, PROGRAMMING, AND BUDGETING OF FIELD OPERATIONS

Critics of American foreign affairs administration also urge the need for improvement in planning, programming, and budgeting of overseas operations. Such operations theoretically pursue basic policy goals but sometimes produce strange and unforeseen alterations therein.

The successful introduction by Secretary of Defense McNamara of a planning, programming, and budgeting system (PPBS) in the Department of Defense increased pressure for improvements in the foreign affairs community. The Department of State's efforts to improve its capability[7] cannot be characterized as successful, principally because of the enormous difficulties involved.

The basic difficulties or limits of prevision in foreign affairs, discussed in Chapter 1, operate with special force here. Dr. Thomas C. Schelling, professor of economics and member of the faculty of public administration of Harvard University, examined State Department problems for the Senate Subcommittee on National Security and International Operations. He concluded that only "the barest minimum standards" of coordination, integration, and rational management can be achieved in foreign affairs. PPBS, he warned, can be used, moreover, to emphasize quantitative data at the expense of more important qualitative considerations. PPBS works best in largely budgetary decisions; but money is not the primary consideration in most major foreign affairs issues. Furthermore, the secretary of state does not ex-

---

[6] The preceding brief summary of Professor McCamy's views, which does not recapitulate all of his interesting and useful suggestions, has been extracted from *Conduct of the New Diplomacy*, pp. 249–266.

[7] See Chapter 6.

ercise enough authority over the budgets of other agencies to assure effective control of their operations; and subordination of the other agencies to the Department of State does not seem feasible. The utility of PPBS in foreign affairs is also limited because it cannot focus on a few programs or objectives, but must evolve a program package for each of the six score nations recognized by the United States. All of these programs must then be considered together, "rather than all countries for a program together."[8]

From the preceding statement and from a similar declaration of former Undersecretary Katzenbach,[9] it is clear that overseas planning, programming, and budgeting cannot be practiced with full effectiveness in the foreign affairs community, first, because of the high proportion of its problems and decisions that cannot be quantified, and secondly, because the community still lacks cohesion. The fact that PPBS requires country programming emphasizes the importance of the Department of State's role as coordinator of basic policy goals to which the several country programs must contribute. It likewise emphasizes the importance of its role as the source of expert knowledge of the nations of the world, which it derives from its Foreign Service, the geographical organization of its line components, and its responsibility for monitoring the research contracts for all agencies in the field of international relations and areas studies.

Review of Established Policy

Nature of the Problem. A highly important area in which improvement in performance could conceivably generate more timely revisions of basic policy, better contingency planning, and more effective overseas planning, programming, and budgeting has still to be explored. External forms and public declarations of policies often bear little relationship to the basic realities of a nation's problems or potential. Such anomalies usually result from cultural lag. Failures to adjust institutions and policies to ideological and technological mutations occur everywhere because entrenched interests resist change. High officials normally cannot keep themselves currently informed of the

---

[8] *Foreign Service Journal*, 45 (March 1968), 4–14, 44–45.
[9] *News Letter*, no. 89 (September 1968), pp. 12–13.

research and intelligence that first suggest such trends. Moreover, they need additional research assistance in the critical, early stages when policy could exploit or adjust to such changes most profitably.

The president shares responsibility for making and reviewing basic policy with the Congress, the secretary of state, the National Security Council, and such other officials as he may designate from time to time. Such division of responsibility inevitably results in some confusion, and the heavy burdens of all the major participants inevitably compel them to focus on problems of the day rather than on retrospective analysis.

The regional bureaus of the Department of State review country policy, and other agencies review policy relating to functions or operations under their control. Responsibility for recommending country and operational policy changes after periodic or spot reviews probably should remain unchanged, but some system for assuring the periodic review of basic policy should be installed at a high and objective level.

Policy makers at all levels and in all agencies feel tender toward their own creations. Despite conscientious efforts to achieve impartiality, they sometimes fail to attain perfect objectivity when reviewing policies they themselves have conceived or sponsored. This generalization applies with special force to regional bureaus, which also display excessive protectiveness toward nations or areas under their jurisdictions.

Periodic reviews of NSC-approved country directives do not fill the need under discussion because they are undertaken principally by officers from the regional bureaus and from operating units of other agencies and do not always examine the underlying assumptions of basic policy. Consequently, they do not achieve adequate range, profundity, or impartiality.

Basic policy review likewise falls outside the scope of the Bureau of Intelligence and Research (INR). Its charter precludes INR from engaging in critiques or analyses of policy, and INR would, in any case, reflect some of the biases of the regional bureaus because of its predominantly regional organization.

The Policy and Coordination Staff will normally exhaust its energies in developing solutions to current problems and lacks time for the systematic review of existing policy. The July 1969 reorganization of the staff and change in its name, emphasizing its coordinating role, can scarcely fail to increase its orientation toward current problems. Moreover, its officers, like other policy makers, tend to become emotionally involved in their contingency plans.

Where then, should the president center responsibility for initiating basic policy review and for collecting and processing the data required? Who should undertake this work? How should it be done? How can the results be presented to the highest policy makers promptly and effectively?

Ideal Locus for Review Responsibility. Responsibility for initiating periodic reviews of established policy assumptions and policy effectiveness might well be located at the level of the Policy Planning and Coordination Staff in the Department of State, where regional loyalties would not impose obstacles to possible assaults on even the most sacred bureaucratic taboos, and where its status would assure that its recommendations would receive prompt and respectful attention. Alternatively, the function might be located in the White House or NSC. This would offer the advantage of further separation from any agency bias; but the locus would not provide as rich resources of experience and continuity, and the staff would be exposed both to the winds of political expediency and distractions of urgent problems.

The Director of a Policy Review Council. The director of a Policy Review Council should be a Foreign Service career minister or ambassador or a distinguished foreign affairs expert with a strong academic and political background. In either case, he should have held at least one high foreign affairs post and should have had broad geographical and functional training or experience. He would need, above all, great perceptivity and sound judgment.

The staff should be excused from all other duties but should enjoy carte blanche to review all basic policies. It should not require many officers, perhaps a dozen at most. They should be chosen from major foreign affairs agencies and public life, representing the principal areas of geographic and functional knowledge. The council's budget should permit the director to contract from the scholarly community for any research unobtainable from INR or other government sources.

The director's seniority, status, and reputation should enable him to review all basic policies, functional, global, or regional, regardless of their sanctity in the eyes of any agency or regional bureau. He and his aides would have to be able to recognize situational changes, scholarly findings, or intelligence that might bear on policy assumptions or effectiveness; to judge when additional research might be needed; and to decide whether the changes or findings might warrant a spot rather than a periodic review. They would exploit promptly all intelligence and other research and all situational changes bearing on policy assumptions and viability to assure that policy still rests on reality rather than on appearance.

Operations Involved in Policy Review. As an initial task, the director would review the State Department's basic policy file and the fundamental assumptions underlying each policy. He would then have to establish, after appropriate consultations, intervals for periodic reviews. An annual cycle might have to be set for policies subject to frequently recurring changes or having such importance in themselves as to require almost continous review. Other categories might be reviewed at considerably longer intervals.

No policy should be pursued for more than five years at the most without taking a hard look at all of the assmptions underlying it and attempting an evaluation of its continued utility. Most guidelines probably should be reviewed more frequently, given the astounding rapidity both of current socio-political change and scientific and technological progress. Relatively frequent assessments of United States policies vis-à-vis the containment of the Soviet Union and Red China, the Middle East, economic assistance aimed at promoting democratic institutions in developing countries, the recognition of *de facto* regimes, self determination, exchanges of persons, maritime territorial limits, regional and functional international organizations, commodity agreements, oil and sugar quotas, special relationships, and many, many others would be necessary.

With cycles of review established, the director would have to program the work of his staff accordingly. He would of course, allot time for the special review of any policies or assumptions suggested by situational developments or required by the president or the secretary of state; for screening intelligence, other research, and major publications; and for attendance at meetings of learned societies and other colloquia likely to yield useful insights.

Upon initiating a review project, the staff would first evaluate all important research produced since the adoption of the policy or the last review thereof to determine whether additional research or intelligence might be needed. The director could then ask INR, other intelligence agencies, or the academic community for additional data or analysis.

The director would next supervise the preparation of a report evaluating, synthesizing, and organizing the data. It would be difficult to overemphasize the importance of presentation to the success of his mission. The format of the report would vary with the nature of the data. A clear and concise abstract or synthesis should accompany every report. Basic documentation should be attached as back-up material, in some cases, but brevity should be sought through synthesis wherever possible. An excellent example of the type of summation envisaged may be found in a *Foreign Affairs* article by former Secretary of Defense Clark Clifford, "A Viet Nam Reappraisal," which reviews United States Vietnam policy.[10]

Completed reports would be sent for action with appropriate recommendations to the secretary of state. Information copies would go simultaneously to appropriate regional bureaus, the Policy Planning and Coordination Staff, and other agencies to permit them to prepare comments or alternate recommendations for transmittal to the secretary. Within a limited period in each case, the secretary would endorse, emend, or disapprove the recommendations but would always send them to NSC or the president.

Conclusions

The foreign affairs agencies of the United States are staffed by an

---

[10] Clark Clifford, "A Viet Nam Reappraisal," *Foreign Affairs*, 47 (July 1969), 601–622. Mr. Clifford reviewed the basic assumptions underlying American policy, especially the unity of the Communist bloc and the domino theory, tested their current validity, and advanced major recommendations for change.

exceptionally large proportion of dedicated, able officials. They work under pressures of heavy responsibility and excessive workloads in an atmosphere of daily crisis. Consequently, responsibilities tend to be discharged in order of their urgency rather than of their importance. All agree that the periodic and systematic review of established policy is highly desirable, indeed, essential; yet this function suffers more neglect than any other of comparable importance. Except for the formalized NSC exercises, relatively few reviews are undertaken until the collapse or drastic erosion of policy gives them the quality of post mortems and deprives them of all save historical value. Yet, the frequent, systematic review of approved policy could yield rich dividends. It would permit the early exploitation of rapidly evolving situations or of important research, either by adopting dynamic measures to advance national objectives or by revising obsolete or ineffective policies with minimal delay.

The proposed review system would offer certain special advantages. It would provide a central focus for this function at a high, objective, and appropriate level in the federal hierarchy. Disassociating it from the performance of any other duties would assure of review being done systematically and periodically. Establishing the function at a high level and reserving the directorship for a truly distinguished foreign affairs specialist would guarantee that all reports receive full consideration. The proposed arrangement would offer the further advantage of giving a unitary quality to review work, which cannot be obtained at present.

Several cognate but important beneficial results could also be anticipated. The department's intelligence arm could be used more effectively with a resultant increase in its morale and efficiency; the Policy Planning and Coordination Staff could devote more of its efforts to longer-range planning because its reviewing burden would be eliminated and because crash planning should diminish if basic policy can be kept more closely related to situational factors; and, finally, the planning and programming of field activities should be facilitated and improved.

17

A Proposal for Reorganizing the High Command of the Department of State

THE NATURE OF THE PROBLEM

Critics of the Department of State often charge that it does not seize opportunities effectively. Sometimes they do not appreciate the complexities of foreign situations and cannot be enlightened because of security considerations; sometimes they fail to realize that ranges of choice did not run from good to bad but from bad to worse. In other cases, human limitations, domestic political considerations, and the basic policies of successive administrations can be cited as the controlling factors in unproductive foreign policy decisions.

Few critics realize that the present volume and complexity of international relations have raised the factor of organization to salient importance. The department grew by accretion rather than design as new functions emerged, and despite successive attempts at rationalization since World War II, important weaknesses persist.

1. Supervisory responsibilities overburden the highest officers.
2. Machinery for reaching prompt and effective decisions requires improvement.
3. The public and officials of other agencies find it difficult to understand the process of foreign policy formulation and execution because of present confusing organizational arrangements.
4. Certain support staffs cannot contribute fully to the development and execution of policy because of their dispersal and dangling organizational status, and some personnel assigned to these staffs resent their inferior status.

Informal arrangements partly remedy some of the deficiencies. High officials of the department, for example, recognize fully the need for coordination and work diligently to achieve it within the existing structure, but this takes valuable time and does not solve other problems. This chapter offers a personal assessment of the organizational problem in the hope that it may generate helpful discussion.

The present organizational chart of the department shows more than a score of agencies, bureaus, staffs, and special assistants reporting to the secretary and the undersecretaries. It suggests that the organization permits excessive dispersal, allows imprecision in defining areas of activity, and impedes effective coordination.

Supervisory burdens of the secretary and undersecretaries should be reduced to provide additional time for reflection on basic policy and for essential relaxation. Unhappily, their representational and negotiating responsibilities cannot be reduced substantially. Improved coordination and supervision of the work of staff units cannot be expected while so many report directly to the secretary and the undersecretaries.

The manifold foreign relations activities of other governmental agencies and the consequent importance of improving interdepartmental relations seem to urge that the Department of State's policy liaison activities come under closer supervision in an organic relationship. The term policy liaison as employed here refers to the activities involved in coordinating, largely through negotiation, departmental policy and operational decisions with those of other agencies. Organizational arrangements obviously have considerable bearing on the speed, efficiency, and, above all, consistency with which these staffs work.

These staffs also require an organizational position in the department corresponding to their importance. Their present dispersal not only impedes coordination but also deprives their personnel of prestige and incentive. For the same reasons the intelligence research and policy planning staffs should be grouped and, in the case of intelligence, elevated in the hierarchy. The British Foreign Office accords policy planning and intelligence and policy liaison bureaucratic parity with policy making, operations, and administration. The department's support staffs should enjoy an analogous position of influence. Not only would their position enhance their effectiveness and status, but it would facilitate recruitment to and specialization in these areas. Moreover, the usefulness of intelligence research could be enhanced if it explored policy implications in a more complementary organizational arrangement embracing the regional bureaus and policy planners.

The Proposal

1. The secretary and the undersecretaries should not exercise direct supervisory responsibility over any staffs or bureaus but should bring their special interests and talents to bear on problems presented to them for solution through the deputy undersecretaries and the counselor. This would not preclude each of these high officials from taking a special interest in particular areas of policy and operations.

2. In line with the recommendations of the Herter Committee and the American Foreign Service Association, the president should appoint a permanent undersecretary as the department's executive officer. This officer would provide an element of continuity in the hierarchy. He would supervise the Executive Secretariat, the Operations Center, and the work of the deputy undersecretaries.

3. The deputy undersecretary for administration should continue to discharge his present supervisory responsibilities over all administrative bureaus and staffs, and should assume direct supervisory responsibility for protocol because he already is responsible for presidential and vice presidential travel arrangements.

4. A deputy undersecretary for political affairs should supervise the

Arms Control and Disarmament Agency, the five regional bureaus, Policy Planning, the proposed Policy Review Staff, and the Bureau of Intelligence and Research.

5. A deputy undersecretary for economic affairs should supervise AID, the Bureau of Economic Affairs, and related units such as Water for Peace, Food for Peace, and Fishing and Wild Life.

6. A deputy undersecretary for policy liaison should supervise the coordination component of the present Policy Planning and Coordination Staff, the bureaus of International Organization Affairs, Congressional Relations, Public Affairs, Politico-Military Liaison, and Scientific and Technological Liaison.

7. A fifth deputy undersecretary should coordinate USIA, the Peace Corps, and the Department of State's educational and cultural relations activities.

DISCUSSION OF THE PROPOSAL

Clarification of Responsibilities. The proposed arrangements would clarify responsibilities by dividing supervisory duties between five well-defined functional areas. Such clarification should improve public and official understanding of the department's organizational structure. Eliminating areas of overlap and uncertainty should enhance operational effectiveness by improving supervision and facilitating clearances. Clearer identification of functions should also permit easier identification of operating deficiencies by functional analysis. Analysis is difficult under the existing organizational plan because functions do not emerge clearly.

Easing the Burdens of the Secretary and Undersecretaries. The proposed delegation of direct supervisory duties would give the secretary and undersecretaries additional time for the consideration of policy questions and for essential recreation. As between the relative importance of having sufficient time for supervision or for reflection preceding policy decisions, the latter obviously should take precedence.

The need to delegate direct supervisory responsibility seems obvious when one reflects on the excessive number of high officials who have direct access to the secretary at present. The delegations suggested would substantially reduce this total. Only the undersecretaries, the permanent undersecretary, the deputy undersecretaries, and the counselor would report to him. The permanent undersecretary could assume most of the burden of direct supervision over the five functional areas.

Execution of the Department's Role in International and Interdepartmental Bodies. The closer coordination of policy and operational liaison staffs should enhance the effectiveness of participation by the secretary, undersecretaries, and other high officials in major international and interdepartmental fora. A single high-level official directing all liaison units could promote more effective vertical and lateral coordination between them, develop a common *esprit,* and promote more effective cooperation.

Increased utilization by the liaison area of its own services and a general improvement in their quality should result. Closer supervision should certainly yield earlier anticipations of needs for supporting intelligence on emerging situations, prompter formulations of departmental proposals for preventive or remedial action by the United States and improved surveillance of areas assigned to the department but often entered by other agencies. Some operating economy through the consolidation of staffs whose responsibilities overlap or merge should also result.

Closer supervision of these staffs would provide an additional guarantee that, regardless of jurisdictional divisions, all important matters of State Department concern receive adequate attention and that all resources are brought to bear simultaneously on any problem. It is essential that the department speak with one voice. An organizational merger of policy liaison staffs should strengthen the department's hand by reinsuring and facilitating the reconciliation of all internal points of view before positions are taken in international and interdepartmental agencies.

Improvement in Quality and Utilization of Policy Planning and Intelligence. The integral linkage of the policy making, policy planning, policy review, and intelligence bureaus should make it feasible to permit intelligence officers to explore fully all major policy and operational influences bearing on their analyses. Intelligence should then become considerably more useful, because present restrictions on the consideration of policy and operational questions by analysts seriously limit the effectiveness of their work.

The proposed tie with the planners and the projected policy review staff should stimulate additional intelligence production in areas of special planning interest and improve its utilization by planners. Since the effectiveness of the regional bureaus and of policy liaison depends largely on the speed and efficiency with which policy planning and intelligence can be brought to bear on problems of the day, highly useful results could be expected from improved and congruent supervision.

Improved Utilization of Support Staffs. The fact that political, economic, and administrative bureaus now have undersecretaries or deputy undersecretaries to represent them, whereas the remaining support staffs do not, reduces the status and influence of the latter. The proposed reorganization, by remedying this deficiency, should give more effective impact to their recommendations and assure wider use of their services. The appointment of a deputy undersecretary for administration immediately opened broader career perspectives to management, administrative, and consular specialists. This improved their status, facilitated recruitment, and produced a general improvement in effectiveness.

The changes proposed here would raise the status, career horizons, and morale of officers in educational and cultural affairs, intelligence, and policy liaison support work, especially those assigned to tasks that have the least immediate or least visible impact on the making and execution of policy; the changes should also make it easier for these officers to use their experience in other areas; and they should encourage excellent people to enter such work and to reach higher achievement when so engaged. Finally, improved public understanding of the character and importance of the intelligence research and policy liaison roles should follow from a clearer organizational recognition of these functions.

The High Command and Decision Making. The measures proposed would create a small, flexible, high command peculiarly suited to the department's needs. The two undersecretaries, the permanent undersecretary, the five deputy undersecretaries, and the counselor would provide the secretary with a superior staff of the size, competence, and grasp of all essential elements required for either consultation or for rapid and informal decision making.

The inner core of this group could give more effective consideration to basic policy problems because the secretary, the undersecretaries, and the counselor would be unhampered by direct supervisory responsibilities and because the closer interaction of intelligence, policy planning, and policy review should result in more perceptive and timely policy studies.

Recurrent tactical crises could also be met more effectively. The flexible group envisaged, capable of rapid, well-informed decision, could move quickly to seize opportunities brought to its attention by better supervised and better coordinated substantive and support units.

As a consultative body the high command could also function more effectively. In all cases, of course, it could call upon functional or area experts for assistance on highly specialized problems.

To conclude, the proposed reorganization should permit decisions to be taken with less delay on the basis of fuller and more carefully analyzed information and more effective consultative liaison. Lower echelons should find it easier to get guidance from above and to clear decisions laterally. The secretary should be able to assign responsibility more easily and precisely to assure the prompt execution of his instructions. Morale and efficiency in the intelligence research and policy liaison bureaus should improve, as should public and official understanding of the process of administering American foreign policy.

18

A Proposal for a Unified Foreign Affairs Service

A broad consensus now exists that civilians staffing foreign affairs positions at home and abroad should be brought into an integrated foreign affairs system with enough functional categories to permit specialists to compete against each other, and flexible enough to permit rapid, temporary expansion to meet emergency workloads. Proposals vary widely in detail, but all concur in the judgment that foreign affairs personnel belong outside the Civil Service, that the era of the generalist ended with World War II, and that major executive positions at home and abroad should be filled by specialists chosen from throughout the system who have demonstrated versatility, management talent, and breadth of conception.[1]

---

[1] No attempt will be made here to catalogue all of the recommendations made by proponents of a more closely related, integrated foreign affairs system or to describe how these proposals differ in detail. The Herter Committee and the Hays Bill envisaged that the Department of State, AID, and USIA should "constitute a family of compatible services" rather than a single service, but endorsed integration of field and home services and the merging of overseas representatives of other civilian agencies into the Foreign Service. The AFSA report generally endorses these concepts except that it does not advocate integration.

The Problem of Reconcentration

No sound argument can be made for reconcentrating all domestic foreign affairs functions in a central agency. President Johnson probably went as far in 1966 as reason and good administrative practice would permit in making the Department of State the manager of foreign affairs activities. The federal system is imperfect, but it also has merits that outweigh many of its imperfections. Americans must learn to live with its defects while exploiting its advantages.

Predominantly domestic agencies now have legitimate interests in foreign affairs. The decentralizing trend that began early in the century and moved much too far toward dispersal of responsibility and impairment of the State Department coordinative powers now seems to have reached a reasonable position again except with respect to certain new agencies engaged exclusively in essentially political foreign affairs activities.

USIA, AID, and ACDA perform special functions inseparably related to the Department of State's primary roles—the coordination and administration of political policy. While they take policy guidance from the department, their separateness increases the burden of coordination, results in considerable duplication of central facilities, and inevitably produces delay, confusion and inefficiency.

ACDA presents no major problem because of its modest size, lack of a field staff, physical location in State Department buildings, and staffing by Foreign Service and departmental officials. But the deputy undersecretary for political affairs, or preferably the proposed deputy undersecretary for policy liaison, could appropriately assume, ex officio, the additional role of director of ACDA, which could, if desired, retain its title but with bureau status.

AID offers less serious problems now that its headquarters also operates from Foggy Bottom; but its work, like ACDA's, could be coordinated more effectively and conducted with lower overhead cost in a chain of command relationship with the deputy undersecretary for economic affairs as its titular head.

USIA, physically separated from the Department of State but more intimately involved in political processes than any major agency other than the Department of State, should again be united integrally with it for optimal performance and for the same reasons that make it desirable to put AID and ACDA in the chain of command. In order to accord proper weight and status to informational and cultural activities, a deputy undersecretary should be named for the information and cultural program. Administrative staffs of all these agencies should be merged and one appropriation voted for the combined agency.

The Peace Corps, because of its unique character, probably should remain outside the department, but its headquarters organization should be staffed preponderantly by foreign affairs personnel seconded by the department to assure that Peace Corps policies coincide in all essential respects with national political policy.

CIA should remain, for obvious reasons, under the National Security Council, but Congress and the president should supervise and control its activities more effectively. No foreign operational activity should be permitted without prior concurrence from the Department of State.

The Rationale for Unifying Field Services

Grave imperfections inhere in the present profusion of agency representation abroad; multiple representation seriously impairs the performance of public business, dissipates revenues, adds to balance of payments difficulties, and overinflates the American presence overseas, thus frustrating policy and operations. Moreover, if the Department of State could coordinate field operations more effectively, problems of domestic coordination would be reduced because field operators also make policy.

The Foreign Service would need no statutory structural modification to accommodate additional specialists. Indeed, it has already adopted the concept that all junior- and middle-grade officers will acquire competence and serve as specialists or technicians, and its midcareer officers now compete for promotion in their special fields rather than by class.

Ample precedents exist for requiring primarily domestic agencies to utilize a unified service representing all civilian components of the executive. President Roosevelt imposed unification in 1939 in compliance with the recommendations of his Commission on Administrative Management, and President Truman took major steps to restore unity in 1945. The unfortunate division of responsibility for foreign affairs administration that occurred between 1947 and 1953 should not be permitted to hamper permanently the effective use of American influence abroad and certainly should not be regarded as having established an immutable institutional pattern.

Unity implies, of course, that the combined service would incorporate the present career field personnel of all foreign affairs agencies. During a transition period and to fill special needs for experts thereafter, it would also use the Foreign Service Reserve as originally conceived to accommodate officers seconded from other departments or agencies or from private life for temporary field service. These officers could serve overseas, subject to full Foreign Service discipline, but would return later to private life or to Civil Service positions in the sponsoring agencies. The Board of the Foreign Service and the Board of Examiners for the Foreign Service would have to include more representatives of the predominantly domestic agencies, as would its oral examining panels and promotion boards. Here, too, ample precedents exist for such multiagency representation.

A broadened program of personnel exchanges between the Department of State and domestic agencies having major foreign affairs responsibilities, especially between bureaus responsible for personnel administration, would also be essential to assure that a unitary, integrated service fully met other agency personnel needs.

CIA representatives, like Peace Corps volunteers, presumably should continue to remain outside the unified structure because CIA serves national defense as well as foreign policy interests. The problem of coordination probably could be solved by giving especially designated officers of the Department of State and certain field officers complete access to all CIA outgoing and incoming communications, including official-informal correspondence. Such access would permit the department and chiefs of mission to comment promptly on CIA intelligence reports and would preclude CIA from undertaking any activity not in accordance with departmental policy, except after review and clearance. It should not stifle CIA initiative, but it certainly would improve the effectiveness of American actions abroad.

To repeat, the structure of a unified foreign affairs service, meeting the needs of all civilian government agencies, except Peace Corps volunteers and the CIA, would not have to depart essentially from the basic structure of the present Foreign Service. Six, eight, or a dozen career ladders or cones might be designated as alternative routes for advancement up to and including FSO-1. Officers showing conspicuous leadership talent, however, should compete against each other in the senior grades if they aspire to generalist positions and to the grades of career minister and ambassador. The present Foreign Service system of rating specialists in the economic, political, consular, and administrative categories in the midcareer grades could be extended to include the senior grades and to categories for cultural, informational, economic assistance, agricultural, transportation, scientific, or other specialists.

The preceding suggestions owe much to the recommendations of those who have studied the problems of American representation abroad but also reflect the writer's personal convictions. They obviously conflict with the views of those who question the administrative or political feasibility of creating a unified, integrated field service. Bureaucratic vested interests certainly would offer strong opposition, as they did in 1939, but surely the experience of the past twenty years has demonstrated amply the grave dangers and waste inherent in the present diversity of overseas representation.

The Problem of Separate Officer Personnel Categories

Before World War II the separate officer categories in the Department of State and the Foreign Service created no serious problems. Agitation for integration, a merger of all field and home services, arose because the Foreign Service Act of 1946 gave Foreign Service officers benefits not enjoyed by the Civil Service and created two large bodies of field officers, in the staff and reserve categories, who aspired to FSO status. The act also failed to provide for enough home service by Foreign Service personnel.

Wristonization solved the problems of rotating field officers into home positions more frequently and of bringing overseas experience to the designated positions. Foreign Service officers now serve about a year at home for each two in the field. It also relieved pressure temporarily for improvement in the status of reserve and staff officers.

Wristonization reduced pressure for integration but did not eliminate morale problems in the Civil Service, the reserve, or the staff, and it failed to establish a unitary system. The large number of dual service positions restricted career opportunities for the Civil Service. Former reserve and staff officers in many areas, who found the competition so difficult as career officers that they were selected out, found it expedient to transfer back to the reserve or staff or at best earned promotion very slowly.

Rapid expansion in the reserve and staff officer contingents after 1962 more than restored the situation that prevailed before integration. But privileges and benefits extended to such employees, staff officers' continued exemption from selection out, and generous promotions seem to have kept reserve and staff morale at an acceptable level, although appointments to the highest executive positions go only to career officers and some prestige still attaches to being a Foreign Service career officer.

Thus the department still supports several personnel systems, and, in America's equalitarian society, reserve, staff, and Civil Service officers will sooner or later demand to share the prestige and few remaining privileges of career officers. Since they already outnumber them and since partial integration programs will only result eventually in further measures subversive of the career principle, a solution should be sought in a single, completely integrated, system in which all will enjoy identical treatment and prestige and in which all who wish to do so may compete for the highest rewards; but the system should preserve the essential elements of careful selection after rigid examinations at lower levels, competitive promotion, and rigid compulsory retirement of the less able.

Such a system should embrace all Foreign and Civil Service employees at home and abroad. This was the spirit that animated the Hays Bill of 1965, which would have established what its proponents chose to describe as a unified, integrated Foreign Service, although the bill fell short of meeting this description.

Field officers certainly should rotate between field and home assignments, and the present system largely meets this objective. Some foreign affairs specialists serving in home agencies should also have field experience. But it must be recognized that foreign service is not everyone's cup of tea, that sending abroad a specialist who lacks certain personal qualities can be disastrous, and that valuable specialists in narrow segments of foreign affairs activities might even resign if compelled to accept field assignments.

Nevertheless, a single, integrated foreign affairs service could reduce or eliminate tensions between home and field employees if domestic employees could serve abroad voluntarily but not under compulsion. All foreign affairs officers should hold identical commissions and receive compensation on the same scale. Presidential commissions probably should be reserved for the highest executive appointments. This, indeed, is the present tendency. All employees on overseas duty should continue to receive allowances and other compensatory fringe benefits. Home employees could opt periodically for overseas duty and vice versa. Thus, neither group would have reasonable ground for complaint about the treatment of their colleagues in the other branch.

The commissioning of all officers as FSO's would eliminate morale problems if standards for administering a career service could be observed thereafter. This need not mean screening out present Civil Service, reserve, or staff officers who cannot compete with FSO's. The present promotion system assures specialists and technicians of equitable treatment. A lengthening of permissible time in class in midcareer grades would further protect the competent but less dynamic officers. It would also serve to protect and encourage officer candidates for more routine consular, administrative, and commercial officer positions. These do not offer career possibilities above the middle grades and do not require more than undergraduate preparation, in contrast to more specialized political, economic, management, and other positions.

On balance, therefore, the arguments for an integrated home and field service seem valid. As suggested earlier, predominantly domestic agencies having limited foreign affairs responsibilities probably would not staff units discharging their foreign affairs work exclusively with foreign affairs officers, but it would be highly desirable if every agency would accept a substantial component, either on exchange or permanent assignment, in positions where expertness in foreign affairs would make their services most useful. The reserve category should be retained for use as originally planned to meet emergency and temporary staffing needs.

The Problem of Specialization

Students of foreign affairs administration now recognize the need for separate cones or career ladders, that is, for functional differentiation, in the Foreign Service or in an integrated, unified service. The variety and complexity of foreign affairs duties not only requires specialists or technicians for optimal performance but also precludes mastery of all fields by any officer, regardless of his ability or industry. Consequently, the generalist-specialist controversy no longer exists. All officers who enter the Foreign Service without a speciality are now programmed to acquire one before leaving the junior grades. But would it not be more intelligent to recruit junior specialists and technicians in the numbers needed rather than to train neophytes at public expense?

Some officers require graduate and even postdoctoral competence in political, economic, public affairs, cultural, management, scientific, labor, and other areas. They obviously should receive commissions in the top junior grades, which probably should be redefined as FSO 5–7. Many technical functions at home and abroad at the junior and midcareer levels can be performed by officers with undergraduate training or less. This is true of much consular, administrative, and commercial work, and of many public affairs, cultural, and economic assistance jobs. More highly trained officers usually find these technical duties unchallenging. Candidates for these positions can be recruited with only the baccalaureate degree and appointed as FSO–8's.

A statutory definition of an integrated, unified, foreign affairs service should assert the principle that all officers, other than reserve officers, serving at home or abroad should be career officers, serve in the same classes, and enjoy the same privileges and immunities, subject to differences in their posts and roles of assignments, but that all should be classified and compete for appointment and promotion by function. This assertion does not mean that innumerable categories would be needed to accomodate all of the specialists and technicians in a unified service. Field specialists seldom find it possible to work in depth, because the number of officers at most foreign posts is too few and the needs for their services too diverse to permit anywhere near the same degree of functional concentration that specialists at home achieve. Moreover, no continuity of service at any field office comparable to the tenure of home office positions can be attained because personnel must be rotated between the field and the home office and between posts.

For example, economists assigned to some posts perform the entire range of economic reporting, negotiation, and representational work, and often some commercial and economic assistance duties as well. Furthermore, an economic specialist may find himself serving in Latin America during one assignment and Northern Europe during the next, as exigencies of the service dictate. Thus, the term specialization when applied to the field officer has a relative rather than an absolute meaning. For this reason and because of the increasingly rapid obsolescence of expert knowledge, specialists in great depth, such as nuclear physicists or national income analysts, can best be supplied where needed by seconding them from home agencies or public life as reserve officers. Such an expert can keep the edge of his professional incisiveness keen by returning home after a foreign tour. This implies, of course, the use of the reserve in the sense originally conceived.

Field functions of a unified service probably could be grouped into no more than a dozen broad categories. But even a unified service would not be large enough to provide full careers for more than a few experts incapable of operating successfully within the total range of their disciplines.

Home agencies obviously need many more specialists and technicians in depth. The Civil Service normally finds it possible to recruit such specialists and technicians into professional grades carrying salaries competing with academic stipends. Such officers usually wish to continue to work in their own fields, and their roles in domestic agencies normally require continuity for optimal performance. The areas in the Department of State requiring relatively narrow specialization and technical expertness can be defined with relative ease. They embrace most of the staffs of the intelligence research, public affairs, legal, educational and cultural, international scientific and technological, security, budget, administrative operations, foreign buildings design, construction, furnishing, and communications units. Many of the desks of protocol, congressional relations, management, international organizations, and economics units likewise require either continuity or expertness in relatively restricted fields.

Domestic employees of a foreign affairs corps could be rated for promotion in subcategories of the field categories because of the higher degree of specialization that pertains in home agencies. In any case, they should compete against each other for promotion rather than against field employees, because the number of promotions awarded should be related in each case to the needs of the home office or the field. But personnel administrators should strive to keep average time in class more or less the same for home and field officers in the same speciality.

Thus, home officers in administrative work might compete by classes in such subcategories as budget and fiscal, accounting, personnel administration, and so on; but field administrative officers with their wider range of duties should compete by FSO classes within the broad administrative category. Average time in class for home and field administrators could be kept close by encouraging home to field transfers and vice versa.

Given the relative scarcity of high-level specialist positions in the field, it seems clear that a senior specialist would have to command enough fields of his speciality to be able to supervise other experts in the area. A field officer wishing to undertake narrow specialization in a functional subcategory probably should be advised to transfer to the domestic branch and to accept occasional field assignments to those few posts where such a specialty could be fully utilized.

Qualifications for reading, speaking, and writing foreign languages should also be fixed by function rather than across the board. Thus, a Foreign Service area specialist normally would have to be increasingly well qualified in reading, speaking, and writing the foreign language of his area to qualify for promotion to midcareer and senior grades. A home area expert might need only a reading knowledge of the area tongue. Field political and economic specialists would have to show relatively high language capabilities even in junior grades; but requirements for field administrative technicians, especially in junior grades, could be modest, and could be waived for home officers.

It might be alleged that setting language and other achievement standards for technicians and specialists at various class levels in a unified foreign affairs service would be difficult. But the advantages would far outweigh any difficulties, and these should not prove excessive if proper use were made of the extensive experience and existing standards files of the Civil Service Commission, which has met far more difficult classification problems.

Every officer upon entering the service would be assigned to a functional category corresponding to his major area of preparation or experience, as indicated by his selection of an optional functional portion of the entrance examination.

Standards for admission into the midcareer and senior classes should appropriately balance requirements for formal training, practical experience, and successful performance. An examination and basic review of attainments and performance should accompany promotion to middle and senior status. All standards should be met by lateral entrants, as well as by officers aspiring to advanced ratings. Every officer entering the junior grades should be able to demonstrate minimal specialist or technical knowledge of some function, except for consular functions for which a reasonably high level of intelligence and good basic education would suffice to permit the candidate to learn while on the job.

Officers should be encouraged to become generalists by displaying superior performance and versatility in their specialty, competence as leaders and supervisors, and both practical and theoretical knowledge of management techniques. A generalist rating would be given only upon entering the senior level. Specialists would continue to compete against each other for promotion, but generalists would thereafter be rated in their FSO classes.

The present requirement that every Foreign Service officer serve in any functional capacity should be modified to encourage the recruitment and retention of competent technicians and specialists. They should be given concrete assurance that they will not be assigned to functions outside their broad field of specialization, unless they themselves volunteer for service or training to enable them to master another specialty or become generalists.

The requirement that any field service officer serve anywhere in the world should be retained. It does not seriously impede recruitment; it permits redeployment to meet emergency needs; and it greatly facilitates the staffing of unhealthful or otherwise unattractive posts.

Five steps could be taken to keep in balance the present Foreign Service or a unified, integrated service.

1. Annual assessments of the requirements for technicians and specialists in each class at home and abroad should be reflected in promotion and recruitment precepts, training programs, recruitment for the reserve, and lateral recruitment.

2. Bonuses or other incentives could be offered to encourage officers to keep abreast of developments in their fields or to move into other fields as needed. The bonuses for substantive and linguistic accomplishment and the existence of the generalist category should permit both the present Foreign Service or a unified, integrated service to meet unexpected fluctuations in the volume and character of its workload, largely through redeployment and with a minimal resort to reserve and lateral recruitment.

3. Reserve officers should be used as originally conceived to meet emergency needs in areas where crisis situations may prevent staffing by the normal processes of recruitment or where an exceptionally high degree of specialization is required.

4. Well-trained lateral entrants should be recruited only after the preceding alternatives are exhausted.

5. As previously posited, field officers should be required to serve, if needed, in all fields of their general areas of expertness but not in other areas. They should be available for world-wide service.

6. Home officers should be encouraged but not required to accept

field assignments as needed, and relatively simple procedures should be established for officers wishing to transfer between the home and field services.

The selection and promotion systems could help appreciably to keep the present or a unified foreign affairs service in balance by basing selection and promotion not so much on the shape of the class pyramid, but on the relative need in each class at home and abroad for various specialists or technicians. Annual assessments of needs for generalists and each category of experts should be made for purposes of recruitment, training, and promotion. Recruitment at all levels should reflect current estimates of requirements for specialists and technicians in order to keep personnel in proper balance, to obviate the need for crash and lateral recruitment, and to hold reserve appointments to a minimum. Success in this endeavor would facilitate the use of the reserve to staff temporary positions or to obtain temporary services of specialists in depth. Annual instructions regarding promotion lists should specify not only the number of officers to be promoted to each class but also the number of specified experts or technicians to be included in the composition of each class list.

Compulsory retirement should cover all employees in a unified service, but time in class should no longer serve as a major criterion. Many career officers have had to leave the Foreign Service because they failed to win promotion within the time spans presently authorized, despite their good performance ratings and despite the fact that their experience represented a valuable asset to the service. Certain functions in a unified service, moreover, will not require high rank or warrant salaries above the median. Officers in such jobs should be released after a relatively short probationary period if they cannot meet service standards but should not be expected to earn more than two or possibly three class promotions before normal retirement.

In contrast, any officers who falls for two years consecutively in the lowest 3 per cent of his class or for four years in the lowest 6 per cent probably should leave the service. But in all such cases, a special board should review the officer's personnel dossier with him on the first occasion of his receiving a low rating to determine whether or not any portion thereof may require correction or amplification. Unfortunately, many officers under the present system have suffered unwarranted blights on their careers because of unfair or careless ratings by superiors or inexplicable gaps or inclusions in their records.

No vast administrative machine would be needed to install and operate a functionally classified personnel system. The Department of State has already introduced a large measure of functional differentiation in the Foreign Service. A unified, integrated service would not vastly complicate the problem of classification. The delineation of areas of specialization and establishment of qualification standards set at entering, intermediate, and senior levels, should not require more than a few months, if the experience of the Civil Service Commission and private consultants were properly used. They should be revised periodically in light of experience and shifts in the character of the workload.

Placement, promotion, in-service training, career planning, and recruitment would all be facilitated and improved by a clearer definition of foreign affairs functions, by the establishment of reasonable standards, and by the preparation of periodic estimates of manpower needs for all functions at all levels. A temporary strengthening of some personnel units might be necessary, and some reallocation of personnel staffs in home agencies might be required, but the global expenses of administering the proposed system should be considerably lower and its efficiency and morale correspondingly higher.

19

Problems of Size and Character

Wise coordinative measures and improvements in organization facilitate foreign affairs administration, but controls and machinery, no matter how ingenious, will not operate effectively with inadequate or excessive staff, or with poorly selected, trained, or motivated personnel. Moreover, skills and talents must be placed to best advantage; employees must keep up with advances in their fields of knowledge; they must rise at rates rapid enough to sustain morale without creating promotion blocks or surpluses; and they must be discharged or retired if they stop achieving.

Political and social considerations also influence personnel policy in a pluralistic society. The geographical representativeness of a corps of public officials inevitably becomes a matter of general concern, and its social representativeness preoccupies minority racial, religious, and nationality groups. American society also has empathetic resources that can be used to great advantage to advance overseas objectives if able minority representatives can be drawn into foreign affairs duties.

Many other problems arise in connection with the establishment of personnel policies. They include determining the linguistic competence needed by various employees, age limits, rates of compensation, fringe benefits, and a myriad of other less important but difficult questions affecting morale and efficiency. Thus, the treatment accorded a few of these matters in this and the following chapters must be regarded as illustrative, suggestive, and impressionistic. The chapters certainly do not pretend to a definitive examination of either the entire range of problems or of those discussed.

The Problem of Bureaucratic Gigantism

The vast size of the foreign affairs establishment impairs its effectiveness almost as much as does dispersion of responsibility. Some of the growth since World War II can be attributed to the expansion in foreign commitments, to the widened scope of international activities generally, and to broadened programs of fringe benefits, especially to those offered overseas employees. But dispersion of responsibility, bureaucratic rivalries, competition leading to duplicating and conflicting activity, and management errors all helped to generate unnecessary inflation.

To what extent is such inflation irremediable? George Kennan observed in 1957, that the size and complexity of the apparatus responded partly to real requirements; but he distinguished between essential mechanical processes, such as the issuance of passports, where staff must expand to meet requirements, and purely intellectual processes, "where bigness runs into the law of diminishing returns." He also pointed to an important distinction between intellectual processes; for example, between intelligence gathering and initial analysis "and the synthesis and final utilization of intelligence." For the first, he admitted a need for large organization; for the second, he urged compactness and intimacy of association. Kennan recommended certain remedial measures to ameliorate the evils of bigness, including "concentration in the hands of the Secretary of State of the authority (under the president's direction) for the entire foreign affairs field, subordinating to him all civilian activity relating primarily to external affairs." He also recommended restoration of personnel and security control to the normal chain of command, that is, the removal of foreign affairs work from Civil Service administration and its organization once more "in accordance with its own specific requirements." He further recommended restoration of a professional service "commensurate in quality with the tasks to be performed."

Kennan concluded that "it would be the height of irrealism to suppose that any of these measures will be—or could be—taken in the intellectual and official climate of the present epoch." The misunderstandings were then too deep and too widely held and vested interests too great. He foresaw that the apparatus would continue to grow with the continued expansion in functions to which it must address itself and because of its own peculiar internal dynamics. Its growth would be limited by the readiness of Congress to provide funds, although its vast size and impenetrability would limit the ability of Congress to appropriate on the basis of exact measurement of what might be required. Hence, the apparatus would become of less value to the president and the secretary of state as a source of immediate guidance and as a vehicle for promulgating policy in important and urgent situations.[1]

Kennan's diagnosis, prognosis, and suggestions for therapy have been summarized in some detail because the diagnosis and suggestions still seem eminently sound, although the prognosis, which most well-informed persons accepted a decade ago, now seems overly pessimistic. After 1961 the secretary of state recovered some coordinative authority and became in a limited sense the manager of foreign affairs administration. Chiefs of mission likewise regained a measure of lost authority, and personnel and security administration now reside once more in the regular chain of command.

A successful effort to unify field services and the home services of the Department of State, AID, USIA, and ACDA would permit major reductions both in personnel stationed abroad and in domestic staffs supporting field operations. It would at once allow elimination of duplicatory administrative services in the field and a substantial reduction in the administrative support load of the Foreign Service. At home of course, the abandonment of separate administrative staffs

---

[1] George F. Kennan, "America's Administrative Response to Its World Problems," in *The American Style: Essays in Value and Performance* (Report on the Dedham Conference of May 23–27, 1957).

supporting field operations and their concentration in a single foreign affairs agency should bring more economy.

The current congressional tendency to reduce foreign economic and military assistance programs, which public opinion apparently supports, also promises to have an important influence on the number of personnel stationed abroad. For the short term, United States balance of payments problems should likewise tend to reduce American overseas private spending and the American military presence abroad where no immediate threat to American interests exists. Both developments should ease foreign affairs workloads. The American ambassador in Brazil in 1967 launched a program originally aimed at reducing his civilian staff by 50 per cent. His efforts probably influenced President Johnson to order substantial cuts in overseas staffs by twenty-one civilian agencies during 1968. President Nixon ordered an additional reduction in 1969.

Many experienced Foreign Service officers had long insisted that there was ample opportunity for effecting such economies even without establishing an integrated, unified service. The writer reduced staffs at the American consulate at Guadalajara and the American embassy at the then Ciudad Trujillo without sacrificing essential services and while clearing up work backlogs. Both operations permitted the release of much office space and reductions in excessive inventories of supplies.[2] The consular officer in charge at Port of Spain reported similar results after a belt-tightening operation in 1961–1962.[3] Ambassadors George Kennan, Ellis Briggs, Henry Villard, and other senior officers testified that missions could operate more effectively with fewer employees.

The preceeding considerations provide no grounds for unbounded optimism that the tide toward gigantism will roll back, but the prospects for pruning overseas staffs appear somewhat brighter today. The

---

[2] In Guadalajara, for example, enough red tape for legal documents reposed in the storeroom to meet estimated needs for a century.

[3] United States, Department of State, *News Letter*, no. 18 (October 1962), pp. 25, 46; see also Leon B. Poullada, "Economy—True and False," *Foreign Service Journal*, 31 (May 1954), 18–21, 58–63.

major reasons for this more hopeful prognosis stem from the realization that gigantism complicates the problem of coordination, multiplies difficulties arising from the American presence abroad, including the current adverse balance of payments, and enhances the ill effects of the negative correlation between size and the "essentially intellectual processes of synthesis and evaluation of information available to the government and of the formulation and execution of high policy."[4]

The optimal size of the field establishment will continue to fluctuate from year to year and crisis to crisis and will grow with the interdependence of the nations and as domestic and foreign affairs in each nation become progressively more intimate. But this growth need not present a serious problem if the government maintains a well-trained career staff capable of using the temporary assistance of specialists and technicians as need may arise. This implies, of course, the use of experts from other agencies and public life as reserve officers. Although nothing is more permanent than a temporary agency, temporary employees rival this dubious distinction. But the problem of expanding and contracting the reserve as originally contemplated will be minimized if most reserve officers come from the home service and other agencies, because such employees would have re-employment rights.

The writer suggests that it certainly would be interesting and conceivably useful, in connection with any effort to estimate the proportion of unnecessary staffing in the American foreign affairs establishment, to compare the number of American civilian foreign affairs employees by functional categories at home and abroad with those required by other great powers to conduct their international relations, especially the Soviet Union, the United Kingdom, France, and the German Federal Republic. Rough surveys made in 1961 of French, British, and West German field deployment suggested that, even after allowing for the greater scope of American commitments, programs, and functional activities, highly disproportionate American staffing then existed, especially in administrative and operational components.

[4] George F. Kennan, "America's Administrative Response," in *American Style*.

The Problem of an Elite or Equalitarian Service

The Foreign Service of the early postwar years displayed elite characteristics that rendered it highly vulnerable to attack by demagogues. Wristonization and other lateral entry programs greatly attenuated its exclusiveness, but the career Foreign Service still retains a more elite character than does the Civil Service. Its members display serious concern about the maintenance of the so-called career principle, and they take pride in their availability for all kinds of duty in all places without regard to office hours. But whether an elite or an equalitarian service best serves the nation will not be decided on the merits of the case. Indeed, pressures of minority groups and the attractions of equalitarian rhetoric rule out an elite corps for an institution without a constituency.

Nevertheless education and educational attainment command great respect in the United States. For this reason a well-qualified foreign affairs service with even higher standards of selection and performance conceivably could emerge. This would not preclude a substantial increase in the representation of minority groups, if proper measures were taken to assist able minority representatives to prepare for the examinations. Indeed, the interpenetration of foreign affairs into every aspect of national life argues most strongly for the mobilization of all intellectual and perceptual resources, without regard to geographic, racial, social, or other criteria.

Thus, the compelling consideration in selecting a foreign affairs service should be whether it represents the best talent available. If adequate public and private funds can be allocated to train promising but underprivileged young people, such an approach will neither restore an aristocratic establishment nor lower entrance standards, which indeed, should be set higher.

Recruitment Levels and Protection of the Career Principle. The Foreign Service created by the acts of 1924 and 1946 operated under the concept that appointments of career officers normally would be to the lowest class of the service. This concept assumed an undifferentiated service in which all officers would function in a wide range of duties and the ablest and best trained would rise to the highest executive positions. It originated when a college degree of any kind represented a considerable academic attainment. Perhaps it would not be far off the mark to equate the relative value of a baccalaureate degree of 1924 with a Ph.D. today. Probably the M.A. degree or its equivalent should now be required of any foreign affairs specialist entering as a junior officer, because he should know research methodology and should have studied in some depth at least one field of his discipline.

The Foreign Service still appoints junior officers with only baccalaureate degrees, but it has constantly expanded the in-service training program to encourage those without advanced degrees or specialized training to improve their capabilities. In-service training is both expensive and wasteful of talent needed for day-to-day operations, because the examination and appointment process should and could provide officers already qualified for specialist roles. Specialists should be given short refresher courses periodically and perhaps sabbatical assignments to academic or other training centers to keep them abreast of current developments, but the public interest clearly will not be served in future by releasing officers from their normal duties and paying salaries and tuition to enable them to complete undergraduate majors or even advanced degrees, if properly trained candidates can be recruited. Surely it would be preferable to offer greater inducements to qualified young persons having graduate training to enter the service to fill specialist positions at beginning salaries equated with those offered by other government agencies, business, and academic employers.

Present recruitment techniques, directed essentially toward the undergraduate, produce a superabundance of such candidates. Even so, there has been an increasing tendency for oral examining panels to recommend candidates having graduate training, and currently over half of the successful candidates receive appointments directly to Class 7.

Some argue that an increase in the educational requirement might cost the service valuable talent because it would result in able officers who now enter with only undergraduate degrees drifting off to other occupations. A few might well be lost if a minimum requirement for graduate training were imposed for specialist candidates, but the gain probably would more than offset the loss.

If this is the age of specialization, administrators must continue to press the Congress for authority to make direct appointments to FSO-6 and possibly to FSO-5, and must recruit more highly trained entrants. The necessary changes would involve reclassifying junior officer grades to include enough classes to permit young, well-trained specialists to enter at competitive salaries. As an interim measure, administrators could recommend for special promotion any highly trained officers already inducted who could meet the new standards. A precedent exists for this because the department reclassified junior officers on duty when it adopted more reasonable standards for direct appointments to FSO-7. Direct appointments of young specialists to FSO-6 and possibly FSO-5 should assure the service an ample supply, providing it directs its recruiting efforts toward the graduate schools, junior faculty members, and research centers.

During a transitional period, generalist officers could either be educated as specialists or assigned to technical work for which their aptitude and experience might qualify them. Specialists appointed in future who want or need additional training, other than refresher courses, should be encouraged to take leave without pay but should not be trained at public expense. Leave without pay to pursue studies leading to specialization might also be granted to technicians appointed to the FSO-8 class.

In-service training should focus on keeping specialists and technicians abreast of current developments in their fields, rather than on educating them in basic specialties or techniques. Such an orientation might even reduce the workload of the Foreign Service Institute by eliminating undergraduate courses and some language training, because functional specialists could be expected to have a world language and area specialists the language of their area. Recruitment of already trained specialists and technicians could scarcely fail to improve efficiency and morale. Moreover, it would greatly reduce the need for reserve and lateral appointments, thus reestablishing the career principle.

These suggestions, of course, imply that specialists will not perform routine technical work in the future except during brief familiarization assignments. These assignments should not be so long as to produce the boredom and disillusionment that have caused some highly motivated and intelligent young people to resign voluntarily from the Foreign Service. Moreover, they should be combined with reporting assignments in order to afford the neophytes opportunities to show their special talents.

Staff and reserve officers have already, in fact, taken over most of the junior and midlevel consular, commercial, and administrative positions. They, too, would also be classified as Foreign Service officers in an integrated, unified service but would compete with each other as technicians.

The Problem of Representativeness

Geographical Representativeness and the Foreign Service Academy Concept. Some congressmen strongly urge the creation of a foreign service academy, modeled on the armed forces academies, to train junior officers. They apparently hope to assure better representation for their districts and to increase the appointments at their disposal. In actuality, the geographical balance of the present career officer corps presents no real problem. The east and west coasts are somewhat overrepresented and the south slightly underrepresented, but there is no glaring inequality. Certainly no problem exists serious enough to warrant incurring the unhappy consequences that inevitably would result from creating a generalist, foreign affairs stereotype entering the service with only baccalaureate preparation and from the hazards of a selection process resting largely on political considerations. Fortunately, the weight of informed opinion both within and outside of the Congress has overwhelmingly rejected this concept.

Social Representativeness—The Economic Problem. Many changes have also occurred in the social representativeness of the Foreign Service since the Rogers Act, which authorized salaries and fringe benefits that permitted any highly motivated, able American to serve in a diplomatic capacity without relying on private resources. Most Foreign Service officers now lack private incomes and come from middle or even working class families. The proportion of officers from very rich families declined sharply between 1924 and 1939 and even more rapidly after 1946. The relative ease with which a promising student can now obtain financial assistance to complete undergraduate and graduate studies has virtually eliminated lack of economic resources as a bar to entrance into a foreign affairs career. A candidate from a family using correct English and offering other cultural advantages still enjoys initial advantages as compared to one from a less favorable situation, but this does not mean that a strongly motivated aspirant from a low-income home cannot win admission. Indeed, family income plays a far less important role today in aiding or hindering a youth aspiring to a foreign affairs career than do other factors that will be discussed below.

Social Representativeness—The Minority Problem. If lack of economic resources hinders but no longer excludes any American from serving his country as a foreign affairs officer, it is equally true that some minority groups remain grossly underrepresented in the Foreign Service and among higher ranking Civil Service contingents of domestic foreign affairs agencies. Women, Jews, Roman Catholics, Japanese-Americans, and descendents of South and Eastern Europeans all overcame prejudices and discrimination, which existed before the Rogers Act. But citizens of Negro, Indian, and Latin American extraction remain underrepresented. This situation, aside from its legal and moral aspects, damages the public interest because it results in failure to exploit their empathetic resources and to use them abroad to help counter propaganda about racial discrimination in the United States.

Two major factors operate to prevent the entry into higher foreign affairs positions of intelligent, highly motivated representatives from these groups. Many come from home environments where no English is spoken, as in the case of citizens of Latin American extraction, or where the English is badly accented, highly ungrammatical, provincial, and quite unsuitable for communication in the foreign affairs community. Such candidates find themselves greatly disadvantaged at the outset, because ability to read, speak, and draft clearly and concisely in English has always been, and unquestionably will continue to be, prerequisite to high performance by foreign affairs officers.

The second obstacle resembles the first. Many minority candidates receive substandard training in the public schools because of segregation and because they reside in states where expenditures for education for both majority and minority elements fall below the national average. Standards of predominantly Negro higher educational institutions also fall well short of the nation's qualitative mean. Records of the Board of Examiners for the Foreign Service reveal clearly that candidates from Southern states, whether of Caucasian or other extraction, do less well in the written examination than do those from the East, West, and Midwest.

Efforts of Presidents Kennedy and Johnson to attract more qualified minority representatives into foreign affairs positions met with only modest success, as recounted earlier. A sound permanent solution to this problem obviously will not be found in lowering selection standards or granting preferences to minority candidates.

The only definitive solution will some from a general elevation of the economic, social, political, and educational opportunities of these groups, a difficult, costly, and lengthy operation. In the meantime, special programs, such as that financed by the Rockefeller Foundation, should be mounted with public funds on a broad national scale to bring forward more able youths.

A special, large-scale, four-year, Federal scholarship program for minority youths should seek to sharpen their verbal skill and otherwise equip them to compete on a basis of complete equality in the Foreign Service and Foreign Service entrance examinations. Like the armed services academy scholarships, they should carry an obligation to enter federal service for a term of years. Such a program, at a per capita cost of $1,500 per year, if extended to, say, two thousand grantees, should annually after five years produce several hundred officers for the Civil Service and at least forty or fifty acceptable minority candidates for foreign affairs positions, or enough to assure reasonable representation in a unified service. Surely $3,000,000 annually to fund these scholarships would represent a very modest price for the empathetic capacity that the federal services would gain, for the opportunity they would afford to increase minority representation without violating the career principle, and for rectifying denials of earlier opportunities to the young grantees and the groups they may represent.

As interim measures, it may be necessary to continue using reserve, presidential, and lateral entry appointments to improve the balance, but such methods may well prove counterproductive in terms of efficiency and race relations if not exercised judiciously on a modest scale. However, they should be continued only until a special training program, such as the one outlined above, begins to produce qualified candidates.

20

Problems of Selection

QUALIFICATIONS OF THE IDEAL OFFICER

What should one look for in a Foreign Service officer? Obviously somewhat different criteria must guide the selection of officers for home and overseas duty. In general, home officers require considerably more knowledge in depth than overseas officers, because of the greater division of labor in the domestic agencies; but personal qualities weigh far more heavily in the ability of an officer to represent his country well and happily overseas.

The basic qualities and characteristics required by the duties and way of life of a Foreign Service officer may be grouped in four broad categories—aptitudes, character traits (including motivation), skills, and substantive knowledge. Officers aspiring to high executive positions must also have leadership potential, but this is a composite of the other attributes melded by ambition. Most of the following observations regarding aptitudes and, to a lesser extent, character traits, relate primarily to the needs of field officers.

Every officer selected under any examination system will be deficient in some qualities, and all will have to be judged competitively. But some aptitudes, such as adaptability; certain character traits, such as loyalty; a minimal knowledge of specified fields of knowledge; and a command of a few essential skills must be regarded as absolutes.

Aptitudes. The ability to perform efficiently after changes of post, of cultural environment, of function or range of specialization, and of hierarchical status probably ranks as an indispensable aptitude for field service. Changes of station occur frequently. Specialists and technicians must also be prepared to work across the spectra of their disciplines rather than in depth. In small and intermediate posts and in emergencies, they must sometimes work outside their disciplines as well. Every officer must face the major financial and psychological adjustments occasioned by home assignments several times during his career.

A sense of humor ranks very high as an asset. Indeed, it often provides an invaluable indication of an individual's adaptability, because appreciation of the ludicrous makes change or incongruity amusing instead of painful or unacceptable. Like good manners, a sense of humor also serves as a lubricant for social situations that might otherwise impair morale.

Somewhat less essential but still highly important for successful field performance are outwardly directed interests and representational capacity. Field officers work in the world and with all of its peoples. They may specialize, but they all represent the nation abroad and they all require some local contacts to perform efficiently. In middle and higher grades even specialists have supervisory, operational, and representational duties. Certain specialists, such as political, commercial, labor, or cultural officers, obviously must be far more gregarious than others.

Every officer serving overseas must also be able to put himself to some extent in the other man's place—to penetrate the intellectual and emotional patterns of others deeply and sympathetically. Reporting officers and negotiators need this aptitude in a superlative degree. Consular, commercial, public affairs, economic assistance, and administrative officers in their daily relationships both with their local staffs and with foreign peoples also perform poorly or well in direct ratio to their empathetic resources. This capability is most difficult to test because it is strongly influenced by acculturation and racial inheritance. Thus, testing sometimes yields results less useful than those which could be anticipated if selection produced a fully representative group capable of exploiting all of the diverse potentialities that the United States' heterogeneous population embraces.

The breadth, range, and unpredictable fluctuations of the workload overseas often require an officer, regardless of his rank or area of specialization, to take more responsibility and to work under far more trying circumstances than those normally encountered at home. Thus, he must have high capacity to concentrate, reason inductively and deductively, and synthesize immense and baffling arrays of facts and hypotheses. The successful officer must also be decisive. Having marshaled his data calmly and logically, he must interpret them in the form of findings or action decisions without undue delay.

Because a field officer works in a constantly shifting ambiance of requirements, he must possess to an uncommon degree the ability to look over the horizon and to identify emerging needs at the earliest possible moment. He must have prescience and sufficient drive to enable him to organize programs to meet such needs. Foresight and initiative normally can be verified only by observation, and not in a written or oral examination. However, if the service focuses more on candidates with graduate degrees, their theses and publications should help oral examiners to appraise their prescience.

The unusual demands and difficulties of foreign affairs work abroad impose exceptionally heavy physical and emotional strain on those who undertake it. Every officer must come to his task in excellent health and with sound physical and emotional equipment. This does not mean that minor physical defects cannot be accepted, but rather that the officer must be emotionally stable and physically able to resist difficult living conditions, exceptional emotional strain, and prolonged periods of overtime activity.

Character Traits and Motivation. The character traits needed for successful performance seem to paraphrase the Ten Commandments and the Scout Law. The most important include maturity, truthfulness, integrity, objectivity, tolerance, steadiness, poise, sound avocational interests, normal habits, ethical acuteness, a sense of social responsibility, loyalty, and real modesty. Maturity, honesty, normal habits, and objectivity probably rank as indispensable. An immoral officer would be dangerous in diplomatic or consular circles, and a prig would find much field work distasteful. Thus, evidence of conspicuous weakness of character raises serious questions about any candidate's suitability.

Motivation often sustains an officer in difficult situations or unpleasant assignments. The successful candidate must demonstrate a lively interest in public affairs, other places and peoples, and the international problems of the United States. He must be willing to serve as a disciplined member of a demanding service. Oral examiners must satisfy themselves that the candidate will not only endure but will also enjoy ways of life alien to his own and that his interests have enough outward direction to make him useful abroad. Married candidates and those about to be married present a special problem because a couple works as a team or does not work well at all. Consequently, examiners must verify that the spouse or fiancée is equally dedicated to a career abroad.

Essential Basic Skills. Foreign Service officers at home and abroad should read, speak, and draft English clearly, concisely, and precisely because the greater portion of their working lives will be spent in attempting to communicate with each other, with other government employees, and with American citizens. Increasing use of quantitative analysis by social scientists now requires that all officers, regardless of their area of specialization, also demonstrate elementary knowledge of mathematical techniques of communication, especially basic statistical method and computer language.

Precision bears an intimate relatioship to verbal and mathematical skills. As Sir Harold Nicolson said very well: "If truthfulness is the first essential for the ideal diplomatist, the second essential is precision." The need to eliminate ambiguity or error from diplomatic or consular communications is too obvious to require expatiation. Even a misplaced comma in a treaty can assume such enormous importance as to make it imperative that candidates demonstrate both respect for accuracy and ability to avoid error. Some officers achieve precision the more easily because they have greater natural endowments of patience and prudence; others attain it only after long discipline. Here habits acquired in graduate school make an invaluable contribution.

Foreign language skills in some degree must be mastered by all officers serving abroad and by many in the domestic component. Specialist candidates and some technicians should demonstrate a working knowledge of at least one world language. Other field technicians could be accepted with more modest linguistic attainments.

Substantive Knowledge. Every Foreign Service officer at home or abroad should possess a basic fund of factual information, in addition to his technical or professional knowledge. He should be able to identify the main currents and figures in United States history, to display broad knowledge of the economic and political geography of his nation, and to demonstrate greater familiarity with his state or region. He should understand the structure, power, and operation of the federal, state, and local governments, and the basic principles upon which the American system and other systems of government rest. He should be generally familiar with the cultural contributions of the United States. Some informational gaps could be accepted, but any candidate not broadly familiar with the entire range of American history, economics, politics, literature, and artistic achievements should be expected to display compensatory knowledge in greater depth in one or more subordinate areas.

Every Foreign Service officer should also be familiar with the major trends of world history since the French Revolution, economic and cultural as well as political, and his interest in other peoples and places should have led him at least to sample the great literatures of alien cultures. A candidate not conversant with national and international events and issues of the day does not belong in foreign affairs work because he obviously cannot possess adequate motivation to serve effectively.

An understanding of modern society also requires a modest acquaintanceship with the broad principles of economics and public administration. Finally, a candidate should possess enough knowledge of the humanities and the hard sciences to prevent embarrassment to his country or himself and to enable him to find additional information should he need it.

The Written Examination

Some critics consider the written examination for Foreign Service officer candidates to be too verbally oriented and too heavily weighted in favor of the history, international relations, political science, or liberal arts major who may be expected to develop into a generalist. It has always been and probably always will be necessary to demand high competence in English usage. Specialists and generalists, officers at home and abroad, all need highly developed verbal skills. Specialization, in fact, greatly accentuates the need for a common, high standard of English usage because it multiplies the importance of coordination and synthesis. Neither can be achieved when specialists and technicians communicate in words of art incomprehensible to persons outside their fields.

That the written examination should test a candidate's factual knowledge outside his own field seems equally indispensable. Few would argue that a specialist or technician should be employed by a foreign affairs agency if unable to demonstrate general knowledge of the history and traditions of his own nation, major trends in world history during the past two centuries, fundamental political and economic theory, and the dynamics of international relations.

The present written examination serves merely as a preliminary screening of candidates' substantive knowledge and does not presume a high degree of specialization or technical skill. Originally the exam sought to uncover bright generalists, but the introduction of optional papers for public affairs and cultural specialists, economists, business administration majors, and administrative and management specialists gives candidates from these disciplines more or less equal opportunities with history, political science, and international relations majors.

A unified, integrated service would have to offer a considerably wider range of options for other technicians and specialists. It certainly would have to lengthen and weigh more heavily the optional examinations for candidates seeking appointment to domestic positions, because their work normally requires higher specialization. Perhaps it should also increase the length and weights of the optional tests administered to field service candidates in order to attract more highly trained technicians and specialists. But the basic knowledge, skills, and aptitudes sections of the written examination probably should never be weighted at less than the specialized tests for domestic candidates or below two thirds of the total weight for field service candidates.

The Oral Examination

Criticism of the oral examining process focuses partly on the rather in-grown character of the examining panels. To some extent this was remedied a few years ago by including representatives of other agencies having foreign affairs responsibilities as members of the three-man oral panels and by inducing a few public members to serve. Both tendencies should be encouraged, the more so if a unified service emerges. Should an integrated service also be established, oral panels examining candidates for the domestic branch probably should contain at least one outside technician or specialist from each candidate's field and one domestic officer, and should examine the candidate intensively to determine his ability to make good use of his specialized knowledge. Oral panels examining candidates for field service should continue to explore personal capabilities and character traits most intensively.

Critics of the oral examination also allege quite justly that its brevity precludes the accurate assessment of personal qualities. Some, like professor McCamy, suggest that the British country-house system would afford more adequate opportunities to explore strengths and weaknesses. The country-house system offers many advantages; but the British only examine orally a few dozen rather than a thousand candidates annually, and the system is both costly and time consuming. Whether the Congress would appropriate for such an elaborate examining program is moot, as is the question of whether the time required to undergo examination would deter any considerable number of able candidates from taking it. The mechanics of conducting such an examination would present major difficulties if extended to the dimensions of the current program, and, should a unified, integrated service be established, the number of oral examinations presumably would increase.

The department could, of course, use the first or probationary assignment more effectively as the final examining stage. But this would involve excessive expense at present because basic orientation and world language training at the Foreign Service Institute follow induction. It might work better should the department introduce flexible language requirements and begin recruiting candidates with professional or technical training.

A more practical approach would seek improvements in the oral itself. Until 1969 the written examination winnowed out, depending on the number of candidates and the places to be filled, between 70 and 85 per cent of those designated to take it. Thus, the panels examined between seven hundred and one thousand candidates annually. They recommended about one third, virtually all of whom were offered appointments, unless they failed the physical examination or security check. Some successful candidates elected not to enter the service for various reasons.

Personnel administrators tried to recruit more minority representatives and specialists in administrative and economic-commercial work by passing more than half of the candidates who took the 1969 written examination. Of the 3,793 candidates, 1,800 who elected Option A for the political or consular "tracks" passed, while 105 candidates passed under Option B for the administrative "track," and 201 under Option C for economic-commercial duty.[1] Specialized oral examining panels reviewed the qualifications of candidates in each of the three categories under instructions to limit recommendations for appointments to specified quotas. This meant that oral examiners of Option A candidates could only recommend about 1 out of 25 candidates.[2] It is to be hoped that this precedent of cheapening the written examination will not be followed in the future.

In connection with the oral examination, candidates should certainly be asked to take a psychological test, which could be monitored by

[1] United States, Department of State, *News Letter*, no. 108 (April 1970), p. 30.
[2] Interview with member of oral examining panel, Austin, Texas, June 1970.

panel secretaries and completed before or after the interview. Such a test need not include questions that would be embarrassing or would raise political difficulties. A well-designed psychological test would fill one of the gaps in the examining system that cannot be closed by a brief oral examination. It would also provide one of the major values of the country-house system.

The candidates to be examined on any given day by an oral panel should convene in one collective examining session and should also attend a social function where conversation could be general and where they could be observed under more relaxed conditions than those prevailing in an examining room. Each candidate should also have more time before the panel during the individual examining session. This implies a 50 to 70 per cent cut in panel workloads and a substantial increase in personnel engaged in such work. But the Foreign Service currently has a surplus of senior officers who could be employed most usefully on panels or in the College Relations Program when not on panel duty. In any case, would not such modest redeployment justify itself amply in light of the task's vital importance and the current downgrading of senior officer assignments?

To conclude, candidates should appear collectively before the panels in one session; individually they should have more time before the panels; panels should observe the candidates in a social situation for at least an hour or two; every candidate should take a standard psychological examination; and an upgrading of recruiting standards should permit greater use of the probationary assignment as the final examining stage. Such procedural changes unquestionably could enhance the utility of the total examining program.

21

Problems of Personnel Training and Organization

THE FOREIGN LANGUAGE PROBLEM

Foreign Service officer candidates under the Rogers Act had to demonstrate their ability to read, draft, and converse in at least one world language before appointment. In 1954, the Foreign Service faced an unprecedentedly heavy workload with a junior officer corps badly depleted by the cessation of recruitment and with middle and senior classes overinflated through integration. As an element of its crash recruitment program, the Department of State dropped the foreign language prerequisite.

After the crisis, some officers, including the writer argued that academic foreign language instruction did not always produce adequate linguistic competence and that reimposing the requirements might exclude otherwise excellent candidates. Today, despite considerable improvement and expansion in academic foreign language programs, the Foreign Service and USIA still admit new officers without requiring them to demonstrate competence in a world language, although they must acquire a working knowledge of one language as probationers or leave the service. Currently, most of the successful candidates display some linguistic competence, and it should soon be feasible to restore a language requirement. It certainly would be most desirable in light of the large investment of money and time currently allocated to junior officers' language training.

As suggested earlier, not all officers require the same degree or kind of linguistic skills, and a functionally differentiated foreign affairs service should set foreign language requirements for technicians, specialists, and generalists at varying levels corresponding to their needs. This in itself would lighten the in-service language training burden, as would increased efforts to recruit more trained specialists from the graduate schools. The language-training role of the Foreign Service Institute will remain highly important, but it should not in future have to prepare junior officers linguistically, although some newly recruited staff support personnel probably will always need initial language training at public expense.

Reintroducing a foreign language requirement should not postpone the attainment of additional representation by minority groups. In fact, candidates of Latin American extraction should find it relatively easy to meet a world language requirement by offering Spanish or Portuguese. Negro candidates show no lack of aptitude in learning foreign languages.

The preceding considerations, together with the growing tendency on the part of American students to spend a year or at least a summer or two abroad, argue strongly that a flexible initial foreign language entrance requirement equated to the needs of each functional role should now be reimposed. Promotion to midcareer and senior grades should also be related partly to linguistic competence in relationship to the functional requirements.

Other Problems Related to In-Service Training

The Foreign Service Act of 1946 for the first time gave the Department of State broad statutory authority to conduct in-service training. Its early programs focused principally on exotic language training, but it initiated modest functional and orientation programs and a large expansion in world language training after 1954. The sophistication and community character of the Foreign Service Institute's curriculum and faculty increased notably during the Kennedy and Johnson administrations, and the percentage of FSO time devoted to training rose from about 1 per cent to about 5 per cent; thus, training programs absorbed the man-year equivalent of 175 to 180 career officers by 1968.

The military services assign roughly 10 per cent of their officers to training programs during times of peace; but the services must do virtually all of their advanced training themselves and the nature of their basic function assures them a surplus of manpower when the nation is not at war. Foreign affairs agencies do not, in theory at least, dispose of superfluous manpower at any time and can recruit specialists from public institutions. Comparisons of the percentage of military officers with foreign affairs officers assigned to training duties, therefore, serve no useful purpose.

The soundest basis for planning an in-service training program geared to the needs of either the present Foreign Service or a unified, integrated service would be on the basis of periodically revised estimates of brush-up requirements for specialists and technicians in major functional fields at junior, intermediate, and senior levels. Initial needs for specialists could be met primarily by recruitment to the junior classes, by promotion, by temporary appointments to the reserve, and occasionally by lateral entry. In-service training should not seek to supply specialists or highly skilled technicians but should focus primarily on keeping officers already in service abreast of current developments in their specialties or technical areas.

The weakness of the present programs, a weakness that reflects no discredit on FSI but rather on the Department of State's personnel management, is that many of its courses offer undergraduate training in specialties that candidates could master before entering the service. This results in great expense to the taxpayer and a heavy drain on manpower needed for current foreign affairs functions.

Officers currently in the Foreign Service or in a unified, integrated service obviously will have to be brought up to a satisfactory level of expertise in some specialty or technical field. But the institute can serve the nation best in future by concentrating on refresher courses and seminars. It should also retain an orientation course for junior officers and other entrants, but such programs need not absorb much instructional effort or a large percentage of service manpower.

A closer association of FSI with ranking academic centers of research and teaching seems highly desirable. A growing tendency in this direction can be discerned and should be encouraged. The use of Foreign and Civil Service officers as instructors in the institute cannot be recommended, except under very special circumstances, but some could serve in administrative roles or perhaps as seminar leaders or coordinators. A major weakness of the old orientation program for junior officers was the uniform dullness of the presentations of most of the Civil and Foreign Service officer lecturers. Expert knowledge does not necessarily accompany ability to teach, and more profitable use might be made of Civil and Foreign Service specialists in informal learning situations.

A functional in-service training program oriented toward the reeducation of technicians and specialists, rather than toward training in fundamentals, should permit substantial savings. If refresher training were combined with home service assignments, no additional travel cost would be entailed, and scheduling should offer no insuperable difficulties because the officer could take the training at any time during the two to four years of his assignment. Savings could also be effected in language training if career plans could include definite recommendations as to the world languages officers should acquire. They could then complete by correspondence or on a part-time basis at least some study of the second or third facility before the need to use it might arise. More use could be made of after-hours study at foreign educational institutions as well. For example, an officer serving anywhere in Europe would have no difficulty in getting excellent instruction, at minimal cost, in world languages. Exotic languages offer special problems, but officers in Paris or London could certainly find excellent instruction in Russian, African, Southeast Asian, and Arabic language and area studies.

FSI should continue its drive to achieve the ideal of a unified, integrated foreign affairs academy serving the entire foreign affairs community. More integration should be encouraged by inviting representatives of still other agencies to offer constructive suggestions on curriculum, course content, and faculty. A dynamic program, designed to make FSI the postgraduate training institute of all American foreign affairs agencies should be drafted with the help of experts from all interested agencies and of academic experts.

The question of whether FSI should operate under special charter, as proposed by President Kennedy, would seem less important should a unified, integrated service emerge. In such a case, FSI probably should function as an integral part of the central foreign affairs management agency. Even under present conditions, the arguments in favor of the present arrangement seem stronger than those for an autonomous institute. Thus, the wisdom of Congress in rejecting the proposal seems sound.

By the same token, the frequently rejected proposal for a foreign affairs academy to select and train junior officers should be buried deeply for reasons advanced earlier. It could only produce stereotypes and procrustean geographic representativeness that would reduce the effectiveness of foreign affairs officers and exclude many able youths from such careers.

The Organization of Personnel Administration

The structure of an operating unit will not assure its success or determine its failure. The morale, quality, and training of a staff are far more important than its organization. Nevertheless, structure can help or hinder efficiency, and frequently organizational changes reduce effectiveness by creating confusion and undermining morale. Foreign affairs personnel administration since World War II has suffered both from bad organization and frequent rearrangements.

Until 1939 the Foreign Service could be administered by a few officers grouped into two small divisions, one concerned with general services, the other with people. Expansion created an obvious need for a larger, more sophisticated personnel staff.

Many Civil Service officers joined the Division of Foreign Service Personnel (FP), and late in 1947 a reorganization gave primary responsibility for assignments to the Employment Branch, which operated through regional sections corresponding to the geographical bureaus of the department. The regional officers made assignments, subject to the final clearance of an Appointments and Assignments Board, but they tended to keep able personnel in their areas and to release only culls or misfits. Moreover, regional section chiefs dominated the board and normally deferred to each other. Although a need in the Foreign Service theoretically could be met by selection from the entire range of officers available, the regional organization restricted such a review in practice to officers available only in the geographical area in which the need arose. It also encouraged the development of regional cliques in the service, the members of which helped each other to choice assignments and promotions. While this obviously did not greatly matter where assignments of area specialists were involved, it imposed severe limits on the proper use of functional specialists and technicians.

Probably the system's greatest weakness derived from its failure to permit employees to pursue career interests as freely as the needs of service might permit. Area officers served as judges and juries on the career development of officers within their area. The system thus failed to provide for service-wide evaluation, career planning, or a proper weighing of individual and service-wide morale problems. A Performance Measurement Section, which attempted officer evaluation, had no responsibility for and negligible influence on assignments and career planning.

Finally, the regional system precluded functional specialization within the Division of Foreign Service Personnel because each area officer had to evaluate every Foreign Service employee in his area, take account of his personal interests and problems, place him, maintain liaison with appropriate regional and operational divisions of the department and other agencies, and perform innumerable cognate tasks.

When the regional scheme was imposed, the writer suggested that a coequal branch should evaluate all personnel, provide monthly or quarterly lists of persons available for promotion, leave, and reassignment on a service-wide basis, and scrutinize personnel actions to assure consideration of developmental problems of the employee. The proposed branch would have certified personnel as suitable for assignment to certain functional activities at specified levels and for work in certain geographic areas, and would have authorized lateral or reserve recruitment for vacancies that could not be filled by transfer or promotion. Appointments or assignments in conformity with certifications of the proposed branch would have been made by employment or regional officers respectively without further clearance, other than that of the Appointments and Assignments Board. Branch chiefs, it was hoped, could negotiate most disagreements, leaving only a few cases for resolution by the personnel chief. The proposal also contemplated a third branch embracing various staffs and sections rendering common services.

Such a functional organization would have facilitated a full review of all available employees to meet every placement need, afforded every Foreign Service employee full career development opportunities limited only by the needs of the service, preserved the career principle by limiting reserve and lateral appointments to positions that clearly could not be filled by officers on duty, and increased the efficiency of the Division of Foreign Service Personnel by permitting its employees to specialize.

Numerous reorganizations of personnel administration between 1949 and November 1967 failed to establish a proper balance between the needs of the job or post and those of the individual.

Career planning and in-service training unquestionably received greater emphasis after 1961, and organizational arrangements for recruitment, assignment, and career planning focus somewhat more on function and the individual today. But the assignments machinery still works under the dominance of regional units.

Thus, it would still seem desirable to adopt a tripodal organizational arrangement with units grouped to serve the needs of the post or position, to further the development of the individual, and to provide common services. Obviously the vast personnel bureaucracy of today differs greatly from the relatively simple staffing arrangements of 1947, but the principles outlined above remain sound. Moreover, the far more sophisticated computer systems available today should make it even easier to operate on the lines suggested.

22

Prognosis

CAN THE UNITED STATES SPEAK WITH ONE VOICE?

Earlier chapters emphasized the unalterable character of many obstacles to the effective coordination of American foreign affairs administration, including the unique American system of checks and balances within a federal structure, the diversity of regional, religious, racial, social, and other loyalties and interests, the unprecedented complexity and range of problems abroad, the interpenetration of domestic by foreign concerns, the inflation in staffs and numbers of agencies involved, and the consequent rise in the political content of foreign affairs administration.

The possibility of constitutional reform to concentrate responsibility or authority remains so remote as to obviate discussion. No support exists for the introduction of ministerial responsibility or for any other scheme to unify the tripartite system. The only post-World War II proposal for constitutional change that aroused lively discussion, the Bricker amendment, would have curtailed the scope of treaties and executive agreements.

Reducing foreign commitments might lighten military and fiscal burdens but not the impact of external developments on American national security and well-being. The planet's continual shrinkage through scientific and technological progress seems destined to complicate American foreign relations increasingly, extend them to additional areas of concern, and bring them ever more intimately into the context of domestic polity.

Consequently, no major contraction could occur either in the number of domestic agencies engaged in foreign affairs administration or in staffs so occupied, even if rational organization and rigid economies could be forced upon them. Under these circumstances, the continued politicization of the bureaucracy seems inevitable.

What do these somber conclusions suggest?

First, *any effective action to enhance the United States' ability to speak with one voice must come from Congress in the form of statutory authorizations and prohibitions and from executive initiative.* Since the executive now initiates most legislation and all administrative law, and, since the president must sign bills into law, by far the greater share of the burden will rest upon him and his appointees.

Second, *some degree of participation must be assumed by virtually every federal agency in foreign affairs administration.* No single agency can ever monopolize this field again, and this poses the question of how coordination can best be achieved.

Interdepartmental committees operating under the rule of unanimity and without effective decision-making powers produce endless delays, watered-down recommendations, and a frightening waste of manpower.

The task force concept developed during the Kennedy and Johnson administrations produced more amply powered interagency committees chaired by senior executives from the agencies primarily responsible, normally the Department of State. They represented a considerable improvement and should probably continue to provide the bulk of coordination and clearance for day-to-day interpretational and operational decisions on both regional functional questions.

But how can such groups best be supervised and their differences reconciled under the National Security Council framework? President Eisenhower established the Planning Board and the Operations Coordinating Board, which President Kennedy abolished, relying somewhat optimistically on his special assistant for national security affairs and the Department of State to fill the gap. President Johnson established the Senior Interdepartmental Group (SIG), chaired by the undersecretary of state, for intermediate coordination and reconciliation of agency viewpoints.

President Nixon reorganized the NSC system as one of his first acts; he abolished SIG, established a NSC Review Group, chaired by his special assistant on national security affairs, to review papers from the Interdepartmental Regional Groups (IRG's) and other papers, and created an Undersecretaries Committee, chaired by the Department of State, to consider matters referred to it by the NSC Review Group or operational matters on which the IRG's cannot reach agreement. He also defined the authority and responsibility of the secretary of state in somewhat less generous language than President Johnson had used in 1966[1]

These changes may imply an intention on President Nixon's part to transfer higher coordinative responsibilities from the Department of State to the White House and to reverse the process of building up the department's authority which the two previous administrations followed. Such a course of action could generate additional resistance to State Department leadership in the intermediate and lower levels of the foreign affairs community and ultimately impair rather than improve coordination because of the politicization of the bureaucracy.

Third, *the major difficulties now involved in coordinating the domestic administration of American foreign relations underscore the grave importance of creating a unitary Foreign Service of the United States as the only official channel of communication and overt operating agency abroad.*

Prospects here do not seem favorable for the immediate future. President Nixon's campaign utterances about the Department of State

[1] United States, Department of State, *News Letter*, no. 94 (February 1969), inner cover and pp. 2–4, 6–7 (hereafter cited as *News Letter*).

However, President Nixon delegated to the secretary of state in February 1970 "responsibility over all activities of executive agencies that relate to U.S. participation in international organizations, programs and conferences" (*News Letter*, no. 106 [February 1970], p. 10).

did not encourage optimism that he might seek to restore more unity to field representation and operations, although his 1969 Air Force Academy commencement address implied that he would look for a more effective and economical instrument to discharge the world-wide mission of the United States, which he specifically endorsed.

Secretary Rogers, early in May 1969 designated then Undersecretary Elliot L. Richardson to chair the Board of the Foreign Service and made the director general of the Foreign Service executive director of the board. He described these changes as "an initial step toward a major and comprehensive review by the new Administration of the entire foreign affairs personnel structure," to take place under the board's auspices.[2] However, the first basic management policy statement of the administration's new deputy undersecretary of state for administration, William B. Macomber, in January 1970 emphasized the importance of developing compatible services in the Department of State, AID, and USIA, rather than a unified service.[3]

The unprecedented activism of the American Foreign Service Association (AFSA) could conceivably have a stimulating effect on the department and possibly on the Congress, which hitherto seldom has heard a voice raised from the career service. Thus, some faint hope may be cherished for the eventual reunification of the Department of State and USIA and for the staffing of overseas positions of all domestic agencies, including the Department of Agriculture, by the Foreign Service, as recommended by the Herter Committee. Advocates of these salutary measures will have to accumulate great pressure and overcome much bureaucratic resistance to achieve them. Little in the present mood or situation warrants optimism, despite the obvious rationality of conducting American affairs abroad in a disciplined manner. Perhaps budgetary stringencies may prevail where common sense has not.

Improved congressional and executive control over CIA's reporting and operational activities may emerge as a more attainable goal. President Nixon wrote to his ambassadors in December 1969 stressing their coordinative role and emphasizing each ambassador's right to "be kept

[2] *Ibid.*, no. 97 (May 1969), pp. 2–5.
[3] *Ibid.*, no. 105 (January 1970), p. 28.

informed to the extent you may deem necessary, of all the information or recommendations reported by any element of the Mission."[4] Congressional discontent with the diminution of its power over American foreign policy and especially over what it regards as excessive exercise of executive initiative could focus on CIA, which offers an easier target than the constitutional powers of the commander in chief. Congressional limitation of CIA's funds, or authority to conduct subversive operations, or unsupervised intelligence activities does not seem unlikely. But here the jealousy of congressional committees for their prerogatives may prevent remedial action.

Can the United States Improve Planning and Decision Making?

The ability of the Department of State to review basic policy, undertake contingency planning, and conduct successful planning-programming-budgeting system work abroad must improve. Unless it learns to plan more effectively, the department cannot hope to discharge its present coordinating role with greater success or to arrive at intelligent decisions more promptly.

Some major obstacles to improvement could be reduced by reorganizing the department's hierarchy to make better use of its policy liaison, intelligence research, and policy planning units, to give the secretary and his senior aides more time for deliberation on major issues, and to improve supervision. The establishment of a policy review staff would also help. The Herter Committee and AFSA both recommended the appointment of an executive undersecretary, but the Nixon administration as well as its two predecessors, has rejected this idea.[5] Virtually all recent studies of foreign affairs administration fault the department's policy planning and organizational arrangements. Since the cost of such a program would be extremely modest, the future may hold some hope for constructive administrative and legislative action along the lines suggested or along others, which further study may commend.

[4] *Ibid.*, no. 104 (December 1969), p. 7.
[5] *Ibid.*, no. 105 (January 1970), p. 29.

A second major thrust toward improved planning and decision making should come from continued intensification of efforts to apply the new techniques of data processing, handling, and retrieval to foreign affairs work. State Department programs of the past decade have been important and fruitful. The department should extend them both in depth and in breadth. Continued research and experimentation on the problem of storing and retrieving substantive data should receive a high priority. The establishment of a foreign affairs data bank supported by and supporting the entire foreign affairs community should be the goal of lateral expansion. The department should press both vertical and lateral expansion of machine data processing and retrieval vigorously to provide the factual basis for improved planning and programming.

The Department of State and other foreign affairs agencies must also make far greater use of academic and other social scientists, both on short assignments and under contractual arrangements. The Office of External Research can contribute even more notably in future than it has in the past to a fruitful collaboration between scholars within and outside the government. The department's role as coordinator of all governmental social science contract research in foreign affairs should also help it to develop closer relationships with and to promote more rapid exploitation of discoveries by the scholarly community. Any real advance in the areas of intelligence research, policy planning, or policy review will depend in large measure on the extent and intimacy of the collaboration here envisaged.

CAN THE UNITED STATES IMPROVE ITS REPRESENTATION ABROAD?

A multiplicity of foreign affairs services, regardless of their individual excellence, cannot hope to avoid duplication of facilities, services, and effort, as well as some divergence in pursuit of common goals. At worst, their efforts become counterproductive. Generally speaking, the most damaging excesses of free-wheeling, which confused and sometimes subverted American overseas efforts during World War II and for a decade thereafter, no longer occur. But the waste of money, manpower, and good will caused by multiagency representation abroad remains so substantial that even a mediocre unitary service probably would serve the United States better than the present plethora.

Happily it would be unnecessary to accept mediocrity. The United States had a career service second to none in 1939, according to the testimony of well-qualified foreign observers. Carefully selected and strictly managed in accordance with the career principle, it performed well and loyally and with high morale within the limits of its generalist capabilities. Faith in the career principle, in fact, represented its greatest strength and its Achilles tendon. It precluded an opening of the middle ranks after the war to accommodate officers needed to staff the new intelligence, information and cultural, foreign assistance, and management functions. Worst of all, it precluded a revision of junior officer selection standards to attract specialists to the lower classes of the service and to permit their appointment at salaries competitive with those paid by the Civil Service and academia. This institutional lag helped to bring about both the emergence of separate functional services and the unhealthy growth and distortion of the sensibly conceived reserve and staff components of the Foreign Service and of the foreign affairs community in general.

Do postwar shortcomings suggest that the career principle should give way to a less rigorous selection, promotion, and compulsory retirement system? By no means. Its misuse or abuse during the past two decades should not obscure its great merits, indeed, indispensability, to an institution requiring a quasi-military discipline and high performance sustained by high morale. The 1924–1939 experience amply demonstrated the value of the principle. Its revival and extension, modified to meet the needs of an integrated, unified Foreign Service of the United States would go far in itself to restore morale among present career officers and to assure high standards of performance and morale generally.

The modifications in selection, promotion, and retirement practices recommended earlier should, in fact, enhance the morale-building potential of the system by removing fear of loss of status through abuse of lateral entry or integration and envy or resentment of superior status or privileges; by assuring all officers doing good work that premature retirement will not be forced upon them; by opening full careers to all specialists; by extending opportunities to compete for the generalist classification and positions to officers from all fields; by equating entrance standards for junior officers more closely to their qualifications and to the needs of the service; and by relating advancement in the service to needs in order to avoid an imbalance in classes and specialties.

Earlier suggestions for improving the quality of the American foreign affairs service contain no revolutionary ideas. Present statutory and administrative law would permit administrators of a unified, integrated service to introduce most of the recommended improvements. They would have to obtain legislation, appropriations, or both, only for the minority scholarship program, for an improved examining system, and for direct appointments of junior officers above the level of FSO-7.

The improvements in the examining program would be relatively inexpensive and could be funded for less than the cost of a few bad selections, in any case for considerably less than the cost of giving world language and undergraduate training to young generalist recruits. Should the president and the Congress accept the need for restoring the Foreign Service of the United States, administrators should not find it difficult to obtain such modest legislative authority and funds. Even if present divisive arrangements continue, they should make every effort to reestablish the career principle in a Foreign Service having the flexibility and dynamism that its role demands.

Deputy Undersecretary of State for Administration William B. Macomber announced a "new personnel program for the '70's" on January 14, 1970. He declared the generalist-specialist controversy ended and promised the early development of a five-category specialist system. Foreign Service officers would staff political, economic-commercial, administrative, and consular positions; Foreign Service Reserve Unlimited (FSRU) officers would staff scientific, medical, security, foreign buildings, communications, and like specialist positions. Other categories of officers (FSSO, FSR, or Civil Service) in dual service positions would be assimilated as FSO's or FSRU's, retained in the Civil Service, removed by attrition, if they elect not to assimilate, or, in some cases, would be terminated. New recruitment would be to areas of specialization, and examinations would emphasize aptitude over "specific academic knowledge."

Promotion and competition would also be by specialties, but officers with executive ability would be developed by cross-specialty and interagency assignments and drawn from the Department of State, AID, and USIA. Macomber also urged a broader role for the Foreign Service Institute, more effective use of planning and coordinating tools and personnel, and many other less important changes.[6] In February 1970 he designated thirteen special task forces to evolve plans for the program.[7] These groups reported in June 1970. Their reports, the *News Letter* announced,[8] would be published with a covering document and distributed to the field and in Washington.

It is still too early (August 1970) to predict which of the many proposals advanced by Macomber will be adopted or, if adopted, in what form. Consequently, it would be futile to try to evaluate them in light of the suggestions put forward in this study. Some obviously would be compatible; others, and particularly those relating to the examination process, would raise serious questions. Probably the main thrust toward the creation of a specialized service, which began under President Kennedy, will be pressed, and this must be applauded; but apprehension remains about the fate of the career principle.

Epilogue

The record of the United States and of its foreign affairs community since World War II provides no basis for despair or even extreme pessimism. Indeed, given American inexperience in the world arena and the unprecedented difficulty of the United States' postwar role, the nation and its servants should take proper pride in their considerable achievements. The American people have held the line and prevented the great catastrophe for a quarter of a century. They have built some sound and, hopefully, durable international institutions.

---

[6] *Ibid.*, pp. 2–5, 28–31.
[7] *Ibid.*, no. 106 (February 1970), p. 6.
[8] *Ibid.*, no. 110 (June 1960), p. 19.

Above all, they have bought time for the processes of history to work their way with the United States and its great antagonist.

The United States has committed serious blunders, but so have other powers. It wasted effort and treasure, but so did they. Has the nation learned from its apprenticeship as a superpower? This question goes to the heart of the problem explored in this volume. Can the United States now, in full realization of the limits of foreign policy and the important role of foreign affairs administration, permit itself the continued luxury of conducting its overseas affairs as a projection of domestic bureaucratic rivalries? Can not the government rationalize the process and unify the institutions that unquestionably bear so largely on national security and well-being? What must be done can be done.

APPENDIX A

Investigations of Foreign Affairs Administration, 1947–1954

Brookings Institution Report, 1951

The Bureau of the Budget commissioned the Brookings Institution to prepare a comprehensive report on foreign policy administration, which appeared in June 1951. The report generally endorsed the recommendations of the Hoover Commission and the secretary of state's committee of 1950. It emphasized the need for mobility and interchangeability in staffs, adequate specialization and training, and greater decentralization of personnel authority, all within the framework of a single civilian foreign affairs system embracing nearly all home and overseas staffs.

The Francis Committee, 1953

Early in the Eisenhower administration, Charles Francis and a group of distinguished businessmen were asked by President Eisenhower's foreign assistance administrator, Harold Stassen, to evaluate Mutual Security Administration operations and concepts. The team reported in March 1953. It criticized sharply the wasteful duplication of administrative facilities in the field; attributed the frustrations of foreign policy administrators and the consequent decline in their morale to the multiplicity of agencies engaged therein; blamed a drop in entrance standards on competition for personnel resulting from the inflated requirements of rival agencies; stated unequivocally that "activities having to do with our foreign relations are a responsibility of the Department of State"; urged that all Mutual Security Administration functions be transferred there; advocated the appointment of an undersecretary of state for economic affairs; and declared flatly that "the Ambassador in each country should be the chief representative of the United States and that all other United States representatives should report to him."[1] This report was never published!

---

[1] United States, Mutual Security Administration, "Evaluation Report, March 24, 1953," letter of Charles Francis et al. to Harold C. Stassen.

ROBERT T. HELLER AND ASSOCIATES INVESTIGATION, 1953–1954

An outside management firm, Robert T. Heller and Associates, was brought in to investigate the department's machinery in February 1953; but its major recommendations, which have never been made public, did not meet with a favorable reception in the department, and the department terminated the contract at the firm's request in March 1954.

WHITE HOUSE FOREIGN AFFAIRS PERSONNEL TASK FORCE, 1954

The White House interagency group of government officials convened in May 1953 under Philip Young as a task force to study personnel arrangements in the field of foreign affairs. It submitted an unpublished report in 1954. This document, which anticipated by eight years major recommendations of the Herter Committee, endorsed generally the proposals of the Rowe-Ramspeck-DeCourcy Committee. It advocated the initial extension of a uniform foreign affairs system outside the Civil Service to the Department of State, Foreign Operations Administration (FOA), and USIA. Each agency was to have authority over its own people, but broad personnel policy was to be made in the Executive Office of the president.

PRIVATE STUDIES AND INVESTIGATIONS, 1947–1954

Private inquiries and research into the problems of foreign policy administration during the period under review probably influenced both the findings and recommendations of public investigations as well as executive and congressional approaches to the solution of some of the problems.

The Woodrow Wilson Foundation financed a study by a distinguished group of experts, chaired by Professor William Yandell Eliott, which issued a perceptive report and series of recommendations in 1952.[2] The report found no substitute for sound presidential leadership but advocated the restoration of the Department of State to a position of primacy among the departments of government in shaping American foreign policy. It also suggested the need for constitutional reform to strengthen the influence of the president.

The report of the Hoover Commission received critical attention from Bradley D. Nash and Cornelius Lynde,[3] two wistful advocates of smaller

[2] William Yandell Elliott, ed., *United States Foreign Policy: Its Organization and Control*.

[3] Bradley D. Nash and Cornelius Lynde, *A Hook in Leviathan: A Critical Interpretation of the Hoover Commission Report*.

government, and from Herman Finer, who contributed a scholarly, theoretical critique.[4] Professor Wallace J. Parks ably explored the administration of foreign economic policy,[5] but inevitably entered the broader field of general administration as well. Professor James L. McCamy[6] and Professor Arthur Macmahon[7] both addressed themselves to the entire field of foreign policy administration and the proliferation of agencies engaged therein. Macmahon also called attention to the danger of divorcing policy and operations. Parks, MacMahon, and McCamy all emphasized the limited value of efforts at field coordination, and the adverse effects of the proliferation of agencies and bureaucratic gigantism on foreign policy administration. All had reservations about the restoration of a unified field service, but their views on this question seemed somewhat ambivalent.

[4] Herman Finer, "The Hoover Commission Reports," *Political Science Quarterly,* 64 (September 1949), 405–419, 574–595.
[5] Wallace J. Parks, *United States Administration of Its International Economic Affairs.*
[6] James L. McCamy, *The Administration of American Foreign Affairs.*
[7] Arthur Macmahon, *Administration in Foreign Affairs.*

APPENDIX B

Investigations of Foreign Affairs Administration, 1955–1961

UNOFFICIAL

The American Assembly dedicated its Ninth Session to a discussion of the representation of the United States abroad. Background papers prepared for the use of participants and subsequently published by Columbia University in 1956 reflected the thinking of many distinguished experts in public and and private life. The Assembly, which worked in this instance under the direction of Henry M. Wriston, recommended manning not only the Foreign Service but also USIA and the International Cooperation Administration with career officers. It also emphasized improved recruitment, career planning, and in-service training of civilian overseas personnel for all agencies by an expanded and more highly developed Foreign Service Institute making full use of universities, colleges, and other facilities.[1]

Wriston also published a volume in 1956 presenting his personal views on the role of diplomacy and the general background and requisite training for the professional diplomat.[2]

Professor G. Dale Fuller's *Training of Specialists in International Relations* analyzed graduate programs in international relations in American universities, emphasizing means of strengthening specialized training programs "to reduce the distortion which is inevitable in overspecialization, while at the same time giving focus to broader education."[3]

Two very perceptive studies by Zara S. Steiner, published in 1958[4] and 1961[5] reported progress in implementing recommendations of the Wriston Committee and pointed out areas for further action. The 1958 study alleged that excessive rapidity of action on the committee's recommendations had

[1] American Assembly, *The Representation of the United States Abroad.*
[2] Henry M. Wriston, *Diplomacy in a Democracy.*
[3] G. Dale Fuller, *Training of Specialists in International Relations.*
[4] Zara S. Steiner, *The State Department and the Foreign Service: The Wriston Report—Four Years Later.*
[5] Zara S. Steiner, *Present Problems of the Foreign Service.*

led to inequities and crisis. Steiner criticized the committee because it had left unresolved the major questions of the generalist-specialist controversy, lateral entry, in-service training, and whether one agency or several should administer foreign affairs. Steiner found the new selection procedures for junior officers less demanding than the former tests and attacked the Committee's recommendation for a more representative service urging that quality should be the first criterion for selection.

Steiner recommended only limited lateral entry because it impaired service morale, few and carefully screened political appointments, larger grants for representation at big posts, broader training opportunities for generalists, and recruitment of more junior area and functional experts in lieu of wide use of lateral entry. She asserted that the middle and upper ranks of the Foreign Service needed specialists and that integration had increased this need without solving the problem of attracting them. She suggested changing promotion policies and establishing separate career ladders to encourage specialization. She found serious weaknesses in the administration of the department and criticized security measures, career planning, promotion, and selection-out; but she concluded that the service "should be given an opportunity to consolidate its ranks before further innovations are made."[6]

Steiner's second study focused on the results of Wristonization. She found that integration had intensified and made the Foreign Service more conscious of the need for specialists without increasing the supply. She again recommended more lateral entry. Although she noted that a shortage of area specialists still existed, Steiner felt that the department's current plans would correct this and that additional functional specialists could be recruited directly from the universities.

She concluded that most Foreign Service officers would continue to be used for traditional diplomatic and representational activities, although many would develop area specialties. The new recruitment drive she felt had sacrificed quality for quantity, by substituting written objective tests for the essay type and dropping the foreign language paper.

She urged that the department grant scholarships to likely Foreign Service candidates, but only at the graduate level, and that it concentrate its recruitment drive on generalists having broader competence than most officers presently enjoyed. Steiner also recommended that ambassadors should come mostly from the career service and that political chiefs of mission be more carefully selected.

[6] Steiner, *State Department and the Foreign Service*, p. 55.

She urged that appropriations for training be increased and that the Foreign Service Institute concentrate on filling present gaps in training. In order to reduce the training load, she recommended that officers be recruited who already had language and other skills. In her final summary, Steiner concluded that the only way for the Foreign Service to increase its competence was to open its ranks to specialists, although this offered the danger of a loss of cohesiveness, overstaffing, and excessive compartmentalization. She asserted that administrative paper work was becoming overwhelming and should be reduced if possible; that more public support should be rallied; and that more funds should be granted for representation at expensive posts.

Official

The Senate sponsored the most important public studies of foreign affairs management undertaken between 1955 and 1961. Its Committee on Foreign Relations published a report in 1958 analyzing State Department reports on its efforts to carry out the Wriston recommendations. This document concluded that the recommendations had been basically sound and that the department had either met or made a good start toward completing all of them. The department, it suggested, lacked information regarding training needs, adequate space for training, and funds for planned expenditure. It commended the Foreign Service Institute's training program but advocated that the Foreign Service accept the concept that good training at intervals is essential in the career of most officers. It urged that a Foreign Service officer should usually not be assigned to a country if he did not have a useful knowledge of its language. It concluded that the disadvantages of a Foreign Service Academy outweighed its advantages. The study characterized FSI's budget of about $5,000,000 per annum as too low in light of the burden imposed by the Wriston program and urged that training money be increased to 10 per cent of salaries and expenditures to take care of the new people and the backlog of training.[7]

Early in 1959, possibly to counter the harmful public effects of the sensational best seller, *The Ugly American*, the Senate Foreign Relations Committee scheduled a special session to hear Dean Harlan Cleveland of the Maxwell Graduate School of Citizenship and Public Affairs, Syracuse University, and two of his colleagues on the subject of foreign affairs personnel.

[7] United States, Congress, Senate, Committee on Foreign Relations, *Recruitment and Training for the Foreign Service of the United States* (staff study), 85th Cong., 2d sess., 1958.

The committee published the transcript of the hearing as a committee print, "The Overseas Americans."[8]

Cleveland summarized the results of a research project then in progress at Syracuse on the education and training of Americans for overseas service, which he described as "a slightly more serious contribution to these matters than . . . 'The Ugly American.' " He found no positive correlation between the number of Americans abroad and the virulence of anti-Americanism; but he suggested that anti-American feelings arose because of excessive American involvement in the internal affairs of other countries, the inflexibility of American foreign policy, undue preoccupation with the Soviet Union to the neglect of other important problems, and the ineffective administration of United States foreign policy. In the latter context he sharply criticized the pluralism in Washington and field operations, asserting that the time "for consolidation of our efforts abroad seems to be at hand," and that "we now have enough experience in foreign operations to know that they have to be consolidated by countries and by regions, because that is the way the world itself is organized."[9]

Professor Gerard J. Mangone outlined the five major elements of effective overseas performance as technical skill and adaptability, job dedication, understanding of political implications, cultural empathy, and organization ability. He asserted that a high correlation between empathic capability and high performance ratings had been uncovered. He recommended "a more integrated process of recruitment and training" and scholarship funds to support private institutions engaged in preparing people for overseas work.

Cleveland, responding to a specific query, rejected the idea of a Foreign Service Academy as entailing a loss of the values that universities independent of government control can offer and because of the advantages to be derived from mixing various specialists in an overseas training course. He criticized undergraduate training for foreign service as inadequate, asserting that "we have to add [elements] . . . at the graduate level." He recommended the inclusion of a period of training abroad as a requirement for a college degree and a broadening of scholarship programs to support students intending to enter overseas service rather than the establishment of a government school. Replying to another question, he said he favored including Foreign Service people, USIA, and ICA people in a common personnel system not only to improve coordination but to increase the breadth of ex-

[8] United States, Congress, Senate, Committee on Foreign Relations, *Hearings* on "The American Overseas," 86th Cong., 1st sess., February 18, 1959.
[9] *Ibid.*, pp. 9, 16.

perience of top administrators through rotation in various functional assignments. He also urged the reincorporation of the Foreign Agricultural Service into the Foreign Service.[10]

In January 1959 the Senate Committee on Foreign Relations also commissioned a series of fourteen important studies of United States foreign policy by well-qualified nongovernmental agencies. These appeared in 1959 and 1960. Studies prepared by the Maxwell Graduate School of Citizenship and Public Affairs and the Brookings Institution addressed themselves directly to problems of foreign policy administration.

The Maxwell study urged more delegation of responsibility to chiefs of mission; much stronger coordination and supervision of field operations by chiefs of mission; the merger of all generalist officers of the Department of State, ICA, and USIA into a broader Foreign Service; a program to improve executive skills of Foreign Service officers; and expanded programs of training for overseas service by American higher education. It argued that foreign operations "must now be seen as a government wide function, not as the exclusive or even primary function of one Cabinet department." Such operations, especially economic and USIA, should remain outside the Department of State to free the secretary from responsibility for "detailed operations" and leave him time to discharge his "real task" as "the President's chief of staff for coordination of the foreign policy aspects of all government activity, including such difficult cases as the Defense Department, the budget process, the setting of monetary, loan and tariff policy, and the disposal of agricultural surpluses." Coordination of overseas operations "should be done to the greatest possible extent by the ambassador in the field, rather than by detailed day-to-day low level clearance among subordinate staff in Washington agencies."[11]

The Brookings study urged the merging of the several national security staffs in the Executive Office (the special assistants for national security affairs, Security Operations Coordination and Foreign Economic Policy, the staffs of the NSC, the OCB, and part or all of the OCDM) into the Office of National Security Affairs under a director similar in status to the director of the budget. It recommended the creation of a secretary of foreign affairs, with general directive authority over political, economic, and information programs within a new Department of Foreign Affairs, embracing the De-

[10] *Ibid.*, pp. 24–25, 27–28.
[11] United States, Congress, Senate, Committee on Foreign Relations, *The Operational Aspects of United States Foreign Policy*, study no. 6, prepared by Maxwell Graduate School, Syracuse University, 86th Cong., 1st sess., 1959, p. 8.

partment of State, ICA, and USIA, but with each component department having a secretary of cabinet rank. It proposed that the new secretary of foreign affairs serve as vice-chairman of the NSC, that regular procedures be established to permit him and his officials to bring their views to bear on major defense decisions, that more exchanges of personnel be arranged between the Department of Defense and civilian agencies, and that civilian officials be given more training in national security problems. The study also called for improved public control over intelligence activities, a further development of contingency planning, and better procedures for evaluation. With regard to the field services, the study recommended greater use of career personnel as ambassadors and international organization representatives, more flexibility in assignments, and more in-service training. It also proposed that the Department of State, USIA, and ICA "work toward a common system" with "more flexible career patterns," including different career ladders. It emphasized the need for specialists but considered that lateral entry should be used as "an auxiliary but not the major means of acquiring them."[12]

The Subcommittee on National Policy Machinery of the Senate's Committee on Government Operations published documents and studies on the substance and administration of national security policy prepared in 1960 by government officials, including Robert Cutler, Gordon Gray, and Sidney Souers, and such private scholars as Walt Rostow, Robert R. Bowie, George Kennan, Henry A. Kissinger, and Hans J. Morgenthau.[13] The study, although expressing a wide diversity of viewpoints, illustrated the complexity of the problem of coordinating national security and foreign policy, basic differences of opinion among experts on the uses of planning and programming, and other differences on the roles of gigantism and agency proliferation in the administration of foreign affairs.

In February 1960 the subcommittee held hearings at which Robert A. Lovett, Robert C. Sprague, James P. Baxter, III, and Thomas J. Watson, Jr., testified. Mr. Lovett, on the whole uncritical of existing policy machinery, asserted nevertheless that our system encourages the assignment of responsibilities without authority, the excessive use of committees, and an undue

[12] United States, Congress, Senate, Committee on Foreign Relations, *The Formulation and Administration of United States Foreign Policy*, study no. 9, prepared by the Brookings Institution, 86th Cong., 2nd sess., 1960, pp. 4–9.

[13] United States, Congress, Senate, Committee on Government Operations, *Selected Materials* prepared for the Subcommittee on National Policy Machinery, 86th Cong., 2d sess., 1960.

urge on the part of peripheral agencies to "get into the act." Sprague, Baxter, and Watson devoted most of their testimony to the communist threat, urging greater flexibility in national security posture and administration. Baxter also spoke for "a better effort in education."[14]

A subcommittee staff study of 1961 criticized the "loss of individual responsibility, excessive compromise, and general administrative sluggishness" attributable to the excessive use of coordinative committee mechanisms arising from what Lovett had called the "foul-up factor" of too widespread participation in the foreign affairs process. It rejected proposals for a super-cabinet or White House super-staff position as more likely to complicate than improve the situation but recommended strengthening the traditional means of executive power by making more effective use of the secretary of state, by improving the cooperation between the Departments of State and Defense, especially at lower echelons, and by bringing the secretaries of state and defense into the budget process before the initial ceiling is established. It proposed the abolition of as many interdepartmental committees as possible and the chairing of remaining committees by the Department of State with the chairman having "more responsibility for decisional action." It also urged the delegation to a single department, usually the Department of State, of responsibility for executing foreign policy decisions, even when several departments participate, and pressed for wider use of joint informal working groups in the first stages of developing policy. The study recommended more training of foreign affairs officials in national security problems and expanded in-service training at a better-supported Foreign Service Institute and other institutions. It stressed the Department of State's need for more specialists, especially for managers and military and technical specialists, and for better policy planning. It advocated contracting out some problems, less travel for the secretary, a wider use of ambassadors-at-large and special representatives in place of the president and secretary, and a modernization of protocol by an international protocol conference.[15]

---

[14] United States, Congress, Senate, Committee on Government operations, *Hearings* before the Subcommittee on National Policy Machinery, 86th Cong., 2d sess., 1960, pp. 12–124.

[15] United States, Congress, Senate, Committee on Government Operations, *Study* submitted by its Subcommittee on National Policy Machinery, 87th Cong., 1st Sess., 1961, pp. 1–10.

APPENDIX C

Long-Term Training Programs Listed for FY-'71[1]

The Department has announced long-term training programs for the fiscal year 1971 (July 1970–June 1971).

The Career Management and Assignment Division in the Office of Personnel—in conjunction with the regional and functional bureaus—has begun the task of selecting candidates for the assignments.

Eligible to compete are all permanent Foreign Service Officers, Foreign Service Staff Officers, Civil Service Officers (General Service Schedule—GS), and Foreign Service Reserve Officers Departmental Employee Standards—FSR/DES.

Foreign Service Reserve Officers on limited appointments who are available for world-wide service are not "ordinarily eligible for long-term training," officials point out. . . .

Each officer's preferences will be weighed on the basis of Service needs, career goals, work experience, academic background, and previous in-Service training.

Applicants selected for university training assignments in non-government institutions will be expected to sign an agreement to remain with the Department for a period of at least three times the length of their training.

Listed below are the programs planned for Fiscal Year 1971:

GENERAL CAREER TRAINING

Diplomats-in-Residence and Senior Seminar—No applications necessary. For officers of FSO Classes Two or above or equivalents.

Training for Senior Responsibilities—(the war colleges and specific university fellowship programs—no applications necessary). Officers are selected who are expected to reach Class One and fill positions in program direction or top functional specialties.

The Senior Training Committee, composed of representatives from the

---

[1] Copied from United States Department of State, *News Letter*, October 1969, pp. 30–33.

operating bureaus and the central personnel system, will develop a rank-order listing of all officers born no earlier than January 1, 1924, who have never been low-ranked while in their present class. As a general rule, this list will consist of the names of eligible FSO-3's, but may also include FSO-2's who have not had senior training and otherwise qualify. GS, FSS and FSR-Domestic officers of equivalent rank who are within the age limit and who have been nominated by their bureaus are also included in the comprehensive list.

Although applications are unnecessary, an interested officer who meets the eligibility criteria may use the accompanying form to indicate his preference for assignment either to an armed service college or a special university program (e.g., Woodrow Wilson School of Public and International Affairs at Princeton, Sloan programs at M.I.T. or Stanford, or the Center for International Affairs [Bowie Seminar] at Harvard).

Courses begin in August or September and run for a full academic year, with the following exceptions: the Imperial Defense College in London, to which a new FSO-2 is normally assigned, begins in January and ends in December; the NATO Defense College in Rome is a six-month course beginning in September and January.

Fellowships—The relatively small number of university fellowships available for a year's unstructured study are primarily awarded to high-potential mid-career officers. Some, like the National Institute of Public Affairs (NIPA) Career Awards, go to officers who have successfully competed against nominees of other federal agencies. The typical candidate for one of these fellowships is an FSO-4 or equivalent, in his early or mid 30's. Ordinarily, those selected will range in grades from FSO-3 through FSO-5 or equivalent.

FSI preparatory courses begin in mid-July for university assignments starting in September or late August. University courses beginning in January are preceded by FSI preparatory courses beginning in December.

Officers who have specific foreign affairs projects in mind (a long paper or book) may apply for a fellowship at the Brookings Institution, at the Johns Hopkins University Center of Foreign Policy Research (SAIS) in Washington, with the Council on Foreign Relations, or with some other qualified institution. Age and class qualifications as well as other information on the Council's Fellowship are described is CA-3344, June 13, 1969. There are no maximum age or class limitations for the other fellowships. Officers interested in such an opportunity should describe their proposed study when applying. Beginning dates are flexible.

Officers who have specific study, writing, or research programs in mind may apply specifying the institutions at which they would like to pursue them, even if no current Department program is scheduled there. The Department may then investigate to see if establishment of a suitable program is feasible.

Internships—The only in-Service training internship program pursued by the Department in recent years has been participation in an inter-agency program administered by the Civil Service Commission to select outstanding young executives as Congressional Interns. Qualifications are the same as for fellowships. The ten-month Congressional Intern Program begins in October.

FUNCTIONAL TRAINING
Administrative/Management

FSI 14-Week Course—A 14-week Administrative Operations and Management course is offered twice a year at FSI, beginning in September and April. This program is designed specifically for promising officers with potential for administrative specialization. The curriculum introduces modern management theory as well as practical approaches to Foreign Service administration in the field. Graduates should expect to receive an on-going assignment in the administrative field. Selections will ordinarily be from candidates in FSO Classes 6 through 3 and equivalents.

University—Graduate-level programs of four months or longer are scheduled for experienced mid-career officers whose performance demonstrates potential to reach program direction positions via the administrative specialty. Candidates selected will range in grade from FSO-6 through FSO-3 and equivalents; the typical candidate is an FSO-5 or FSO-4, or equivalent, in his early 30's, who has served one or more tours in an administrative capacity. Starts are in September and January, some via preparatory training at FSI. Candidates for this training may be required to take the Admission Test for Graduate Study in Business which is offered several times each year in the U.S. and abroad. They should expect assignments in the administrative field following completion of the training.

Economic/Commercial

FSI 22-Week Course—An intensive 22-week course in economics at FSI covering economic theory, money and banking, public finance, international trade, etc., starts in January and July. The course is directed to Foreign Service needs and is designed to equip graduates with the equivalent of an undergraduate major in economics. Applicants for the course do not necessarily commit themselves to pursue a career specialty in economics. They should, however, expect to receive an on-going assignment from the course to a position with substantial economic content. The typical candidate for this training is an FSO-5, or equivalent, in his early 30's with minimal or no formal education in economics who has shown promise as a substantive officer. Students who are high achievers in this course are excellent candidates for later university graduate-level training in economics. Selections are ordinarily from candidates in FSO grades 6 through 4, or equivalents, who are not more than 38 years old.

University—Graduate-level programs for superior mid-career officers who aspire to reach the program direction level via career specialization in economics and/or who intend to become economics specialists in such fields as international trade and finance, economic development, etc., begin with preparatory training at FSI in July, followed by an academic year at a university. Applicants must have a strong academic background in economics or have satisfactorily completed the FSI 22-week economics course. Selections will ordinarily be from candidates in FSO Classes 4, 5, and 6, or equivalents, not more than 38 years old, who have served at least one assignment as an economic officer and have had some exposure to economic theory within the past five years.

Political-Military

Five-month courses at the Armed Forces Staff College (Norfolk) begin each August and January. The course ranges from weapons technology through foreign affairs, but emphasizes the joint staff planning (including political considerations) of military operations. Applicants do not necessarily commit themselves to pursue career specialization in political-military affairs. Following completion of the course, they may, however, be assigned to positions with substantial political-military content such as POLADS, DOD exchange, USRO, J/PM, and so forth. FSO-4's and 5's with political experience, between 32 and 40, are ordinarily considered for this program.

Systems Analysis

This is a government-wide program administered by the National Institute of Public Affairs for the development of managerial talent to use systematic analysis in carrying out Departmental responsibilities, and for those who wish to specialize in analysis as a function. The program consists of an academic year at a leading university starting in July with preparatory training, and includes intensive work in such subjects as economic analysis, operations research, and quantitative methods in general. Graduates of the program will probably be assigned in the Department to both substantive and administrative positions. The typical candidate is an FSO-5, or equivalent, in his early 30's, with some background or experience in economics and/or mathematics. Selections are ordinarily from candidates in FSO Classes 6 through 4 or equivalents.

Labor

The program is divided into (1) a Washington-based segment (September-February) which includes training in the Departments of State and Labor as well as field trips and (2) an academic segment (February-June) consisting of 13 weeks at the Harvard Trade Union Program, followed by ten days with an American labor union local. Graduates of this program will specialize in labor work during their mid-career years and can expect to serve as labor officers in political sections or in labor attaché positions. A typical candidate for the program would be an FSO-5, about 32 years of age, who has had some labor reporting experience. Selections will ordinarily be from candidates of FSO Class 6 through 4 or equivalents.

Petroleum

A special program of two to five months is tailored to the individual officer's background and his on-going assignment. It consists of consultation at the Departments of State and Interior and field visits to oil companies. Graduates will receive assignments as petroleum reporting officers or attachés. Selections are ordinarily from candidates of FSO Classes 4 or 5, or equivalents. Timing of starts is flexible.

Science and Foreign Affairs

An academic year at a university begins in September and encompasses a survey of contemporary scientific achievements and their relation to public policy with emphasis on foreign affairs. Graduates of the program will receive assignments in science attaché or science reporting positions abroad or in International Scientific and Technological Affairs (SCI) in the Department. The candidate should normally be a new FSO-5, or equivalent, who has a good academic record in the natural sciences or engineering. He should be able to handle quantitative concepts. Selections will ordinarily be from candidates between 26 and 38 years of age, with ranks of FSO-6 through 4, or equivalent.

Population Studies

Ford-Foundation-supported university study of the problems arising from pressures of population on resources, particularly as they affect the developing world, and of U.S.-supported programs of family planning abroad, begins with preparatory study in July. Graduates of the program will normally be assigned to positions in Washington and the field, with the Department of State or on detail to AID, where officers with this training are needed. The typical candidate for this training is an FSO-4, or equivalent, in his mid-30's, with an economic background gained through education or experience. Selections will ordinarily be from candidates in FSO Classes 5 through 3, or equivalents.

Geographical Area

These programs ordinarily conducted at American universities lead to, or reinforce, a substantive specialization in a geographic area of the world and are inter-disciplinary in content. Although most candidates for these programs are either economic or political officers, other officers who intend to pursue their functional specialties in a particular geographic area during most of their career will also be considered.

Applicants must have achieved a 3/3 tested rating in at least one major language of the area and have already served there, with the exception of Atlantic Affairs training for which prior service is not a requirement.

The ideal candidates for all area programs are FSO-5, or equivalent, about 32 years of age, with at least four years of service experience. Officers between the ages of 28 and 36 in FSO grades 6 to 4 are ordinarily selected for area training programs.

The geographic areas include Latin America, Atlantic Affairs, Eastern Europe and USSR, Near East and North Africa, Africa, Sub-Sahara; South Asia, Southeast Asia, and East Asia.

University area training begins in mid-July with a series of preparatory courses at FSI prior to September university enrollment. (FSI preparatory training begins in December for January enrollment.)

Senior Area Research Fellow

The University of Michigan has provided a Foreign Service fellowship for a senior mid-career officer to serve for an academic year as a research fellow in its Center for Chinese Studies. Similar programs might be developed for experienced specialists in other geographic areas at appropriate universities.

Applicants must have a 3/3 tested rating in at least one major language of the area; have already served more than one tour there; and be interested in doing independent study and research, possibly leading to publication. The typical candidate will be Class 3 or 4, or equivalent.

Hard Languages and Area Specialization Training

Training in hard languages at FSI is preceded by three weeks of intensive area study and is regularly accompanied throughout by continuing area study. The training is intended for officers who are prepared to serve a significant part of their careers in regions where the language is spoken. Hard language enrollments are directly geared to anticipated vacancies abroad.

Where the usefulness of the language is limited to one or two posts (e.g., Finnish, Amharic) graduates may expect to serve two tours, not necessarily consecutive. Graduates of programs in languages which are useful at several posts, particularly in languages requiring more than one year's study, should be prepared to spend most of their careers in their area specialty. A few officers with high language aptitude may be selected for dual language-area specialization. Examples of such dual specializations are China and Russia, Near East and East Europe, and China and Japan.

Selection criteria include a good language aptitude index (generally 60 or above on the Modern Language Aptitude Test) and success in previous language study. The ideal candidate is a Class 6 officer under 30 years of age. Officers above Class 4 or older than 36 are ordinarily ineligible.

Within-step salary increases are offered as an incentive for the study of certain languages (3 FAM 873).

Training usually varies from 27 weeks, including three weeks of intensive area study, to two years. Most assignments start in August, though several languages have a second starting date later in the fiscal year.

Hard languages which may be offered in FY 1971 are Afrikaans, *Amharic, Arabic (elementary, beginning and advanced), *Bengali, Berber, Bulgarian, *Burmese, Cambodian, Chinese (Mandarin and Cantonese, elementary and advanced), Czech, Finnish, Greek, Hebrew, Hindi, Hungarian, Indonesian, Japanese (elementary and advanced), *Korean (elementary and advanced), *Lao, Malay, *Nepali, Persian, Polish, Romanian, Russian (elementary and advanced), Serbo-Croatian, *Singhalese, *Somali, Swahili, *Tamil, Thai, Turkish, Urdu, and *Vietnamese.

(*Denotes probable incentive languages to be recognized by the Department for study in FY 1971, pending possible revision of 3 FAM 873.1.)

APPENDIX D

The Flow of Policymaking in the Department of State[1]

The Department of State is an organism that is constantly responding to a vast assortment of stimuli. A new Soviet threat to Berlin, a forthcoming conference of Foreign Ministers of the Organization of American States, a request from Poland for credit, a solicitation for support of a candidacy for the Presidency of the United Nations General Assembly, a plea from an ambassador that the head of the government to which he is accredited be invited to visit the United States officially, a refusal by another government to permit the duty-free importation of some official supplies for a U.S. consulate, a request from the White House for comment on the foreign affairs section of a major presidential address, an earthquake in the Aegean creating hardships which it appears the U.S. Navy might be able to alleviate, a request for a speaker from a foreign policy association in California, a transmittal slip from a Member of Congress asking for information with which to reply to a letter from a constituent protesting discriminatory actions against his business by a foreign government, letters from citizens both supporting and deploring the policy of nonrecognition of Communist China, a continuing inquiry by a press correspondent who has got wind of a top secret telegram from Embassy Bonn on the subject of German rearmament and is determined to find out what is in it, a demand by a Protestant church group that the Department take steps to prevent harassment of their coreligionists in a foreign country, a request by a delegation of a federation of women's clubs for a briefing on southeast Asia and suggestions as to how its members might be useful in their planned tour of the area, a request from Consulate General Brazzaville for a revision of cost-of-living allowances, a visit by a commission of inquiry into the opera-

---

[1] Extract of Appendix C by Charlton Ogburn, Jr., from United States, Congress, Senate, Committee on Foreign Relations, *United States Foreign Policy: The Formulation and Administration of United States Foreign Policy*, Study No. 9, prepared by the Brookings Institution, 1960.

tions of U.S. foreign aid programs, a notification from the staff of the National Security Council that a revision of the National Security Council paper on dependent areas is due, a telegram from a U.S embassy in the Near East declaring that last night's flareups make a visit by the Assistant Secretary for Near Eastern and South Asian Affairs, now in mid-Atlantic, inopportune at the moment, a warning by a European Foreign Minister of the consequences should the United States fail to support his nation's position in the Security Council, and a counterwarning by an African representative at the United Nations of the consequences should the United States do so—this is a sample of the requirements made of the Department of State in a typical day. Of course it does not include the oceans of informational reports that come into the Department by telegram and air pouch or the countless periodicals from all parts of the world that arrive by sea.

What is required to begin with is that the flow be routed into the right channels. This does not apply to press correspondents and foreign embassy officials; they usually know where to go without being directed. For the rest, almost every piece of business—every requirement or opportunity for action—comes within the Department's ken first as a piece of paper. These pieces of paper—telegrams, dispatches (or "despatches," as the Department prefers to call them), letters—must be gotten as speedily as possible into the hands of the officers who will have to do something about them or whose jobs require that they know about them.

The telegram and mail branches of the Division of Communication Services, a part of the Bureau of Administration, receive the incoming material and, after decoding and reproducing the telegrams, indicate on each communication the distribution it should receive among the bureaus or equivalent components of the Department. If, in the case of a letter or a dispatch, there are not enough copies to go around, the recipients are listed one after another and receive it consecutively, the original going first to the bureau responsible for taking whatever action the document requires. With telegrams, the deliveries are simultaneous. Several score copies of a telegram may be run off. A yellow copy, called the action copy, like the original of a dispatch or letter, goes to the bureau responsible for taking any necessary action; white copies go to all others interested.

A telegram (No. 1029, let us say) from a major U.S. embassy in Western Europe reports the warning of the Foreign Minister of X country that a grave strain would be imposed on relations between X and the United States should the latter fail to vote with X on a sensitive colonial issue in the United Nations General Assembly. Such a telegram would have a wide distribution. The action copy would go to the Bureau of European Affairs. The action copy of a telegram to the same purpose from the U.S. delegation to the United Nations in New York, quoting the X delegation, would go to the Bureau of International Organization Affairs. This is a matter of convention.

Information copies of a telegram of such importance would go to all officers in the higher echelons—the Secretary of State (via the executive secretariat), the Under Secretaries, the Deputy Under Secretaries, the counselor. They would also go to the Policy Planning Staff, to the Bureau of African Affairs because of the involvement of certain territories within its jurisdiction, to the Bureau of Far Eastern Affairs and the Bureau of Near Eastern and South Asian Affairs because the telegram concerns the incendiary question of European peoples' ruling non-European peoples, and of course to the Bureau of Intelligence and Research. Other copies would go to the Department of Defense and the Central Intelligence Agency. The executive secretariat would doubtless make certain that the Secretary would see the telegram. In addition, its staff would include a condensation in the secret daily summary, a slim compendium distributed in the Department on a need-to-know basis. If classified top secret, it would be included in the top secret daily staff summary, or black book, which goes only to Assistant Secretary-level officials and higher.

In the bureaus, incoming material is received by the message centers. There a further and more refined distribution would be made of telegram 1029. Copies would go to the Office of the Assistant Secretary (the so-called front office), to the United Nations adviser, to the public affairs adviser (since the United States is going to be in for trouble with public opinion in either one part of the world or the other), and to whatever geographic office or offices may seem to have the major interest. In the Bureau of International Organization Affairs, this would be the Office of United Nations Political and Security Affairs. Another copy, however, might go to the Office of Dependent Area Affairs.

In the Bureau of European Affairs, the yellow action copy of the telegram goes to the Office of Western European Affairs and thence to the X country desk, where it is the first thing to greet the desk officer's eye in the morning. As it happens, the desk officer was out the evening before at an official function where he discussed at length with the first secretary of the X embassy the desirability of avoiding any extremes of action in the United Nations over the territory in question. In the front office of the Bureau, the

THE FLOW OF POLICYMAKING IN THE DEPARTMENT OF STATE 371

staff assistant has entered in his records the salient details of the problem the Bureau is charged with and has passed the telegram on to the Assistant Secretary.

The following scenes are now enacted:

The X country desk officer crosses the hall to the office of his superior, the officer-in-charge, and the two together repair to the office of the Director of the Office of Western European Affairs. The three officers put in a call to the Assistant Secretary for European Affairs and tell his secretary that they would like as early an appointment as possible.

The Director of the Office of United Nations Political and Security Affairs (UNP) telephones the Director of the Office of Western European Affairs (WE). He says he assumes WE will be drafting an instruction to the U.S. embassy in X to try to dissuade the Foreign Office from its course, and that UNP would like to be in on it. He adds that they had thought of getting the U.S. delegation to the United Nations (US Del) to present this view to the X mission in New York but that there seemed to be no point in doing so since the latter would already be advising its government to take account of world opinion.

After the Secretary's morning staff conference, where the matter is discussed briefly, a conference is held in the Office of the Assistant Secretary for European Affairs to decide on a line to take with the X government. The X desk officer is designated to prepare the first draft of a telegram embodying it. The draft is reviewed and modified by his officer-in-charge and the Office Director for Western European Affairs.

The telegram instructs the U.S. embassy in X to make clear to the X government our fear that its projected course of action "will only play into hands extremists and dishearten and undermine position elements friendly to West" and suggests that the X government emphasize its policy to take account of the legitimate aspirations of the indigenous population of the territory in order to improve the atmosphere for consideration of the problem by the General Assembly. The Assistant Secretary, after scrutinizing and approving the telegram, finds it necessary only to add the Bureau of Near Eastern and South Asian Affairs to the clearances. Those already listed for clearance are the Deputy Under Secretary for Political Affairs, the Bureau of International Organization Affairs, and the Bureau of African Affairs. He says it can be left to the Deputy Under Secretary for Political Affairs to sign the telegram; he does not see that the telegram need go higher.

It remains for the drafting officer to circulate the telegram for approval by those marked for clearance. In the Bureau of African Affairs the telegram is termed extremely gentle to the X government but is initialed as it stands. The Office of United Nations Political and Security Affairs (UNP) wishes to remind X that the United States, setting an example of its adherence to the principle of affording the widest latitude to the General Assembly, had even accepted on occasion the inscription of an item on the agenda accusing the United States of aggression. The X desk officer states, however, that WE would not favor such an addition, which might only further antagonize the X government. Thereupon, UNP, yielding on this point, requests deletion of a phrase in the telegram seeming to place the United States behind the X contention that the question is not appropriate for discussion in the United Nations. The drafter of the telegram telephones the Director of the Office of Western European Affairs who authorizes the deletion, having decided that he can do so on his own without referring the question to his superior, the Assistant Secretary.

With that, the Director of the Office of United Nations Political and Security Affairs initials the telegram for his Bureau, and the X desk officer "hand carries" the telegram (in the departmental phrase), with telegram 1029 attached, to the Office of the Deputy Under Secretary for Political Affairs and leaves it with his secretary. At 6 o'clock he is informed by telephone that the Deputy Under Secretary has signed the telegram (that is, signed the Secretary's name with his own initials beneath) without comment. The desk officer goes to the fifth floor, retrieves it, and takes it to the correspondence review staff of the executive secretariat, where the telegram is examined for intelligibility, completion of clearances, conformity with departmental practices, etc., before being sped to the Telegram Branch for enciphering and transmission.

The next morning, all offices of the Department participating in the framing of the telegram receive copies of it hectographed on pink outgoing telegram forms. The telegram, bearing the transmission time of 8:16 p.m., has entered history as the Department's No. 736 to the embassy in X. The X desk officer writes "telegram sent," with the date, in the space indicated by a rubber stamp on the yellow copy of the original telegram 1029, and the staff assistant in the front office makes an equivalent notation in his records. The yellow copy is then sent on to the central files, whence in time it will probably be consigned to the National Archives. Only the white copies may be kept in the Bureau's files.

In this case, however, no one is under any illusion that the matter has been disposed of. Scarcely 24 hours later comes a new telegram 1035 from the embassy in X reporting that, while the X government may possibly make some concessions, it will certainly wage an all-out fight against inscription of the item and will expect the United States to exert itself to marshal all the negative votes possible. The question is, what position will the United States in fact take and how much effort will it make to win adherents for its position? No one supposes for a moment that this explosive question can be decided on the bureau level. Only the Secretary can do so—as the Secretary himself unhappily realizes.

At the end of a staff meeting on Berlin, the Secretary turns to the Assistant Secretary for Policy Planning and asks him to give some thought within the next few days to the alternatives open on the question. The official addressed sets the wheels in motion at once. A meeting is called for the next morning. Attending are: the Assistant Secretary for Policy Planning himself and several members of his staff (including the European and African specialists), the Director of the Office of United Nations Political and Security Affairs, the Western European officer-in-charge, the X desk officer, a member of the policy guidance and coordination staff of the Bureau of Public Affairs, and two intelligence specialists, namely, the Director of the Office of Research and Analysis for Western Europe and the Director of the Office of Research and Analysis for the Near East, South Asia, and Africa.

The discussion explores all ramifications of the issues involved and is generally detached and dispassionate. The object of the meeting is to help clarify the issues so that the Policy Planning Staff may be sure all relevant considerations are taken into account in the staff paper it will prepare for the Secretary.

The Secretary is in a difficult position. The President's views on what course of action to take are somewhat different from his. The Congress is also of divided view, with some Members impressed by the irresistible force of nationalism among dependent peoples, others by the essential role of X in NATO and European defense. The ambassadors of some countries pull him one way, others another. One of the Nation's leading newspapers editorially counsels "restraint, understanding and vision." At the staff meeting he calls to arrive at a decision, the Secretary perceives that his subordinates are as deeply divided as he feared. He takes counsel with each—the Assistant Secretaries for Policy Planning, European Affairs, African Affairs, and Near Eastern and South Asian Affairs. At the end he sums up and announces his decision. Thereupon the following things happen:

The Assistant Secretaries take the news back to their bureaus.

An urgent telegram is sent to the U.S. Embassy in X reporting the decision.

Telegrams are sent to embassies in important capitals around the world instructing the ambassador to go to the Foreign Office and present the U.S. case in persuasive terms.

A similar telegram is sent to the U.S. delegation in New York for its use in talks with the delegations of other United Nations members.

Conferences attended by representatives of the geographic bureaus concerned, of the Bureau of Public Affairs, and of the U.S. Information Agency, are held. Afterward, the representatives of the U.S. Information Agency return to their headquarters to draft guidances to the U.S. Information Service establishments all over the world. Such guidances tell how news of the U.S. decision is to be played when it breaks.

The more important the problem, the more the upper levels of the Department become involved. In a crisis—one brought about, say, by the overthrow of A, a Western-oriented government in the Middle East—the Secretary himself will take over. However, the bulk of the Department's business is carried on, of necessity, by the lower ranking officers. Even when a crisis receives the Secretary's personal, day-to-day direction, the desk officer and the officer-in-charge are always at hand to provide the detailed information only specialists possess, while in the intelligence bureau, country analysts and branch chiefs will be putting in 10-hour days and 6- or 7-day weeks. Generally, moreover, the crisis will have been preceded by a good deal of work on the part of lower level officials.

In the case suggested, it was apparent for some time that all was not well in A. The U.S. Embassy in A was aware of growing discontent with the regime through its indirect contacts with the opposition political elements, from information from Cairo, from evidences of tension, from clandestine publications. Additional straws in the wind were supplied by the public affairs officer in A both to the embassy and to the U.S. Information Agency because of his special contacts among professional groups. On the strength of these reports and of dispatches from American foreign correspondents in the area, and equipped with analyses from the Bureau of Intelligence and Research, all pointing in the same direction, the desk officer at a staff meeting of the Office of Near Eastern Affairs imparts his disquiet. He is directed to prepare a memorandum which, if convincing in its presentation, the Office Director undertakes to put before the Assistant Secretary.

What the desk officer has in mind will require national action, so what he drafts takes the form of a memorandum to the Secretary. It embodies a statement of the problem, the actions recommended, a review of the facts bearing upon the problem, and a conclusion. At the end are listed the symbols of the offices of the Department from which concurrences must be sought. Backing up the memorandum will be supporting documents, especially telegrams from the embassy, each identified by a tab. The mass fills a third of an in-box.

The problem is defined as that of strengthening the present pro-Western regime of A. By way of recommendation, the desk officer is especially sensitive to the problems and needs of the country for which he is responsible. He calls for more detachment of the United States from A's rival, B, expediting U.S. arms deliveries to A and the supply of certain recoilless rifles and jet fighter planes the A government has been requesting, support for A's membership in various United Nations agencies, a Presidential invitation to the Prime Minister of A to visit the United States. Much of what the memorandum recommends has to be fought out in the Bureau and even in the Office since it conflicts with the claims of countries (and the desk officers responsible for them) in the same jurisdiction. While neither the Office Director nor the Assistant Secretary doubts that support of B is a handicap in the region, they consider that a proposal for a radical departure would simply doom the memorandum by preventing anyone from taking it seriously.

As it finally leaves the Bureau with the Assistant Secretary's signature, the memorandum is considerably revised, and further change awaits it. The Department of Defense cannot provide the desired recoilless rifles and jet fighters. The Bureau of International Organization Affairs cannot offer any undertakings at this stage with respect to the question of membership in United Nations agencies. The Deputy Under Secretary for Political Affairs rules out a request of the President to invite the A Prime Minister for an official visit because the number of those invited is already too large.

Among recommendations in memorandums to the Secretary, as among salmon battling their way upstream to the spawning grounds, mortality is heavy. Almost everywhere in the world, things are far from satisfactory, but the United States cannot be doing everything everywhere at the same time. And A, far from seeming to cry out for attention, looks like the one Middle Eastern country about which it is not necessary to worry.

Then the uprising occurs in A. Early in the morning, the officer-incharge of A and one other country is awakened by the ringing of the telephone. In a flash, before his feet have touched the floor, he has visualized every conceivable disaster that could have befallen his area and has picked the overthrow of the monarchy in C as the most likely. Or did the security people find a top secret document under his desk?

On the telephone, the watch officer at the Department tells him that a "Niact" (a night action telegram, which means "Get this one read immediately even if you have to rout someone out of bed") is coming off the machine and it looks serious—he had better come down. En route, the officer-in-charge turns on his car radio and picks up a news broadcast, but nothing is said about A. Uncle Sam has beaten the press agencies.

At the Department, he finds the telegram wholly decoded and reads the hectograph master. There is revolution in A. The top leadership has been either murdered or banished. The officer in charge could legitimately awaken the Assistant Secretary, but for the moment it seems there is nothing that can be done, so he decides to hold off until 6 a.m. and then call the Office Director and put it up to him. He does, however, call the A desk officer and tell him to get on his way. To share his vigil beside the watch officer's window there is a representative of the executive secretariat, who will have the telegram ready for the Secretary to read immediately on his arrival. In the Bureau of Intelligence and Research—it being now after 4 o'clock—the morning briefers have arrived to go over the night's take and write up items of importance, with analyses, for the Director's use in briefing the Secretary's morning staff conference. The briefer for the Office of Research and Analysis for the Near East, South Asia and Africa—a GS11 specialist on India—takes one look at the Niact on A and gets on the telephone to the A analyst.

By the time the Secretary has stepped from his black limousine and headed for the private elevator a good deal has happened. In the Bureau of Near Eastern and South Asian Affairs, everyone concerned with A from the Assistant Secretary down, and including the officer-in-charge of Baghdad Pact and Southeast Asia Treaty Organization affairs and the special assistant who serves as a policy and planning adviser, has been in conference for an hour laying out the tasks requiring immediate attention. Two more Niacts have come in from A, one reporting that so far no Americans are known to have been injured but offering little assurance with respect to the future. The Assistant Secretary has already put in a call to the Director of Intelligence Research to ask that all possible information on the new leader of A and his connections be marshaled and that the Central Intelligence Agency be informed of the need. For the rest, the following represent the Assistant Secretary's conception of what should be done first:

1. The Department of Defense must be apprised of the Department of State's anxiety and be requested to have transport planes in readiness at nearby fields for the evacuation of Americans if necessary in accordance with prearranged plans. There must be consultation on what instruments are available if American lives have to be protected by force.

2. The U.S. embassy in C, a friendly neighbor of A's to which the Niacts have been repeated, will be heard from at any moment, and the Special Assistant for Mutual Security Coordination in the Office of the Under Secretary for Economic Affairs and, also, the Office of International Security Affairs in the Department of Defense will have to be alterted to the possibility of emergency military assistance for C.

3. Anything in the pipeline for A should be held up. The Special Assistant for Mutual Security Coordination must be advised of this.

4. The possibility of a demonstration by the U.S. 6th Fleet in support of C's independence and integrity will have to be discussed with the Department of Defense.

5. A crash national intelligence estimate will be requested of the Central Intelligence Agency, provided the Agency does not consider the situation too fluid for a formal estimate to be useful.

6. The public affairs adviser will get in touch with the Bureau of Public Affairs, the departmental spokesman and the U.S. Information Agency to agree on the kind of face the United States will put on the affair.

7. The B Ambassador will probably have to be called in and apprised of the critical need for his government's acquiescence in overflights of B for the purpose of getting supplies to C. The B and C desk officers had better get busy immediately on a draft telegram to embassy B (repeat to C) setting forth the case the ambassador should make urgently to the B Foreign Office.

At 9:12, anticipating that he will be called to accompany the Secretary to the White House, the Assistant Secretary instructs his secretary to cancel all his appointments for the day, including one with the dentist but excepting his appointment with the C ambassador. ("Mr. Ambassador, you may assure His Majesty that my Government remains fully determined to support the sovereignty and territorial integrity of his nation.")

At 9:14, 1 minute before the scheduled commencement of the staff meeting, the Assistant Secretary joins his colleagues in the Secretary's anteroom, prepared to hear the estimate of the Director of Intelligence and Research and to give his own appraisal and submit his plan of action.

LIST OF ABBREVIATIONS

ACDA:	Arms Control and Disarmament Agency
AEC:	Atomic Energy Commission
AFSA:	American Foreign Service Association
AID:	Agency for International Development
ARA:	Bureau of Inter-American Affairs
BEW:	Board of Economic Warfare
BEX:	Board of Examiners for the Foreign Service
CAMO:	Consolidated Management Organization
CCPS:	Comprehensive Country Programming System
CIA:	Central Intelligence Agency
CIAA:	Office of the Coordinator for Inter-American Affairs
CM:	career minister
COM:	chief of mission
CS:	Civil Service
DCM:	deputy chief of mission
DLF:	Development Loan Fund
EDB:	Economic Defense Board
EEC:	European Economic Community
FA:	Division of Foreign Service Administration
FAA:	Federal Aviation Administration
FAIME:	Foreign Affairs Information Management Effort
FAPS:	Foreign Affairs Programming System
FAS:	Foreign Agricultural Service
FBI:	Federal Bureau of Investigation
FOA:	Foreign Operations Administration
FP:	Division of Foreign Service Personnel
FS:	Foreign Service of the United States
FSI:	Foreign Service Institute
FSIO:	Foreign Service information officer
FSL:	Foreign Service local employee

FSO:	Foreign Service officer
FSRO:	Foreign Service reserve officer
FSRU:	Foreign Service reserve officer unlimited
FSS:	Foreign Service Staff
FSSO:	Foreign Service staff officer
FY:	fiscal year
GAO:	General Accounting Office
GATT:	General Agreement on Trade and Tariffs
GNP:	gross national product
GS:	General Service
HEW:	Department of Health, Education and Welfare
ICA:	International Cooperation Administration
ILO:	International Labor Organization
INR:	Bureau of Intelligence and Research
INS:	Immigration and Naturalization Service
IPU:	International Postal Union
IRG:	Interdepartmental Regional Group
IRS:	Internal Revenue Service
MAAGS:	military assistance advisory groups
MUST:	Manpower Utilization System and Techniques
NASA:	National Aeronautics and Space Administration
NEA:	National Education Association
NSC:	National Security Council
OCB:	Operations Coordinating Board
OEO:	Office of Economic Opportunity
OFF:	Office of Facts and Figures
OLL:	Office of Lend-Lease Administration
O/SNS:	Substantive Information Systems Program
OSS:	Office of Strategic Services
OWI:	Office of War Information
PER/CMA:	Office of Personnel, Career Planning and Management Division
PHS:	Public Health Service
PPBS:	planning-programming-budgeting system
RIF:	reduction in force
SEC:	Securities and Exchange Commission
SID:	Senior Interdepartmental Group
S/PC:	Policy Planning and Coordinating Staff

SWNCC:	State-War-Navy Coordinating Committee
UNRRA:	United Nations Relief and Rehabilitation Administration
USIA:	United States Information Agency
USIS:	United States Information Service
WHO:	World Health Organization

BIBLIOGRAPHICAL NOTES

PART I

Illustrations of the excruciating difficulties and dilemmas encountered in administering American foreign affairs may be found in Sheldon Appleton, *United States Foreign Policy: An Introduction with Cases*; Lawrence S. Kaplan, *Recent American Foreign Policy: Conflicting Interpretations*; Bernard Brodie, *Strategy in the Nuclear Age*; all of George Kennan's works, but especially his *American Diplomacy, 1900–1950*; Henry A. Kissinger, *The Necessity for Choice: Prospects for American Foreign Policy* and *Nuclear Weapons and Foreign Policy*; Kurt London, *How Foreign Policy Is Made*; Walt W. Rostow, *The United States in the World Arena: An Essay in Recent History*; Kenneth W. Thompson, *American Diplomacy and Emergent Patterns*; and Henry M. Wriston, *Diplomacy in a Democracy*. Thomas L. Hughes's article "On the Causes of Our Discontents" also repays reading.

Uncited studies consulted in the field of psychological problems, including those posed by communications, include Satish K. Arora and Harold D. Laswell, *Political Communication: The Public Language of Political Elites in India and the United States*; Herbert C. Kelman, *International Behavior*; Klaus Knorr and Sidney Verba, eds., *The International System*; Joseph H. de Rivera, *The Psychological Dimension of Foreign Policy*; and David J. Singer, ed., *Human Behavior and International Policy*.

In the cognate area of decision-making processes, many useful insights are found in Joseph Frankel, *The Making of Foreign Policy: An Analysis of Decision Making*; Dean Pruitt, *Problem Solving in the Department of State*; Burton M. Sapin, *The Making of Foreign Policy*; Richard C. Snyder, H. W. Bruck, and Burton M. Sapin, *Foreign Policy Decision Making: An Approach to the Study of International Politics*; Richard C. Snyder and James A. Robinson, *National and International Decision Making*; and Harold Stein, ed., *Public Administration and Policy Development: A Case Book*.

Manfred Halpern, *The Morality and Politics of Intervention*; David L. Larson, ed., *The Puritan Ethic in United States Foreign Policy*; and Robert E. Osgood, *Ideals and Self Interest in American Foreign Relations* contain many illustrations of the inhibiting roles of ethics, beliefs, and ideologies.

Much data for the discussion of presidential and congressional powers in Chapter 2, and in Chapters 8 and 9 of Part III, has been drawn from uncited authorities. Authors and works consulted on the presidency and congressional-presidential relationships include Dean Acheson, *A Citizen Looks at Congress*; Edwin S. Corwin, *The President: Office and Powers, 1787–1957* and *The President's Control of Foreign Relations*; Robert A. Dahl, *Congress and Foreign Policy*; Louis W. Koenig, *The Chief Executive*, *Congress and the President*, and *The Invisible Presidency*; R. E. Neustadt, *Presidential Power*; and Nelson W. Polsby, *Congress and the Presidency*.

Especially useful studies on the Congress include the American Academy of Political and Social Science symposium report, *Congress and Foreign Relations*; Holbert N. Carroll, *The House of Representatives and Foreign Affairs*; George Grassmuck, *Sectional Biases in Congress on Foreign Policy*; Richard F. Fenno, *The Power of the Purse*; and Kenneth N. Waltz, *Foreign Policy and Democratic Politics: The American and British Experience*.

J. M. Juran, *Bureaucracy: A Challenge to Better Management*, first drew my attention to the political content of administration. Other works in the bibliography, especially Burton M. Sapin, *The Making of United States Foreign Policy*, reveal clearly the growing politicization of administration as does the perceptive introduction to Gene E. Raney, ed., *Contemporary American Foreign Policy: The Official Voice*. An article by Graham T. Allison, "Conceptual Models and the Cuban Missile Crisis" (*American Political Science Review*, 63, no. 3 [September 1969], 689–718), sheds revealing light on both the political role of the bureaucracy and the decision-making processes.

Part II

In the drafting of Chapters 3–5, in addition to the authorities cited, the following were consulted: William Barnes and John Heath Morgan, *The Foreign Service of the United States: Origins, Development and Functions;* W. Wendell Blancké, *The Foreign Service of the United States*; Keith C. Clark and Laurence J. Legere, eds., *The President and the Management of National Security*; Wayne S. Cole, *An Interpretive History of American Foreign Relations*; Katherine Crane, *Mr. Carr of State: Forty-seven Years in the Department of State*; Herbert Emmerich, *Essays on Federal Reorganization*; Eleanor Lansing Dulles, *American Foreign Policy in the Making*; Louis L. Gerson, *John Foster Dulles as Secretary of State, 1953–1959*; John E. Harr, *The Professional Diplomat*; Cordell Hull, *The Memoirs of Cordell Hull*; Warren F. Ilchman, *Professional Diplomacy in the United States, 1779–1939*; Tracy H. Lay, *The Foreign Service of the United States*; Arthur W. Macmahon, *Memorandum on the International Information Program of the United States*; Martin W. Moser, "The Personnel System of the Foreign Service of the United States: An Analysis and Evaluation of the Foreign Service Officer Corps"; Robert E. Sherwood, *Roosevelt and Hopkins—An Intimate History*; and Graham H. Stuart, *The Department of State*.

Although the preponderance of the material in Chapters 6 and 7 was derived from the Department of State *News Letter* and other official sources, six Foreign Affairs Personnel Studies published by the Carnegie Endowment for International Peace, which contain data supplementing the Herter Committee Report, were most useful. These include two studies by John E. Harr, *The Anatomy of the Foreign Service: A Statistical Profile* and *The Development of Careers in the Foreign Service*; Arthur G. Jones, *The Evaluation of Personnel Systems for U.S. Foreign Affairs*; Regis Walther, *Orientation and Behavior Style of Foreign Service Officers*; Robert E. Elder, *Overseas Representation and Services for Federal Domestic Agencies*; and Frances Fielder and Godfrey Harris, *The Quest for Foreign Affairs Officers: Their Recruitment and Selection*. Burton M. Sapin, *The Making of United States Foreign Policy*, was frequently consulted when this and subsequent sections were drafted.

Part III

The authorities listed in the note for Chapter 2 were consulted for Chapters 8 and 9 as well. Useful information about the intelligence function was found in Hanson W. Baldwin, *The Price of Power*; Roger Hilsman, Jr., *Strategic Intelligence and National Decisions*; Robert Holt and Robert W. van de Velde, *Strategic Psychological Operations and American Foreign Policy*; William M. McGovern, *Strategic Intelligence and the Shape of Tomorrow*; Andrew M. Scott, *The Revolution in Statecraft: Informal Penetration*; and H. Bradford Westerfield, *The Instruments of America's Foreign Policy*. Comments on the role and management of intelligence were limited to modest and fully documented proportions because of statutory restrictions.

Additional uncited works on the presidency and the Executive Office consulted in preparing Chapter 9 include J. I. Coffey and Vincent P. Rock, "The Presidential Staff"; Richard F. Fenno, *The President's Cabinet*; Alexander and Juliet George, *Woodrow Wilson and Colonel House*; and Aaron Wildarsky, *The Politics of the Budgetary Process*.

Uncited authors whose works provided data incorporated in Chapter 10 include Thomas A. Bailey, *The Art of Diplomacy*; Willard L. Beaulac, *Career Ambassador* and *Career Diplomat: A Career in the Foreign Service of the United States*; Wendell Blancké, *The Foreign Service of the United States*; Chester Bowles, *Ambassador's Report*; Ellis Briggs, *Farewell to Foggy Bottom*; Alexander de Conde, *The American Secretary of State: An Interpretation*; John P. Davies, *Foreign and Other Affairs*; Donald Dunham, *Envoy Unextraordinary*; John P. Leacacos, *Fires in the In-Basket: The ABC's of the State Department*; Luke T. Lee, *Vienna Convention on Consular Relations*; Elmer Plischke, *Conduct of American Diplomacy*; Don K. Price, ed., *The Secretary of State*; E. Wilder Spaulding, *Ambassadors Ordinary and Extraordinary*; Charles W. Thayer, *Diplomat*; Charles A. Thomson and Walter H. Laves, *Cultural Relations and U.S. Foreign Policy*; Henry S. Villard, *Affairs at State*; and Temple Wanemaker, *American Foreign Policy Today*. The uncited works consulted in preparing Part II also provided useful data.

Comments on USIA in Chapter 11 and elsewhere derive in part from the American Assembly's *Cultural Affairs and Foreign Relations*; Edward W. Barrett, *Truth Is Our Weapon*; Wilson P. Dizard, *The Strategy of Truth: The Story of the U.S. Information Service*; and John W. Henderson, *The United States Information Agency*.

The following authorities on the foreign assistance administration were consulted: George Liska, *The New Statecraft: Foreign Aid in American Policy*; John D. Montgomery, *Foreign Aid in International Politics*; John D. Montgomery and William J. Siffin, eds., *Approaches to Development: Politics, Administration and Change*; and Joan M. Nelson, *Aid, Influence, and Foreign Policy*.

Uncited authorities on national security administration whose works were consulted in drafting Chapter 12 include Donald G. Brennan, ed., *Arms Control, Disarmament, and National Security*; Robert A. Goldwin, ed., *America Armed: Essays on United States Military Policy*; Paul Y. Hammond, *Organizing for Defense: The American Military Establishment in the Twentieth Century*; Charles Hitch and Roland N. McKean, *The Eco-*

nomics of Defense in the Nuclear Age; Samuel P. Huntington, *The Common Defense*; William R. Kintner, with Joseph L. Coffey and Raymond J. Albright, *Forging a New Sword*; Burton M. Sapin and Richard C. Snyder, *The Role of the Military in American Foreign Policy*; Timothy W. Stanley, *American Defense and National Security*; and Alfred Vagts, *Defense and Diplomacy*.

Little monographic literature exists on the foreign affairs roles of either the federal domestic agencies or the state and local governments, although some works, such as Don Whitehead's *The FBI Story*, give incidental treatment to such activities.

In contrast, Chapter 15 owes much to a growing body of literature that seeks to delimit, define, and describe the role of public opinion. Gabriel Almond's *The American People and Foreign Policy* broke much new ground. Other authorities include Thomas A. Bailey, *The Man in the Street: The Impact of American Public Opinion on Foreign Policy*; Doris A. Grabner, *Public Opinion, the President and Foreign Policy*; Norman R. Luttbeg, ed., *Public Opinion and Public Policy: Models of Political Linkage*; Lester Markel, ed., *Public Opinion and Foreign Policy*; and James N. Rosenau, ed., *Domestic Sources of Foreign Policy*. Bernard C. Cohen explored the role of the press in *The Press and Foreign Policy*; and Raymond A. Bauer, Ithiel de Sola Pool, and Lewis A. Dexter examined the role of the business community in *American Business and Public Policy: The Politics of Foreign Trade*. Louis L. Gerson, *The Hyphenate in Recent American Politics and Diplomacy*, addressed himself to an appraisal of the relative importance of such pressure groups. John A. S. Granville and George Berkeley Young, *Politics, Strategy and American Diplomacy: Studies in Foreign Policy, 1873–1937*, examined the impact of party politics on foreign policy before World War II; and Richard W. Cottam, *Competitive Interference and 20th Century Diplomacy*, illustrated the influence aliens can and do exert in foreign affairs administration.

Part IV

The observations and recommendations embodied in Chapters 14–21 derive primarily from personal experience and from the entire range of works previously cited or referenced in these notes. A few additional uncited works also provided useful data or insights They included the following: American Academy of Political and Social Science, *Resources and Needs of American Diplomacy*, Annals, 180; Chris Argyris, *Some Causes* of *Organizational Ineffectiveness within the Department of State*; Brookings Institution, *Research for Public Policy: Brookings Dedication Lectures*; Sir Douglas Busk, *The Craft of Diplomacy: How to Run a Diplomatic Service*; John E. Harr, *The Professional Diplomat*; Henry M. Jackson, *The Secretary of State and the Ambassador*; Sir Harold Nicolson, *Diplomacy*; Achilles N. Sakell, *Careers in the Foreign Service*; and Smith Simpson, *Anatomy of the State Department*.

BIBLIOGRAPHY

OFFICIAL DOCUMENTS

United Kingdom. *Report of the Committee on Representational Services Overseas* (Plowden Committee Report). Command Paper 2276. London: Her Majesty's Stationery Office, 1964.

U.S. Bureau of the Budget. *Organization and Coordination of Foreign Economic Activities.* Washington, D.C.: Government Printing Office, 1961.

U.S. Commission on Organization of the Executive Branch of the Government (First Hoover Commission). *Concluding Report.* Washington, D.C.: Government Printing Office, 1949.

——— (Second Hoover Commission). *Intelligence Activities and Overseas Economic Operations.* Washington, D.C.: Government Printing Office, 1955.

U.S. Congress. House of Representatives. Committee on Foreign Affairs. *The Foreign Service Act of 1946 (Public Law 724, 79th Congress) as Amended to October 17, 1960.* 79th Cong., 1960.

———. Committee on Government Operations. *Hearings.* 83rd Cong., 1st Sess., December 2–4, 1953.

U.S. Congress. Senate. Committee on Foreign Relations. *Administration of the Department of State.* 86th Cong., 2d sess., 1960.

———. *Developments in Military Technology and Their Impact on United States Strategy and Foreign Policy.* Study No. 8, prepared by the Washington Center of Foreign Policy Research of Johns Hopkins University, 86th Cong., 1st sess., 1959.

———. *Economic, Social, and Political Change in the Underdeveloped Countries and Its Implications for United States Policy.* Study No. 12, prepared by the Center for International Studies, Massachusetts Institute of Technology, 86th Cong., 2d sess., 1960.

———. *The Formulation and Administration of United States Foreign*

Policy. Study No. 9, prepared by the Brookings Institution, 86th Cong., 2d sess., 1960.

———. *Hearings* on "The American Overseas," statement by Dean Harland Cleveland and others from Maxwell Graduate School, Syracuse University. 86th Cong., 1st sess., February 18, 1959.

———. *The Operational Aspects of United States Foreign Policy*. Study No. 6, prepared by Maxwell Graduate School, Syracuse University, 86th Cong., 1st sess., 1959.

———. *Organization for Economic Cooperation and Development*. 87th Cong., 1st sess., 1961.

———. *Recruitment and Training for the Foreign Service of the United States* (staff study). 85th Cong., 2nd sess., February 28, 1958.

———. *Worldwide and Domestic Economic Problems and Their Impact on the Foreign Policy of the United States*. Study No. 1, prepared by the Corporation for Economic and Industrial Research, Inc., 86th Cong., 1st sess., 1959.

———. Committee on Government Operations. *Hearings* before the Subcommittee on National Policy Machinery. 86th Cong., 2d sess., 1960, 1961.

———. *Organization of Federal Executive Departments and Agencies*. Report No. 26, 89th Cong., 2d sess., April 25, 1966.

———. *Selected Materials*, prepared for the Subcommittee on National Policy Machinery, 86th Cong., 2d sess., 1960.

———. *Study* submitted by the Subcommittee on National Policy Machinery, 87th Cong., 1st sess., 1961.

U.S. Department of Defense, National War College. "The Anatomy and Character of National Power," by Karl W. Deutsch. *Forum*, 6, Fall 1968.

———. *Directory of Staff, Faculty and Graduates of the National War College*. Washington, D.C.: National War College, 1965–.

U.S. Department of State. *The Biographic Register*. Washington, D.C.: Government Printing Office, 1960–1963.

———. *Bulletin*, 55–62 (1966–1970).

———. *The Computer and Foreign Affairs: Some First Thoughts*. Washington, D.C.: Government Printing Office, 1966.

———. *The Country Team: An Illustrated Profile of Our American Missions Abroad*. Publication No. 8193. Washington, D.C.: Government Printing Office, 1967.

———. Departmental Order 782 (January 26, 1939), 1218 (January 15, 1944), 1301 (December 20, 1944).

———. *Foreign Service List.* Washington, D.C.: Government Printing Office, 1946–1970.

———. *The Foreign Service of the United States: Origins, Development and Functions.* Washington, D.C.: Government Printing Office, 1961.

———. *How Foreign Policy Is Made.* Rev. ed. Publication No. 7707. Washington, D.C.: Government Printing Office, 1965.

———. *International Affairs: A List of Current Social Science Research by Private Scholars and Academic Centers.* Office of External Research, 1965–1968.

———. *Memorandum on the Postwar International Information Program of the United States.* Publication No. 2438. Washington, D.C.: Government Printing Office, 1945.

———. *News Letter,* 1–110 (May 1961–June 1970).

———. *Papers Available.* Office of External Research, 1967–1970.

———. *Register.* Washington, D.C.: Government Printing Office, December 1909.

———. "A Report to the Secretary of State by the Secretary's Advisory Committee on Personnel, August, 1950." Multigraph, 43 pages.

———. "Summary of Employment." PER/CMA, Reports and Statistics Section, May 23, 1969.

———. *Telephone Directory.* Washington, D.C.: Government Printing Office, 1965–1970.

———. *This Worked For Me . . . Mission Chiefs Pool Useful Ideas and Techniques.* Washington, D.C.: Department of State, 1964.

——— (Report of Wriston Committee). *Toward a Stronger Foreign Service: Report of the Secretary of State's Public Committee on Personnel, June, 1954.* Publication 5458. Washington, D.C.: Government Printing Office, 1954.

U.S. General Services Administration. National Archives and Records Service, Office of the Federal Registrar. *United States Government Organization Manual, 1969–70.* Rev. ed. July 1, 1969. Washington, D.C.: Federal Registrar, 1969.

U.S. Library of Congress. *Reorganization of the Executive Branch of the Government of the United States: A Compilation of Basic Information and Significant Documents, 1912–1947.* Legislative Reference Service, Public Affairs Bulletin No. 66. Washington, D.C.: Government Printing Office, 1949.

U.S. Mutual Security Administration. "Evaluation Report, March 24, 1953."

Letter of Charles Francis et. al., to Harold C. Stassen, Multigraph, 15 pages.

U.S.President's Advisory Committee on Management. *Report to the President.* Washington, D.C.: Government Printing Office, 1952.

U.S. President's Committee on Administrative Management (Brownlow Committee). *Report.* Washington, D.C.: Government Printing Office, 1937.

BOOKS AND MONOGRAPHS

Acheson, Dean. *A Citizen Looks at Congress.* New York: Harper, 1957.

Almond, Gabriel. *The American People and Foreign Policy.* New York: Harcourt, Brace & World, 1950.

American Academy of Political and Social Science. *Congress and Foreign Relations.* Annals, 289. Philadelphia: American Academy of Political and Social Science, 1953.

———. *Resources and Needs of American Diplomacy.* Annals, 380. Lancaster, Pa.: American Academy of Political and Social Science, 1968.

———. *Theory and Practice of Public Administration: Scope, Objectives, and Methods.* Monograph, no. 8. Lancaster, Pa.: American Academy of Political and Social Science, 1968.

American Assembly. *Cultural Affairs and Foreign Relations.* Englewood Cliffs, N. J.: Prentice-Hall, 1963.

———. *The Representation of the United States Abroad.* New York: American Assembly, School of Business Administration, Columbia University, 1956.

Appleton, Sheldon. *United States Foreign Policy: An Introduction with Cases.* Boston: Little, Brown, 1968.

Argyris, Chris. *Some Causes of Organizational Ineffectiveness within the Department of State.* Center for International Systems Research, Occasional Papers, No. 2, Department of State Publication 8180. Washington, D.C.: Department of State, 1967.

Arora, Satish K., and Lasswell, Harold D. *Political Communication: The Public Language of Political Elites in India and the United States.* New York: Holt, Rinehart and Winston, 1969.

Bailey, Thomas A. *The Art of Diplomacy.* New York: Appleton-Century-Crofts, 1968.

———. *The Man in the Street: The Impact of American Public Opinion on Foreign Policy.* New York: Macmillan, 1948.

Baldwin, Hanson W. *The Price of Power.* New York: Harper, 1948.

Barnes, William, and Morgan, John Heath. *The Foreign Service of the United States: Origins, Development, and Functions.* Historical Office, Bureau of Public Affairs, Department of State. Washington, D.C.: Government Printing Office, 1961.
Barrett, Edward W. *Truth Is Our Weapon.* New York: Funk & Wagnalls, 1953.
Bauer, Raymond A., Pool, Ithiel de Sola, and Dexter, Lewis A. *American Business and Public Policy: The Politics of Foreign Trade.* New York: Atherton, 1963.
Beaulac, Willard L. *Career Ambassador.* New York: Macmillan, 1951.
―――. *Career Diplomat: A Career in the Foreign Service of the United States.* New York: Macmillan, 1964.
Black, Eugene R. *The Diplomacy of Economic Development.* Cambridge, Mass.: Harvard University Press, 1960.
Blancké, W. Wendell. *The Foreign Service of the United States.* New York: Praeger, 1969.
Bloomfield, Lincoln P. *The United Nations and U. S. Foreign Policy.* Rev. ed. Boston: Little, Brown, 1960.
Bowles, Chester. *Ambassador's Report.* New York: Harper, 1954.
Brennan, Donald G., ed. *Arms Control, Disarmament, and National Security.* New York: Braziller, 1961.
Briggs, Ellis. *Farewell to Foggy Bottom.* New York: David McKay, 1964.
Brodie, Bernard. *Strategy in the Missile Age.* Princeton, N. J.: Princeton University Press, 1959.
Brookings Institution. *The Administration of Foreign Affairs and Overseas Operations.* Washington, D.C.: Government Printing Office, 1951.
―――. *Administrative Aspects of United States Foreign Assistance Programs.* Washington, D.C.: Government Printing Office, 1957.
―――. *Governmental Mechanisms for the Conduct of United States Foreign Relations.* Washington, D.C.: Government Printing Office, 1949.
―――. *Research for Public Policy: Brookings Dedication Lectures.* Washington, D.C.: Government Printing Office, 1961.
Busk, Sir Douglas. *The Craft of Diplomacy.* New York: Praeger, 1969.
Callières, F. de. *De la manière de négocier avec les souverains.* Paris, 1716.
Carroll, Holbert N. *The House of Representatives and Foreign Affairs.* Pittsburgh: University of Pittsburgh Press, 1958.
Childs, J. Rives. *American Foreign Service.* New York: Holt, Rinehart & Winston, 1948.
Clark, Keith C., and Legere, Laurence J., eds. *The President and the Man-*

agement of National Security: A Report by the Institute for Defense Analyses. New York: Praeger, 1969.

Cleveland, Harlan, Mangone, Gerard J., and Adams, John C. *The Overseas Americans.* New York: McGraw-Hill, 1960.

Cohen, Bernard C. *The Press and Foreign Policy.* Princeton, N.J.: Princeton University Press, 1963.

Cole, Wayne S. *An Interpretive History of American Foreign Relations.* Homewood, Ill.: Dorsey, 1968.

Committee on Foreign Affairs Personnel (Herter Committee). *Personnel for the New Diplomacy.* Washington, D.C.: Carnegie Endowment for International Peace, December 1962.

Coplin, William D., ed. *Simulation in the Study of Politics.* Chicago: Markham Publishing Co., 1968.

Corwin, Edward S. *The President: Office and Powers, 1787–1957.* 4th ed. New York: New York University Press, 1957.

———. *The President's Control of Foreign Relations.* Princeton, N.J.: Princeton University Press, 1917.

Cottam, Richard W. *Competitive Interference and 20th Century Diplomacy.* Pittsburgh: University of Pittsburgh Press, 1967.

Crane, Katherine. *Mr. Carr of State: Forty-seven Years in the Department of State.* New York: St. Martin's Press, 1960.

De Conde, Alexander. *The American Secretary of State: An Interpretation.* New York: Praeger, 1962.

Dahl, Robert A. *Congress and Foreign Policy.* New York: Harcourt, Brace, 1950.

Davies, John P., Jr. *Foreign and Other Affairs.* New York: W. W. Norton, 1964.

Dizard, Wilson P. *The Strategy of Truth: The Story of the U.S. Information Service.* Washington, D.C.: Public Affairs Press, 1961.

Djumena, Asep Wiria. "The Foreign Service: Problems of Recruitment, Selection, and Training." Ph.D. dissertation, Indiana University, 1964.

Dulles, Eleanor Lansing. *American Foreign Policy in the Making.* New York: Harper, 1968.

Dunham, Donald. *Envoy Unextraordinary.* New York: John Day, 1944.

Elder, Robert E. *Overseas Representation and Services for Federal Domestic Agencies.* Foreign Affairs Personnel Study No. 2. New York: Carnegie Endowment for International Peace, 1965.

———. *The Policy Machine: The Department of State and American Foreign Policy.* Syracuse, N. Y.: Syracuse University Press, 1960.

Elliot, William Yandell, ed. *United States Foreign Policy: Its Organization and Control.* New York: Columbia University Press, 1952.

Emmerich, Herbert. *Essays on Federal Reorganization.* University: University of Alabama Press, 1950.

Fenno, Richard F., Jr. *The Power of the Purse.* Boston: Little, Brown, 1966.

———. *The President's Cabinet.* Cambridge, Mass.: Harvard University Press, 1959.

Fielder, Frances, and Harris, Godfrey. *The Quest for Foreign Affairs Officers: Their Recruitment and Selection.* Foreign Affairs Personnel Study No. 6. New York: Carnegie Endowment for International Peace, 1966.

Frankel, Joseph. *The Making of Foreign Policy: An Analysis of Decision Making.* Oxford: Galaxy Books, 1967.

Fuller, G. Dale. *Training of Specialists in International Relations.* Washington: American Council on Education, 1957.

George, Alexander and Juliette. *Woodrow Wilson and Colonel House.* New York: John Day Company, 1956.

Gerberding, William P. *United States Foreign Policy: Perspectives and Analysis.* New York: McGraw-Hill, 1966.

Gerson, Louis L. *The Hyphenate in Recent American Politics and Diplomacy.* Lawrence: University of Kansas Press, 1964.

———. *John Foster Dulles as Secretary of State, 1953–1959.* New York: Cooper Square Publishers, 1968.

Goldwin, Robert A., ed. *America Armed: Essays on United States Military Policy.* Chicago: Rand McNally, 1969.

Graber, Doris A. *Public Opinion, the President, and Foreign Policy.* New York: Holt, Rinehart and Winston, 1968.

Granville, John A. S., and Young, George Berkeley. *Politics, Strategy, and American Diplomacy: Studies in Foreign Policy, 1873–1917.* New Haven, Conn.: Yale University Press, 1966.

Grassmuck, George. *Sectional Biases in Congress on Foreign Policy.* Baltimore: Johns Hopkins Press, 1951.

Graves, W. Brooke, ed. *Reorganization of the Executive Branch of the Government of the United States: A Compilation of Basic Information and Significant Documents, 1912–1947.* U. S. Library of Congress, Legislative Reference Service, Public Affairs Bulletin No. 66. Washington, D.C.: Government Printing Office, 1949.

Guetzkow, Harold, et. al. *Simulation in International Relations.* Englewood Cliffs, N. J.: Prentice-Hall, 1963.

Halpern, Manfred. *The Morality and Politics of Intervention*. New York: Council on Religion and International Affairs, 1963.

Hammond, Paul Y. *Organizing for Defense: The American Military Establishment in the Twentieth Century*. Princeton, N. J.: Princeton University Press, 1961.

Harr, John E. *The Anatomy of the Foreign Service: A Statistical Profile*. Foreign Affairs Personnel Study No. 4. New York: Carnegie Endowment for International Peace, 1965.

———. *The Development of Careers in the Foreign Service*. Foreign Affairs Personnel Study No. 3. New York: Carnegie Endowment for International Peace, 1965.

———. *The Professional Diplomat*. Princeton, N. J.: Princeton University Press, 1969.

Henderson, John W. *The United States Information Agency*. New York: Praeger, 1969.

Hilsman, Roger, Jr. *Strategic Intelligence and National Decisions*. Glencoe, Ill.: The Free Press, 1956.

Hitch, Charles, and McKean, Roland N. *The Economics of Defense in the Nuclear Age*. Cambridge, Mass.: Harvard University Press, 1960.

Holt, Robert T., and van de Velde, Robert W. *Strategic Psychological Operations and American Foreign Policy*. Chicago: University of Chicago Press, 1960.

Holt, W. Stull. *Treaties Defeated by the Senate*. Baltimore: Johns Hopkins Press, 1933.

Howe, Fisher. *The Computer and Foreign Affairs: Some First Thoughts*. Department of State. Washington, D.C.: Government Printing Office, 1966.

Hull, Cordell. *Memoirs of Cordell Hull*. New York: Macmillan, 1948.

Huntington, Samuel P. *The Common Defense*. New York: Columbia University Press, 1961.

Ilchman, Warren F. *Professional Diplomacy in the United States, 1779–1939*. Chicago: University of Chicago Press, 1961.

Jackson, Henry M., ed. *The Secretary of State and the Ambassador: Jackson Subcommittee Papers on the Conduct of American Foreign Policy*. New York: Praeger, 1964.

Johnson, E. A. J., ed. *The Dimensions of Diplomacy*. Baltimore: Johns Hopkins Press, 1964.

Jones, Arthur G. *The Evolution of Personnel Systems for U. S. Foreign*

Affairs. Foreign Affairs Personnel Study No. 1. New York: Carnegie Endowment for International Peace, 1965.

Juran, J. M. *Bureaucracy: A Challenge to Better Management.* New York: Harper, 1944.

Kaplan, Lawrence S. *Recent American Foreign Policy: Conflicting Interpretations.* Homewood, Ill.: Dorsey, 1968.

Kelman, Herbert C. *International Behavior.* New York: Holt, Rinehart & Winston, 1965.

Kennan, George F. *American Diplomacy, 1900–1950.* New York: New American Library, Mentor, 1952.

———. *Memoirs (1925–1950).* Boston: Little, Brown, 1967.

Kindleberger, Charles P. *American Business Abroad.* New Haven, Conn.: Yale University Press, 1969.

Kintner, William R., in association with Joseph L. Coffey and Raymond J. Albright. *Forging a New Sword.* New York: Harper, 1958.

Kissinger, Henry A. *The Necessity for Choice: Prospects for American Foreign Policy.* New York: Harper, 1961.

———. *Nuclear Weapons and Foreign Policy.* New York: Council on Foreign Relations, 1957.

Knorr, Klaus, and Verba, Sidney, eds. *The International System.* Princeton, N.J.: Princeton University Press, 1961.

Koenig, Louis W. *The Chief Executive.* New York: Harcourt, Brace & World, 1968.

———. *Congress and the President.* Glenview, Ill.: Scott, Foresman, 1965.

———. *The Invisible Presidency.* New York: Holt, Rinehart, and Winston, 1960.

Larson, David L., ed. *The Puritan Ethic in United States Foreign Policy.* Princeton, N.J.: Van Nostrand, 1966.

Lay, Tracy H. *The Foreign Service of the United States.* New York: Prentice-Hall, 1925.

Leacacos, John P. *Fires in the In-Basket: The ABC's of the State Department.* Cleveland: World Publishing Co., 1968.

Lee, Luke T. *Consular Law and Practice.* New York: Praeger, 1961.

———. *Vienna Convention on Consular Relations.* Durham, N.C.: Rule of Law Press, 1966.

Liska, George. *The New Statecraft: Foreign Aid in American Foreign Policy.* Chicago: University of Chicago Press, 1959.

London, Kurt. *How Foreign Policy is Made*. Princeton, N.J.: Van Nostrand, 1949.
Luttbeg, Norman R., ed. *Public Opinion and Public Policy: Models of Political Linkage*. Homewood, Ill.: Dorsey, 1968.
McCamy, James L. *The Administration of American Foreign Affairs*. New York: Knopf, 1950.
———. *Conduct of the New Diplomacy*. New York: Harper, 1964.
McGovern, William M. *Strategic Intelligence and the Shape of Tomorrow*. Chicago: Regnery, 1961.
Macmahon, Arthur W. *Administration in Foreign Affairs*. University: University of Alabama Press, 1953.
———. *Memorandum on the Postwar International Information Program of the United States*. Department of State Publication No. 38. Washington, D.C.: Government Printing Office, 1945.
Markel, Lester, ed. *Public Opinion and Foreign Policy*. New York: Harper, 1959.
Marshall, Charles Burton. *The Limits of Foreign Policy*. New York: Henry Holt, 1954.
May, Ernest R., ed. *The Ultimate Decision: The President as Commander-in-Chief*. New York: Braziller, 1960.
Montgomery, John D. *Foreign Aid in International Politics*. Englewood Cliffs, N.J.: Prentice-Hall, 1968.
Montgomery, John D., and Siffin, William J., eds. *Approaches to Development: Politics, Administration and Change*. New York: McGraw-Hill, 1966.
Moser, Martin W. "The Personnel System of the Foreign Service of the United States: An Analysis and Evaluation of the Foreign Service Officer Corps." Ph.D. dissertation, University of Maryland, 1952.
Nash, Bradley D., and Lynde, Cornelius. *A Hook in Leviathan: A Critical Interpretation of the Hoover Commission Report*. New York: Macmillan, 1950.
Needler, Martin C. *Understanding Foreign Policy*. New York: Holt, Rinehart and Winston, 1966.
Nelson, Joan M. *Aid, Influence, and Foreign Policy*. New York: Macmillan, 1968.
Neustadt, Richard E. *Presidential Power*. New York: Wiley, 1960.
Nicolson, Harold. *Diplomacy*. London: Oxford University Press, 1963.
———. *The Evolution of Diplomatic Method*. New York: Collier, 1966.

Osgood, Robert E. *Ideals and Self Interest in American Foreign Relations.* Chicago: University of Chicago Press, 1953.
Parks, Wallace J. *United States Administration of Its International Economic Affairs.* Baltimore: Johns Hopkins Press, 1951.
Plischke, Elmer. *American Diplomacy: A Bibliography of Biographies, Autobiographies, and Commentaries.* College Park: University of Maryland Press, 1957.
———. *American Foreign Relations: A Bibliography of Official Sources.* College Park: University of Maryland Press, 1956.
———. *Conduct of American Diplomacy.* Princeton, N. J.: Van Nostrand, 1950.
Polsby, Nelson W. *Congress and the Presidency.* Englewood Cliffs, N. J.: Prentice-Hall, 1964.
Price, Don K., ed. *The Secretary of State.* Englewood Cliffs, N. J.: Prentice-Hall, 1960.
Pruitt, Dean. *Problem Solving in the Department of State.* Monograph Series No. 2. Denver, Colo.: University of Denver, 1964–1965.
Pusey, Merlo. *The Way We Go To War.* Boston: Houghton Mifflin, 1968.
Rainey, Gene E., ed. *Contemporary American Foreign Policy: The Official Voice.* Columbus, Ohio: Merrill, 1969.
Ransom, Harry Howe. *Central Intelligence and National Security.* Cambridge, Mass.: Harvard University Press, 1958.
Rivera, Joseph H. de. *The Psychological Dimension of Foreign Policy.* Columbus, Ohio: Merrill, 1968.
Robinson, James A. *Congress and Foreign Policy-Making: A Study in Legislative Influence and Initiative.* Rev. ed. Homewood, Ill.: Dorsey, 1962.
Rosenau, James N., ed. *Domestic Sources of Foreign Policy.* New York: Free Press, 1967.
———. *International Politics and Foreign Policy.* New York: Free Press, 1961.
Rostow, Walt W. *The United States in the World Arena: An Essay in Recent History.* New York: Harper, 1960.
Sakell, Achilles N. *Careers in the Foreign Service.* New York: Henry Z. Walck, Inc., 1963.
Sapin, Burton M. *The Making of United States Foreign Policy.* New York: Praeger, 1966.
Sapin, Burton M., and Snyder, Richard C. *The Role of the Military in American Foreign Policy.* New York: Doubleday, 1954.

Schlesinger, Arthur M., Jr. *The Bitter Heritage*. Boston: Houghton Mifflin, 1966.

———. *A Thousand Days: John F. Kennedy in the White House*. Boston: Houghton Mifflin, 1965.

Scott, Andrew M. *The Revolution in Statecraft: Informal Penetration*. New York: Random House, 1965.

Seckler-Hudson, Catherine. *Bibliography on Public Administration Annotated*. Washington, D.C.: American University Press, 1953.

Servan-Schreiber, Jean Jacques. *The American Challenge*. New York: Atheneum, 1968.

Sherwood, Robert E. *Roosevelt and Hopkins—An Intimate History*. New York: Harper, 1948.

Simpson, Smith. *Anatomy of the State Department*. Boston: Houghton Mifflin, 1967.

Singer, David J., ed. *Human Behavior and International Policy*. Chicago: Rand McNally, 1965.

Snyder, Richard C., and Robinson, James A. *National and International Decision-Making*. New York: Institute for International Order, 1961.

Snyder, Richard C., Bruck, H. W., and Sapin, Burton. *Foreign Policy Decision-Making: An Approach to the Study of International Politics*. New York: The Free Press of Glencoe, 1962.

Sorenson, Theodore C. *Decision-Making in the White House: The Olive Branch or the Arrows*. New York: Columbia University Press, 1963.

———. *Kennedy*. New York: Harper, 1965.

Spaulding, E. Wilder. *Ambassadors Ordinary and Extraordinary*. Washington, D.C.: Public Affairs Press, 1961.

Stanley, Timothy W. *American Defense and National Security*. Washington, D.C.: Public Affairs Press, 1956.

Steiner, Zara S. *Present Problems of the Foreign Service*. Policy Memorandum No. 23. Princeton, N. J.: Center of International Studies, 1961.

———. *The State Department and the Foreign Service: The Wriston Report—Four Years Later*. Policy Memorandum No. 16. Princeton, N. J.: Center of International Studies, 1958.

Stern, Harold, ed. *Public Administration and Policy Development: A Case Book*. New York: Harcourt, Brace & World, 1952.

Stuart, Graham H. *American Diplomatic and Consular Practice*. 2nd ed. New York: Appleton-Century-Crofts, 1952.

———. *The Department of State*. New York: Macmillan, 1949.

Thayer, Charles W. *Diplomat*. New York: Harper, 1959.

Thompson, Kenneth W. *American Diplomacy and Emergent Patterns*. New York: New York University Press, 1962.

Thomson, Charles A., and Laves, Walter H. *Cultural Relations and U. S. Foreign Policy*. Bloomington: Indiana University Press, 1963.

Vagts, Alfred. *Defense and Diplomacy*. New York: King's Crown Press, 1956.

Villard, Henry S. *Affairs at State*. New York: Crowell, 1965.

Walther, Regis. *Orientations and Behavior Styles of Foreign Service Officers*. Foreign Affairs Personnel Study No. 5. New York: Carnegie Endowment for International Peace, 1965.

Waltz, Kenneth N. *Foreign Policy and Democratic Politics: The American and British Experience*. Boston: Little, Brown, 1967.

Wanamaker, Temple. *American Foreign Policy Today*. New York: Bantam Books, 1964.

Westerfield, H. Bradford. *Foreign Policy and Party Politics: Pearl Harbor to Korea*. New Haven, Conn.: Yale University Press, 1955.

———. *The Instruments of America's Foreign Policy*. New York: Crowell, 1963.

Whitehead, Don. *The FBI Story*. New York: Random House, 1956.

Wildavsky, Aaron. *The Politics of the Budgetary Process*. Boston: Little, Brown, 1964.

Wise, David, and Ross, Thomas B. *The Invisible Government*. New York: Random House, 1964.

Wriston, Henry M. *Diplomacy in a Democracy*. New York: Harper, 1956.

———. *Executive Agents in American Diplomacy*. New York, 1929.

ARTICLES

Alger, Chadwick F. "The External Bureaucracy in United States Foreign Affairs." *Administrative Science Quarterly*, 7 (June 1962), 50–78.

Allison, Graham T. "Conceptual Models and the Cuban Missile Crisis." *American Political Science Review*, 63, no. 3 (September 1969), 689–715.

Anderson, Dillon. "The President and National Security." *Atlantic Monthly*, 197 (January 1956), 2–3.

Bissell, Richard M., Jr. "America's Administrative Response to Its World Problems." In *The American Style: Essays in Value and Performance* (A report on the Dedham Conference). New York: Harper, 1958.

Clifford, Clark M. "A Viet Nam Reappraisal." *Foreign Affairs*, 47, no. 4 (July 1969), 601–622.

Coffey, J. I., and Rock, Vincent P. "The Presidential Staff." Mimeographed. National Planning Association, December 15, 1960.

Cutler, Robert. "The Seamless Web." *Harvard Alumni Bulletin*, 57 (June 4, 1955), 449–451.

Deutsch, Karl W. "The Anatomy and Character of National Power." *The National War College Forum*, 6 (Fall 1968).

Diebold, John. "Is the Gap Technical?" *Foreign Affairs*, 46 (January 1968), 276–291.

Evans, Allan. "A View of Personnel Administration." (Department of State) *News Letter*, no. 90 (October 1968), pp. 18–19.

Finer, Herman. "The Hoover Commission Reports." *Political Science Quarterly*, 64 (September 1949), 405–419, 579–595.

Foreign Service Journal, 7–47 (1940–1970).

Galbraith, John Kenneth. "How to Control the Military." *Harper's Magazine*, 238, no. 1429 (June 1969), 31–46.

Hoffman, Stanley. "The American Style: Our Past and Our Principles." *Foreign Affairs*, 46, no. 2 (January 1968), 362–376.

Hughes, Thomas L. "On the Causes of Our Discontents." *Foreign Affairs*, 47 (July 1969), 653–667.

Katzenbach, Nicholas de B. "Administration of Foreign Policy." (Department of State) *News Letter*, no. 79 (November 1967), pp. 2–5.

Kennan, George F. "America's Administrative Response to Its World Problems." In *The American Style: Essays in Value and Performance* (A report on the Dedham Conference). New York: Harper, 1958.

"The Long-Term View from the 29th Floor." *Time*, December 29, 1967, pp. 56–59, 63.

McConaughy, John B. "International Law as Practiced in State Courts." *South Carolina Law Quarterly*, 10 (Winter 1958), 189–224.

May, Ernest. "The Development of Political-Military Consultation in the United States." *Political Science Quarterly*, 70 (June 1955), 161–180.

Morgan, George, "Planning in Foreign Affairs: The State of the Art." *Foreign Affairs*, 39 (January 1961), 271.

Morgan, Thomas E. "Congress and the Foreign Service." (Department of State) *News Letter*, no. 39 (July 1964), pp. 10, 47.

Poullada, Leon B. "Economy—True and False." *Foreign Service Journal*, 31, no. 5 (May 1954), 18–21, 58–63.

Randall, Clarence B. "The Advisory Committee on International Business Problems." (Department of State) *News Letter*, no. 30 (October 1964), pp. 14–16, 28.

Rockefeller, Nelson A. "Policy and the People." *Foreign Affairs*, 46 (January 1968), 231–241.

Sherwood, Foster K. "Foreign Relations and the Constitution." *Western Political Quarterly*, 1 (1948), 386–399.

Sutton, Francis X. "American Formulations and U.S. Public Diplomacy." Address by Deputy Vice President of Ford Foundation (July 22, 1968). New York: Ford Foundation, 1968.

Tulchin, Joseph S. "Inhibitions Affecting the Formulation and Execution of the Latin American Policy of the United States." *Ventures*, no. 2 (Fall 1967), pp. 68–80.

Walker, Lannon. "Our Foreign Affairs Machinery: Time for an Overhaul." *Foreign Affairs*, 47 (January 1969), 309–320.

INDEX

ACDA: organization and roles of, 23, 120, 229; relation of, to State, 229, 295, 300, 301, 315
Acheson, Dean: 176, 196
Act of 1856: 53–54
Act of 1906: 57, 62
Adams, John Quincy: 48, 51
administration. SEE foreign policy (U.S.) administration
administrative law: 36–38
Advisory Commission on Information: 229
Advisory Commission on Inter-Governmental Relations: 229
Advisory Panel on a National Academy of Foreign Affairs, Presidential: 118, 154
Africa: new U.S. roles in, 110
agreements, interagency: 191
agricultural attachés: 245
AID: relation of, with State, 37, 119, 120, 127, 223, 300, 301, 315; programs and roles of, 43, 119, 120, 225 and n.; organization and staff of, 119, 155–159, 217 n., 223–225 *passim*; relations of, with FS, 214, 215, 223, 225, 226; patronage in, 223–224
Albania: 8
Algeria: 8
Allen, George: 131
Almond, Gabriel: 256 n.
ambassadors (U.S.). SEE chief of mission (COM)
America First: 271
American Academy of Political and Social Science: 39
American Assembly: 354
American Battle Monuments Commission: 249
American Chemical Society: 270
American Civil Liberties Union: 270
American Communist Party: 273, 274

American Foreign Service Association (AFSA): 164–166, 294, 299 n., 344–345
American Historical Association: 270
American Political Science Association: 270
American Red Cross: 250
Americans for Democratic Action: 270
Anderson, Dillon: 110
Anderson, Jack: 259
anglophiles: 267
anticommunism: 20
Antitrust Division (Justice): 247
Appointments and Assignments Board (State): 339, 340
Arab states: 11
Arms Control and Disarmament Agency. SEE ACDA
assistant secretaries of state: 128, 370–376 *passim*
Atomic Energy Commission (AEC): 239–240
attachés: 214, 215
attorney general: 247
Ausland, John C.: 281
auxiliary officers (FS): 78 and n., 82

Ball, George: 117, 200
Batista, Fulgencio: 20
Baxter, James P., III: 359
Bay of Pigs (invasion): 6, 186, 273
Berle, Adolph: 117
Berlin blockade: 26
BEX: legislative history of, 81, 132; work of, 103–106, 131–132, 139–142, 147–149, 228, 319–323, 332; role of, proposed, 302, 323–333
Bill of Rights: 34
binational centers (USIS): 221, 222
Block, Herbert (Herblock): 259
Board of Economic Warfare: 76, 80
Board of Examiners for the Consular Service: 58

Board of Examiners for the Diplomatic Service: 58
Board of Examiners for the Foreign Service. SEE BEX
Board of Foreign Service Personnel: 81, 132
Board of Governors of the Federal Reserve System: 246
Board of Immigration Appeals (Justice): 247
Board of Geographic Names (Interior): 245
bolsheviks: 5
Border Patrol (Justice): 247
Bowie, Robert W.: 359
Bowles, Chester: 117, 200
Bricker amendment (proposed): 341
Briggs, Ellis: 316
Brinkley, David: 261
British empire: 12
Brodie, Bernard: 259
Brookings Institution: 351, 358–359
Buchwald, Art: 259
budget cuts. SEE reduction in force
Bullitt, William: 72
Bundy, McGeorge: 183
Bureau of African Affairs (State): 110
Bureau of Congressional Relations (State): 176, 198, 295
Bureau of Cultural Affairs (State): 199, 221
Bureau of Customs (Treasury): 242
Bureau of Economic Affairs (State): 198, 295
Bureau of Intelligence and Research (State). SEE INR
Bureau of Inter-American Affairs (State): 223
Bureau of International Organization Affairs (State): role of, 197; in proposed reorganization, 295; in flow of policy making, 370–373, 375–376
Bureau of Narcotics (Treasury): 242
Bureau of Prisons (Justice): 247
Bureau of Public Affairs (State): 199, 373, 374, 377
Bureau of Security and Consular Affairs (State): 199
Bureau of the Budget (Executive Office): and 1946 Foreign Service Act, 93 and n.; and 1965 FS budget review, 120–121; as part of executive office, 180, 183–185
Bureau of the Public Debt (Treasury): 242
business corporations: influence of, 262–265
Byrnes, James: 195

cabinet (U.S.): 189
cabinet system: 177
Calderhead, William D.: 149 n.
Cambodia: 30 n.
Canal Zone Government: 249
career ambassadors (FS): 113. SEE ALSO chief of mission (COM)
Career Development and Counseling Staff (State): 137
career ladders: 83
career officer. SEE Foreign Service officer
career principle: in U.S. consular and diplomatic services, 57, 58, 61–62. SEE ALSO Foreign Service personnel policy
career reserve officers (USIA): 130, 131, 132, 146, 161
Carnegie Endowment for International Peace: 118
Charlesworth, James C.: 39–40
chief of mission (COM): appointments as, 1774–1924, 48, 51, 54–55, 58; appointments as, 1925–1969, 66–67, 114, 160–161 and n., 208; roles of, 119, 193, 211, 228; personal staffs of, 211
China, Peoples Republic of: 25
Chinese-Americans: 268–269
CIA: history and roles of, xvii, 180, 186–188, 273, 377; suggestions regarding, 301–303, 344–345 passim
Ciudad Trujillo (Santo Domingo): U.S. Embassy at, 316
Civil Service: role of, in State, xvi, 31, 83, 94, 303, 348; effects of reform of, on field services, 54
Civil Service Commission: 309, 312
Clark, Kenneth: 140, 147 n.
Cleveland, Grover: 57
Cleveland, Harlan: 44, 117, 356–358
Clifford, Clark: 290 and n.
Coast Guard (Transportation): 245
collective security: 17
Commentary: 259
commercial attachés: 244
Commission on Administrative Management, Presidential: xii, 301, 302
Commission on International Rules of Judicial Procedure: 230
communication: as limiting factor, 13–16; electronic systems of, used by State, 124–126. SEE ALSO mass media
communists: 271, 273
Comprehensive Country Programming System (CCPS): 123, 285–286
computer: role of, 40, 125 and n., 126
conference diplomacy: 7
Conference on Minority Employment (State): 147
Congress (U.S.): constitutional powers

INDEX 407

of, 17, 22, 24–25, 27–32, 186–188 *passim;* relations of, with executive, 42, 49–50, 55–60, 74, 169–177 *passim;* techniques of, influencing foreign affairs, 169–171; bipartisanship in, 172; informational sources of, 172; foreign travel of, 174–175
Congress of Vienna: 209
Consolidated Administrative Service Center: 133
Consolidated Management Organization (CAMO): 133
Consular Service (U.S.): history of, 1775–1924, 48–49, 51–55, 57–59, 61–63; roles of, 1775–1924, 52–53, 63; director of, 59; agencies of, 62 and n. SEE ALSO Foreign Service
—after 1924: merger of, into FS, 63; officers of, 208–209, 210, 211; immunities and privileges of, 209–210; agencies of, 210; consulates and consulates general in, 210, 213–214, 216
Continental Congress: 48
contingency planning, civilian. SEE Department of Defense; policy planning
Controller of the Currency: 242
Coolidge, Calvin: 67, 181
coordination (administrative): origin and nature of problem, xiii–xiv, 73–77, 114, 192, 231–232, 343–344 *passim;* and compatibility among foreign affairs agencies, xvii, 115–116, 130–133; presidential techniques of, 110–111, 118–122, 175–176, 186–190; other executive techniques of, 120–129, 176, 190–194, 370, 373, 377 *passim;* congressional techniques of, 176–177; interagency, 191. SEE ALSO president (U.S.)
Coordinator for Inter-American Affairs: 76, 80, 222
Coordinator for the Alliance for Progress (U.S.): 223
Council of Economic Advisers (Executive Office): 185
Council on International Educational and Cultural Affairs: 128
counselor of embassy: 62
counselor of the Department of State: 59
Country Analysis and Strategy Paper: 123–124, 285–286
country directors (State): 128
country house examining system: 282 and n., 331–332
country team: 192
Crockett, William: xvi, 117, 137
Cronkite, Walter: 261

Cuba: 8
Curtiss-Wright case: 33
Cutler, Robert: 110, 359
Czechoslovakia: 8

data processing and retrieval: 124–126, 346
decision making. SEE policy making
Defense Materials Service (General Services Administration): 240
De Gaulle, Charles: 8, 264, 267
Department of Agriculture: FAS of, xii, 90, 111, 244–245; as threat to FS monopoly, 68–70; and proposed reunification with FS, 344
Department of Commerce: xii, 68–70, 242–244
Department of Defense: influence of, on foreign affairs, 23, 26, 225, 231–237, 375, 377; established, 31, 88; personnel of, 217 n., 238 and n., 239; and contingency planning, 235 and n.
Department of Foreign Affairs: 48
Department of Health, Education and Welfare: 248–249
Department of Justice: 247
Department of Labor: 247–248
Department of State: and politico-military affairs, 126 and n., 295; public relations of, 134–135; proposal for reorganization of, 294–298
—administration and organization: roles of administrators in, 31–32, 70–71, 79, 85, 94, 142–147; organization of, 1909–1945, 59–60, 69–71, 77–79; organization of, 1946–1969, 84–87, 94, 126–133, 152–154 *passim;* security in, 96–97, 112; communications in, 124–126, 369–370, 372, 375–376
—history: authorities on, xii, xiv; from 1790–1939, 50, 55–56, 58; from 1939–1969, 75–80, 84–91, 94–166 *passim*
—personnel: Civil and FS components of, xvi, 59, 95, 100 and n., 145 and n., 200–201; numbers, 1790–1918, 50, 55, 58, 61; morale of, 68, 83–84, 92–97, 102, 111–113, 160–166 *passim;* numbers, 1919–1969, 70–71, 77, 84, 95, 145; special assistants of, 122, 370, 372, 377
—personnel programs: exchanges of, xvii, 79, 109, 113–114, 133–134, 191–192; compatibility of, xvii, 115–116, 130–133; integration of, 98–99, 102–104, 129–131, 142–143, 146–147, 200. SEE ALSO BEX
—roles and problems: in guidance and

support of other agencies, xii, 37, 88–90, 113, 129 and n., 213–250 *passim*; nature and range of problems of, xiii, 73–74, 76–77, 89, 94, 368–369; war-time roles of, 61, 75, 77, 78; general description of, 109–110, 195–200, 368–377; coordinative role of, 120–129, 176, 189–194, 370, 373–377 *passim*; policy planning in, 122–123, 281–288, 295, 345–346 *passim*; policy making in, 197 and n., 198, 345–346, 368–377 *passim*. SEE ALSO policy making
Department of the Air Force: 237 and n., 238
Department of the Army: 237 and n., 238
Department of the Interior: 69–70, 245
Department of the Navy: 23, 68, 87, 88, 237 and n., 238
Department of the Treasury: 68, 241–242, 246
Department of Transportation: 245–246
deputy chief of mission: 211–212
deputy undersecretary of state: for administration, 199–200; role of, proposed, 294–295; in flow of policy making, 370–372, 375
desk officer (State): 128, 370–376 *passim*
Development Loan Fund: 119
Diebold, John: 263 n.
diplomatic missions (U.S.): roles and history of, 1775–1893, 49, 51, 53, 55; current roles, 211–215, 316, 368–369, 371–377 *passim*
Diplomatic Service (U.S.): from 1775–1924, 48–51, 53–59, 61–63; secretaries of, 51, 58. SEE ALSO Foreign Service
diplomats: technique of, 14; responsibility of, 177; precedence of, 209; immunities and privileges of, 209. SEE ALSO Foreign Service officer
disarmament: 17
Division of Foreign Quarentine (PHS): 248
Division of Functional Intelligence (State): 283
Division of International Health (PHS): 248
Dominican Republic: 25–26, 29
Dulles, Allen: 186
Dulles, John Foster: 97, 186, 196
Dungan, Ralph: 183, 234
Duvalier, François: 20

East Germany: 25
Economic Defense Board: 76

economic development: 20. SEE ALSO AID
education: U.S. system of, 251–253; influence of groups in, on foreign policy, 270
Eire: 171
Eisenhower, Dwight David: reorganizes foreign affairs agencies, xii, 89–90, 94; coordinative activities of, 88, 110–111, 185, 342–343; economy program of, 95–96; administrative style of, 186, 196; views of, on military-industrial complex, 232–233; mentioned, 37, 124, 131, 181, 242
Elliott, William Yandell: xiv
embassies (U.S.). SEE diplomatic missions (U.S.)
Emmerich, Herbert: 41
Euratom: 239
European Economic Community: 5
examination (FS). SEE BEX
executive agreements: 24
executive assignments system, federal: 134
Executive Office: 180, 182–189. SEE ALSO president (U.S.)
Executive Secretariat (State): 294, 370, 372, 376
Export-Import Bank: 246

fascists: 271
FBI (Justice): 199, 242, 247
Federal Aviation Administration (Transportation): 240, 245
Federal Civil Defense Administration: 249
Federal Commerce Commission: 246
Federal Highway Administration: 245
Federal Maritime Administration: 246
Federal Power Commission: 246
Federal Railroad Administration (Transportation): 245
Federal Reserve Board: 242
federal scholarship program (proposed): 323–324
Federal Trade Commission: 246
Feldman, Meyer: 183
Fisheries and Wildlife, Special Assistant for (State): 295
Food for Peace: 121
Ford Foundation: 148
Foreign Affairs: 259
foreign affairs data bank (proposed): 346
Foreign Affairs Information Management Effort (Faime): 128
Foreign Affairs Programming System (FAPS): 123, 285–286
Foreign Affairs Scholars Program: 148

INDEX 409

Foreign Agricultural Service (FAS): xii, 90, 111, 244, 344
Foreign Area Research Coordination Group: 128 and n.
foreign assistance. SEE AID; International Cooperation Administration
foreign buildings program (State): 58, 84
Foreign Claims Settlement Commission: 229
Foreign Commerce Service: xii, 69–70, 243
Foreign Office (British): 294
foreign policy (U.S.): coordination of, with national security policy, 26, 110–111, 185–186, 191, 231–232, 342–343; basic, defined, 280–281, 286–291
—administration: need for more research in, xiii, xvii; limits of, 3–21; legal basis of, 36–38; extra-legal basis of, 38–39; theory of, 39–42, 77, 231–232; investigations of, 97–100, 113–114, 118, 164–165, 299 and n., 351–360; problems of, 279–340 *passim*; prognosis for improvement in, 341–350
—, influences on: of foreign groups, 34–35, 172, 271–274, 370, 373, 377; of local governments, 34, 251–255; of general public, 34, 256–259, 279–280; of mass media, 172, 256, 259–262, 373, 374; of pressure groups, 172, 256, 262–271, 274; of military-industrial complex, 232–235; of political parties, 256, 261–262; of Americans overseas, 257–259; of economic interest groups, 262–267; of nationality groups, 267, 268; of racial groups, 267–269; of religious groups, 269–270; of professional groups, 270; of ideological groups, 270–271
Foreign Service: roles and duties of, xvii, 75, 77–79, 109–110, 201–216, 348; criticism of, 74, 93; directors general of, 81, 94, 153, 199; Negroes in, 148–149, 268, 322–324 *passim*. SEE ALSO Foreign Service officer
—administration: support role of, xiii, xvii, 68–70, 129 and n., 133 and n., 201, 205–206 and n., 214–216; security system of, 96–97, 112; inspection service of, 199
—history: authorities on, xii, xiv; from 1924–1961, 63–64, 72, 80–84, 89–113 *passim*; from 1961–1970, 115–119, 129–134, 136–166 *passim*
—organization: changes in, 31–32, 63–64, 66, 80–84, 129, 132, 143–147; in field offices, 71, 210–216
—personnel policy: history of, 1961–1970, 31–32, 132–164, 207, 338–340, 348–349; and specialization, 41, 83, 114, 141–143, 306–312, 319–322 *passim*; history of, 1924–1961, 63–67, 78–79, 94–99, 102–109; career principle of, 63, 68, 92–97, 142–147, 318–321; and compensation, 64, 66, 68, 81 and n., 112 and n., 161; and promotion, 64–66, 79, 82, 143–146, 150–151, 203
—personnel programs: interdepartmental exchanges as, xvii, 79, 109, 113–114, 133–134, 191–192; compatibility of, xvii, 115–116, 130–133; fringe benefits of, 64, 67–68, 81 and n., 112 and n., 161, 206; in-service training as, 1925–1942, 64–65; lateral entry as, 67, 80–81, 104, 142–144, 200, 208, 318; integration as, 98–99, 102–104, 129–131, 142–143, 146–147, 200, 207, 208, 303–304. SEE ALSO BEX
—Reserve: as subject of interagency agreements, 37; and 1946 FS Act, 82–83; and 1962 reorganization, 143–144; staffing levels of, 145, 207–210 *passim*; and 1965 changes, 145–146; reserve officers unlimited of, 146, 207, 348; proposed use of, 302–312 *passim*; and 1970 reorganization, 348–349
—Staff: strength of, 23, 67, 84, 95–96, 106, 145 and n.; noncareer vice consuls of, 67; local (alien) employees of, 67, 159–160, 208; morale of, 68, 83–84, 92–97, 102, 110–113, 160–166 *passim*, 304; auxiliary officers of, 78 and n., 82; and 1946 FS Act, 82, 83–84; and 1962 reorganization, 144; representativeness of, 147–150, 321–324; categories of, 207–208, 210; as proportion of U.S. overseas employees, 217 and n., 218; criticism of size of, 314–317
foreign service (Interior): 69–70, 245
foreign service academy (proposed): 108, 321
Foreign Service Act of 1946: provisions and defects of, 80–84, 93 and n., 184, 335; amendments to, 104, 113, 140, 146–147
Foreign Service Institute (FSI): history and evaluation of, xvii, 82, 106–108, 154–159, 199, 207; programs of, 107–108, 154–160, 335–336, 361–367 *passim*; proposed changes in, 113–114, 319–320, 334–338, 349
Foreign Service officer: roles of, xvi–xvii, 100 and n., 207–211, 348; status of, lowered, 31–32, 143–146 *passim*; views

of, on foreign affairs administration, 164–166, 316; qualifications of, optimal, 325–330. SEE ALSO Foreign Service
—appointments and force levels: junior officer appointments, 64, 105 and n., 140; numbers of, 64, 67, 68, 78, 84, 95, 106, 145; lateral appointments, proportion of, 208. SEE ALSO BEX
—characteristics: strengths and weaknesses, xvi, 63, 75–76, 83, 93–94; language competence, 65 and n., 67, 105, 108 and n., 156 and n., 157, 334–335; elitism, 93, 318; recent activism, 164–166
—and personnel rules: probation, 64, 66–67, 332; promotion, 64–66, 79, 82, 143–146, 150–151, 203; prohibition on marriages of, to aliens, 72; compulsory retirement, 82, 113, 151–152; commissioning, 208–209
Foreign Service School (State): 64–65
Formosa: 26
Formosa Straits Resolution: 170, 175
France: 317
Francis Committee: 351
Franco, Francisco: 269
Franklin, Benjamin: 48, 272
freedom of the press: 260
free enterprise system: 20
FSIO(USIA): 130, 220 and n. SEE ALSO USIA
FSRO. SEE Foreign Service Reserve
FSRU. SEE Foreign Service Reserve
FSSO. SEE Foreign Service Staff
Fullbright Resolution: 170

Galbraith, John Kenneth: 233–234
Gallatin, Albert: 51
General Accounting Office: 169, 170
generalists: 309
General Services Administration: 240
German-Americans: 267
German Federal Republic: 317
Gerry, Elbridge: 51
gigantism: in foreign affairs agencies, 41, 73–74, 90–92, 314–317 *passim*
Gonzalez, Henry B.: 130
good neighbor commissions: 254
Goodwin, Richard: 15, 183
Gordon, Kermit: 120
Gorgas Memorial Institute: 250
Grant, Ulysses Simpson: 54
Gray, Gordon: 359
Greek-Turkish aid program: 192 and n.
Guadalajara, (Mexico): American Consulate at, 316
Guatemala: 273

Gulf of Tonkin Resolution: 170, 175

Haiphong: 21
Harding, Warren Gamaliel: 181
Harper's Magazine: 259
Harriman, Averill: 192 n., 200
Hays, Wayne L.: 174
Hays Bill: 130, 299 n., 304
Henderson, Loy: xvi, 103
Herblock (Block, Herbert): 259
Herter, Christian: 117, 118, 195
Herter Committee: recommendations of, 129, 132, 136–137, 152–154, 294, 299 n.; views of, rejected, 144, 154, 345
Hilsman, Roger: 117
Hiss, Alger: 96, 170
Hitler, Adolf: 271, 273
Hoffman, Stanley: 16–17
Hoover, Herbert: 67, 181
Hoover, Herbert, Jr.: 98
Hoover Commission: 98
Hopkins, Harry: 76, 182
House, Edward M.: 182
House of Representatives (U.S.): 173–174. SEE ALSO Congress (U.S.)
Hull, Cordell: 70, 195
Humphrey, George M.: 242
Hungary: 8, 275

ILO: 247
Immigration and Naturalization Service (INS): 199, 247
Indians, American: 322–324 *passim*
Indians, East: 11
information. SEE CIA; INR; intelligence; intelligence community
information program. SEE USIA
INR: role of, 127, 198, 370, 373, 376, 377; proposal regarding, 287, 291, 295
in-service training. SEE Foreign Service; Foreign Service Institute (FSI)
integration. SEE Foreign Service personnel programs
intelligence: 172. SEE ALSO CIA; INR
intelligence community: 186, 187, 236, 237.SEE ALSO CIA; INR
interagency agreements: 191
Interagency Committee on International Aviation: 127
interagency personnel exchanges: xvii, 79, 109, 113–114, 133–134, 191–192
Interdepartmental Committee on Scientific Research and Development: 250
Interdepartmental Regional Groups: 121 and n., 343
Internal Revenue Service: 242

INDEX 411

International Atomic Energy Organization: 239
International Cooperation Administration: 89, 119
International Development Association: 170
international expositions: 254
International Hydrographic Organization: 236
international law: 35
International Meteorological Organization: 236
IPU: 249
Ireland (Eire): 171
Irish-Americans: 267
Isabel II (of Spain): 54
isolationism: 17
Israel: 11, 171

Japan: 259
Japanese-Americans: 268–269
Jay, John: 51
Jefferson, Thomas: 48
Johnson, Lyndon Baines: administrative style of, 37, 116–117, 182–183, 196; coordinative activities of, 116, 120–122, 186, 191, 193, 300, 343; personnel policies of, 130–132, 134–135, 147–150, 160–161 and n., 323; mentioned, 9, 25, 173, 181, 266, 274
Johnston, Eric: 266
Joint Automated Data Processing Requirements Coordinating Committee: 128
Joint Chiefs of Staff: 26
Joint Intelligence Board (U.S.): 187, 237
Joint State and Navy Neutrality Board: 232
Jones, Roger W.: xvi, 117, 129, 147, 154
judiciary, U.S. federal: 32–34, 177–178
Jusserand, Jean Jules: 272

Katzenbach, Nicholas de B.: xi, 117, 286
Kennan, George: 284, 314, 316, 359
Kennedy, Edward: 182
Kennedy, John Fitzgerald: administrative style of, 37, 116–117, 182–183, 196, 272; coordinative activities of, 115–116, 118–120, 134–135, 185–186, 193, 226, 343; personnel policies of, 118–119, 139, 147–149, 154, 160–161 and n., 268, 323; mentioned, 181, 186, 243, 338
Kennedy, Joseph P.: 182
Kennedy, Robert: 182
King, David S.: 281
King, Rufus: 51

Kipling, Rudyard: 11
Kissinger, Henry A.: 359
Krock, Arthur: 259
Ky, Nguyen Cao: 279 n.

land reform: 20
lateral entry. SEE Foreign Service personnel programs
Laurens, Henry: 48
League of Women Voters: 270
Leahy, William (Admiral): 76, 182
Lebanon: 26
Legal Adviser (State): 199
Legislative Reference Service (Library of Congress): 172
Lindsay, John Vliet: 255
Lippman, Walter: 259
Livingston, Robert: 51
lobbyists: 265, 267, 274
local governments: and foreign affairs, 34, 251–255
Lovett, Robert A.: 359, 360

McCamy, James L.: 259, 282–285 and n. *passim*
McCarthy, Joseph: 96, 104
McKinley, William: 57
McLane-Ocampo Treaty: 29
Macomber, William B.: 117, 334, 348–349
majority leader (U.S. Senate): 173
Mangone, Gerard J.: 357
Manifest Destiny: 49, 56
Mann, Thomas C.: 120
Manpower Act of 1946: 80–81 and n., 200
Manpower Utilization System and Techniques (MUST): 137
Marshall, Charles Burton: 3, 17–19
Marshall, George C.: 196
Marshall, John: 51
mass media: 172, 256, 259–262
Maxwell Graduate School of Citizenship and Public Affairs: 358
Mexican-American Boundary Commission: 249–250
Mexican-Americans: 147 and n., 267–268 and n., 322–324 *passim*
Mexico: 11, 29
military (U.S.): roles of, xii–xiii, 43, 239. SEE ALSO Department of Defense
Military Air Transport Command: 235
military assistance advisory groups (MAAGS): 225
military-industrial complex: 232–235
Millis, Walter: 259
Mindzenty, Cardinal: 275
ministers plenipotentiary. SEE chief of

mission (COM)
missionaries: 269
Monroe, James: 51
Monroe Doctrine: 20
Monroney Resolution: 170
Morgenthau, Henry: 76, 182, 242, 359
Morris, Gouverneur: 51
Morrow, Dwight W.: 272
Moses-Linthicum Act of 1931: 66
Mossadeq government: 273
Munich analogy: 12
Murrow, Edward: 261
Mutual Assistance Program: 24

Napoleon III: 9
NASA: 234, 240
National Academy of Foreign Affairs (proposed): 118, 154
National Academy of Sciences: 250
National Advisory Council on International Monetary and Financial Problems: 242
National Aeronautics and Space Council: 188
National Archives: 270
National Council of Churches: 269
National Interdepartmental Seminar (FSI): 159
Nationality Act: 35
National Research Council: 250
National Science Foundation: 250
National Security Act of 1947: 88
national security agencies: 88, 231–240
National Security Council Review Group: 343
national security policy: impact of, on foreign policy, 23, 26, 87, 235; coordination of, with foreign policy, 26, 110–111, 185–186, 191, 231–232, 342–343
National War College: 88
nazi groups: 271
NEA: 270
New Yorker: 259
New York Times: 259
Niact: 376
Nicholson, Sir Harold: 328
Nixon, Richard Milhouse: coordinative activities of, 160–161 and n., 186, 191, 193, 343–344; mentioned, 30 n., 170, 181, 183
North Korea: 21, 25, 26
North Vietnam: 21, 25
Novosan, Phoumi: 274 n.
NSC: role of, 26, 110–111, 185–186, 287, 291; history of, 88, 110, 185–186, 191, 342–343; mentioned, 31, 231, 232, 288

office director (State): 128, 370–376 *passim*
Office of Alien Property (Justice): 247
Office of Economic Opportunity: 149 and n.
Office of Emergency Preparedness (Executive Office): 88, 188
Office of External Research (State): 346
Office of Facts and Figures: 76
Office of Functional and Biographic Intelligence (State): 283
Office of International Aviation (State): 127
Office of International Finance (Treasury): 242
Office of International Labor Affairs (Labor): 248
Office of International Science and Technical Affairs (State): 127–128 and n., 199, 283, 295
Office of International Security Affairs (Defense): 377
Office of Lend-Lease Administration: 76, 77, 80
Office of Manpower and Budget (Executive Office): 183–185
Office of Politico-Military Affairs (State): 126 and n., 295
Office of Science and Technology (Executive Office): 188
Office of Strategic Services: 76, 80
Office of the General Counsel (Treasury): 242
Office of the Special Representative for Trade Negotiations (Executive Office): 188–189
Office of the Undersecretary for Monetary Affairs (Treasury): 242
Office of War Information: 76, 80
officer-in-charge (State): 371, 373, 374, 375
Ogburn, Charlton: 368–377
open diplomacy: 7
Open Door Policy: 20
Operations Center (State): 123, 294
Operations Coordinating Board: creation of, 88, 185; role of, 110–111; abolished, 119, 185; mentioned, 342–343
Orrick, William H., Jr.: 117

Pakistan: 11
Panama Canal Company: 249
Peace Corps: 36, 120, 226–228, 301–303
Pérez Jiménez, Marcos: 20
Performance Measurement Section (State): 137, 339

INDEX 413

Perkins, Dexter: 259
Perkins, James A.: 118
permanent (executive) undersecretary of state (proposed): 153, 294, 345
personnel. SEE Foreign Service, personnel policy, personnel programs
Phillips, William: 67
PHS(HEW): 248
Pinckney, Thomas: 51
Pinkney, William: 51
Planning Board (NSC): 88, 119, 185, 342–343 *passim*
Poinsett, Jules: 272
Point Four Program. SEE AID
Poland: 8
Policy and Coordination Staff (State): 283–284, 287–288, 291. SEE ALSO policy planning; Policy Planning Staff
policy making: role of administrators in, xi, 14, 23, 26–27, 31–32, 39–44, 74, 180, 342; in State, 197 and n., 198, 345–346, 368–377 *passim*
policy planning: in State, 85, 122–123, 281–283, 295, 345–346; by the military, 26, 235 and n.
Policy Planning Staff: 85, 122–123, 370, 373
Policy Review Council (proposed): 286–291
political accommodation: 17
political parties: 256, 261–262
Port of Spain (Trinidad): 316
Portugal: 268
Post Office Department: 249
Poullada, Leon B.: 316 n.
PPBS: 123–124, 285–286. SEE ALSO policy planning
president (U.S.): as reorganizer of foreign affairs agencies, xii, 69–70, 79–80, 89–90, 111, 116, 129–133; appointments of, 22–24, 50–51, 77, 196, 200; powers and roles of, 22–30, 179–181; travel of, 129; as coordinator, 175–176, 179–180, 185–186, 189–190, 342–343; administrative styles of, 180–182, 195–196; influence of election of, on foreign affairs, 257. SEE ALSO chief of mission (COM); under individual presidents
Presidential Advisory Panel on a National Academy of Foreign Affairs: 118, 154
presidential agents (U.S.): 50–51, 77
press: 259–260, 373, 374
pressure groups: 172, 256, 262–271
privileges: diplomatic and consular, 209–210
proliferation and growth: of foreign affairs agencies, xvi, 73–74, 88–92, 113, 346
public (general): 34, 256–259, 279–280
public affairs officer (USIS): 43, 220–223
public affairs sections (USIS): 220–223
publications: influence of, on foreign affairs, 259–260, 373, 374
Pueblo, USS: 8, 21
Puerto Ricans: 147 and n., 267–268 and n., 322–324 *passim*

Railway Wage Board: 275
Raisuli (Moroccan bandit): 275
reciprocal trade agreements: 24
reduction in force: under Eisenhower, 95–96; in 1962, 160; in 1968, 162–163
refugee program (State): 109
regional bureaus (State): 128, 287, 295, 370–377
Reorganization Plan No. 2: xii, 69–70
Reorganization Plan No. 7: 89, 94, 111
Reorganization Plan No. 8: 89, 94, 111
resident diplomatic officer (State): 59
Reston, James: 259
Revolution of Rising Expectations: 7, 14, 41
Rhodesia: 268
Richardson, Elliot L.: 344
Rimestad, Idar: 117
Robert T. Heller and Associates: 352
Robinson, James A.: 171–174
Rockefeller, Nelson A.: 262
Rogers, William Pierce: 126 n., 344
Rogers Act of 1924: structures FS, 35; provisions of, 63–64, 334; amended, 66; mentioned, 48
Rojas Pinilla, Gustavo: 20
Roman empire: 12
Roosevelt, Franklin Delano: reorganizes foreign affairs administration, xii, 69–70, 301; attitude of, toward FS and State, 67, 69–70, 72, 76, 232; administrative style of, 76, 182, 232, 242; mentioned, 260, 274
Roosevelt, Theodore: 57, 58, 180
Rostow, Eugene: 117
Rostow, Walter W.: 117, 200, 359
Rovere, Richard: 259
Rowe-Ramspeck-DeCourcy Committee (State): 98
Rumania: 8
Rush, Richard: 51
Rusk, Dean: 116–117, 120, 160, 176, 196, 234

Saint Lawrence Seaway Development Corporation: 245
Saltzman, Charles: 103
Schelling, Thomas C.: 285–286
Schlesinger, Arthur M., Jr.: views of, on limits of foreign policy, 14–15, 18, 274 n.; statements of, on Kennedy's attitude toward FS and State, 119, 160, 183, 185–186; influence of, 183, 259
science adviser (State): 109
science reporting: by FS, 109
secretary of defense: 234
secretary of state: as policy maker, 176, 195–196, 343, 370–371, 373–376 *passim*; proposal to ease burdens of, 291–298
secretary of the treasury: 241–242
Secret Service (Treasury): 242
Securities and Exchange Commission: 249
Selective Service System: 249
Senate (U.S.): powers of, 22–32, 174 *passim*; Committee on Foreign Relations of, 160–161, 187–188; studies for, 356–360. See also Congress (U.S.)
Senior Interdepartmental Group: 121 and n., 343
Servan-Schreiber, Jean Jacques: 264
Sevareid, Eric: 261
Seward, William H.: 29
Shriver, Sargent: 182
Sickles, Daniel: 54
sister city program (AID): 254
Smith, Howard K.: 261
Smith, W. Bedell: 99
Smithsonian Institution: 250
Social Security Administration: 201–202, 248–249, 275
Sorenson, Theodore: 183
Souers, Sidney: 359
South Korea: 259
South Vietnam: 26, 259
Spain: 171, 269
special assistant for national security affairs (Executive Office): 88, 182–183, 191, 231, 343
Special Committee Investigating National Defense Programs (U.S. Senate): 170
specialists: roles of, 41, 83, 306–308; need for, 83, 100–101, 104, 114, 306–307; recruitment and selection of, 140–141, 309–310, 319–321, 330–333. See also Foreign Service Reserve
special purpose consular post (FS): 210–211
spoils system: 54
Sprague, Robert C.: 359
Standard Oil of New Jersey: 263 and n.

states (U.S.): roles of, 34, 122, 251–255; executives of, influence foreign affairs, 255
State-War-Navy Coordinating Committee (SWNCC): 87, 232
statutes: as bases for U.S. administration, 35–36, 62, 140–141, 146. See also under individual statutes
Steeves, John M.: 151
Steiner, Zara S.: 354–356
Stettinius, Edward: 195
Stroessner, Alfredo: 20
Substantive Information Systems Program (State): 125
Subversive Activities Control Board: 249
summit diplomacy: 7
Supreme Court (U.S.): 32–34, 177–178

Taft, William Howard: 58
Taiwan: 259
Talleyrand, Charles Maurice, Comte de: 272
Tariff Commission: 30, 242, 246
task forces: 123, 191
technical assistance. See AID
Third Reich: 273
Thompson, William (Big Bill, mayor of Chicago): 255
Tripoli: 29
Trist, Nicholas: 43
Trujillo, Rafael Leonidas: 25, 274
Truman, Harry S.: coordinative activities of, 79–80, 88, 179, 181, 302; administrative style of, 179, 181, 196; mentioned, 9, 170, 260

Undersecretaries Committee (NSC): 343
undersecretaries of state: roles of, 70, 86–87, 370, 377; executive, proposed, 153, 294, 345
unified foreign affairs service (proposed): agency and staff components of, 299–311; prospects and rationale for, 301–303, 315–316, 343–345; personnel policies of, 304–312, 330–333; roles of generalists and specialists in, 306–312 *passim*; career principle in, 347–349
Union of South Africa: 268
United Kingdom: 317
United Nations: 370, 371, 374
UNRRA: 80
USIA: relations of, with State, xvii, 37, 155–159, 214–216, 220–223, 300–301, 344 *passim*; organization and staffing of, 31, 89, 116, 130–131, 217–220; roles of, 217–223, 374, 377; binational centers, information centers, and li-

braries of, 221–222, 275; relations of, with Advisory Commission on Information, 229
USSR: 6, 9, 11, 317

Vandenberg Resolution: 170
Vatican: 269
Versailles Treaty: 17, 29
Veterans Administration: 201–202, 249, 275
Villa, Francisco (Pancho): 275
Villard, Henry: 316
Voice of America (USIA): 218

War Department: 23, 68, 87–88. SEE ALSO Department of Defense; Department of the Army
Washington, George: 49
Washington Post: 259
watch officers (State): 376
Water for Peace: 121–122, 295
Watson, Thomas J., Jr.: 359
White, Harry: 273

White House Staff (Executive Office): 37, 182–183, 288
WHO: 248
Wiesner, Jerome: 183
Wilson, Henry Lane: 272
Wilson, Woodrow: 29, 58, 182
Winant, John Gilbert: 28, 192 n.
women: in FS and State, 147–150 *passim*
Working Group and Committee on Population Matters: 128
World Court: 29
world government: 17
World War I: 61
World War II: 73–79 *passim*
Wriston, Henry: 99, 259
Wriston Committee: 99–102, 112, 129, 144
Wristonization: 98–99, 102–115, 147, 200, 207, 208, 303–304

Yalta Agreements: 17
Young, Phillip: 352

Zionists: 255, 267